SWIFT STUDIES, 1965–1980

GARLAND REFERENCE LIBRARY
OF THE HUMANITIES
(VOL. 386)

SWIFT STUDIES, 1965-1980
An Annotated Bibliography

Richard H. Rodino

GARLAND PUBLISHING, INC. • NEW YORK & LONDON
1984

Library of Congress Cataloging in Publication Data

Rodino, Richard H.
  Swift studies, 1965-1980.

  (Garland reference library of the humanities ;
v. 386)
  Includes bibliographical references and index.
  1. Swift, Jonathan, 1667-1745—Bibliography.
I. Title. II. Series.
Z8856.R6 1984   [PR3726] 016.828′509   82-49113
ISBN 0-8240-9197-3

Printed on acid-free, 250-year-life paper
Manufactured in the United States of America

CONTENTS

PREFACE

This bibliography covers studies of the life and writings of Jonathan Swift published from 1965 to 1980, continuing the work begun by James E. Tobin and Louis A. Landa in *Jonathan Swift: A List of Critical Studies Published from 1895–1945* (New York: Cosmopolitan Science and Art, 1945), which was updated by James J. Stathis in *A Bibliography of Swift Studies 1945–65* (Nashville: Vanderbilt U. Press, 1967). Because Stathis listed 659 items for his 20-year period, 1945–65, while the present volume contains nearly 1300 entries for only fifteen years from 1965–1980, it is tempting to speculate that interest in Swift has swelled with the poststructuralist and reader-response temper of the present critical times. However, documentary evidence of comparative bloatage is lacking. My preliminary research in the leading annual bibliographies suggests that in 1980 Swift was being studied at about the same rate George P. Mayhew described in 1965: more frequently than Dryden or Pope, about as much as Samuel Johnson, Wordsworth, and Chaucer, and consistently surpassed only by Shakespeare and Milton.

The organization of this volume continues that of the 1965 Stathis bibliography, though a few of the distinctions he drew then seem slightly less telling now. Section One lists Bibliography, Canon, and Editions, with the last assigned to a separate subsection of its own. Sections Two and Four, Biography and Poetry, respectively, are still overwhelmingly useful as discrete categories. And yet, Swift's life has never been thoroughly separated from his writings; similarly, it is less common than ever to see Swift's poetry treated as utterly different in tone and purpose from his prose satires. The 1970's and 1980's appear to have put more stress on the continuity of Swift's vision and motives than the formalism of the 1940's, 50's, and 60's. On the other hand, a recent body of publication expressly on Swift's verses, including a bibliography by David M. Vieth and five other books in 1976–82 (not to mention a forthcoming *Essential Articles* volume on Swift's poetry from Archon Press), gives the Poetry Section some integrity and usefulness still in 1980. This may be less true when the present volume is updated twenty, fifteen, or even ten years hence.

Section Three, General Criticism, lists studies of Swift's entire career, of his satirical methods in general, or discussions of three or more works, whose main purpose is to generalize. Studies that treat only two or three works in considerable detail are for the most part cross-listed in two or more of the specialized categories in Section Five.

Section Five, specialized studies of Prose Works, has grown less symmetrical since 1965. Fewer critics address *The Mechanical Operation of the Spirit* by itself, preferring to include it in general discussions, especially those which focus also on *The Battle of the Books* and *A Tale of a Tub*. Criticism of the *Battle*, on the other hand, continues to be a modestly thriving industry, especially in Germany, where Hermann J. Real and others have been definitively editing and annotating. *Polite Conversation*, too, though more slenderly represented than other major texts, did continue to draw specialized treatment, enough to warrant a category all its own.

Swift's religious writings were generally the stickiest to store away. Enough specialized criticism of the religious tracts and sermons appeared to justify (almost) a separate category for them. And yet, with the exception of the sermons, the major texts which might comprise this new category, especially *An Argument Against Abolishing Christianity*, were all voluminously treated in studies better classified elsewhere. Section Six, devoted to *Gulliver's Travels* alone, predictably makes up about one-fourth of the entire volume.

The backbone of the research procedure for this volume was an original search of the most important journals listed in the *MLA Directory of Periodicals* or picked up elsewhere. Among the invaluable annual bibliographies consulted were the *MLA International Bibliography*, *The Eighteenth Century: A Current Bibliography*, of which I have been a contributing editor for six years, and the indispensable *Scriblerian*. I have tried to be exhaustive in covering English and American criticism, but undoubtedly managed only to be comprehensive. Coverage of foreign language scholarship, especially French, Italian, German, Russian, Rumanian, and Japanese, is as extensive as possible. The forms of transliterated titles have been taken from the best sources available in each individual case; most conflicts were resolved in favor of the Harvard librarians' versions.

A few remarks on the mechanics of this bibliography: It attempts to list more reviews than usual, at least for major books. In many cases, reviews are described as "favorable," "severe," "with factual corrections," and so on, to simplify the task of anyone seeking out a balanced set of judgments on any particular book. Important reviews of articles are noted as well, since eighteenth-century studies have the benefit of at least four regular sources of them: *The Eighteenth Century: A Current Bibliography*, the *Scriblerian*, and the annual reviews of restoration and eighteenth-century scholarship in *Philological Quarterly* and *Studies in English Literature 1500-1900*. When a rare item is described as "Noted by . . ." rather than "Reviewed by . . . ," I have had only secondhand information about the item and have had to rely on the source cited. Reprints of older books and articles are not generally listed in the body of this bibliography, with a few exceptions for special landmarks included in important new collections. However, a sample of the more useful other reprints is included at the end of this preface. At the end of each section, pertinent items from other categories are cross-referenced.

The research for this volume owes much to the staff of Dinand Library at Holy Cross and to the resources of Widener Library at Harvard and to the Boston Public Library. The diligence and intelligence of my undergraduate research assistants, Therese Broderick, John Luiz, Marie Faulkner, and Elaine Feloney, made this bibliography possible. Shirley Adams worked on the index and other chores.

Marion Meilaender and James Kee carefully read parts of the manuscript. Maurice A. Geracht supplied many items and commented on a number of them. Margo Wilson translated Gaelic material. James Woolley, R.S. Pendexter, John R. Clark, Hermann J. Real, Heinz Vienken, Richard J. Panofsky, Alamgir Hashmi, George A. Test, and B. Eugene McCarthy called attention to items that would otherwise have been overlooked. David M. Vieth sent the manuscript of his *Swift's Poetry 1900-1980: An Annotated Bibliography of Studies* (Garland, 1982) to me a full year before it was published. For this and other kindnesses from a great Swift scholar, I am profoundly grateful.

To the late Reuben A. Brower, with whom I first studied Swift, I owe more debts than I can ever acknowledge adequately.

The research for and writing of this volume over three years was supported by a semester's leave from Holy Cross College, which also made available the word-processing facilities that produced this book.

To all of these, and especially to my wife, Denise, my mother, Nan Elizabeth, and my family and friends, who offered patience and encouragement during three years of what often seemed like drudgery, I offer my gratitude.

A Sample of Books and Articles Reprinted in 1965–1980.

Ball, F. Elrington. *Swift's Verse: An Essay.* London: John Murray, 1929. Reprinted Folcroft, Pa.: Folcroft Press, 1969; New York: Octagon Books, 1970. Pp. xv + 402.

Berwick, Donald M. *The Reputation of Jonathan Swift 1781–1882.* Philadelphia, 1941. Reprinted New York: Haskell House, 1965.

A Catalogue of Books and Manuscripts by Jonathan Swift, D.D. Exhibited in the Old Schools of the University of Cambridge. To Commemorate the 200th Anniversary of His Death, October 19, 1745. Cambridge: Cambridge U. Press, 1945. Reprinted Folcroft, Pa.: Folcroft Press, 1971.

Craik, Henry. *The Life of Jonathan Swift.* 2 vols. 2d. ed. 1894. Reprinted (essays in Literature and Criticism, 31) New York: Burt Franklin, 1969.

Davis, Herbert. *The Satire of Jonathan Swift.* New York: Macmillan, 1947. Reprinted Westport, Ct.: Greenwood Press, 1979. Pp. 109.

Dennis, Nigel. *Jonathan Swift: A Short Character.* London: Macmillan, 1964. Reprinted London: Weidenfeld and Nicolson, 1965; New York: Collier Books, 1967. Pp. 160.

Ehrenpreis, Irvin. *The Personality of Jonathan Swift.* London: Methuen; New York: Barnes & Noble, 1958. Reprinted 1969. Pp. 179.

Firth, C.H. "The Political Significance of *Gulliver's Travels.*" *Proceedings of the British Academy,* 9 (1919), 237–59. Reprinted Gloucester, Ma.: Peter Smith, 1974. Pp. 23.

Freeman, Martin A. (ed.). *Vanessa and Her Correspondence with Jonathan Swift. The Letters Edited for the First Time from the Originals.* London: Selwyn & Blount; Boston: Houghton Mifflin, 1921. Reprinted Folcroft, Pa.: Folcroft Press, 1969; 1974; Norwood, Pa.: Norwood Editions, 1976. Pp. 216.

Gold, Maxwell B. *Swift's Marriage to Stella: Together with Unprinted and Misprinted Letters.* Cambridge, Ma.: Harvard U. Press, 1937. Reprinted New York: Russell & Russell, 1967.

Greenberg, Robert A. (ed.). *Gulliver's Travels: An Authoritative Text, the Correspondence of Swift, Pope's Verses on Gulliver's Travels, Critical Essays.* New York: Norton, 1961. Reprinted 1970.

Hubbard, Lucius L. *Contributions Toward a Bibliography of* Gulliver's Travels. Chicago, 1922. Reprinted (Burt Franklin Bibliography and Reference Series, 152) New York: Burt Franklin, 1968. Pp. xiii + 189; 25 plates.

Jackson, Robert Wyse. *Swift and His Circle: A Book of Essays.* 1945. (Essays Index Reprint Series.) Reprinted Freeport, N.Y.: Books for Libraries Press, 1969. Pp. ix + 112.

Jeffrey, Francis Lord. *Jonathan Swift, D.D.* London: Longman, Brown, Green, and Longman, 1853. Reprinted Folcroft, Pa.: Folcroft Press, 1969. Pp. 92.

Johnson, Maurice. *The Sin of Wit: Jonathan Swift as a Poet.* Syracuse: Syracuse U. Press, 1950. Reprinted New York: Gordian Press, 1966. Pp. xvii + 145.

King, Richard Ashe. *Swift in Ireland.* 1895. Reprinted Folcroft, Pa.: Folcroft Press, 1969.

Landa, Louis A., and James Edward Tobin (comps.). *Jonathan Swift: A List of Critical Studies Published from 1895-1945. To Which Is Added Remarks on Some Swift Manuscripts in the United States by Herbert Davis.* (Eighteenth Century Bibliographical Pamphlets.) New York: Cosmopolitan Science and Art Service Co., 1945. Reprinted New York: Octagon Books, 1974. Pp. 62.

Moriarity, Gerald P. *Dean Swift and His Writings.* 1893. Reprinted New York: Haskell House, 1970. Pp. 341.

Murry, John Middleton. *Jonathan Swift: A Critical Biography.* London: Jonathan Cape, 1954. Reprinted New York: Farrar, Strauss and Giroux, 1967. Pp. 508.

Paulson, Ronald. *Theme and Structure in Swift's* Tale of a Tub. New Haven: Yale U. Press, 1962. Reprinted Hamden, Ct.: Archon, 1969; 1972.

Price, Martin. *Swift's Rhetorical Art: A Study in Structure and Meaning.* (Yale Studies in English, 123.) New Haven: Yale U. Press, 1953. Reprinted New York: Arcturus Books; Carbondale and Edwardsville: Southern Illinois U. Press; London and Amsterdam: Feffer and Simons, 1973.

Quintana, Ricardo. *The Mind and Art of Jonathan Swift.* New York and London: Oxford U. Press, 1936. Reprinted Gloucester, Ma.: Peter Smith, 1965.

Rossi, Mario M., and Joseph M. Hone. *Swift, or the Egoist.* London: Gollancz; New York: E. P. Dutton, 1934. Reprinted Folcroft, Pa.: Folcroft Press, 1969; 1976.

Stephen, Leslie. *Swift.* 1882. Reprinted (Gale Library of Lives and Letters) Detroit: Gale Research Co., 1968.

Van Doorn, Cornelius. *An Investigation into the Character of Jonathan Swift.* 1931. Reprinted Folcroft, Pa.: Folcroft Press, 1968; 1970.

Williams, Harold. *Dean Swift's Library with a Facsimile of the Original Sale Catalogue and Some Account of Two Manuscript Lists of His Books.* Cambridge U. Press, 1932. Reprinted Folcroft, Pa.: Folcroft Press, 1969. Pp. vii + 93 + 16.

Williams, Kathleen. *Jonathan Swift and the Age of Compromise.* Lawrenceville: U. of Kansas Press, 1958. Reprinted 1965; 1968.

Wilson, C. H. *Swiftiana.* 2 vols. 1804. Reprinted Folcroft, Pa.: Folcroft Press, 1972. Pp. 232; 237.

LIST OF ABBREVIATIONS

ECCB	*The Eighteenth Century: A Current Bibliography*
ECS	*Eighteenth-Century Studies*
ELH	*ELH: A Journal of English Literary History*
ELN	*English Language Notes*
HLQ	*Huntington Library Quarterly*
JEGP	*Journal of English and Germanic Philology*
JHI	*Journal of the History of Ideas*
MLN	*Modern Language Notes*
MLQ	*Modern Language Quarterly*
MLR	*Modern Language Review*
MP	*Modern Philology*
N&Q	*Notes and Queries*
PBSA	*Papers of the Bibliographical Society of America*
PLL	*Papers on Language and Literature*
PMLA	*Publications of the Modern Language Association of America*
PQ	*Philological Quarterly*
RES	*Review of English Studies*
SEL	*Studies in English Literature 1500–1900*
SP	*Studies in Philology*
SVEC	*Studies on Voltaire and the Eighteenth Century*
TLS	*Times Literary Supplement* (London)
TSLL	*Texas Studies in Literature and Language*

INTRODUCTION
"Capable of Being in Uncertainties, Mysteries, Doubts"

Swift is the most controversial of writers. Practically every major text has its colliding schools of interpretation, and the major developments of criticism from 1965–1980 have been in acquiring self-consciousness about these controversies and in learning to take disagreements seriously. In 1980, these developments had by no means reached maturity. The period from 1965 to 1980 is filled with Swiftian cries of alarm that the controversy and contradiction among us must be making someone look foolish. Can't we ever agree on the "best" answers? (Think, for example, how impatient, even patronizing, became the late 1970's discussion of James Clifford's apparently relativistic "hard" and "soft" school concepts for *Gulliver's Travels*.) Swift critics have never felt easy with pluralistic readings of their hero, partly because Swift scholarship has maintained close ties with the history of ideas, but mostly because the study of Swift since the 1930's has been heavily influenced by psychological assumptions, closely connected to pursuit of an author's coherent consciousness.

To a theoretical eye, therefore, criticism of Swift's writing can appear to be late blooming. Traditional biographical approaches to *Gulliver's Travels*, for instance, did not lose pre-eminence until the early 1950's.[1] In fact, the most important work in Swift studies up to 1950, without a major rival, was Ricardo Quintana's aptly titled *The Mind and Art of Jonathan Swift* (1936).[2] Though New Criticism was blooming on most other vines during the 1940's, not until 1955 did Quintana publish his own epochal conversion to formalist premises, *Swift: An Introduction*, staking out the next ten years of Swift criticism.[3] Even in the 1950's, Irvin Ehrenpreis's *The Personality of Jonathan Swift* (1958) was a center of discussion; in fact, his combative discounting of persona for personality (re-emphasized in 1963) was probably *the* liveliest center of discussion.[4] In the next decade, the first two volumes of Ehrenpreis's ensuing biography, *Swift: The Man, His*

Works, and the Age (1963, 1967), were unsurpassed as sources for critical argument.[5] Even in the past fifteen years, such landmarks as W.B. Carnochan's *Lemuel Gulliver's Mirror for Man* (1968) and C.J. Rawson's *Gulliver and the Gentle Reader* (1973),[6] though evidently propelled by interests in technique and reader response, have nevertheless declared themselves ultimately concerned with the mind behind the manipulation, sometimes called the "biographical presence" of Swift. Even when biographical criticism was finally fading a bit for many Swift critics, by the early 1950's, only sometimes did they replace it with the formalist analysis blossoming throughout the rest of the literary establishment. Just as often, and with equal relish, they also returned to re-pruned and re-grafted arguments from the History of Ideas.[7]

New Critical formalism, as I mentioned, came comparatively late to Swift studies. Quintana's foundational essay on method, "Situational Satire," seemed pivotal to Swift critics as late as 1948, when New Criticism had already been stretching its wings for nearly a decade. The greatest formalist critics in eighteenth-century studies—Reuben A. Brower, Maynard Mack, Earl Wasserman, William K. Wimsatt—wrote on Pope rather than on Swift. Brower, for example, made no secret of the tepid satisfactions his exemplary New Critical method and talents wrenched from Swift's verse ("when it even *is* poetry," Brower used to moan). Quintana, the uncontested leader of Swift studies, officially converted to formalist rhetorical criticism in 1955, just two years before Northrop Frye's devastating body-blow to New Criticism in *The Anatomy of Criticism*, and also just two years before Frank Kermode could be seen performing an autopsy on the battered body in *The Romantic Image*.[8] Maurice Johnson's famous second thoughts about his approach to Swift's poetry are instructive along this line. His pioneering study, *The Sin of Wit* (1950), analyzed line after line, poem after poem, following respectable formalist premises.[9] But by 1973 Johnson was motioning younger critics back onto the well-trodden biographical paths. In fact, Johnson's advice to study the "biographical presence" in Swift was already widely heeded by 1973 and continued to dominate criticism of Swift's poetry in the 1970's.[10]

Similarly, thorough-going post-structuralist analyses of Swift started to appear in measurable quantities only at the end of the 1970's, just beginning really near the end of the period covered by this volume.[11] Elsewhere, by 1980, leading American post-structuralists, such as

J. Hillis Miller, were already announcing that deconstruction had been born, had flourished, and was now dying. Perhaps because American post-New Critical theory from Frye to Bloom has been dominated by those trained in and primarily interested by Romantic literature, Swift studies, from such a spacious vista, can have the look of a theoretical late bloomer.

However, the apparent diffidence of Swift studies cannot simply be chalked up to a general complacency in eighteenth-century studies. Consider how beloved to post-structuralists are Defoe and Richardson, to take just two examples. Consider, too, how appetizing some of Swift's writings must be to post-structuralist critics. *A Tale of a Tub* virtually deconstructs itself from underneath you; *Gulliver's Travels* has long been famous for foiling attempts to arrive at its "meaning." Even an outspoken limiter of pluralism like Wayne C. Booth finds *A Modest Proposal* nearly indeterminate, or at least a hard knot for unravelers of determinate meaning.[12] What might be worth stressing is how the attractions of Swift's work for deconstruction seem to have weakened the urgency with which post-structuralists have thought to pursue it. This routine quality in Swift's works of blockage, of freeplay, of decentering, of reader entrapment, of a text falling into crumbs, may be responsible for the misleading appearance of old-fashionedness of many Swift critics. *They* were forced long ago to find their own languages for describing what Roland Barthes recently called the "Text of bliss: the text that imposes a state of loss, the text that discomforts (perhaps to the point of a certain boredom), unsettles the reader's historical, cultural, psychological assumptions, the consistency of his tastes, values, memories, brings to a crisis his relations with language."[13]

Post-structuralism's flabbier and often more uneasy bedfellow, reader-response criticism, has been better represented in the period 1965–1980, though here, too, a variety of old-fashioned determinance and intentionality has usually predominated. Thus Quintana, dean of the "mind and art" approach, found little to disapprove of in the recent work of C.J. Rawson, who strikes many Swiftians as their most advanced voice in reader-response criticism. As Quintana recognized, Rawson's approach is largely psychoanalytical, showing us a consistent eighteenth-century figure through modern lenses.[14] Rawson would undoubtedly agree. Though his work is viewed as radical by some Swiftians, exciting by nearly all, his brilliant analyses are underpaved with familiar assumptions (battled against by such radical reader-response theorists as Stanley Fish) that an author's personality can and should be distinguished from a reader's experience.

Complaints about this pragmatism and conservativism have not been lacking. William Kinsley recently shook Swift scholarship by the lapels: ". . . we leap to interpret individual episodes more or less plausibly so as to support an overall view of the book that we have arrived at by processes that would hardly bear inspection, or at least are seldom offered for inspection. We don't stop to make our assumptions explicit or to consider what results our methods would produce if applied to other episodes."[15] However, if individual analyses are sometimes infuriatingly smug about *meaning*—what it is, how you acquire it, and how you then verify it—Swift studies collectively has continuously presented some of the most explicit challenges to determinate meaning in all of literary studies. I am thinking here of the tendency of Swift criticism, on whatever text, to fall into well-defined debates over meaning, with rival presentations of the same evidence and competing validity claims. This tendency is easily documented in every area of Swift scholarship, but for this introduction, I have picked out five representative controversies that flourished in the period 1965–1980. One or two are famous, but all are instructive. Far from being irritating evidence of perversity or indecisiveness, these conflicts clarify extraordinarily well how the critical premises we begin with pre-determine the meaning we find. The disagreements, far from being dead ends, strike me as potentially among the most salutary developments in all Swift scholarship.

Persona or Personality in *A Tale of a Tub*

Roughly half the writings devoted to *A Tale of a Tub* have disagreed about a stunningly fundamental question. Do the *Tale*'s opinions and descriptions come from Swift's own personality, or from a dramatically consistent persona whom Swift disowns and actually makes into the object of the satire? The other half of writings on the *Tale* in 1965–1980 continued undisturbed with source hunting and theme tracing—Hopewell Selby tracing metaphors of confinement and isolation, Leslie Mechanic finding patterns of food consumption and gluttony, Ricardo Quintana locating Descartes at the heart of IX, ii, Charles Scruggs adding information about Lucretius, Eugene Bud Korkowski noting figures of containment, W.B. Carnochan focusing on Swift's proverb lore, Thomas L. Canavan scrutinizing traditions of Puritan invective, and so forth.[16]

However, a definite struggle for control of terms preoccupied the other half. Ronald Paulson's ground-breaking argument, or one like it, for the consistent identity of Swift's Taleteller, underpinned most *Tale* criticism until the mid-1970's.[17] The speaker is regarded as a dramatized persona (grubstreet hack, madman, or modern virtuoso), entirely distinguishable from Swift, who embodies in the content, style, and structure of his *Tale* the genuine targets of Swift's satire. A good example is Jay Arnold Levine's much-reprinted 1966 article, which called the *Tale* an "olio, a fricasee, a ragout," but then confidently asserted that the "fictive author of the *Tale*—whom modern critics have variously labelled the Hack, the Madman, the Grub-Street Author, the Fool(s), and the Ingénu—is a Bentlyan Critic in a very special sense; that his 'authorship' explains the form of the work."[18] This same impulse to find an organic wholeness to the work through a coherent narrative persona was a central assumption in the work of, for example, Robert H. Hopkins (the Hack is an impersonation of Hobbes), John Hayman (1970) (Swift's persona is both like and unlike Shaftesbury's), Robert C. Elliott (an emphatic argument that Swift uses, rather than identifies with, his personae), Pat Rogers (1972) (the *Tale* is a conspicuous satiric example of *excess of form*, the Taleteller "a half-educated incompetent"), and Raymond Anselment (1973) (everything about the Hack represents the despised "Modern writer"). Michael DePorte brought in fresh scholarship in eighteenth-century notions of madness to label the narrator an unstable madman and thus answer objections that the persona appears inconsistent or shows traces of Swift leaking through. This novelistic or dramatically coherent view of the *Tale*'s narrator was carried to its extreme in Marjorie Beam's systematic comparison (1976) of "him" with Hamlet![19] However, the most concentrated expression of this general view was contained in John R. Clark's *Form and Frenzy* (1970), which thoroughly advanced the premises of an earlier essay by Clark, "treating the *Tale* centripetally as a single and complete work of mimetic art," narrated by a madman.[20]

Clark's book, not mere formalism, but also scholarship of a high order, provoked sharp rebuttal from certain quarters. C.J. Rawson complained that Clark missed Swift's self-implication in mad contradictions and polarities (a point most tellingly made by Kenneth Burke, and another continuing bone of contention). Robert Martin Adams nagged that Clark's scholarship rubbed tough Swiftian passages into soft, explicit statements. In his review, Gardner Stout reiterated his whole-hearted opposition (1969, 1973) to modern persona theories of Swift: only "by listening to the *Tale* as spoken by Swift, *in propria persona*, however varied his tone and pose, [can] we . . . avoid misreading the shifting complexities of his brilliant satire as a tale told by an idiot."[21] Stout's view was therefore a version of psychological criticism, closely related to phenomenology: "By reading the *Tale* as spoken by Swift, we can share his experience of that condition and, like him, dis-cover our faces in the *Tale*'s satiric glass." Stout's insistence that "Swift is the speaker throughout," closely followed the lines of Irvin Ehrenpreis's 1963 challenge to personae criticism of Augustan satire. Provocative enough to prompt a long symposium in *Satire Newsletter*, Ehrenpreis's well-known protest replaced persona with the author's own "ironical pose, which wins its literary effect only to the degree that it is seen through."[22]

In 1965, William John Roscelli had anticipated Stout's method to an extent, by advancing a long argument about Swift's problems in satirizing religion in the *Tale* without needing to refer to a narrative presence other than the author's.[23] John Traugott's 1971 essay insisted that neither persona nor scholarly paraphernalia accounts for the "mad voices" of the *Tale*; they are found in all men, a truth Swift discovered about himself when his defensive snobbery about Sir William Temple led him to write subversively accurate mimicry of vulgarian types. Traugott relished (*contra* F.R. Leavis) Swift's self-licensing as a fool and the *Tale*'s sharp "potpourri of attitudes"—all, however, presumably close to those actually held by Swift himself.[24] Cary Nelson's apparently *avant garde* essay of 1973 turned out, on this score, to be partly traditional psychological pronouncement: "The horror in Swift is a contamination phobia, an image of Swift himself frozen in the knowledge that he has already succumbed to corruption."[25] Likewise, all of Denis Donoghue's points about Swift's rhetoric depended upon the assumption that "This is the Hack, but it is also Jonathan Swift."[26]

This frank disagreement, like most, has prompted some rethinking about the inadequate terminology that underlies the conflict. By 1970

Frank Kinahan was explicitly discounting both the persona and the "personality" schools: "It would seem a thankless task to try to determine which of the two [Swift or the Hack] is actually speaking, for in fact, they are both speaking at the same time. The voices bounce off each other and back, and their interaction produces an echo which is a voice in its own right."[27] Alan Fisher (1974) termed Swift's presence as "mysterious" and located the mystery in the *Tale*'s ambiguous pleasures: "The critical question becomes, then, how is it possible to have fun while at the same time one is contemplating the void?"[28] David Vieth's way out of the conflict was to acknowledge a more or less coherent narrative presence but to deny the reader any sure distance from it: "According to the 'official' interpretation, the unnamed speaker of the *Tale* is a bad modern writer who is implicitly condemned for violating traditional norms of aesthetics, morality, and plain common sense. Again, we encounter a 'reversible meaning,' for these indistinct, implicit norms are less 'real' than the speaker himself, whose perceptions, though solipsistic, possess more immediacy than anything else in the *Tale*."[29]

Earlier, in 1973, Neil Schaeffer articulated another reader-response answer: assigning distinct responsibility for statements is less important than recognizing how Swift's satire works by stymieing or trapping its audience. Schaeffer was especially successful in explaining how a thematic critic such as F.R. Leavis and a persona critic such as Robert C. Elliott, each confessing he had fallen into Swift's trap, could nevertheless arrive at precisely opposite interpretations of the *Tale*'s famous "fool among knaves" passage without being guilty of careless reading. Shaeffer's explanation was that Swift's satire works by encouraging its readers to look for and rely upon simple inversions so that it can rub their noses in that inadequate presumption.[30] The most thoroughgoing alternative to the either-or choice of persona or "personality" was offered in Frederik N. Smith's 1979 book *Language and Reality in Swift's* A Tale of a Tub, where the Hack's convoluted verbosity is admitted but seen as constantly undercut by Swift's own concrete mater-of-factness.[31] The meaning or effect of this double style is changeful, from repudiation of the Hack's emptiness, to a sneer at the lowness of reality itself. Smith's conclusions leaned away from a subject-bound hermeneutic: "The responsibility for distinguishing between sanity and insanity, truth and error, is in the *Tale* turned over to us." However, for Smith, as for the "personality-ists," Swift's partial identification with the mad Hack proves Swift did not care to write about modern insanity from the safe position of modern insanity. Smith's analyses, carefully distinguishing Swift's statements from those of the Hack, remain in most respects as arbitrarily "objective" as the analyses of the two "establishment" schools.

"A Fool Among Knaves"

The fortunes of Section IX of the *Tale* (the "fool among knaves" passage) are closely related to the persona question, and in 1965–1980 returned to their pre-1950's status. Put another way, F.R. Leavis's pioneering statement of indignation is once again alive and well, as it ought to be: "What is left? The next paragraph begins significantly: 'But to return to Madness.' This irony may be critical, but 'critical' turns out, in no very long run, to be indistinguishable from 'negative.' The positives disappear."[32] The list of "positives" proposed to answer Leavis has been contradictory enough to build a semi-permanent foundation under his question. For instance, two of our most formidable critics are at loggerheads over the "fool among knaves" passage. Irvin Ehrenpreis (1963) saw the "positives" lying ultimately with the party of knaves: "The real proposition here is that man's moral essence or reason—his inside—is infinitely more important than his physical accidents—the outside. Reason and judgment are therefore analytical or introspective, while the sense, passions and imagination (when divorced from the understanding) may be tricked by appearances. It is better to be sadly wise and know oneself, Swift really says, than to be complacently self-deceived."[33] On the other hand, Denis Donoghue (1967) defined the "positive" as the state of being a fool, an allusion, as he sees it, to Swift's hero, Sir William Temple: "To be a fool among knaves is consciously and conscientiously to seek the life of the garden, rejecting the life of the world which, in this Epicurean setting, is the work of knaves."[34]

It is not difficult to discern that each critic is arriving at the interpretation that his *a priori* assumptions have allowed him to reach. Ehrenpreis's "real" interpretations are based on an understanding of Anglican thought, while Donoghue's derive from biographical assumptions. Outright conflicts like this one have tended to prompt a slew of "middle ground" interpretations, which insist that both extremists are partly right and partly wrong, giving Swift studies its characteristic triangular shape. However, even when critics resist these determinate ideas of meaning, and ultimately decide that the passage's primary effect is to *resist* interpretation, to make decisions knotty, disagreements likely, questions about its motives nag on. Is Swift expressing something about himself? Did he intend to express just that, and not something else? If not self-expression, then are the motives of the text benign? The psychological answer was spelled out by Robert M. Adams in 1958: "Standing apart from his society, and with special horror from those who had rebelled against it, Swift achieved at bitter expense an especially acute and individual insight into it."[35] Much, perhaps most, criticism addressing this passage in 1965–1980 followed these general psychological lines, at some point reducing the text to Swift's either intentional or unwitting self-expression.

By the same token, most alternative approaches before 1970—such as seeing this satiric dilemma as Swift's friendly inducement to the reader—are still reductive in other ways. We have not yet mastered the equivalent of a null hypothesis in scientific method, in which the choice of question is such that either a yes or a no answer is in error; unask the question, what does this passage *really* mean, we need to say; the context of the question is too small for the truth of the answer. Even the best answers to date about the paradoxes of Section IX have been a trifle too small. Witness the powerful view, articulated by William Empson in 1935, that the choice itself is a trap; that is, that acquiescing to either-or structures may block us from deeper understanding: "It is because of the strength given by this antagonism that it seems to get so safely outside the situation it assumes, to decide so easily about the doubt which it in fact accepts. This may seem a disagreeable pleasure in the ironist but he gives the same pleasure more or less secretly to his audience, and the process brings to mind the whole body of their difficulty with so much sharpness and freshness that it may give the strength to escape from it."[36] Deriving meaning, especially from a form so apparently irresolute about its sense, seems an irresistible need for critics. John R. Clark (1969) preemptorily dismissed any view of Swift as "helpless neurotic, attracted by Credulity as well as by Curiosity, and eviscerated upon the horns of his dilemma."[37] Clark accepted the Hack's definition of the sane mind (which elects to pass life adhering to the "common forms") in Section IX as marking off a third alternative of decision and self-possession. This, conveyed through his "artistic aloofness," is the "natural position" Swift himself is advocating.

Another way out of the seeming impasse is illustrated by Robert H. Hopkins's (1966) close attention to the phrase *"in a Commonwealth"* in the title of Section IX, which allowed Hopkins and later Alan S. Fisher (1974) to describe the "fool among knaves" paradox as mockery of Hobbist thinking, rather than as a universal human condition. Thus they were able to posit a normative non-Hobbist reader whose values coincide with those of Swift. Swift is rather a "wry jester" than a gloomy presence.[38] Ricardo Quintana (1974), who sought to be fair to the passage's complexity, but who also wanted a determinate meaning, constructed the idea of a double audience "consisting of those who could and would follow the ridicule in all the modes of its delivery . . . and those who were going to be reduced to stupid rage."[39] Neil Schaeffer's reader-attack argument was also representative of the bedrock resistance in some circles to viewing Swift's irony as universal denial. He concluded by distinguishing the "fools" and "knaves" of Section IX from the "sensible men" whom he believes are rendered implicitly by the text.[40]

Blasphemy or Blessing in "The Lady's Dressing Room"

One of the primary contributions of twentieth-century Swiftian criticism has been to lift from Swift's shoulders the burden of misanthropy or misogyny embodied in characters such as Gulliver or Strephon of the scatological poems. Unfortunately, this service is often performed in the name of positive affirmations the texts seem uninterested in making, aiming rather for blockage or difficulty. "The Lady's Dressing Room" (1730) has been one of Swift's two or three most-discussed poems, partly because Strephon's putative delusions often strike soft-school readers as paralleling Gulliver's escapades.

Strephon is a compulsive idealist, says the soft school, who insists upon repeatedly shocking himself by a most meticulous survey of his "goddess's" dressing room. His tortured revulsion, the wages of inadequate sublimation or compulsive anality, is by no means that of Swift, nor need it be shared by readers. James L. Tyne representatively viewed the poem as a cautionary illustration of how idealization will lead to frustration, then to demoralization.[41] On the other hand, hard-school interpretations have depended upon seeing a contradiction in the final lines of the poem, which Christine Rees put thus: "The speaker implicitly condemns both Strephon's original illusion and his violent disillusion as ferments of a diseased imagination, but his own insinuating answer is no less ironic, and no more tenable."[42] What should we make of the concluding advice to hold our noses and ignore the confusion and excrement that underpaves Order and Tulips?

> When *Celia* in her Glory shows,
> If *Strephon* would but stop his Nose;
> (Who now so impiously blasphemes
> Her Ointments, Daubs, and Paints and Creams,
> Her Washes, Slops, and every Clout,
> With which he makes so foul a Rout;)
> He soon would learn to think like me,
> And bless his ravisht Eyes to see
> Such Order from Confusion sprung,
> Such gaudy Tulips rais'd from Dung.[43]

The varieties of the soft-school reading are legion and have often been based on positivistic historical assumptions. Source-hunters, like Harry M. Solomon, or John F. Sena, for instance, need a soft-school interpretation to deflect attention from the reader's participation in the making of meaning. Solomon, who wanted to explain the poem as mockery of verses by a poet Swift despised, Tom D'Urfey, posited Swift relying on "an audience of initiated readers who can share his contempt at a dual superficiality." Sena muzzled the ending with a medical tradition that treated "love melancholy" by forced disillusionment. Similarly, Felicity Nussbaum operated by some standard assumptions about Swift himself in order to hear the ending trying to "release men from passion and its attendant madness."[44]

Versions of Norman O. Brown's 1959 articulation of this view were still pervasive in 1965–1980: Swift is urging upon Strephon the notion that sublimation is still possible and necessary.[45] Donald Greene countered that Swift's argument was actually that all beauty is born of chaos and imperfection; Swift was not urging sublimation, that is, but rather Christian acceptance of reality.[46] John M. Aden seconded Greene's view with some modifications: "if Strephon would but discount the argument from his sense . . . he could, like the poet, find the spectacle of beauty out of such noisome origins a source of wonder, and not, as he has, of despair."[47] Susan Gubar also assumed that this text offered a super-highway to Swift's most genuine beliefs, and, prompted by her feminist agenda, wrote the most vehement attack on Swift himself since Orwell and Middleton Murry (with whose literary assumptions she shares much): "Swift describes his own inability to accept the ambiguities and contradictions of the human condition, portraying his failure in the figure of the repulsive female."[48]

A significant variation on this soft-school psychological reading was advanced by Peter J. Schakel who argued that although Swift was trying hard to write comically at the end of "The Lady's Dressing Room," he simply failed. Anything that smacks of contradiction or denial in the final lines is a sign that "Swift was unable to dissociate himself sufficiently from his material."[49] Thomas B. Gilmore, who participated in a well-known quarrel with Schakel and Greene, actually read the poem not very dissimilarly ("What is now clearer to me, thanks to Schakel, is the legitimacy of seeing Swift's comedy, however qualified its success, as the essential token of his maturity, and of valuing it the more as an earned outcome of the conflict within him").[50] In carrying this sort of author-bound interpretation to its extreme, C.J. Rawson approached the hard-school position (about which, more below), pointing to the special "urgency and truth" in Swift's inability or unwillingness to compromise or reconcile "the reality of the flayed woman and the gutted beau" with the need for decent repression.[51]

Although the points of difference among these critics were significant, all shared two important soft-school assumptions: Swift's own values are manifestly not those of Strephon, and are more or less identical with those of the poem's narrator. A third premise they shared was that "The Lady's Dressing Room" must somewhere, somehow *mean* something; furthermore, that meaning is separable from, not created by, the contradictory tugs readers may encounter in the final lines. The hard school, on the other hand, seemed to believe, with greater or lesser enthusiasm for the idea, that explaining what "The Lady's Dressing Room" means is fundamentally similar to describing what it *does* to its readers. Along these lines, there were a number of seemingly moderate or "spongy" (Clifford's word) positions. Louise Barnett, for instance, agreed with the hard school (Rees, A.B. England, Richard H. Rodino, for example) that the narrator's final position is untenable. But because she believed readers ought to see through the unreliableness of both the narrator and Strephon from the start, Barnett was able to postulate a firm and unambiguous, though implicit, stance taken by the author Swift.[52] The moderate school, that is, did not ignore the interpretive difficulties of the poem's ending and did not necessarily attribute those difficulties to Swift's self-expression, deliberate or inadvertent. It was interested, however, in guiding those difficulties safely to closure. Peter Briggs's (1979) typical moderate view was that the ending provides a "positive, though cautionary and skeptical, moral" about the need to see tulips and dung as complementary, not contradictory. Paul C. Davies's similar interpretation employed the term "reconcile" to account for the ending's insistence on both goddesses and greasy whores.[53]

While the moderate critics attempted to reduce the ending's obstacles to thematic statements, hard-school interpreters were busy explaining them as parts of the reading process. The assumption underlying this view was that the poem's "meaning" is not, strictly speaking, detachable from the experience of reading it. "Meaning," in this sense, is the event of perceiver encountering the unusually stressful, open-ended signals given off by the text. Rawson's essay, noted above, recognized the poem's resistance to closure (it does not compromise or reconcile), but insisted that this openness is an act of self-revelation by some recoverable consciousness, which we may call Swift. A.B. England went further towards holding his eye on the process of the poem, for the most part refusing to collapse the ending into meaning where it is rather designed for resistance. His insights, quite advanced when first published in 1966, remained attached, however, to the terminology of subjective expression rather than reader response: "Swift on the one hand establishes a morally evaluative framework that often seems capable of bringing its subject matter to a kind of order by placing it firmly within a coherent ethical structure. But he also at several points in the poem renders that subject matter in such a way as to suggest that it is not being entirely subdued by the rationalizing framework, and that it is in the end too radically disturbing and unruly to be subject to that kind of ordering containment."[54]

Christine Rees (1973), to a greater degree than England, swung the focus to the reader's experience of the poem's difficulties: "Swift has forced 'Confusion' upon the reader too intimately and menacingly in the whole poem for 'Order' to be anything other than an abstract and highly satiric compensation. . . . His actual rejection of the nature/art compromise is confirmed by the final image."⁵⁵ My own 1978 article on the scatological poems emphasized the experience of vexation and dislocation into which the final lines push their reader: "the speaker is ingratiating and plausible as a satirist in order to startle us with the sudden revelation that his moral scorn of Strephon has concealed an equally repugnant grossness. Reality is vastly imperfect, and certainly must be accommodated, but one shrinks from calling a 'pocky Quean' a goddess, or smiling luridly while holding one's nose. Such 'order' is 'ravishment,' illusory and degrading. . . . 'The Lady's Dressing Room' does not simply delineate the ambiguities and dilemmas of the 'fair and foul' female paradox, it forces the reader to redeem himself from complacency."⁵⁶ In short, the hard-school critics' key assumption was that the experiences and responses leading readers to construct interpretations were no less important than the hypostatized meanings they might arrive at. This allowed them to analyze "The Lady's Dressing Room" without necessarily forcing a determinate meaning from it.

The *Project for the Advancement of Religion*: Tract or Travesty?

The tendency of Swiftians to argue for directly contradictory interpretations is, as we have seen, little short of breathtaking. Take the recent brouhaha over the *Project for the Advancement of Religion and the Reformation of Manners* (1709). In 1967 Leland Peterson was able to argue, at length, in the most prominent journal in English studies (*PMLA*), that a treatise accepted for centuries as a sincere, direct proposal for political and moral reform was, in actuality, "not only a satiric thrust against the Society for the Reformation of Manners and projectors, not only another shocking exposure of nominal Christianity (like the *Argument*), but chiefly a political satire designed to embarrass the Whig Ministry."⁵⁷ Peterson's argument, which seemed to imply, as one non-admirer put it, "centuries of misinterpretation by many critics," relied chiefly on seeing Swift's evident advocacy of hypocrisy as outrageous and unacceptable and therefore as ironical.

Peterson proceeded by four stages: first, by surveying a history of eighteenth-century attitudes towards hypocrisy; second, by establishing that Swift's (presumably more reliably genuine) opinions in his sermons and in his *Argument Against Abolishing Christianity* contradict a pious reading of the *Project*; third, by analyzing certain formal features of the *Project* to show they are characteristic of Swiftian satire, including the flavor of the persona, the parody of royal proclamations, and the self-defeating legalistic and logical language; and, fourth, by implying that an historical analysis of the Whig ministry in 1709 would reveal vulnerably targets for the *Project's* satirical insinuations.

Over the next few years, Peterson's argument was attacked vigorously on the first two of these grounds, less emphatically on the last two. Phillip Harth's rebuttal (1969) was based on learned assumptions about Swift's own likely beliefs. High Anglicans could have and would have approved a distinction between public and private moral acts, Harth insisted, and so in Swift's eyes the *Project* would not be proposing hypocrisy at all. Jan R. Van Meter also argued from external ideas about Swift's own probable morality, but in addition supplied formalistic readings of "the whole of the *Project*" to discredit Peterson's claims about its satiric effect. The *Project's* speaker ought not to be lumped with the naively perverse Modest Proposer as a loony "projector," Van Meter objected, nor would Swift would have minded endorsing hypocrisy as the agency of goodness. John Kay rebutted Peterson by constructing his own, differing history of attitudes towards hypocrisy—from comments by Archbishops Sharp and Tillotson and by Robert Nelson.[58] (Peterson's contradictory sources had also included Tillotson, as well as William Sherlock, Daniel Defoe, Henry Sacheverell, and Queen Anne herself.)

On the other hand, even Harth admitted that in Peterson's reading the targets of Swift's satire are mostly plausible (he objected only to the alleged ridicule of Queen Anne); and no one has successfully denied that the *Project* does employ many of the devices familiar from Swift's most brilliant ironical satires.

The point, I think, is not that each of these arguments is equally worthy of belief. Tests for the sufficiency of evidence are not altogether comparative. Trained critics will impose standards for the quality and completeness of evidence before giving assent to any argument. However, each response and counter-response in the little *Project* controversy has been a double blessing, augmenting the fullness of our understanding of the *Project* and its context but also proving that the *Project* belongs to a great many putative "contexts," some of them directly contradictory. What we have gained is an invaluable reminder of how any critic's imposition of a "context"—formalistic, historical, moralistic—on any text is fraught with presumptions. Critical readers always contribute to the meaning of texts by choosing particular contexts for their readings, necessarily rejecting other contexts as less interesting or useful without undermining their truth value. Peterson's consistently able defense of his interpretation implicitly denied stability and determinate meaning to the text of the *Project*, as well as to our critical tradition's standards of historical and biographical context. Peterson wrote: "when we consider the audience for the *Project* (the Queen members of the court, the ministry, Parliament), and the last days of the Whig ministry during Queen Anne's reign, the *Project* takes on meanings far beyond the reformation of manners. In the context of its time, it is a genuinely complex work." Is even an ingenious reader or an impressively learned reader a perfectly transparent receiver of an organically unified meaning or experience? May we insist that a text means what it says, when it is not even repeating the same things to different readers? Or is the text a "picnic, to which the author brings the words and the reader brings the meaning?" These hard questions became the most formidable work of criticism in the 1970's and have continued to dominate the criticism of the 1980's.

Hard and Soft Schools on *Gulliver's Travels*

Everyone is familiar with James Clifford's "hard and soft schools" for interpreting *Gulliver's Travels*, a marking of indeterminacy coordinates that was without a doubt the chief development between 1965 and 1980 in criticism of the *Voyages*. From this sort of surveying, we at least learned to recognize some of the different soils in which competing meanings might grow. Familiarity breeds contempt, of course, and despite Clifford's salutary arguments for teaching literature (and understanding it) by way of controversy, the volume of irritable reaching after fact and certainty has grown since the early 1970's.[59] Yet, like a beautifully flawed hierarchy in mathematics, revealed by Gödel's theorem, the discussion of Book IV keeps slipping delightfully into strange loops, through which alert observers may hold two mutually contradictory understandings in mind at once, or at least in effortless mental alternation.

Clifford's largest questions were "should *Gulliver's Travels* be considered as a single, isolated work of art, or as an integral part of Swift's total output as a writer? Second, what are Swift's overall goals, if it is possible to discover them? And does he ever in his other works present an easily attainable norm?" Then he suggested four main categories of disagreement: "(1) the meaning of the Yahoos, (2) the meaning of the Houyhnhnms, (3) the significance of Captain Mendez, and (4) the interpretation of the ending." Clifford summarized his survey in the following way: Neither side any longer sees the Yahoos as a crazy slander on human beings; current hard and soft theories now accept them as the limits to which men might degenerate. The Houyhnhnms are seen by soft-school critics as either merely rational, not ideal, or as cold inhuman beings, lacking Christian benevolence, or else as merely prelapsarian perfection, irrelevant to men. Hard schoolers, on the other hand, are convinced that the rational horses do indeed represent some kind of ideal. Captain Pedro de Mendez, the virtuous Portuguese sea captain, is shrugged off by the hard school; however, the soft school views him as Swift's strategically placed, carefully considered model for human behavior. Soft-school critics see the ending of Book IV as comic or satiric, with Gulliver a main butt of the satire, along with the reader, for being taken in by Gulliver's misanthropy.[60] In this brief update of Clifford's study there is space only for a rollcall of work since 1965.

Although, as Clifford said, the Yahoos were one front on which the battle was cooling, John J. McManmon (1966) disputed the conventional wisdom that the pessimism of *Gulliver's Travels* is rooted in universal Christian doctrine about fallen human nature, correcting a number of careless generalizations about Christian thought.[61] Curt A. Zimansky (1966), in the footsteps of R.S. Crane, outlined the more traditional historical method that allows us to understand Swift's "satirical formula": "man is distinguished from animals by his gift of reason, and is no better than a beast unless he uses that reason." Donald Keesy (1979) sought to correct the view that Swift is depicting man as ultimately in a viable middle state between Houyhnhnms and Yahoos. The most thorough study of the Yahoos' symbolic significance, by James E. Gill, also shed the most light on Book IV's eternal teasing: even where the dominant impulse of the narrative is toward conclusive identification of man and Yahoo, constant hints are given of the gap between them. The construction of Book IV, Gill argued, continually begs readers to fix symbolic meanings to Yahoo and Houy-hnhnm yet also blocks all attempts to do so.[62]

On the subject of the Houyhnhnms, hard-school critics were generally more spirited than were their soft-school counterparts. However, some of the most cogent soft-school discussion attacked the horses' economic policies. Michael Wilding (1973), Peter Thorpe (1969), and Ann Cline Kelly (1976) argued, in different ways, that the Houyhnhnms' society is founded on economic oppression, and is thereby disqualified as a norm in the satire.[63] However, Louis Landa's even more thorough study of the Houyhnhnms' economics argued that their simple agrarian society rebukes the consumer-oriented, luxurious, service trade-riddled English economy, providing comfort for the hard school.[64] Other soft-school attacks on the Houyhnhnms were fairly familiar. For Steward LaCasce (1970), even Gulliver's Houyhnhnm master becomes less and less ideal or even attractive in his thinking and speaking, while John H. White (1966) blamed Swift's horses for displaying typically human mental processes—snap judgments and preoccupation with Gulliver's superficial form.[65] Hugo Reichard (1967) went so far as to accuse Gulliver of learning snobbery from the rational horses.[66] W.K. Thomas (1968) felt Swift was ridiculing the doctrine of moral self-sufficiency through the contented Houyhnhnms, while John B. Radner (1977) saw Gulliver's initial infatuation with the Struld-bruggs as foreshadowing the inadequate values and understanding underlying his later deluded admiration of the Houyhnhnms.[67]

On the hard school side, main emphasis was put on identifying presumably unassailable utopias that resemble Houyhnhnmland. Accordingly, William Halewood (1965) pointed out parallels between Book IV and Plutarch's "Life of Lycurgus"; M.M. Kelsall (1969) argued effectively that the six ideal heroes cited in Book III, chapter vii (the "one ideal picture in the *Travels* which even the most sophisticated critics would find difficult to read ironically"), resemble the Houy-hnhnms in crucial ways; A. S. Knowles, Jr. (1974) suggested that Book IV is a form of retirement literature, within the tradition "that reaches back to the Sabine farm of Horace," making it highly unlikely that Swift is satirizing the horses; Gerald J. Pierre (1975) found echoes of Sir William Temple's *Of Heroic Virtue* which describes the superiority of Chinese culture, an identification also advanced by Fumiko Takase (1980); John F. Reichert (1968) discovered a "markedly Platonic cast" to Houyhnhnmland, more an illustration of Plato's republic than a satire on deism or Cartesianism or neo-stoicism.[68]

Other hard-school arguments on behalf of the Houyhnhnms included William H. Halewood's and Marvin Levich's (1965) position that Swift more or less accepted a rational definition of man derived from contemporary cliché, and he "fully approved of the Houyhnhnm life of reason and conceived of it as fully possible for man."[69] John N. Morris (1972) pointed out that the Houyhnhnms' sanity is not truly repulsive at all, but rather is merely "insufficiently childish for our tastes."[70] The case against reading the Houyhnhnms as complex characters in a novel was summarized by W.E. Yeomans (1966): Swift combines burlesque and solemn elements in the horses, allowing them to be "altogether subservient to his intellectual purposes," with much Menippean precedent behind him.[71] Ralph W. Rader (1974) similarly argued that although horses performing human-like tasks seems ludicrous, this is a minor risk for Swift, "compared with the need to maintain the imaginative probability of the fictional premise essential to the special satiric attack."[72] Robert M. Philmus (1973) also asserted the worthiness of Houyhnhnmland by ascribing a dialectical relationship between the horses' utopia and the preceding three books of the *Travels*; Houyhnhnmland is itself "the thing which is not," expressing not lies, but transcendent truths.[73]

On the role of Pedro de Mendez, little news was announced except the suggestion by John S. Phillipson (1969) that Swift "anticipated a development of modern psychiatry" by giving Gulliver, in both the personality and the dwelling of the Portuguese sea captain, a "half-way house" on his return from confinement to the world outside. The hard-school answer was stated best by Conrad Suits (1965): Mendez's virtues merely reveal the "hopeless distance between even the best human beings and rational creatures."[74]

On Gulliver's apparent misanthropy at the ending, its function and development, the soft school has traditionally had the edge, however, for the most part treating Gulliver as a psychologically whole, novelistic character. Terry Cook's article (1980) was representative, arguing that the first three voyages carefully represent Gulliver's distorting perceptual and moral norms, so that his failures occupy the ironic foreground of Book IV; Hugo M. Reichard's "Gulliver the Pretender" (1965) was an even more thoroughgoing attack on Gulliver's delusions and excesses.[75] Not far behind in psychoanalyzing Gulliver's deviousness and perverseness were Everett Zimmerman (1974) and John A. Vance.[76] Gorman Beauchamp (1974) blamed Gulliver for abdicating the philosopher's duty to enlighten others when he "returns from the cave" as in Plato's allegory (although, didn't Gulliver attempt to enlighten us in his book titled "Travels into Several Remote Nations of the World"?). There were numerous further attacks on Gulliver's personality and character flaws. Robert M. Otten (1969) assigned all four books to Gulliver's coherent motive of eradicating Yahooism in England; Raymond Bentman (1971) proposed that Gulliver's raging and inconsistent behavior at the ending demonstrates the futility of attempting to live by pure ideals; Fred M. Fetrow (1977) suggested that Gulliver's deteriorating self-knowledge is documented by the changing nature and number of souvenirs he carries back from his voyages, while Joseph F. Trimmer (1971) suggested similarly that study of Gulliver's interaction with each captain may help us in judging Gulliver's variable reliableness.[77] Along only slightly different lines, Charles Pullen (1971) saw Gulliver, whatever he might symbolize, as a novelistic character of some substance, so that the reader watches "not only a good man, but an intelligent and scientifically-trained man under the pressure of increasingly bewildering shifts of perception."[78] Steven M. Cohan (1974) put the assumptions of this side of the argument in a usefully extreme way, claiming that "The power of Gulliver's four imaginary voyages is not that of a satire, but of a fiction."[79]

On the opposing side, the argument against reading the *Travels* as a novel has never slackened. A companion piece on Gulliver to Yeoman's caveats about the Houyhnhnms was written by Raymond J. Smith, Jr. (1965): Although it is barely possible to study Gulliver as a novelistic character, Swift's main intent is to manipulate him as an instrument of satire.[80] Donald Greene usefully restated the classic hard-school insistence that Swift intends Gulliver to be plausible, so that readers will identify with him and "undergo the same painful process of re-education that he does."[81] Ricardo Quintana also contributed a hard-school defense of the non-novelistic "range of mood and voice" in *Gulliver's Travels*, including Swift's "rhetoric of realism," his utopias, his "comedy of exclusion," and absurdity through entrapment.[82] Conrad Suits (1965), in perhaps the best all-around hard-school essay, showed that Gulliver does draw valid inferences from the evidence before him. Of the ending generally, Suits declared: if the "conclusion is in any sense a retraction on Swift's part or anything but one lash the more, then I am a sorrel nag."[83]

Attempts to reach behind the insistent either-or contradictions of the hard and soft schools grew numerous by 1980. H.D. Kelling and Steward LaCasce were among those who explicitly attacked Clifford's "hard" and "soft" school distinctions. Kelling saw both Houyhnhnms and Yahoos as metaphors, making Swift's own opinion of them indeterminable, a view also developed expansively in 1978 by James E. Gill.[84] LaCasce perceived a more fundamental opposition than hard and soft schools, between criticism based on "philosophic" assumptions concerning the nature of man and criticism based on "theological" assumptions. The former sees Book IV as a classical dichotomy of mind and matter, resolvable through either stoic resignation of a *via media* fashioned through natural philosophy. The latter treats the Yahoos as symbols of the passions corrupted by the prior condition of sin, the Houyhnhnms as Christian ideals; resolution is possible through compassion and hope.[85]

One of the most influential movements away from the impasse was W.B. Carnochan's (1968) argument that *Gulliver's Travels embodies*, rather than comments on, tensions inherent in seventeenth and eighteenth-century literary theory, insisting upon a "duality of feeling in every important case," from its readers, but also managing to express Swift's deep-seated fear of uncertainty.[86] Carnochan's interpretation implicitly values and incorporates both soft and hard readings. C.J. Rawson (1968) analyzed the ways Swift disconcerts his readers, denying them distance from his satiric targets and from his satiric values. What *Gulliver's Travels* intends to *mean* is no more important than the way it works to render its readers vulnerable and thereby more receptive.[87]

Additional attempts to steer around or through the hard and soft schools' scrimmage line included (among many others) those of Peter Thorpe (1967) (Swift plants fragments of his "norm" throughout *Gulliver's Travels*, allowing readers to bring them together by examining the interplay between Gulliver and his foils); A.K. Easthope (1967) (Gulliver's character is merely a trap: the reader laughs too easily, only to find Gulliver melting "back into the verbal world he came from"); Alexander W. Allison (1968) (claims to steer "an appropriate middle course" between "pro- and anti-Houyhnhnm positions," but then describes the Houyhnhnms as "faintly ridiculous throughout"); Pierre Nordon (1968) (the reader participates in the disgusting developments of Book IV but also retains some distance from the satiric victims); Robert M. Philmus (1971) (through Gulliver's repudiation of saying "the thing which is not," Swift is warning the reader against abuse of interpretation precisely because interpretation is always necessary); Grant Holly (1979) (discussions of determinate meaning may be almost irrelevant to *Gulliver's Travels*: "Swift's text makes signifying its subject, by implying a vast textuality which incorporates the reader and which, therefore, he can participate in but is no longer free to comment on"); Anthony J. Hassall (1979) (Swift puts the reader into a position similar to Gulliver's—blundering about, getting his bearings, learning the language); and Alain Bony (Gulliver has no objective reality independent of the reader's own needs and illusions; *Gulliver's Travels* is a journey into the reader's deepest self).[88]

A discussion of this sort could go on and on with Swift's writings. Does "The Day of Judgement" invite the religiously orthodox part of its audience smugly to deride the other, Dissenting, part? Or is the final dismissal a devastating joke played on all humankind? (Any discussion of this problem has to begin with textual difficulties.)[89] Or, in *A Modest Proposal*, can it possibly be that we are hearing Swift express his own opinions? Isn't it, well, *safer* to assume that a persona is speaking? The status of even that assumption was jolted severely in 1965–1980, however. David Nokes, for one, identified many of the proposer's opinions as those articulated elsewhere, in presumably non-ironical contexts, by "Swift" himself.[90] In fact, the list in this volume of all the "meanings" ascribed to *A Modest Proposal* in the last fifteen years is lengthy, contradictory, and might tell us much about ourselves as critics. Everywhere, both Swift's writings and the critical disputes surrounding them are signalling us about the different ways readers read and then go on to organize and express their responses. The best criticism published in 1965–1980 managed to be self-conscious and explicit about its assumptions, expectations, and methods of analysis.

A final example. In his verses on his own death, is Swift making fun of himself? Nominating himself for the future Nobel prizes in Literature and Peace? Teaching his readers something about the futility of life in the great world? Setting up his readers for a rude little shock? All of the above? None?[91]

Notes

1. See Milton Voigt, *Swift and the Twentieth Century* (Detroit: Wayne State U. Press, 1964).

2. Ricardo Quintana, *The Mind and Art of Jonathan Swift* (New York and London: Oxford U. Press, 1936; rept. with additional bibliographical material, 1953; rept. Gloucester, Ma.: Peter Smith, 1965).

3. Ricardo Quintana, *Swift: An Introduction* (New York and London: Oxford U. Press, 1955).

4. Irvin Ehrenpreis, *The Personality of Jonathan Swift* (London: Methuen; New York: Barnes & Noble, 1958; rept. 1969).

5. Item 172.

6. Items 906, 391.

7. See Milton Voigt, *Swift and the Twentieth Century*, ibid; Ricardo Quintana, *Swift: An Introduction*, ibid., and Item 388.

8. Northrop Frye, *The Anatomy of Criticism: Four Essays* (Princeton: Princeton U. Press, 1957); Frank Kermode, *The Romantic Image* (New York: Random House, 1957). For the best post-formalism history of American criticism to date, see Frank Lentricchia, *After the New Criticism* (Chicago: U. of Chicago Press, 1980).

9. Maurice Johnson, *The Sin of Wit: Jonathan Swift as a Poet* (Syracuse: Syracuse U. Press, 1950; rept. New York: Gordian Press, 1966).

10. Item 537.

11. See, for example, Items 977, 907, 780, 892.

12. Item 781.

13. Roland Barthes, *The Pleasure of the Text*, trans. Richard Miller (New York: Hill & Wang, 1975), p. 14.

14. Item 388.

15. William Kinsley, "Gentle Readings: Recent Work on Swift," *ECS*, 15 (1982), 442–53. Other well-documented complaints include John M. Aden, "Satire or Sense: A Subtler Mixture," *Sewanee Review*, 89 (1981), 441–47; also Item 977.

16. Items 412, 688, 699, 705, 682, 654, 653.

17. Ronald Paulson, *Theme and Structure in Swift's* Tale of a Tub (New Haven: Yale U. Press, 1962; rept. Hamden, Ct., 1969, 1972).

18. Item 685.

19. Items 671, 669, 297, 700, 649, 664, 650.

20. Item 656.

21. C.J. Rawson, *RES*, n.s. 22 (1971), 214–16; Robert Martin Adams (Item 238); Gardner D. Stout, Jr., *JEGP*, 71 (1972), 135–40. See also Items 712, 711.

22. Irvin Ehrenpreis, "Personae" (Item 294); "The Concept of the Persona in Satire: A Symposium" (Item 240).

23. Item 702.

24. Item 713.

25. Item 690.

26. Item 286.

27. Item 678.

28. Item 667.

29. Item 715.

30. Item 703.

31. Items 708, 709.

32. Item 348.

33. Item 172.

34. Item 286.

35. Robert M. Adams, *Strains of Discord: Studies in Literary Openness* (Ithaca, N.Y.: Cornell U. Press, 1958), p. 157.

36. William Empson, *Some Versions of Pastoral* (London: Chatto and Windus, 1950; first pub. 1935), p. 62. Empson is not, by the way, discussing *A Tale of a Tub* per se, but rather structures similar to that of the "Fool Among Knaves" passage.

37. Item 658.

38. Items 671, 667.

39. Item 699.

40. Item 703.

41. Item 607.

42. Item 570.

43. The quotation is from Item 115.

44. Items 602, 593, 552.

45. Norman O. Brown, *Life Against Death* (Middletown, Ct.: Wesleyan U. Press, 1959), pp. 179–201; rept. in *Swift: A Collection of Critical Essays*, ed. Ernest Tuveson (Englewood Cliffs, N.J.: Prentice-Hall, 1964), p. 37. Similar readings are common; see, for example, Items 485, 515.

46. Item 521.

47. Item 470.

48. Item 522. Ellen Pollak's published answer to Gubar in *Signs*, 3 (1978),

728–33, suggested that Swift is rather using anti-feminine images to reveal the inadequacy of his society's view of women (Item 522). An even clearer example of a priori value judgments running rough-shod over analysis is Item 480.

49. Items 587, 584.

50. Item 519. In an exchange with Greene (Swift is recommending "good sense") and Schakel ("the scatological poems show us a more human Swift, fallible, uncertain, struggling—trying to work through his feelings, but not succeeding entirely"), Gilmore himself acknowledged the similarity of his reading to Schakel's but disputed its close ties with Greene's (Item 519).

51. Item 562.

52. Item 476.

53. Items 483, 492.

54. Items 499, 504.

55. Item 570.

56. Item 575.

57. Item 862.

58. Items 862, 852. Donald Green (Item 862) added a reminder of La Rochefoucauld's grim acknowledgment of hypocrisy.

59. James L. Clifford, "Argument and Understanding: Teaching Through Controversy," *Eighteenth-Century Life*, 5, no. 3 (Spring 1979), 1–7. See, for example, Items 1007, 989, 878.

60. Item 911.

61. Item 1029.

62. Items 1183, 915, 988, 950.

63. Items 1176, 1144, 991.

64. Item 1010.

65. Items 1006, 1174.

66. Item 1091.

67. Items 1142, 1086.

68. Items 965, 992, 998, 1068, 1138, 1092.

69. Item 966.

70. Item 1041.

71. Item 1181.

72. Item 1085.

73. Item 1066.

74. Items 1065, 1134.

75. Items 914, 1090.

76. Items 1184, 1160.
77. Items 886, 1057, 890, 939, 1153.
78. Item 1078.
79. Item 912.
80. Item 1126.
81. Item 958.
82. Item 1082.
83. Item 1134.
84. Items 989, 950.
85. Item 1007.
86. Item 906.
87. Item 391.
88. Items 1145, 933, 878, 1051, 1067, 977, 970, 892.
89. Items 35, 74, 28, 51, 577.
90. Item 860.
91. Many approaches to "Verses on the Death of Dr. Swift" are analyzed by David M. Vieth (Item 623).

Swift Studies, 1965–1980

SECTION 1

Bibliography, Canon, Editions

A. Bibliography, Canon

1. Adams, Robert Martin. "Jonathan Swift, Thomas Swift, and the Authorship of A Tale of a Tub." MP, 64 (1967), 198-232.

   See the reservations of Dipak Nandy, "Jonathan Swift, Thomas Swift, and the Authorship of A Tale of a Tub" (Item 65); and of Denis Donoghue, "Appendix A: The Authorship of 'A Tale of a Tub'," Jonathan Swift: A Critical Introduction (Item 286).

   Adams's suggestion that Jonathan Swift's first cousin, Thomas Swift, collaborated with him on the Tale is based on (1) internal evidence; (2) assertions made in various editions about the circumstances of composition and publication; and (3) biographical facts concerning the relations of Thomas and Jonathan Swift.

2. Aden, John M. "Swift, Pope, and 'the Sin of Wit'." PBSA, 62 (1968), 80-85.

   Aden dates "The Author Upon Himself" between 31 May 1714, when Swift left London, and 4-11 July, when he was visited by Pope at Letcombe, based on an apparent borrowing by Pope of the phrase "the sin of wit" and on the splenetic tone of "The Author Upon Himself," which seems to display Swift's lack of distance early in his retirement. Speculative.

3. Beasley, Jerry C. English Fiction 1660-1800: A Guide to Information Sources. (English Information Guide Series, 14.) Detroit: Gale Research, 1978. Pp. xvi + 313.

   Pp. 253-67 list 100 items under Editions, Selections and Specialized Collections, and Individual Works, and include very brief annotations.

4. Béranger, Jean. "Emile Pons, Editeur de Swift." Etudes Anglaises, 22 (1969), 177-79.

   A brief discussion of Pons's edition of Swift's Oeuvres for Gallimard, including his view of Gulliver's Travels as concerned with moral and metaphysical, rather than political, questions,

the authority of his notes (which occasionally side with Denis
Johnston or Sybil Le Brocquy against Irvin Ehrenpreis), and the
underused resources of his files.

5. Blackwell, Basil. "The Shakespeare Head Swift." University Review
   (Dublin), 4 (1967), 89-90.

   A brief history of the standard edition, thirty years in the making.

6. Bond, Donald F. (comp.). The Eighteenth Century. (Goldentree
   Bibliographies in Language & Literature.) Northbrook, Ill.: AHM
   Publishing, 1975. Pp. xvi + 184.

   Lists 205 recent Swift studies.

7. Carnochan, W.B. "Swiftiana: Beardsley's Illustrations of Swift."
   Scriblerian, 9 (1976), 57-60.

   Reproduces some of Beardsley's schoolboy drawings for Battle of the
   Books and A Tale of a Tub.

8. Catalogue of the Kildare Exhibition to Commemorate the 300th
   Anniversary of the Birth of Dean Swift (1667-1745). [1967.] Pp.
   1-12; illustrations.

   An exhibition presented at Celbridge, County Kildare, 23-30 April
   1967, and at Robertstown, County Kildare, 30 July-13 August 1967, by
   the Irish Georgian Society, the Kildare Archaeological Society, and
   Robertstown Muintir na Tire.

9. Clifford, James L., and I. Ehrenpreis. "New Light on Swift and His
   Family." TLS, April 21, 1966, p. 356.

   Reprints an unpublished letter in which Swift rails on about members
   of his family.

10. Davis, Herbert. "David Nichol Smith." Pp. 1-16 of Studies in the
    Eighteenth Century: Essays Presented at the David Nichol Smith
    Memorial Seminar, Canberra 1966. Edited by R.F. Brissenden.
    Canberra: Australian National U. Press; Toronto: U. of Toronto
    Press, 1968.

    Includes a brief reminiscence of Nichol Smith's insights into
    editing Swift.

11. Daw, C.P. "The Date of Swift's Hints Towards an Essay on
    Conversation." Scriblerian, 8 (1976), 119-21.

    A possibly unique copy of the Hints assigns the date 1708 to the
    work.

12. Daw, C.P. "A Tentative Date for Swift's 'Sleeping in Church'." N&Q, 216 (1971), 330-31.

    Based on its scriptural quotations, the sermon was delivered 16 August 1724.

13. Dowling, John. "Swift in Spain (1747)." Scriblerian, 11 (1979), 143.

    Reports on how Swift's works were censored by the Inquisition.

14. Downie, J.A. "Dr. Swift's Billetdoux." Scriblerian, 11 (1979), 143-45.

    Not written by Swift, this letter uses "the cases of Latin declension to convey a sexual message" and demonstrates an "extensive contemporary knowledge of Swift's 'trifles'."

15. Downie, J.A. "Editor Extraordinaire." Scriblerian, 13 (1980), 2-4.

    A pointedly critical assessment of Sir Harold Williams's narrowmindedness as interpreter and his imprecision as editor of Swift's Poems, Journal to Stella, and Correspondence.

16. Downie, J.A., and Pat Rogers. "Newer Light on Pope and Swift?" Scriblerian, 11 (1978), 57-58.

    A reply to Robert P. Maccubbin, "Unique Scribleriana Transferred 1969-1970," Scriblerian, 4 (1971), 38-39.

    Corrects a mistaken attribution to Swift.

17. Eddy, Donald D. "Jonathan Swift's Copy of the Comoediae Sex of Terence." Cornell Library Journal, 1 (1966), 40-41.

    A volume purchased by Swift from the auctioned library of Charles Bernard on April 11-16, 1911.

18. Elias, A.C., Jr. "The First Printing of Orrery's Remarks on Swift (1751)." Harvard Library Bulletin, 25 (1977), 310-21.

    A thorough study of the printing history of Orrery's Remarks, revealing the extent of Orrery's self-aggrandizement, often at Swift's expense.

19. Elias, A.C., Jr. "The Pope-Swift Letters (1940-41): Notes on the First State of the First Impression." PBSA, 69 (1975), 323-43.

    A minutely detailed account of Pope's extraordinarily meticulous control over the printing process.

20. Ellis, Frank H. "Swift's Seventh Penny Paper." TLS, May 10, 1974, p. 506.

    See the reply by David Woolley (Item 107).

    Attributes to Swift and reproduces a propagandist poem printed in 1712. Woolley replies that Williams and Davis had already excluded the poem.

21. Falle, George. "Sir Walter Scott as Editor of Dryden and Swift." University of Toronto Quarterly, 36 (1967), 161-80.

    Scott's edition of Swift, inferior to his editing of Dryden, was nevertheless a milestone for the nineteenth century—this, despite Scott's arbitrary emendations, ignoring of textual complexities, overhasty attributions, and tone deafness to irony and wit.

22. First Line Index of English Poetry 1500-1800 in Manuscripts of the Bodleian Library. 2 Vols. Oxford: Clarendon Press, 1969.

    Lists 21 poems attributed to Swift.

23. Foxon, D.F. English Verse, 1701-1750: A Catalogue of Separately Printed Poems with Notes on Contemporary Collected Editions. Vol. I: Catalogue. Vol. II: Indexes. London and New York: Cambridge U. Press, 1975. Pp. xxviii + 924; vi + 302.

    Rev. in review art. by James Woolley in MP, 75 (1977), 59-73; by Ian Jack in RES, n.s. 28 (1977), 473-75.

    Supplements and supersedes Teerink-Scouten for Swift's verse.

24. Gabriner, Paul. ("Hebrew Translations of Gulliver's Travels.") Scriblerian, 7 (1974), 6-7.

    Seven translations in Hebrew have appeared since 1922. Only one (by Menachem Mendel Mibashan, 1922) is complete; Mibashin's fondness for Biblical style "makes Gulliver sound like God in the original Genesis."

25. Gaskell, Philip. From Writer to Reader: Studies in Editorial Method. Oxford: Clarendon Press, 1978. Pp. xiv + 268.

    Rev. (favorably) by D.F. Foxon in RES, n.s. 30 (1979), 237-39; (favorably) by J.R. Banks in Critical Quarterly, 21, no. 1 (Spring, 1979), 88-91; (favorably) by Jack Stillinger in JEGP, 78 (1979), 422-24; by Johan Gerritsen in English Studies, 61 (1980), 552-53.

    Extracts from Directions to Servants, from the Rothschild and

Forster Mss., illustrate the editorial process and lead to evaluation of the London 1745 and Faulkner editions.

26. Goldgar, Bertrand A. "Swift's 'Character of Sir Robert Walpole'." N&Q, 221 (1976), 492-93.

    Swift's poem did appear in his lifetime (under the title "The Riddle," and signed "J.C.--Sevens the Main") in Common Sense, 14 April 1739. See Peter J. Schakel's discovery of a 1733 printing (Item 84).

27. Guide to Literary Manuscripts in the Huntington Library. San Marino, Ca.: Huntington Library, 1979. Pp. ix + 539.

    Pp. 449-51 list Swift materials.

28. Gulick, Sidney L. "No 'Spectral Hand' in Swift's 'Day of Judgement'." PBSA, 71 (1977), 333-36.

    A reply to Leland D. Peterson (Item 74). (See below.)

29. Guskin, Phyllis J. "Political Implications of Thomas Swift's Sermon Noah's Dove (1710)." Eighteenth-Century Life, 1 (1975), 46-50.

    Guskin argues that Noah's Dove is not conclusive proof of Thomas Swift's authorship of A Tale of a Tub.

30. Halsband, Robert. "Jonathan Swift and Swiftiana at Columbia." Columbia Library Columns, 16, no. 3 (May 1967), 19-23.

    Reproduces Swift's translation of Catullus's "Lesbia mi dicet semper male."

31. Harris, John. "Swift's The Publick Spirit of the Whigs: A Partly Censored State of the Scottish Paragraphs." PBSA, 72 (1978), 92-94.

    The discovery of a text intermediate between the first, uncensored issue and the edition that completely excised the Scottish paragraphs reveals an interesting attempt by Swift to mute rather than to silence entirely his inept attack against the Scots.

32. Holzknecht, G.K. "Swift and the Text of A Tale of a Tub." English Studies, 54 (1973), 470-78.

    Makes the case for the authority of the first edition text over that of the fifth edition. The "Apology," added to the fifth edition, along with a number of alterations, replaces "a text written by a penetrating satirist" with "the second thoughts of an ambitious clergyman." Includes a list of variants.

33. Jarrell, Mackie Langham. "'Ode to the King': Some Contests, Dissensions, and Exchanges among Jonathan Swift, John Dunton, and Henry Jones." TSLL, 7 (1965), 145-59.

    Jarrell supplements the internal evidence for Swift's authorship of "Ode to the King," sketches a few suggestive circumstances, and provides the intriguing information that, in "Ode to the King" as in Swift's other early poems, echoes of Dryden's All for Love "are so numerous that they may be read as an inadvertant signature."

34. Jenkins, Clauston. "The Ford Changes and the Text of Gulliver's Travels." PBSA, 62 (1968), 1-23.

    Claiming that Charles Ford's changes have been undeservedly ignored, Jenkins documents that the changes represent revision as well as restoration, providing valuable insight into Swift's method of working.

35. Johnson, Maurice. "Text and Possible Occasion for Swift's 'Day of Judgement'." PMLA, 86 (1971), 210-17.

    Replied to by W.B. Carnochan, "The Occasion of Swift's 'Day of Judgement'," PMLA, 87 (1972), 518-20; and by Charles R. Sleeth, PMLA, 88 (1973), 144-45.

    With fine economy, Johnson (1) traces the obscure textual history of Swift's "greatest poem"; (2) argues that the specific occasion of the poem indicates that it was read not as universal satire but as an attack upon dissenting sects; (3) redates the poem to 1732 or 1733 on the grounds that it was a response to renewed attempts to repeal the Test Act; (4) supplies further evidence of Swift's authorship. Carnochan and Sleeth argue that nevertheless the poem may and ought to be read as a satire on all mankind.

36. Koon, Helene. "A Lilliputian Poem." ELN, 7 (1969), 107-10.

    Makes the case for Swift's authorship of "A Poem to his Majesty King George II on the present State of Affairs in England with Remarks on the alterations expected at Court, after the Rise of the Parliament"--written in "Lilliputian verse" to satirize the King's accession.

37. Kwan-Terry, John. "Chinese Travels." Scriblerian, 11 (1978), 4-6.

    Reports on Chinese translations of Gulliver's Travels.

38. Lamont, Claire. "A Checklist of Critical and Biographical Writings on Jonathan Swift, 1945-65." Pp. 356-91 of <u>Fair Liberty</u> Was All <u>His Cry: A Tercentenary Tribute to Jonathan Swift 1667-1745.</u> Edited by A. Norman Jeffares. London: Macmillan; New York: St. Martin's Press, 1967.

    Covers the same material as the bibliography of James J. Stathis (Item 89), but without annotation.

39. Landa, Louis A. "Swift." Pp. 38-41 of <u>The English Novel: Select Bibliographical Guides.</u> Edited by A.E. Dyson. Oxford: Oxford U. Press, 1974.

    A bibliographical essay commenting on the voices and motives of Swift's satire and providing a list of references.

40. Lenfest, David S. "A Checklist of Illustrated Editions of 'Gulliver's Travels', 1727-1914." <u>PBSA</u>, 62 (1968), 85-123.

    Complete listings for 48 illustrated editions in England, Holland, Germany, Spain, France, Sweden, Italy, Russia, and the U.S.

41. Love, H.H.R. <u>Swift and His Publishers: A Tale Delivered to Friends of the Monash University Library on November 11, 1968 with a Short-Title Catalogue of Early Editions of Swift and Swiftiana in the Monash University Library.</u> Monash: Monash U., 1969. Pp. 1-40.

42. Luce, J.V. "A Note on the Composition of Swift's Epitaph." <u>Hermathena</u>, 104 (Spring 1967), 78-81.

    Notes the frequency with which "the greatest epitaph in history" has been misquoted and suggests that Swift's source may have been Dryden's characterization of Juvenal in "A Discourse Concerning ... Satire," perhaps explaining the inelegances in Swift's Latin.

43. MacCarvill, Eileen. "Jonathan Swift, Aodh Buí Mac Cruitín and Contemporary Thomond Scholars." <u>North Munster Antiquarian Journal</u>, 11 (1968), 36-46.

    Swift collaborated (1714-24) on an Irish History with Aodh Buí Mac Cruitín who may have influenced Swift's 1723 journey through the south of Ireland.

44. Maccubbin, Robert P. "Unique Scribleriana Transferred 1969-1970." <u>Scriblerian</u>, 4 (1971), 38-39.

    See the corrections of J.A. Downie and Pat Rogers, "Newer Light on Pope and Swift?" <u>Scriblerian</u>, 11 (1978), 57-58.

    Includes letters by Swift.

45. Maccubbin, Robert P. "Unique Scribleriana Transferred 1970-71."
    <u>Scriblerian</u>, 5 (1972), 56-57.

    Including Swiftiana.

46. Maccubbin, Robert P. "Unique Scribleriana Transferred 1971-1973."
    <u>Scriblerian</u>, 6 (1973), 46-48.

    Including a few incidental items by Swift.

47. Maccubbin, Robert P. "Unique Scribleriana Transferred 1973."
    <u>Scriblerian</u>, 7 (1974), 53-56.

    Including a volume of Swift's letters and some Swiftiana.

48. Maccubbin, Robert P. "Unique Scribleriana Transferred, 1974-75."
    <u>Scriblerian</u>, 8 (1976), 121-24.

    Including a number of Swift items.

49. Maner, Martin W. "An Eighteenth-Century Editor at Work: John Nichols
    and Jonathan Swift." <u>PBSA</u>, 70 (1976), 481-99.

    An account of how one eighteenth-century editor proceeded in
    locating and identifying works, in making attributions, in
    soliciting help, and in dealing with competition from other editors.

50. Matlack, Cynthia S., and William F. Matlack. "A Statistical Approach
    to Problems of Attribution: <u>A Letter of Advice to a Young Poet</u>."
    <u>College English</u>, 29 (1968), 627-32.

    This criticism of Louis T. Milic (Item 365) sets forth a general
    methodology for quantitative stylistic approaches to authorship
    problems. Incidentally, the authors disparage Milic's attribution of
    <u>A Letter of Advice</u> to Swift and pronounce their gloom on the
    prospect of this work ever being firmly established or repudiated on
    the basis of internal evidence.

51. Mayhew, George. "Swift's 'On the Day of Judgement' and Theophilus
    Swift." <u>PQ</u>, 54 (1975), 213-21.

    A newspaper clipping found in Sir Walter Scott's papers, perhaps
    earlier than the 1774 <u>St. James Chronicle</u> printing, reconfirms the
    authenticity of the latter text.

52. Mayhew, George P. "Jonathan Swift's 'On the Burning of Whitehall in
    1697' Re-examined." <u>Harvard Library Bulletin</u>, 19 (1971), 399-411.

Argues for Swift's authorship of the unfinished poem "On the Burning of Whitehall in 1697"--an attribution also made by Sir Walter Scott, but not accepted by Sir Harold Williams. The issues concerning authorship are whether Scott possessed an autograph copy and whether the poem endorses the beheading of Charles I.

53. Mayhew, George P. "Jonathan Swift's 'Prefermts of Ireland', 1713-1714." HLQ, 30 (1966), 297-305.

An autograph copy of Swift's plan for filling eight of the twenty-two bishoprics of the Church of Ireland with Tories.

54. Mayhew, George P. Rage or Raillery: The Swift Manuscripts at the Huntington Library. San Marino: Huntington Library, 1967. Pp. xviii + 190.

Rev. (with another work) by Francis Doherty in RES, n.s. 19 (1968), 200-02; (favorably) by M.J. Weedon in N&Q, 213 (1968), 229-30; (favorably) by Miriam K. Starkman in South Atlantic Quarterly, 67 (1968), 183-84.

Mayhew describes the contents of the Huntington manuscripts (often little-known, fragmental, or seemingly trivial works), their history and provenance, and--most rare and most welcome--their significance in relation to a wide view of Swift's life and works.

55. Mayhew, George P. "Swift's Political 'Conversion' and His 'Lost' Ballad on the Westminster Election of 1710." Bulletin of the John Rylands Library, 53 (1971), 397-427.

Internal and circumstantial evidence supports Charles Main's attribution of "A Dialogue Between Captain Tom and Sir H--y D--n C--t" as Swift's first published work as a Tory.

56. McKelvie, C.L. "The 'Bickerstaff' Pamphlet at Armagh." Scriblerian, 7 (1975), 123.

The rare first edition of "The Accomplishment of the First of Mr. Bickerstaff's Predictions" (1708) (Teerink 495), reported lost by Herbert Davis, is at the Armagh Public Library.

57. McKelvie, C.L. "Scriblerians' Books in Armagh Public Library." Scriblerian, 8 (1975), 56.

Notes, in addition to the famous corrected Gulliver's Travels, a copy of Temple's Miscellanea from Swift's library.

58. McKelvie, C.L. "Some Books from Swift's Library." Hermathena, 120 (Summer 1976), 30-34.

Describes the Armagh Public Library's first edition of Gulliver's
Travels corrected by Swift, together with a few other holdings.

59. Milham, Mary E. "The Art of Cookery." TLS, July 2, 1970, p. 726.

See the reply by Margaret Boddy, "The Art of Cookery," TLS, Aug.
21, 1970, p. 928.

A rare edition of William King's The Art of Cookery is entitled "The
second part of the Tale of a Tub" and attributed to "the Author of
the Tale of a Tub." Boddy opines that the edition was pirated.

60. Moore, John Robert. "An Unrecorded Drapier Poem." Yearbook of
    English Studies, 2 (1972), 115-17.

Moore does not attribute this attack on Wood's coinage to Swift.

61. "The Morrison Collection." Scriblerian, 1, no. 2 (Spring 1969),
    32-33.

The collection purchased by the San Antonio College Library from
Lois G. Morrison includes six items either attributed to Swift or of
Swiftiana.

62. Morton, Richard. "The Eighteenth-Century Collection at McMaster
    University, Hamilton, Ontario." Scriblerian, 3 (1971), 77-78.

Includes several Swift items.

63. Munby, A.N.L., and Lenore Coral (comps.). British Book Sale
    Catalogues 1676-1800: A Union List. London: Mansell, 1977. Pp. xxv
    + 146.

Includes the auction catalogue for Swift's library.

64. Murtuza, Athar. "Twentieth-Century Critical Responses to Swift's
    'Scatological Verse': A Checklist." Bulletin of Bibliography, 30
    (1973), 18-19.

This list unfortunately came too early, since the renewed interest
in Swift's poetry encouraged important reconsiderations of Swift's
scatology in the late 1970's.

65. Nandy, Dipak. "Jonathan Swift, Thomas Swift, and the Authorship of A
    Tale of a Tub." MP, 66 (1968), 333-37.

Attacks several details of Robert Martin Adams's case for
collaborative authorship (Item 1), without however attempting to
refute Adams's thesis itself.

66. "A New Book from Swift's Library." <u>Bulletin</u> <u>of</u> <u>the</u> <u>John</u> <u>Rylands</u>
    <u>Library</u>, 62 (1980), 262-64.

    Reports on the discovery, by Hermann J. Real and Heinz J. Vienken,
    of a copy of Freart's <u>Parallèle</u> <u>de</u> <u>l'Architecture</u> <u>Antique</u> <u>et</u> <u>de</u> <u>la</u>
    <u>Moderne</u> that was once in Swift's possession.

67. Nokes, David. ["Cambridge University Library Swiftiana."]
    <u>Scriblerian</u>, 8 (1975), 56.

    Notes the location (Manuscripts Room, Add. 7788-Williams) of Sir
    Harold Williams's working papers--"twenty-two boxes of Swiftiana."

68. "The Osborn Collection at Yale." <u>Scriblerian</u>, 3 (1970), 33-34.

    See the response by James D. Woolley, <u>Scriblerian</u>, 3 (1971), 81.

    The Osborn Collection includes three poems in manuscript that are
    attributed to Swift but were not included by Harold Williams.

69. Osborn, James M. "Swiftiana in the Osborn Collection at Yale."
    <u>University</u> <u>Review</u> (Dublin), 4 (1967), 72-83.

    "Although none of these Swiftiana in the Osborn Collection with the
    exception of the Temple estate papers and the Bolingbroke letter
    [concerning <u>History</u> <u>of</u> <u>the</u> <u>Last</u> <u>Four</u> <u>Years</u> <u>of</u> <u>the</u> <u>Queen</u>] adds much
    to knowledge of Swift's life and times, their existence and location
    should be placed on record."

70. Parks, Stephen. "Unique Scribleriana Transferred, 1976." <u>Scriblerian</u>
    10 (1977), 58-59.

    Including Stella's autograph word book.

71. Parks, Stephen. "Scribleriana Transferred, 1977-1978." <u>Scriblerian</u>,
    11 (1978), 51-54.

    Including four items of Swiftiana.

72. Parks, Stephen. "Scribleriana Transferred, 1978-1979." <u>Scriblerian</u>,
    11 (1979), 56-59.

    Including two rare items of Swiftiana.

73. Parks, Stephen. "Scribleriana Transferred, 1979-1980." <u>Scriblerian</u>,
    13 (1980), 48-50.

    Including a group of four letters to Orrery, four single letters, a
    first edition of <u>A</u> <u>Tale</u> <u>of</u> <u>a</u> <u>Tub</u>, the unauthorized first edition of

A <u>Meditation</u> upon a <u>Broom-stick</u>, and a first edition of <u>Gulliver's</u>
<u>Travels</u>.

74. Peterson, Leland D. "The Spectral Hand in Swift's 'Day of
    Judgement'." <u>PBSA</u>, 70 (1976), 189-219.

    See the reply by Sidney L. Gulick (Item 28).

    Peterson explains the existence of five versions of the poem by
    arguing that the 16-line, 1773 "Friend's" version (a comparatively
    clear attack on dissenters, rather than on the human race) is the
    one Swift wrote, while the others represent successive revisions by
    one or more "ghosts," chiefly Chesterfield. Gulick attacks the
    slenderness of Peterson's evidence and doubts whether Chesterfield
    was capable of making changes of such high quality. The argument is
    an important one indeed, since the choice of text determines whether
    the poem should be read as a specific satire on dissenting sects or
    a universal attack on mankind. However, with this exchange, the
    question is still up in the air.

75. Peterson, Leland D. "A Variant of the 1742-1746 Swift-Pope
    <u>Miscellanies</u>." <u>PBSA</u>, 66 (1972), 302-10.

    Includes a brief printing history of the thirteen-volume set of
    <u>Miscellanies</u>, a list of the variants in the Old Dominion University
    set, and the implication that the <u>Miscellanies</u> is still in a state
    of bibliographical chaos.

76. Potter, Lee H. "The Text of Scott's Edition of Swift." <u>Studies in
    Bibliography</u>, 22 (1969), 240-55.

    Potter gives a thorough account of Scott's editorial practices and
    accounts for Scott's use of Nichols's 1801 edition even after the
    1808 version was available.

77. Quintana, Ricardo. "A Modest Appraisal: Swift Scholarship and
    Criticism, 1945-65." Pp. 342-55 of <u>Fair Liberty Was All His Cry: A
    Tercentenary Tribute to Jonathan Swift 1667-1745</u>. Edited by A.
    Norman Jeffares. London: Macmillan; New York: St. Martin's Press,
    1967.

    A survey of Swift scholarship and criticism from 1945 to 1965
    including editions, bibliographies, biographical items, general
    books on Swift, books on Swift's satire or on some particular work.
    A section on "Modern Trends" points to studies of Swift's
    <u>Weltanschauung</u>, hard and soft schools of interpretation of
    <u>Gulliver's Travels</u>, renewed interest in the <u>Tale</u> and in Swift's
    poetry, and stylistic and rhetorical analyses.

78. Roberts, Philip. "The Original of a Swift Letter." <u>N&Q</u>, 215 (1970),
    287-88.

The autograph letter by Swift to George Lyttelton, 5 June 1739, differs from the version printed in the Williams edition. A transcription is included.

79. Rogers, Pat. "The Case of Pope v. Curll." The Library, 5th ser., 27 (1972), 326-31.

Describes the circumstances of Pope's action against Curll for the pirated edition of Swift's Literary Correspondence, for Twenty-Four Years--the first important test regarding copyright in personal letters.

80. Rothenberg, Albert, and Bette Greenberg (comps.). The Index of Scientific Writings on Creativity. Folkestone, Kent, 1974. Nos. 2011-14, 2763-89.

Noted in Scriblerian, 9 (1977), 146.

Lists several medical and psycholanalytic studies of Swift and Pope.

81. Rousseau, G.S., and David Woolley. "A New Letter of Swift to Marcus Antonius Morgan, July [1735]." Harvard Library Bulletin, 18 (1970), 94-97.

The only existing letter from Swift to the target of his bitter attack in "The Legion Club" shows no trace of that animosity and should therefore be assigned to 1735, not 1736 as George Mayhew had dated it.

82. Saxena, P.K. ["Gulliver's Travels in India."] Scriblerian, 3 (1971), 51.

Lists ten translations of the Travels in Bengali, from abridged editions for children to complete translations for adults. Only one of the translations (by Lila Majumdar, 1966) is from the period 1965-1980.

83. Schakel, Peter. "A Brief Bibliography of Recent Swift Studies." Johnson Society of the Central Region Newsletter, March, 1980, pp. 3-4.

Reviews recent criticism of Swift's poetry.

84. Schakel, Peter J. "'The Character of Sir Robert Walpole': A Previously Unnoticed Publication." PBSA, 70 (1976), 111-14.

"The Character of Sir Robert Walpole" was printed while Swift was alive, in Robin's Panegyrick. Or, the Norfolk Miscellany (1733). See Bertrand A. Goldgar's discovery of a 1739 printing (Item 26).

85. Schultz, H.D. "English Literary Manuscripts in the Huntington
    Library." HLQ, 31 (1968), 251-302.

    Lists the Swift items held by the Huntington Library, many of which
    were analyzed so thoroughly by George P. Mayhew (Item 54).

86. Shinagel, Michael (ed.). A Concordance to the Poems of Jonathan
    Swift. Ithaca and London: Cornell U. Press, 1972. Pp. xxvi + 978.

    Rev. by George P. Mayhew in Scriblerian, 5 (1973), 100-01; by
    Colin J. Horne in MLR, 69 (1974), 376-77; (favorably) by Paul J.
    Korshin in Computers and the Humanities, 7 (1973), 219-20.

    Although one might quibble that Shinagel chose to use the Harold
    Williams edition of the poems over the cheaper and shorter Herbert
    Davis edition, his sensible handling of eccentricities of language
    and his accuracy and thoroughness make this one of the finest
    concordances to eighteenth-century poetry.

87. Shipley, John B. "A Note on the Authorship of The Whale." RES, n.s.
    18 (1967), 166-69.

    Endorses Hervey's attribution of "The Whale" (1737) to Chesterfield.

88. Slepian, Barry. "George Faulkner's Dublin Journal and Jonathan
    Swift." Library Chronicle, 31 (1965), 97-116.

    Lists items written by and about Swift for the Dublin Journal.

89. Stathis, James J. (comp.). A Bibliography of Swift Studies
    1945-1965. Nashville: Vanderbilt U. Press, 1967. Pp. xii + 110.

    Rev. (with other works) by Colin J. Horne in MLR, 64 (1969),
    401-03; by Hilbert H. Campbell in PBSA, 61 (1967), 392-93; by
    Peter J. Schakel in PQ, 47 (1968), 436-38.

    Supplements the bibliography covering 1895-1945 by James E. Tobin
    and Louis A. Landa; includes annotations and lists of book reviews,
    but no introduction in deference to Milton Voigt's Swift and the
    Twentieth Century (1964). Schakel's review is exemplary in its
    thoroughness and includes a supplementary list of additional items.

90. Sterne, Noel. "A Mistaken First Publication Date of a Poem by
    Swift." N&Q, 214 (1969), 338.

    Swift's imitation of Horace, Ode III, 2, first appeared, with
    variations, in Volume II of Miscellaneous Poems by Several Hands
    (1730), compiled by David Lewis.

91. Swift and His Age: A Tercentenary Exhibition. Dublin: National
    Gallery of Ireland, 1967. Pp. 56.

    Lists portraits of Swift and his circle, of eighteenth-century
    Dublin, as well as books, coins, medals, and other Swiftiana.

92. "Swift and Pope in the Boston Atheneum (Part I)." Scriblerian, 4
    (1971), 33-34.

    A partial list of Swift's works in the Boston Atheneum.

93. Thompson, Paul V. "An Unpublished Letter by Swift." The Library, 5th
    ser., 22 (1967), 57-66.

    A transcript, in John Forster's hand, of a letter dated 11 July 1726
    to Delany concerning Delany's hopes for the deanery of Cloyne,
    Swift's bleak evaluation of his own chances for promotion, and
    Swift's promise to Stella not to obligate himself to Walpole for
    preferment.

94. Vieth, David M. "Swift: Poetical Works." N&Q, 220 (1975), 562-63.

    Replaces "Satira" in the Davis and Williams editions of "The Lady's
    Dressing Room," l. 132, with "Statira," found in eighteenth-century
    texts. (This may be an allusion to Nathaniel Lee's tragedy The Rival
    Queens.) The restoration heightens the contrast between the virtuous
    Queen Statira and the "pocky" actress who plays the role--a contrast
    also repeated in the pun on "quean" and "queen."

95. Walther, Karl Klaus. "Erste Deutsche Ubersetzungen von Swifts
    Gullivers Reisen." ("Early German Translations of Swift's
    Gulliver's Travels.") Marginalien: Zeitschrift für Buchkunst und
    Bibliophilie, 59 (1975), 48-53.

    A report on the first two German translations of the Travels
    (Hamburg and Leipzig, 1727).

96. Weedon, Margaret. "An Uncancelled Copy of the First Collected
    Edition of Swift's Poems." The Library, 5th ser., 22 (1967),
    44-56.

    Swift's textual changes and arrangements were extensive, and he left
    out five poems altogether. The essay includes a summary table of
    cancellations by Swift.

97. Weinglass, D.H. "An Uncollected Letter from Swift to Mrs.
    (Pendarves) Delany." N&Q, 224 (1979), 548-49.

    Printed in the Monthly Mirror for March 1797, the letter is full of classic Swiftian raillery: "The apology you make in the post[s]cript is, in few words, a compound of falsehood and affection. You are ashamed, you say, of your blunders: and I cannot observe one."

98. Weitzman, Arthur J. "Addendum to Teerink and Scouten: Another Edition of Swift's Poems." PBSA, 67 (1973), 62-64.

Reports a 1731 edition of Cadenus and Vanessa, "Baucis and Philemon," and "The Journal of a Modern Lady of Quality," not recorded in Teerink-Scouten.

99. White, P.J. (ed.). Swift Tercentenary Commemoration. Trim, Co. Meath: Swift Commemoration Committee, 1967. Pp. 2 + 9.

100. Williams, Aubrey L. "'A vile Encomium': That 'Panegyric on the Reverend D--n S--t'." Pp. 179-90 of Contemporary Studies of Swift's Poetry. Edited by John Irwin Fischer and Donald C. Mell, Jr. With David M. Vieth as Associate Editor. Newark, Del.: U. of Delaware Press, 1981.

The internal and external evidence Williams presents against Swift's authorship of "A Panegyric on the Reverend D--n S---t, In Answer to the Libel on Dr. D--y, and a certain Great L--d" (1730) seems conclusive. See also Item 104.

101. Wolf, Edwin 2nd, and John Freehafer. "Scriblerian Publications at the Library Company of Philadelphia." Scriblerian, 2 (1969), 30-31.

Includes Bickerstaffiana and other Swift apocrypha.

102. Woolley, David. "Swift's Copy of Gulliver's Travels: The Armagh Gulliver, Hyde's Edition, and Swift's Earliest Corrections." Pp. 131-78 + plates of The Art of Jonathan Swift. Edited by Clive T. Probyn. New York: Barnes & Noble; London: Vision Press, 1978.

Woolley's case for the authenticity of the corrections in the Armagh Library's copy of Gulliver's Travels includes Swift's liking for special, large-paper editions of his works; a report by the second owner of the book that the changes were in Swift's hand; the reliableness of the auction catalogue; the limitations of modern textual editors, including Harold Williams's dislike of having his opinions challenged; a very extensive study of Swift's handwriting; significance in the content of the changes that is "not apparent on a casual inspection"; and the immediate publication of more than one-fourth of the changes in the first authorized Irish reprint of Gulliver's Travels. Appendices give Charles Ford's letter to Benjamin Motte of 3 January 1727 and the collation of the changes sent by Williams to Herbert Davis in 1940.

103. Woolley, David. "Swift's Seventh Penny Paper." <u>TLS</u>, May 17, 1974, p. 528.

    A reply to Frank H. Ellis (Item 20). (See above.)

104. Woolley, James. "Arbuckle's 'Panegyric' and Swift's Scrub Libel: The Documentary Evidence." Pp. 191-209 of <u>Contemporary Studies of Swift's Poetry</u>. Edited by John Irwin Fischer and Donald C. Mell, Jr. With David M. Vieth as Associate Editor. Newark, Del.: U. of Delaware Press, 1981.

    Woolley supports Aubrey Williams's case (Item 100) against Swift's authorship of "A Panegyric on the Reverend D--n S---t" by citing the corroborating opinion of an eighteenth-century reader, by analyzing handwriting and textual variants, and by supporting George Faulkner's testimony as to the authorship of James Arbuckle. He goes on to identify, with inconclusive evidence, "An Answer to Dr. D--y's Fable of the Pheasant and the Lark" as the "scrub libel" Swift said he wrote against himself.

    See also Items 235, 357, 951, 1017, 1018, 1019, 1025, 1115.

B. Editions

105. Armellini, Bruno (trans.). <u>Una Modesta Proposta e Altri Scritti Satrici</u>. Milan: Sugar, 1967.

    Includes <u>An Argument Against Abolishing Christianity</u>, <u>The Bickerstaff Papers</u>, <u>Directions to Servants</u>, and "Meditation on a Broomstick."

106. Asimov, Isaac (ed.). <u>The Annotated Gulliver's Travels</u>. New York: Clarkson N. Potter, 1980. Pp. xxii + 298.

    Copiously illustrated (with designs from the eighteenth to the twentieth century) and annotated.

107. Barzun, Jacques (intro.). <u>Gulliver's Travels</u>. Illustrated by Warren Chappell. New York: Oxford U. Press, 1977. Pp. xxxii + 300.

    Reprints the Blackwell text.

108. Beaumont, Charles (ed.). <u>A Modest Proposal</u>. (Merrill Literary Casebook Series.) Columbus, Ohio: Charles E. Merrill, 1969. Pp. xii + 130.

Includes the following critical essays: William Makepeace Thackeray, from The English Humourists of the Eighteenth Century; Sir Henry Craik, from The Life of Jonathan Swift, Dean of St. Patrick's Dublin; J.W. Johnson, "Tertullian and A Modest Proposal"; Louis A. Landa, "A Modest Proposal and Populousness"; Oliver W. Ferguson, "Swift's 'Saeva Indignatio' and A Modest Proposal"; Edward W. Rosenheim, Jr., from Swift and the Satirist's Art; Ricardo Quintana, "Situational Satire: A Commentary on the Method of Swift"; Maurice Johnson, "The Structural Impact of A Modest Proposal"; Martin Price, from Swift's Rhetorical Art; Charles Beaumont, "The Classical Rhetoric of A Modest Proposal"; Edward Corbett, "A Method of Analyzing Prose Style with a Demonstration Analysis of Swift's A Modest Proposal."

109. Bliss, Alan (ed.). "A Dialogue in Hybernian Stile Between A and B" and "Irish Eloquence." (Irish Writings from the Age of Swift, 6.) Dublin: Cadenus Press, 1977. Pp. 102.

Rev. (favorably) by Alan Ward in N&Q, 223 (1979), 252-54; (with other works) by C.J. Rawson in Yearbook of English Studies, 10 (1980), 278-79.

Bliss's introduction is a valuable description of the linguistic and social history of Hibernian English.

110. Bosse, Malcolm J. (intro.). A Tale of a Tub, A Full and True Account of the Battel Fought Last Friday between the Antient and the Modern Books in St. James's Library, A Discourse Concerning the Mechanical Operations of the Spirit. (Foundations of the Novel Series.) New York and London: Garland, 1972. Pp. 9 + 322.

The 1704 edition.

111. Brewster, William T. (intro.). Gulliver's Travels. New York: Franklin Watts, 1969. Pp. xxviii + 356.

An "Ultratype" edition, with generous type and spacing for easier reading. Also a bowdlerized edition, with zealous deletion of scatological passages.

112. Brezianu, Andrei (trans.). Jurnal Pentru Stella: 1710-1713. [Journal to Stella.] Bucarest: Univers, 1973. Pp. xxxii + 549.

Rev. (favorably) by Virgil Nemoianu in Scriblerian, 7 (1974), 5-6.

Annotated and illustrated, with a short bibliography and introduction. Nemoianu's review is interesting on Brezianu's decision to borrow his stylistic effect from eighteenth-century Rumanian writers.

113. Brezianu, Andrei (trans.). Povestea unui poloboc. Satire si alte
     pamflete. [A Tale of a Tub. Satires and Other Pamphlets.]
     Bucarest: Edit. Univers, 1971. Pp. 380.

     Noted in Scriblerian, 4 (1972), 54-55.

     The first Rumanian translation of the Tale, along with the Battle of
     the Books, Mechanical Operation of the Spirit, Polite Conversation,
     The Drapier's Letters, and other works.

114. Brilli, Attilio (ed.). Swift, I Viaggi di Gulliver. [Gulliver's
     Travels.] (I Grandi Libri.) Milan: Garzanti, 1975. Pp. xx + 277.

     Rev. in review art. ("L'anatomia swiftiana") by Giuseppe Sertoli
     in Nuova Corrente, 67 (1975), 276-312; in Scriblerian, 11 (1978),
     10.

     "Mr. Brilli's Introduction is founded on the best modern editions of
     Swift's work and a serious understanding of his life. The
     translation reproduces the thrust and tone of Swift's writing."
     (Scriblerian)

115. Davis, Herbert (ed.). Swift: Poetical Works. (Oxford Standard
     Authors.) London: Oxford U. Press, 1967. Pp. xxx + 682.

     Rev. in review art. ("Recent Studies in the Restoration and
     Eighteenth Century") by Frank Brady in SEL, 8 (1968), 551-72;
     (favorably) by Maurice Johnson in Scriblerian, 1, no. 1 (Autumn,
     1968), 27-28; (with another work) by Pierre Danchin in English
     Studies, 52 (1971), 178-80; by W.A. Speck in N&Q, 214 (1969),
     395-98.

     Davis's one-volume edition lacks the extensive background notes,
     lists of variants, and remarks on publishing history of Sir Harold
     Williams's three-volume Clarendon Press edition (1937; 1958). It is
     far easier to read, however, and infinitely more convenient to
     carry. Davis reprints most of Williams's texts, but does make
     several valuable corrections. He also prints all names in full,
     which sometimes has the effect, as Maurice Johnson remarked, of
     "trying to rescue the Dean from his lifelong habit of arch
     playfulness."

116. Daw, C.P. (intro.). Swift's Miscellanies in Prose and Verse (1711).
     (Scolar Students' Facsimiles.) Menston, Yorkshire: Scolar Press,
     1972. Pp. 416.

     Facsimile reprint.

117. Directions to Servants: 1745. (Scolar Students' Facsimiles.)
     Menston, Yorkshire: Scolar Press, 1971. Pp. 94.

118. A Discourse from 'A Tale of a Tub,' 1704; and A Meditation Upon a
     Broomstick, 1710. (Scolar Students' Facsimiles.) Menston,
     Yorkshire: Scolar Press, 1970. Pp. 51.

119. Dixon, Peter, and John Chalker (eds.). Gulliver's Travels.
     Introduction by Michael Foot. Harmondsworth: Penguin Books, 1967.

120. Dubashinsky, J.A. (ed.). "Puteshestviya Gullivera" Dzhonatana
     Svifta. [Gulliver's Travels.] Moscow: Vysshaja Shkola, 1969. Pp.
     111.

     Noted by Leonid M. Arinshtein in Scriblerian, 2 (1970), 39.

     "[C]overs ground that is well known (for example, the political
     aspects of the tale)." (Arinshtein)

121. Ehrenpreis, Irvin (supervised by). The Prose Works of Jonathan
     Swift. Vol. XIV: Index. Compiled by William J. Kunz, Steven
     Hollander, and Susan Staves. Under the Supervision of Irvin
     Ehrenpreis; Addenda, Errata, Corrigenda. Edited by Herbert Davis
     and Irvin Ehrenpreis. 1968. Pp. xv + 384. Vols. XV-XVI: Journal to
     Stella. 1974. Pp. lxii + 368; 369-801. (Shakespeare Head Edition.)
     Oxford: Basil Blackwell.

122. Ellis, Frank H. (ed.). A Discourse of the Contests and Dissentions
     Between the Nobles and the Commons in Athens and Rome. Oxford:
     Clarendon Press, 1967. Pp. viv + 270.

     Rev. (favorably) by C.J. Rawson in RES, n.s. 19 (1968), 75-77;
     (favorably) by Francis E. Moran in Seventeenth-Century News, 26
     (1968), 11; (favorably) in review art. ("The Text and Context of
     Swift's Contests and Dissentions") by Edward Rosenheim, Jr. in MP,
     66 (1968), 59-74; by W.A. Speck in N&Q, 213 (1968), 230; by Pierre
     Danchin in English Studies, 52 (1971), 74-76; by Colin J. Horne in
     MLR, 63 (1968), 942-43; (with other works) by Maurice Johnson in
     Satire Newsletter, 5 (1968), 175-78.

     This edition is based (though with several changes) on the first
     edition of 1701, not the corrected version of 1735 that Herbert
     Davis relied upon. Ellis's detailed discussion of the political
     history of 1697-1702 is superb.

123. Ellis, Frank H. (ed.). Poems on Affairs of State: Augustan Satirical
     Verse 1660-1714. Vol. VII: 1704-1714. New Haven and London: Yale
     U. Press, 1975. Pp. xlii + 732; plates.

     Rev. (with another work) by William Kinsley in Scriblerian, 9
     (1977), 122-23; (with another work) by Pat Rogers in MLR, 72
     (1977), 402-05; (with other works) by Malcolm Kelsall in RES, n.s.
     28 (1977), 348-50; by H.T. Dickinson in N&Q, 221 (1976), 366-67.

147. Skoumal, Aloys (trans.). <u>Gulliverovy cesty</u>. [<u>Gulliver's Travels</u>.]
     Illustrated by Cyril Bouda. Praha: Albatros, 1970. Pp. 336.

     See the review of Skoumal's often-reprinted translation by Martin
     Hilský in <u>Scriblerian</u>, 5 (1972), 9-10.

     A republication of the 1931 Czechoslovakian translation by Aloys
     Skoumal, with his postscript and commentary.

148. Skoumal, Aloys (ed.). <u>Zakletý duch</u>. [<u>A Conjured Mind</u>.] Praha, 1967.

     Noted in <u>Scriblerian</u>, 4 (1971), 6-7.

     Czechoslovakian edition of selected works in three parts: Educator
     (including the <u>Argument</u>); Politician (including <u>The Drapier's
     Letters</u>, IV, and <u>A Modest Proposal</u>); Man (including <u>Verses on the
     Death of Dr. Swift</u>, and <u>Journal to Stella</u>).

149. <u>A Tale of a Tub: The Battle of the Books: The Mechanical Operation
     of the Spirit</u>. London: Fraser, 1970.

     A luxury edition.

150. Turner, Paul (intro. and annot.). <u>Gulliver's Travels</u>. Oxford: Oxford
     U. Press, 1971. Pp. 379.

     The text is from the Davis edition of <u>Prose Works</u>, from the 1735
     Faulkner edition.

151. Williams, Harold (ed.). <u>The Correspondence of Jonathan Swift</u>. Vol.
     IV: 1732-36; Vol. V: 1737-45. Oxford: Clarendon Press, 1965. Pp.
     xx + 560; xii + 404.

     Rev. by Kathleen Williams in <u>RES</u>, n.s. 17 (1966), 207-08; by
     Pierre Danchin in <u>English Studies</u>, 46 (1965), 427-35; by Denis
     Donoghue in <u>The New Statesman</u>, May 14, 1965, p. 766; in <u>TLS</u>, May
     27, 1965, p. 424; by Richmond P. Bond in <u>MLR</u>, 61 (1965), 291-92.

152. Williams, Kathleen (ed.). <u>A Tale of a Tub and Other Satires by
     Jonathan Swift</u>. (Everyman's University Library.) London: Dent; New
     York: E.P. Dutton, 1975. Pp. xxxii + 279.

     Rev. by C.J. Rawson in <u>N&Q</u>, 222 (1976), 516-18.

153. Woolley, James (preface by). "The Place of the Damn'd ... & The
     Devil's Reply." Dublin: Trinity Closet Press, 1980. Pp. 8.

     Reprints the anonymous reply to "The Place of the Damn'd" for the first time since 1731. "The Devil's Reply," based on a rather thorough misreading of Swift's poem, argues that to compare Hell with Dublin is to lessen its threat, since the author himself quite <u>likes</u> Dublin and thinks others might also!

154. Agnew, Jean. "The Delanys and Their Links with Clogher and Derryvullan." Clogher Record, 7 (1970), 221-35.

A brief history of Clogher, of Swift's great friend, Patrick Delany, and especially of his gifted wife, Mary Pendarves Delany.

155. Archibald, Douglas N. "The Words upon the Window-pane and Yeats's Encounter with Jonathan Swift." Pp. 176-214 of Yeats and the Theatre. Edited by Robert O'Driscoll and Lorna Reynolds. Toronto: Macmillan-Hunter, 1975.

Yeats sketched three Swifts in his play: the public man (who "oil'd many a spring that Harley moves"), the lover of Stella and Vanessa, and the legendary "driv'ler and a show." More important, Swift as Tory gloomist and Irish patriot haunted Yeats's mind and help him find his own voice. The most original part of the essay is a survey of several Yeats poems whose language reveals that "haunting."

156. Astaldi, Maria Luisa. Tre Inglesi Pazzi. [Three English Madmen.] Milano: Rizzoli Editone, 1974. Pp. 334.

Rev. by Mario Praz in Tempo, 9 (1974), 3.

Biographical sketches of Swift, Johnson, and Beckford, including a non-scholarly, uncritical, sentimental impression of Swift's "troubled" personal life. Elaborate scenes and invented dialogues are the wonderworks and most solid elements of this fabulist's narratives.

157. Becker, Isidore H. "The Genial Side of Jonathan Swift." Lock Haven Review, 14 (1973), 104-12.

Stresses Swift's affection for his friends, his generosity, and his conviviality, citing Hawkesworth almost exclusively.

158. Beckett, J.C. Confrontations: Studies in Irish History. Totowa, N.J.: Rowman and Littlefield, 1972. Pp. 175.

Pp. 111-22 are "Swift: The Priest in Politics." In 1708 and 1709,

Swift's conduct was governed by his regard for the welfare of the
church. In 1710, however, Swift's actions arose primarily from his
own desire for position and influence. The dualism in Swift's
position highlights his refusal to sacrifice the church for the sake
of political unity and his essential pessimism about the church's
future.

159. Berrie, Francoise. "Swift et l'Ecosse." Les Langues Modernes, 62
     (1968), 490-95.

     Describes Swift's well-known dislike of the Scots in well-known
     ways.

160. Brady, Charles A. "Reach Me My Mask: A Tale of Jonathan Swift."
     Eire-Ireland, 2, no. 3 (Fall 1967), 12-33.

     Silly fictionalized version of Swift's everyday life in Dublin.

161. Broes, Arthur T. "Swift the Man in Finnegans Wake." ELH, 43 (1976),
     120-40.

     Joyce saw Swift primarily as "an exemplar of the Fall of Man, his
     life and death an illustration of the weaknesses of the human
     condition."

162. Butler, T.R. Fitzwalter. "Dean Swift and the Butlers." Journal of
     the Butler Society (Dublin), 1 (1970-71), 159-65.

     Sketches Swift's relations with Ormande.

163. Carpenter, Andrew. "Archbishop King and Swift's Appointment as Dean
     of St. Patrick's." Long Room, 11 (1975), 11-13.

     Sketches King's (thwarted) plan to block Swift from the deanship.

164. Carroll, Paul Vincent. Farewell to Greatness! Edited by Robert
     Hogan. ("Lost Play" Series, 3.) Dixon, Ca.: Proscenium Press,
     1966.

     Rev. by William J. Feeney in Eire-Ireland, 2, no. 2 (Summer 1967),
     120-21.

     Highlights conflicts in Swift's life from 1711 to Stella's death in
     1728.

165. Ceretti, Olga. "Jonathan Swift: soltanto scherno per amore."
     Historia, July, 1968, pp. 94-99.

166. Cullen, Sara. "In the Sheridan Country: Rambles Round Quilca."
     Drumlin: A Journal of Cavan, Leitrim and Monaghan, 1 (1978),
     43-48.

167. Daiches, David (ed.). "Swift." Pp. 507-09 of The Penguin Companion
     to English Literature. London: Penguin; New York: McGraw-Hill,
     1971.

     Pp. 507-09 are a biographical summary.

168. Davis, Herbert. "Swift's Character." Pp. 1-23 of Jonathan Swift
     1667-1967: A Dublin Tercentenary Tribute. Edited by Roger McHugh
     and Philip Edwards. Dublin: Dolmen Press; London: Oxford U. Press,
     1967.

     More accurately, "Swift's Character of Himself": this is a survey of
     Swift's self-portraits, with special attention to the irony and
     indirection of Verses on the Death of Dr. Swift, the connection
     between Swift's "worst passions" and his poetry-writing, and his
     (angry) insistence on seeing the truth.

169. Deford, Miriam Allen. "Swift and Stella: An Unsolved Mystery Story."
     Modern Age, 11 (1967), 400-06.

     A grotesque account of Temple as Stella's father (though not
     Swift's), of Swift's mother causing his Oedipal "spiritual disease,"
     of "the idol and terror of London drawing-rooms," of Vanessa being
     dealt a "death-blow" by both Swift and Stella, and of a man who
     "feared and hated" women.

170. Downie, J.A. "Dr. Swift's Bill." N&Q, 223 (1978), 42-43.

     This newly found item "Sheds light not only on Swift's acquaintance
     with Shakespeare; it confirms his obsession with the everyday
     problem of feeding himself."

171. Duthie, Elizabeth. "'And "Swift" Expires a Driv'ler and a Show'."
     N&Q, 222 (1977), 250.

     The source of Samuel Johnson's famous portrayal is a 1743
     Gentlemen's Magazine item. The following year a retraction (of the
     insinuation that Swift was insane) was printed.

172. Ehrenpreis, Irvin. Swift: The Man, His Works, and the Age. Vol. 2:
     Dr. Swift. Cambridge, Mass.: Harvard U. Press; London: Methuen,
     1967. Pp. xvii + 782.

     Rev. (favorably) by Colin J. Horne in MLR, 64 (1969), 646-47;
     (with reservations) by Ricardo Quintana in ELN, 6 (1968-69),

136-40; (favorably) by George Mayhew in South Atlantic Quarterly, 68 (1969), 137-39; in review art. ("Recent Studies in the Restoration and Eighteenth Century") by Frank Brady in SEL, 8 (1968), 551-72; (favorably) by Pierre Danchin in English Studies, 49 (1968), 566-70; (favorably) by C.J. Rawson in RES, n.s. 19 (1968), 440-42; in review art. ("Ehrenpreis's Swift: The Biographer as Critic") by Phillip Harth in MP, 67 (1970); (favorably) by Denis Donoghue in New York Review of Books, Jan. 16, 1969, pp. 10-12; (with another work) by W.A. Speck in N&Q, 214 (1969), 395-98; (favorably) by Robert C. Steensma in Scriblerian, 1, no. 1 (Autumn, 1968), 24-26; by P.K. Elkin in Journal of the Australasian Universities Language and Literature Association, 35 (1971), 102-03; by A.R. Humphreys in Hermathena, 110 (1970), 101-02.

This second volume of Ehrenpreis's biography covers the years 1699-1714--biographically the most intriguing period of Swift's life, though none of his most important works was written during this time (except, perhaps, A Tale of a Tub, analyzed extensively in Vol. 1). Ehrenpreis adds newly researched facts to almost jargon-free psychological analysis of Swift's motives, meticulous untangling of political threads, and critical analysis of Swift's writing that is not infrequently the best to date. When the final volume and index are published, this will be the standard biography of Swift for our generation.

173. Elistratova, A.A. "The Champion of Freedom." Izvestija, Nov. 30, 1967.

Noted in Leonid Arinshtein in Scriblerian, 2 (1970), 39.

Written "in honor of the great satirist" by "the most prominent Russian student of English literature in the eighteenth century." (Arinshtein)

174. Finch, G.J. "The Earl of Orrery and Swift's 'Genius'." Theoria, 44 (1975), 55-63.

Orrery's account of Swift anticipates, in a negative way, our own current critical uncertainties about the existence of a "firm centre" to Swift's life and works.

175. Foss, Michael. The Age of Patronage: The Arts in England 1660-1750. Ithaca: Cornell U. Press, 1971. Pp. x + 234; plates.

Contains many scattered references to Swift's English career in a detailed study of the relations of writers to political structures.

176. French, David P. "The Identity of C.M.P.G.N.S.T.N.S." Pp. 1-9 of Jonathan Swift: Tercentenary Essay. (U. of Tulsa Department of English Monograph Series, 3.) Tulsa: U. of Tulsa, 1967.

John Geree, a sometime friend of Swift, is offered here as the author of a 1757 Gentlemen's Magazine article that identified Swift and Stella as the illegitimate children of Sir William Temple.

177. Gheorghiu, Mihnea. "Irlanda Nimic despre cei vii daca nu-i adevarat." ["About the Living Nothing But the Truth."] Secolul XX, 15, no. 2 (1972), 57-60.

Swift's murky relationship with Stella somehow symbolizes his equivocal love of Ireland.

178. Goldberg, Gerald Y. Jonathan Swift and Contemporary Cork. Line Drawings by Szymon. Foreword by Cearbhaill O'Dalaigh. Cork: Mercier Press, 1967. Pp. 120.

Rev. in TLS, July 4, 1968, p. 707.

Less valuable on Swift than on Cork, this volume includes chapters on Swift and Vanessa, on the preferment of Thomas Sheridan, on Swift's own hopes for advancement, on The Drapier's Letters, and on Swift's "freedom of the city" of Cork.

179. Gould, William (ed.). "Jonathan Swift." Pp. 417-21 of Lives of the Georgian Age 1714-1837. Compiled by Laurence Urdang Associates. New York: Barnes & Noble, 1978.

A useful brief life.

180. Graham, Edward. "Smedley and Swift--'Further Reasons for Their Enmity'." PQ, 48 (1969), 416-20.

The "further reasons" are Smedley's pamphlet attacking the Test Act and his exploitation of a lapse of argumentation in Swift's A Letter Concerning the Sacramental Test Act.

181. Griffith, Philip Mahone. "Middleton Murry on Swift: 'the Nec Plus Ultra of Objectivity'?" D.H. Lawrence Review, 2 (1969), 60-67.

Attacks Murry's biased view of Swift's life, especially his queasiness at scatology and his contemptuous uneasiness with Swift's celibacy.

182. Hagstrum, Jean H. Sex and Sensibility: Ideal and Erotic Love from Milton to Mozart. Chicago and London: U. of Chicago Press, 1980. Pp. xix + 350.

This survey of Restoration and eighteenth-century attitudes towards Eros includes several pages ("Swift's Vanessa and Stella," pp. 145-59) of speculation about Swift's "psycho-sexual energy" and discusses briefly, and on more solid ground, Swift and Stella's "friendship plus (intimate love without the final intimacy)."

183. Harvey, Sir Paul (comp. and ed.). "Swift." Pp. 791-93 of The Oxford Companion to English Literature. Oxford: Clarendon Press, 1967.

Pp. 791-93 are a biographical outline. Pp. 71, 247, 359, and 798, are brief identifications of Battle of the Books, the Drapier's Letters, Gulliver's Travels, and A Tale of a Tub, respectively.

184. Hayley, R.L. "The Scriblerians and the South Sea Bubble: A Hit by Cibber." RES, n.s. 24 (1973), 452-58.

A passage in Cibber's play The Refusal attacks Gay, Arbuthnot, and Pope, along with Swift, for their eager speculations in the South Sea Bubble.

185. Hilles, Frederick W. "Dr. Johnson on Swift's Last Years: Some Misconceptions and Distortions." PQ, 54 (1975), 370-79.

This defense of Johnson's fairness as a biographer points to his close reliance, concerning the end of Swift's life, on Hawkesworth, the fairest previous biographer. The famous line, "And Swift expires a driv'ler and a show,--" is accounted for by Johnson's emulative needs in following Juvenal's tenth satire.

186. Jackson, Robert Wyse. "Dean Swift, the Liberties King." Pp. 40-45 of The Liberties of Dublin. Edited by Elgie Gillespie. Dublin, 1973.

Noted in Scriblerian, 8 (1975), 10.

The "Liberties" is the oldest part of Dublin, the area surrounding St. Patrick's.

187. Jackson, Robert Wyse. "Stella: Her Relationship with Jonathan Swift." Pp. 375-94 + plates of North Munster Studies: Essays in Commemoration of Monsignor Michael Moloney. Edited by Etienne Rhynne. Limmerick: The Thomond Archaeological Society, 1967.

Stresses Swift's immaturity and "old maidishness" in his relations with Vanessa and Stella, as well as Stella's "bitter loneliness and impatience" during Swift's time away from her; defends the notion of Maxwell Gold (Swift's Marriage to Stella, 1937) that an unconsummated marriage ceremony took place.

188. Jeffares, A. Norman. "Swift and the Ireland of His Day." Irish University Review, 2 (1972), 115-32.

General story of the religious, political, and intellectual

atmosphere of Swift's Ireland, mostly during his early years before England.

189. Kay, Donald. "To the Very Hour of Death: The Friendship of Addison and Swift." Aevum, 47 (1973), 332-35.

A very general account of Swift's and Addison's literary, political, and personal relations, with stress on mutual admiration.

190. Ketrick, Paul J. "Jonathan Swift: Great Wit or Blest Madman?" Pp. 31-38 of Jonathan Swift: Tercentenary Essays. (U. of Tulsa Department of English Monograph Series, 3.) Tulsa: U. of Tulsa, 1967.

Lists a "catalogue of items which have caused controversy concerning symptoms of insanity in the mind of Swift": excessive gravity, hiding of authorship, attitudes toward science, religion, pride, insolence, obscurity, cruelty, paradoxical nature, attitude against humanity.

191. Korshin, Paul J. "The Earl of Orrery and Swift's Early Reputation." Harvard Library Bulletin, 16 (1968), 167-77.

Orrery's annotations to two copies of his biography suggest that his motive was not deliberate malice but an aristocratic inability to understand or appreciate Swift's taste for vulgarity or his abuse of the human species, coupled with a misguided attempt to redress sensationalism by knocking Swift off the pedestal of blind adulation.

192. Landa, Louis A. "Jonathan Swift: 'Not the Gravest of Divines'." Pp.38-60 of Jonathan Swift 1667-1967: A Dublin Tercentenary Tribute. Edited by Roger McHugh and Philip Edwards. Dublin: Dolmen Press; London: Oxford U. Press, 1967.

Rept. as pp. 63-85 of Essays in Eighteenth-Century English Literature. Princeton: Princeton U. Press, 1980.

Argues that Swift's notorious "pessimism" as a churchman--not uncommon among the embattled clergy of the times--was a natural outgrowth of the seriousness with which Swift took his decanal duties and of his historical and economic determinism.

193. Le Brocquy, Sybil. Swift's Most Valuable Friend. Dublin: Dolmen Press; London: Oxford U. Press; Chester Springs, Pa.: Dufour Editions, 1968. Pp. 128.

Rev. (severely) by Francis Doherty in RES, n.s. 20 (1969), 505-06; (with reservations) by Pierre Danchin in English Studies, 52 (1971), 559; (with other works) by Colin J. Horne in MLR, 67 (1972), 170-72.

A largely invented account of Swift and Stella, perpetuating unproven theories of their blood kinship and of Swift's collapse into "wild disorder" and "disaster" upon Stella's death.

194. Le Brocquy, Sybil. A View of Vanessa, a Correspondence with Interludes, for the Stage. Dublin: Dolmen Press; London: Oxford U. Press 1967. Pp. 80.

Rev. in TLS, Nov. 16, 1967, p. 1083.

195. Lee, Gerard A. "The Dublin of Jonathan Swift." Dublin Historical Record, 21 (1967), 53-66.

An unscholarly, but often charming, description of the physical appearance of Dublin in Swift's time.

196. Longfield, A.K. "Longfields of Kilbride and a Link with Swift." Journal of the County Kildare Archaeological Society, 15 (1971), 29-37.

Nothing new about Swift.

197. MacCarvill, Eileen. "Swift and the Vanhomrighs." Journal of the County Kildare Archaeological Society, 14 (1967), 95-126.

198. Mayhew, George. "Swift and the Tripos Tradition." PQ, 45 (1966), 85-101.

This essay elaborates on the origins and evolution of the satiric, mock-academic Tripos and strongly implies Swift's participation in two such exercises, though it does not make this a definite conclusion. Nor does it have space to take on the intriguing question of what, if any, influence the Tripos may have had on Swift's later art.

199. Mayhew, George P. "A Portrait of Jonathan Swift." HLQ, 29 (1965), 287-94.

A 1742 letter by Swift's friend, the Rev. William Dunkin D.D., gives a brief physical description of Swift and refers to a now lost oil portrait of him by the contemporary Dublin artist Francis Bindon.

200. McCarthy, Muriel. "Swift and the Primate of Ireland: Marsh's Library in the Early Eighteenth Century." Dublin Historical Record, 27 (1974), 109-12.

Marsh irked Swift by requiring a pre-ordination testimonial of good behavior from him and by dashing Swift's hopes to be Dean at Derry and Bishop of Cork. Ironically, Swift eventually became Governor of Marsh's Library and even asked to be buried next to Marsh.

201. McElrath, Joseph R., Jr. "Swift's Friend: Dr. Patrick Delany." _Eire-Ireland_, 5, no. 3 (Autumn 1970), 53-62.

A brief summary of their relationship, especially their poetical exchanges.

202. McHugh, Roger. "The Life of Jonathan Swift." Pp. 9-24 of _Swift Revisited_. Edited by Denis Donoghue. Cork: Mercier; Hatboro, Pa.: Folklore Associates, 1968.

For a general audience, with special attention to Swift's career in Ireland.

203. Meyers, Jeffrey. "Autobiographical Reflections in Johnson's 'Life of Swift'." _Discourse_, 8 (1965), 37-48.

Johnson's choice of anecdotes about Swift and the way he generalizes about facts of Swift's life not only dissociate him from Swift, but from all that he feared in Swift: deafness and death, solitude and madness.

204. Meyers, Jeffrey. "Swift, Johnson, and the Dublin M.A." _American Notes and Queries_, 4 (1965), 5-6.

Some of Johnson's hostility to Swift may be explained by the mix-up of 1739: Johnson (mistakenly) thought Swift had the power to obtain an M.A. for him but had simply refused to do so.

205. Moore, J.N.P. "Swift's Philanthropy." Pp. 137-56 of _Jonathan Swift 1667-1967: A Dublin Tercentenary Tribute_. Edited by Roger McHugh and Philip Edwards. Dublin: Dolmen Press; London: Oxford U. Press, 1967.

The story of St. Patrick's Hospital, Dublin, founded by Swift. Moore also discusses Swift's own illnesses and stresses Swift's "intelligent, creative response to his neurotic fear" of disorders of the mind.

206. Moreau, Pierre. "L'Homme-cheval." _Europe_, 463 (1967), 120-31.

The remaining puzzles about Swift's life include his Irishness, his obsession with power, his failed preferment, his attitude towards the Jacobites, and his relations with women. Moreau posits that Swift was an anti-mercantilist conservative, whose ideal of moderate reasonableness is expressed in the Houyhnhnms.

207. Mouravjev, Vladimir. <u>Jonathan Swift</u>. Moscow: Prosvestchenie, 1968.
     Pp. 304.

     Noted by Leonid Arinshtein in <u>Scriblerian</u>, 1, no. 2 (Spring,
     1969), 3-4; by V. Kharitonov in <u>Vosprosy Literatury</u>, 12 (1968),
     219-21.

     More a series of interpretations than a source of new facts about
     Swift's life, this Russian biography stresses "Swift's sober
     evaluation of the social and personal limits to man's moral power."
     (Arinshtein)

208. Patterson, Emily H. "Swift's Marginal Allusions to the Atterbury
     Case." <u>Anglia</u>, 92 (1974), 395-97.

     Patterson takes issue with Edward Rosenheim, Jr. (Item 218),
     documenting that Swift <u>did</u> believe in Atterbury's innocence by three
     notes Swift left in history books identifying Atterbury with
     innocent men.

209. Prahl-Lauersen, Vagn. "Jonathan Swift, mennesket bag satirkeren."
     ["Jonathan Swift, the Man behind the Satirist."] <u>Extracta</u>, 2
     (1969), 281-87.

     Noted (severely) by Birgitta Steene in <u>Scriblerian</u>, 5 (1972), 8.

     "[S]ubstantially a historical enumeration of basic episodes in
     Swift's life." (Steene)

210. Rafroidi, Patrick. "Swift et l'Irlande." <u>Les Langues Modernes</u>, 62
     (1968), 484-89.

     Stressing Swift's "Irishness" (here something like contradictoriness
     and <u>ad hoc</u> attitudes), Rafroidi argues that Swift was neither an
     anti-capitalist nor an anti-colonist.

211. Rawson, C.J. "Biographical Introduction." Pp. 9-16 of <u>Focus: Swift</u>.
     Edited by C.J. Rawson. London: Sphere Books, 1971.

     Perhaps the best very brief biographical sketch.

212. Reynolds, James. "Jonathan Swift--Vicar of Laracor." <u>Riocht na
     Midhe: Records of the Meath Archaeological and Historical Society</u>,
     4 (1967), 41-54.

213. Rhynehart, J.G. "A Dean Swift Relic." <u>Irish Booklore</u>, 1 (1971), 259.

     A cradle, labelled as that of Swift, was reportedly on display in a
     Sussex church in the village of Brede.

214. Richman, Jordan. "Subjectivity in the Art of Eighteenth Century Biography: Johnson's Portrait of Swift." Enlightenment Essays, 2 (1971), 91-102.

     Mostly a survey of Johnson's predecessors in Swiftian biography, this essay does not really support its large claims for Johnson's achievement in his Life of Swift.

215. Riely, Elizabeth G. "The Duchess of Marlborough on Swift." Scriblerian, 7 (1974), 1-3.

     In a series of unpublished letters, Sarah, Duchess of Marlborough, commented sardonically, disgustedly, and finally wistfully, on her husband's nemesis.

216. Rogers, Pat. "Anthony Henley and Swift." American Notes and Queries, 8 (1970), 99-101; 116-19.

     A few further facts about Swift's Whig friend.

217. Rogers, Pat. "The Dunce Answers Back: John Oldmixon on Swift and Defoe." TSLL, 14 (1972), 33-43.

     The invective against Swift of a Dunciad victim is surveyed, with no claims made for its influence on anybody.

218. Rosenheim, Edward, Jr. "Swift and the Atterbury Case." Pp. 174-204 of The Augustan Milieu: Essays Presented to Louis A. Landa. Edited by Henry Knight Miller, Eric Rothstein, and G.S. Rousseau. Oxford: Clarendon Press, 1970.

     Swift voiced his opinion of the Atterbury prosecution in Gulliver's Travels, Book III, chapter 6, and in "Upon the horrid Plot discovered by Harlequin." This very detailed account of the case accepts that Swift had no great belief in Atterbury's innocence but describes his disgust at the trumped-up prosecution, especially the motives of informers. On Swift's belief in Atterbury's innocence, see Emily H. Patterson (Item 208).

219. Rowse, A.L. Jonathan Swift: Major Prophet. New York: Scribners; London: Thames and Hudson, 1975. Pp. 240.

     Rev. (severely) by Jenny Mezciems in MLR, 72 (1977), 904-05; (severely) in review art. ("Recent Studies in Augustan Literature") by William Kupersmith in PQ, 55 (1976), 533-52; (severely) by Leland D. Peterson in Scriblerian, 9 (1976), 44-45; (favorably, and with other works) by A. Norman Jeffares in Sewanee Review, 85 (1977), 301-17; (severely) by Irvin Ehrenpreis in New York Review of Books, June 24, 1976, pp. 19-20; by C.L. McKelvie in Hermathena, 120 (1976), 89-91.

In this biography for a popular audience, Rowse devises frequent
parallels between Swift's times and our own, is thirty years behind
in some areas of scholarship, and is confidently opinionated
everywhere. Not for scholarly use.

220. Russo, John Paul. Alexander Pope: Tradition and Identity. Cambridge,
     Ma.: Harvard U. Press, 1972. Pp. 241.

     Pp. 176-98 ("A Living Image: Swift") describe the famous friendship
     between Swift and Pope.

221. Sawyer, Paul. "Swift, Mist, and a Lincoln's Inn Fields Benefit."
     N&Q, 222 (1977), 225-28.

     Although Sawyer concludes differently, the evidence he presents
     suggests mutual backpatting between Swift and Mist.

222. Seymour, William Kean. Jonathan Swift: The Enigma of a Genius: A
     Biographical Outline. Farnham, Surrey: Moor Park College, 1967.
     Pp. x + 34; plates.

     Rev. in TLS, Oct. 5, 1967, p. 941; by James Turner in Contemporary
     Review, 211 (1967), 54-55.

     Hardly a reliable biographical sketch; sample judgments: "Swift was
     a forerunner of the Age of Reason"; "he developed misanthropy into a
     habit."

223. Simms, J.G. "Dean Swift and County Armagh." Seanchas Ard Mhacha
     [Journal of the Armagh Diocesan Historical Society], 6 (1971),
     131-40.

     Mostly a summary of Swift's relations with the Achesons.

224. Simms, J.G. "Ireland in the Age of Swift." Pp. 157-75 of Jonathan
     Swift 1667-1967: A Dublin Tercentenary Tribute. Edited by Roger
     McHugh and Philip Edwards. Dublin: Dolmen Press; London: Oxford U.
     Press, 1967.

     A useful general account of political, social, and economic
     conditions, emphasizing early eighteenth-century Ireland as a nation
     of contrasts: widespread poverty but pockets of individual wealth;
     extreme legislation, indifferently enforced; a vigorous, persecuted
     Catholic Church and a stagnant established Church of Ireland;
     presbyterians migrating while catholics stayed to endure ever worse
     conditions; English colonists treated as badly as Irishmen;
     undeveloped resources, but a flourishing capital city and sea-ports;
     vigorous and constructive intellectuals with little or no effect on
     government.

225. Stéphane, Nelly. "Chronologie de Swift." Europe, 463 (1967), 167-72.

An outline of important dates in Swift's life.

226. Trauberg, L. "'Bezumie' Doktora Svifta." ["The Madness of Swift."]
Voprosy Literatury, 20 (1977), 113-27.

227. Warncke, Wayne. "Samuel Johnson on Swift: The Life of Swift and
Johnson's Predecessors in Swiftian Biography." Journal of British
Studies, 7, no. 2 (May 1968), 56-64.

The conventional stress here is on Johnson's departure from
Hawkesworth's comparative objectivity in favor of Orrery's
moralistic censure.

228. Wilson, T.G. "Pooley's Portrait of Swift." Dublin Magazine, 8, nos.
1-2 (Spring/Summer 1969), 47-50.

The portrait of Swift as an undergraduate at Trinity was located in
the possession of K.G.F. Balfour. Wilson opens with the egregious
comment that "while the shelves of the bookshops remain stacked with
unsold volumes of his writings, the man in the street remains firmly
convinced that Swift was disgusting, lecherous and mad."

229. Wilson, T.G. "Swift in Trinity." Dublin Magazine, 5, no. 2 (Summer,
1966), 10-22.

Stresses Swift's interest in the Dublin Philosophical Society,
despite his antagonism to Descartes.

230. Wilson, T.G. "Swift's Personality." Pp. 15-41 of Fair Liberty Was
All His Cry: A Tercentenary Tribute to Jonathan Swift 1667-1745.
Edited by A. Norman Jeffares. London: Macmillan; New York: St.
Martin's Press, 1967.

Orig. pub. in Review of English Literature, 3, no. 3 (July, 1962).

Comments on Swift's medical history; his psychological make-up
("undoubtedly a psychopath"); his scatological obsession; and his
relations with women (normal to a fault).

231. Winnett, A.R. Jonathan Swift, Churchman. Farnham, Surrey: Moor Park
College, 1968. Pp. iv + 16; plates.
Excuses the bad taste of Swift's writings in the name of his "true
Christian piety."

232. Winton, Calhoun. "Steele, Swift, and the Queen's Physician." Pp.
138-54 of The Augustan Milieu: Essays Presented to Louis A. Landa.

Edited by Henry Knight Miller, Eric Rothstein, and G.S. Rousseau. Oxford: Clarendon Press, 1970.

Sketches Swift's deteriorating relations at court, 1710-14.

233. Wittkop, Justus Franz. Jonathan Swift in Selbstzeugnissen und Bilddokumenten. ['A Portrait of Jonathan Swift Based Upon His Own Works and Contemporary Illustrations.] (Rowohlts Monographien, 242.) Hamburg: Rowohlt, 1976. Pp. 154.

Noted in Scriblerian, 9 (1976), 89.

Numerous short essays on periods of Swift's life and on particular works. No new evidence or interpretation.

234. Wolff-Windegg, Philipp. Swift. Stuttgart: Ernst Klett Verlag, 1967. Pp. 314.

Rev. by Helmut Castrop in Archiv für das Studium der Neueren Sprachen, 208 (1972), 386-87; by Virgil Nemoianu in RITL, 18 (1969), 322-23.

This German effort shows the need for the second volume of Irvin Ehrenpreis's biography, which appeared simultaneously. Includes a very brief bibliography.

235. Woolley, David. "Forster's Swift." Dickensian, 70 (1974), 191-204.

Contains information about Forster's huge workshop of materials on Swift's life.

236. Woolley, James. "Thomas Sheridan and Swift." Pp. 93-114 of Studies in Eighteenth-Century Culture. Vol. 9. Edited by Roseann Runte. Madison: U. of Wisconsin Press for the American Society for Eighteenth-Century Studies, 1979.

An enlightening account of Sheridan's engaging personality, ingenious punning, and other word play, along with Swift's ambivalent feelings towards him.

See also Items 18, 43, 53, 80, 270, 315, 317, 319, 320, 329, 331, 339, 357, 731, 732, 741, 745, 753, 828, 830, 880, 1043, 1089.

General Criticism

237. Adams, Robert M. The Roman Stamp: Frame and Facade in Some Forms of Neo-Classicism. Berkeley, Los Angeles, London: U. of California Press, 1974. Pp. v + 254.

Pp. 145-60 ("Swift and Bentley") criticize Swift's role in the Ancients-Moderns controversy (without specifically discussing The Battle of the Books). Swift disguised his arrogance with humility; he "despised literature"; he was hostile to modern mathematics and philosophy because "his abilities in those directions were moderate and his training abominable"; his art is principally "to limit, to define, and to aim a whole long passage like a flung javelin toward a precise (generally destructive) point." Although he was shallower than other major contributors to the controversy, specificially Boileau and Richard Bentley, Swift paradoxically remains more highly regarded today--ironically illustrating the superiority of a Modern position: knowledge is cumulative (and so Bentley became outdated), but art is individual (and so Swift's satire is still unequaled). Included is the fresh opinion that Swift's opinion of Milton was not unlike that of Bentley.

238. Adams, Robert Martin. "The State of the Dean." Hudson Review, 23 (1970), 578-84.

A review essay, including Denis Donoghue, Jonathan Swift: A Critical Introduction (1969), John R. Clark, Form and Frenzy in Swift's Tale of a Tub (1970), and Matthew Hodgart, A New Voyage to the Country of the Houyhnhnms (1970).

239. Alexander, Jean. "Yeats and the Rhetoric of Defilement." Review of English Literature, 6, no. 3 (July 1965), 44-57.

Locating the source of Yeats's fascination with Swift in "the disparity between physical ugliness and ideal passion," this essay goes on to make a series of loose connections between Yeats's and Swift's literary modes.

240. Anderson, William S., William F. Cunningham, Jr., Guy Davenport, Arthur Efron, Leonard Feinberg, William N. Free, D.J. Greene, Robert A. Kantra, William Kinsley, Norman Knox, Philip Pinkus, Edward Rosenheim, Jr., A.H. Scouten, William Stafford, J.P.

Sullivan, Howard D. Weinbrot, Norman Yates, Paul Zall. "The Concept of the Persona in Satire: A Symposium." Satire Newsletter, 3 (1966), 89-153.

The discussion was prompted by Irvin Ehrenpreis's 1963 article "Personae," Restoration and Eighteenth-Century Literature: Essays in Honor of Alan Dugald McKillop, ed. Carroll Camden (Chicago: U. of Chicago Press, 1963). Many of the contributors mention Swift, with A Modest Proposal as the predictable favorite.

241. Arinshtein, Leonid M. "Recent Swift Scholarship in Russia." Scriblerian, 2 (1970), 39-40.

A very brief overview.

242. Arinshtein, Leonid M. "Swift's Literary Reputation in Russia." University Review (Dublin), 4 (1967), 84-88.

Reports Swift's unfailing popularity in Russia.

243. Arita, Masaya. "Swift no shukyo to dotoku ron." ["Swift on Religion and Morality."] English Language and Literature (Chuo U.), 17 (1977), 1-29.

Noted by Zenzo Suzuki in Scriblerian, 10 (1977), 9.

"The Sentiments of a Church-of-England Man, A Project for the Advancement of Religion and An Argument against Abolishing Christianity are discussed in terms of neutralism, realism and conservatism." (Suzuki)

244. Atherton, James S. The Books at the Wake: A Study of Literary Allusions in James Joyce's Finnegans Wake. London: Faber and Faber, 1959; New York: Viking, 1960. Expanded and Corrected, Mamaroneck, N.Y.: Paul P. Appel, 1974.

Pp. 114-23 are "Swift: A Paradigm of a God," in which Swift's unique presence in Finnegans Wake is described.

245. Bà, Paolo. "J. Swift e la cultura del suo tempo." Il Lettore di Provincia, 4, no. 14 (September 1973), 13-20.

A nosegay of footnotes on the English intellectual milieu between 1660 and 1740, gathered for the Italian undergraduate.

246. Ball, David. "La Définition Ironique." Revue de Litterature Comparée, 50 (1976), 213-36.

Proceeding from Denis Donoghue's observation that Swift's favorite tactic was to demonstrate "that a complex A was 'nothing but' a simple B," Ball argues that Voltaire (and Swift, in his more complex satires, including Book IV of Gulliver's Travels) followed an analogous method of re-defining human nature by simplification.

247. Ball, David. "Vers une théorie de l'ironie: perspectives sur Swift." Etudes Anglaises, 29 (1976), 1-14.

Rev. in review art. ("Augustan Studies in 1976") by William Kupersmith in PQ, 56 (1977), 470-97.

A curiously unhelpful attempt to diagram oppositions in ironic statements.

248. Battestin, Martin C. The Providence of Wit: Aspects of Form in Augustan Literature and the Arts. Oxford: Clarendon Press, 1974. Pp. x + 331.

Rev. in review art. ("The Surface of Fact") by Martin Price in Sewanee Review, 85 (1977), 639-51; by Robert Voitle in MP, 75 (1977), 84-86; (favorably) by Benjamin Boyce in South Atlantic Quarterly, 75 (1976), 132; (with reservations) by Irène Simon in English Studies, 58 (1977), 355-58; (favorably) by Lawrence Lipking in Scriblerian, 7 (1975), 105-07; in review art. ("Exuberant Mixtures: Some Recent Studies in the Eighteenth Century") by Patricia Carr Brückmann in University of Toronto Quarterly, 46 (1976), 83-91; (unfavorably) by Douglas Brooks in MLR, 71 (1976), 135-36; (with reservations) by Ronald Paulson in Studies in Burke and His Time, 17 (1976), 234-40.

Pp. 215-69 are "Swift and Sterne: the Disturbance of Form." In his poetry, Swift is an anomaly, travestying conventional views of universal Order. However, in A Tale of a Tub, Swift's eccentricities point to a core of belief which defines confusion and reveals the satirist to be the advocate of traditional forms and values. In other words, Swift is defining Truth by its opposite.

249. Beattie, Lester M. "The Lighter Side of Swift." Pp. 35-50 of Six Satirists. (Carnegie Series in English, 9.) Pittsburgh: Carnegie Institute of Technology, 1965.

Because the shock of the "morose and caustic reflections of Swift's wry humor" has "lost something of its voltage, from repetition, or from our lessened squeamishness," Beattie surveys a few of Swift's "little excursions ... into the side roads of gaiety," including the Journal to Stella, and Books I-III of Gulliver's Travels. The essay consists of waves of the hand at jocularity and "bright happenings."

250. Beaumont, Charles Allen. Swift's Use of the Bible: A Documentation and a Study in Allusion. (University of Georgia Monographs, 14.) Athens, Ga.: U. of Georgia Press, 1965. Pp. vii + 68.

Rev. by Miriam K. Starkman in <u>Georgia Review</u>, 21 (1967), 275-76;
(severely) by James H. Sims in <u>South Atlantic Quarterly</u>, 65
(1966), 551-53.

Beaumont's conclusions are that Swift associated excessive quoting
from the Bible with pomposity and tried to avoid biblical references
in many works, including his correspondence. Swift's personae quote
the Bible most often as a means of developing their characters. For
example, the Drapier quotes heavily, as do the personae of <u>A Tale of</u>
<u>a Tub</u> and <u>The Mechanical Operation of the Spirit</u>. Bible quotations
in <u>The Examiner</u> have the effect of establishing the moral character
and persuasiveness of the speaker. That Gulliver does not quote from
the bible at all may indicate Swift's sympathy with him. This book
has been criticized for slipshod scholarship and unfocused
interpretation.

251. Benstock, Bernard. "Joyce's Swift: Synthetical but not Serene."
      <u>Dublin Magazine</u>, 10, no. 2 (Summer 1973), 21-32.

Emphasizes "the degree to which Swift <u>as a person</u> haunts the book"
(<u>Finnegans Wake</u>), in an irreverent characterization as a lecherous
old man. Joyce, who liked to equate his own blindness with Swift's
"madness," imitated Swift's tone of ironic detachment and his
satiric incisiveness.

252. Béranger, J. "Critique swiftienne du tricentenaire." ["Tricentenary
      Swift Criticism."] <u>Etudes Anglaises</u>, 22 (1969), 159-76.

Reviews the following: Herbert Davis, <u>Swift: Poetical Works</u>;
Margaret Weedon, "An Uncancelled Copy of the First Edition of
Swift's Poems"; Mackie L. Jarrell, "Ode to the King"; Frank H. Ellis
(ed.), <u>A Discourse of the Contests</u>; Louis T. Milic, <u>A Quantitative</u>
<u>Approach to the Style of Jonathan Swift</u>; Richard I. Cook, <u>Jonathan</u>
<u>Swift as a Tory Pamphleteer</u>; and George P. Mayhew, <u>Rage or Raillery?</u>

253. Béranger, Jean. "Swift et le Parlement." ["Swift and Parliament."]
      <u>Etudes Anglaises</u>, 25 (1972), 116-31.

Balance is the key to Swift's attitude towards Parliament, both in
Book II of <u>Gulliver's Travels</u> and elsewhere. Swift's conservatism
and "rage for order" is always qualified by his scepticism about
human institutions.

254. Bloom, Edward. "Apotropaic Visions: Tone and Meaning in Neoclassical
      Satire." <u>HLQ</u>, 38 (1974), 35-52.

In the course of very general remarks on satiric intentions, tones,
and responses, Bloom points to the cleansing, restorative properties
of Swift's indignation, as if Swift's methods and motives were
uniform in all his satires.

255. Bloom, Edward A., and Lillian D. Bloom. <u>Satire's Persuasive Voice</u>. Ithaca: Cornell U. Press, 1979. Pp. 306.

Rev. in review art. ("Satire or Sense: A Truer Mix") by John M. Aden in <u>Sewanee Review</u>, 89 (1981), 441-47; by Raman Selden in <u>Scriblerian</u>, 12 (1979), 44-45; (severely) by John R. Clark in <u>ELN</u>, 17 (1979-80), 218-22; (with reservations) by Pat Rogers in <u>N&Q</u>, 226 (1981), 81-82; in review art. ("Uncertainties of Satire") by Patricia Meyer Spacks in <u>MLQ</u>, 40 (1979), 403-11.

Swift is cited throughout to illustrate various points, without much sustained discussion. Pp. 87-90 compares the personae of <u>Gulliver's Travels</u> ("an evolving though not altogether full-bodied character") and <u>A Modest Proposal</u> ("a murky, disturbing presence"); pp. 135-36 discuss why the <u>Tale</u> was misread as an attack on orthodox Protestantism.

256. Bloom, Edward A., and Lillian D. Bloom. "The Satiric Mode of Feeling: A Theory of Intention." <u>Criticism</u>, 11 (1969), 115-39.

Stresses the positiveness and regenerativeness of Swift's intentions ("the sense of good will"), with scattered references to many of his works.

257. Bouvier-Ajam, Maurice. "Swift et Son Temps." ["Swift and His Age."] <u>Europe</u>, 463 (1967), 33-46.

A quick outline of French scholarship on Swift, together with a survey of eighteenth-century English history as told by French historians.

258. Brezianu, Andrei. 'Smerita Jalba: Situare şi Context." <u>Secolol XX</u>, 15, no. 2 (1972), 40-42.

259. Brilli, Attilio. <u>Retorica della Satira</u>. [The Rhetoric of Satire.] Bologna: Il Mulino, 1973. Pp. 202.

Noted in <u>English Miscellany</u>.

A "thorough study of Scriblerian satire."

260. Brilli, Attilio. <u>Swift o dell'Anatomia</u>. [Swift or Anatomy.] Firenze: Sansoni, 1974. Pp. 166.

Rev. by Paul Kirby in <u>Scriblerian</u>, 8 (1975), 13-14; in review art. ("L'anatomia swiftiana") by Giuseppe Sertoli in <u>Nuova Corrente</u>, 67 (1975), 276-312.

Satire as dismemberment and dissection, "articulated in a preface plus chapters on anatomic illustrations, dissection, coronations and

discoronations, strategies of language, and lists of references to
Swift's works and an index of names." (Kirby)

261. Broes, Arthur T. "Swift's Works in Finnegans Wake." English Studies
     in Canada, 5 (1979), 167-86.

     Documents Joyce's extensive allusions to Swift's works, especially
     to A Tale of a Tub.

262. Brown, Daniel R. "Swift and the Limitations of Satire." Dublin
     Magazine, 9 (1972), 68-78.

     The salutary stress here on the peculiar tendency of satire to
     thwart itself (by fostering the complacent superiority of its
     readers) is combined with some egregious complaints—e.g., "Of
     course the Drapier's letters did help stop Wood's coins. But the
     atom bomb was still invented." Pace W.H. Auden.

263. Brown, Daniel Russell. "Swiftian Scatology." Books and Bookmen, 17,
     no. 1 (October 1971), 18-23.

     The author declares his approval of the theories of Norman O. Brown,
     concluding that "scatological is not so much morality as taste."

264. Bullitt, John M. "Swift's 'Rules of Raillery'." Pp. 93-108 of Veins
     of Humor. (Harvard English Studies, 3.) Edited by Harry Levin.
     Cambridge, Ma.: Harvard U. Press, 1972.

     Maps Swift's characteristic uses of raillery, for compliment and for
     amusement, and occasionally for the purpose of "parallel satire," in
     which the remarked eccentricities of Swift's correspondent
     constitute a rebuke to the rest of the world. See also Items 435,
     596.

265. Byrd, Max. Visits to Bedlam: Madness and Literature in the
     Eighteenth Century. Columbia: U. of South Carolina Press, 1974.
     Pp. xvii + 200.

     Rev. (with another work) by Patricia Meyer Spacks in MP, 73
     (1976), 305-10; in review art. ("Exuberant Mixtures: Some Recent
     Studies in the Eighteenth Century") by Patricia Carr Brückmann in
     University of Toronto Quarterly, 46 (1976), 83-91.

     Pp. 58-87 are on Swift. Reading Swift's early odes, we sense the
     unshaken assumption that truth and shareable standards are fixed.
     But in A Tale of a Tub Swift makes a tentative identification of
     satirist and victim, sane man and madman, which he confirms at the
     end of his career in "The Legion Club." The principal texts in this
     discussion are the Tale and Gulliver's final voyage.

266. Carnochan, W.B. "Augustan Satire and the Gates of Dreams: A Utopian Essay." Studies in the Literary Imagination, 5, no. 2 (October 1972), 1-18.

"City Shower," the scatological poems, "The Day of Judgement" are examples of how "Augustan satire is a continuous struggle between the realms of dream and waking," a fantasy in which "the world of quotidian reality submits to the solvent powers of the satirical imagination." Augustan satire (here evidently different from other sorts of satire) has closer ties to nightmares than to the formal realism of novels.

267. Carnochan, W.B. Confinement and Flight: An Essay on English Literature of the Eighteenth Century. Berkeley, Los Angeles, and London: U. of California Press, 1977. Pp. xi + 201.

Rev. (with reservations) by Dennis Todd in Criticism, 20 (1978), 220-21; (with reservations) by John Traugott in Scriblerian, 10 (1978), 120-21; (favorably) by David W. Tarbet in ECS, 12 (1979), 549-52; (favorably) by Ronald Paulson in JEGP, 77 (1978), 443-48; (favorably) by Jenny Mezciems in MLR, 75 (1980), 363-65; (with reservations) by Robert H. Bell in MLQ, 39 (1978), 76-77; in review art. ("Fiction and Its Discontents, 1977") by J. Paul Hunter in PQ, 57 (1978), 493-526; in review art. ("Recent Studies in the Restoration and Eighteenth Century") by G.S. Rousseau in SEL, 18 (1978), 553-93.

In the course of this study of the "modernist" metaphors of prison and of escape, Carnochan describes Gulliver's movement "from fluency to blockage, from speech to speechlessness"; points out that what is most striking about "A Description of the Morning" is "the way it suspends motion and falls away into silence"; notes that "A Description of a City Shower" comes to a crescendo of movement that is merely recycling, not purgation ("the final triplet leads nowhere"); and remarks on Swift's images of height and depth, rise and fall, in A Tale of a Tub.

268. Carnochan, W.B. "The Consolations of Satire." Pp. 19-42 of The Art of Jonathan Swift. Edited by Clive T. Probyn. New York: Barnes & Noble; London: Vision Press, 1978.

Beginning with the premise that what pleases us in satire is "the display of controlled aggression," Carnochan describes Swift's creation of compensatory gratifications out of his and others' most threatening pains. Modern psychoanalytic theory is invoked judiciously to shed light on examples including the Bickerstaff Papers, A Modest Proposal, Gulliver's Travels, and a number of poems, especially "Apollo: or A Problem Solved," and "Death and Daphne."

269. Carpenter, Andrew. The Irish Perspective of Jonathan Swift. (Wuppertal Gesanthochschule, 13.) Wuppertal: Peter Hammer Verlag, 1978. Pp. 20.

Presents a more enthusiastic Irish partisan than is the standard
view of Swift. For Carpenter, Swift's outrage at the English
economic and political oppression of Ireland fed not only into his
life, but directly into the dread visions of his later works,
including Gulliver's Travels (which, Carpenter further asserts,
takes its tone from Irish fantastical oral stories).

270. Clarke, Austin. "A Sermon on Swift." Massachusetts Review, 9 (1970),
     309-12.

     The title work of a volume of poems published in Dublin by Bridge
     Press, 1968.

271. Clayborough, Arthur. The Grotesque in English Literature. Oxford:
     Clarendon Press, 1965.

     Rev. (unfavorably) by James T. Boulton in N&Q, 212 (1967), 37-38;
     (with reservations) by G.D. Josipovici in RES, n.s. 18 (1967),
     102-03; (favorably) by W.J.M. Bronzwaer in Neophilologus, 51
     (1967), 212-13; (unfavorably) by Ulrich Weisstein in JEGP, 66
     (1967), 114-16; (favorably) by A.J. Herbert in MLR, 62 (1967),
     690-91; by Valerie Owen in British Journal of Aesthetics, 6
     (1966), 208.

     Pp. 112-57, "Swift: The Fantasy of Extreme Logic," identifies the
     "narrative uncertainty" of Gulliver's Travels and A Tale of a Tub as
     the result of a "regressive-progressive opposition" in Swift's own
     personality. The core of ambivalence in Swift's mingling of the
     absurd, the humorously allegorical, and the ideal "gives expression
     to the enduring paradox of human nature."

272. Coudert, Marie-Louise. "Le trois rires: Rabelais, Swift, Voltaire."
     Europe, 463 (1967), 93-98.

     A quick sketch of three distinct varieties of laughter.

273. Coulling, Sidney M.B. "Carlyle and Swift." SEL, 10 (1970), 741-58.

     The focus here is on Carlyle who, despite his lifelong admiration
     for Swift's writing, was too much the "true humorist" to push irony
     to its ultimate point or to derive from it the universal
     significance that Swift's irony achieves.

274. Cunningham, Sandy. "Bedlam and Parnassus: Eighteenth-Century
     Reflections." Essays and Studies by Members of the English
     Association, 24 (1971), 36-55.

     Comments, mostly with reference to Pope, on the parallelism between
     madness and the impulse to write satire. The complaint, included

here, in 1971, that critics insist on finding in Swift "little to
cause lasting perplexity," seems so outdated by 1980 as to suggest
that the mid-twentieth century may have taken Swift less seriously
than any previous critical age.

275. Daishi, Hori. "Swift and Goya." Rising Generation (Tokyo), 113
     (1967), 768-70.

     Noted in Scriblerian, 1, no. 1 (Autumn 1968), 6.

     "Show [sic]similarities between Swift and Goya in their highly
     individual satire." (Scriblerian) The essay is in Japanese.

276. Davies, Hugh Sykes. "Irony and the English Tongue." Pp. 129-53 of
     The World of Jonathan Swift: Essays for the Tercentenary. Edited
     by Brian Vickers. Cambridge, Ma.: Harvard U. Press; Oxford: Basil
     Blackwell, 1968.

     A discussion of how Swift exploited for ironic purposes the
     restricted vocabulary he advocated for the English language. A
     Modest Proposal is the chief example analyzed.

277. Davies, Paul C. "Augustan Smells." Essays in Criticism, 25 (1975),
     395-406.

     Davies's main thesis, that for the Augustans smell is a primary test
     of falsity, is briefly used to good effect on "The Lady's Dressing
     Room" and parts of Gulliver's Travels.

278. Davis, Herbert. "Introduction." Pp. ix-xix of Jonathan Swift
     1667-1967: A Dublin Tercentenary Tribute. Edited by Roger McHugh
     and Philip Edwards. Dublin: Dolmen Press; Oxford and New York:
     Oxford U. Press, 1967.

     The last published words on Swift by the great Swiftian.

279. Davis, Herbert. "Swift's Use of Irony." Irony in Defoe and Swift.
     Los Angeles: William Andrews Clark Memorial Library, 1966.

     Rept. as pp. 221-43 of Stuart and Georgian Moments. Edited by Earl
     Miner. Berkeley: U. of California Press, 1972; as pp. 154-70 of
     The World of Jonathan Swift: Essays for the Tercentenary. Edited
     by Brian Vickers. Cambridge, Ma.: Harvard U. Press; Oxford: Basil
     Blackwell, 1968.

     Rev. (with reservations) by A.L. Soons in Seventeenth-Century
     News, 28 (1970), 70; (with reservations) by C.J. Rawson in N&Q,
     212 (1967), 432-34.

     Davis's focus here is on the way Swift risked being misunderstood

and on his intermittent, not consistent, use of masks. The essay
includes a fine statement of the hard school line on Gulliver.

280. Davis, Lennard, Brent Harold, Richard Ohmann, Barry Phillips, and
      Jack Weston. "The Period Course: Eighteenth-Century British
      Literature." Radical Teacher, 7 (March, 1978), 6-11.

      A guide to Marxist teaching: "you can teach A Tale of a Tub ... and
      show how the concept of madness in religion and in secular knowledge
      is a version of the naked self-interest of individualism, dominated
      by the cash-nexus, and accelerated by the recent transition to
      capitalism"; "You can balance the students' tendency to picture
      [Swift] as an early 1970's movement activist by pointing to the
      aristocratic and authoritarian nature of his solutions, as well as
      to his retrogressive view of history."

281. Daw, C.P. "Swift's Favorite Books of the Bible." HLQ, 43 (1979),
      201-12.

      To wit: St. Paul's First Epistle to the Corinthians, because it
      deals more with instruction than with comfort, confronts the problem
      of disunity in the church, and emphasizes the inadequacy of human
      understanding; and the Gospel of Matthew, because it was generally
      endorsed by orthodox Anglican divines, and because Swift preferred
      direct historical narrative to interpretation and elaboration.

282. Daw, Carl P., Jr. "Swift and The Whole Duty of Man." American Notes
      and Queries, 8 (1970), 86-87.

      Notes Swift's allusions to The Whole Duty in The Drapier's Letters,
      Directions to Servants, and Examiner, No. 14.

283. De Labriolle, Marie-Rose. "Swift." Pp. 369-76 of Le Pour et contre
      et son temps. Vol. 2. (Studies in Voltaire and the Eighteenth
      Century, 35.) Oxford: Voltaire Foundation at the Taylor Institute,
      1965.

      General survey of life and works, with emphasis on Swift's French
      reputation.

284. Dobrée, Bonamy. "The Jocose Dean." Pp. 42-61 of Fair Liberty Was All
      His Cry: A Tercentenary Tribute to Jonathan Swift 1667-1745.
      Edited by A. Norman Jeffares. London: Macmillan; New York: St.
      Martin's Press, 1967.

      Rept. as pp. 28-46 of Swift: Modern Judgements. Edited by A.
      Norman Jeffares. London: Macmillan, 1969; Nashville, Tenn.:
      Aurora, 1970.

      The immense gaiety that offset or sustained Swift's indignation is

documented in letters, poems, A Tale of a Tub, the Argument Against
Abolishing Christianity, the Bickerstaff Papers, and even the
Drapier's Letters ("it is as though he were always, not searching
for, but overtaken by the ridiculous through the sheer make-up of
his nature"), and Gulliver's Travels.

285. Donoghue, Denis (ed.). Jonathan Swift: A Critical Anthology.
(Penguin Critical Anthologies.) Harmondsworth and Baltimore:
Penguin, 1971. Pp. 455.

Rev. (with other works) by Philip Roberts in N&Q, 218 (1973),
430-31.

Includes: Part I, "Contemporaneous Criticism," to 1751; Part II,
"The Developing Debate," to 1934; Part III, "Modern Views," to 1968.
Modern essays include: Irvin Ehrenpreis, "Swift and the Comedy of
Evil"; Geoffrey Hill, "Jonathan Swift: The Poetry of 'Reaction'";
Denis Donoghue, "The Sin of Wit"; C.J. Rawson, "Gulliver and the
Gentle Reader"; Hugh Kenner, from The Counterfeiters; Hugh Sykes
Davies, "Irony and the English Tongue."

286. Donoghue, Denis. Jonathan Swift: A Critical Introduction. London and
Cambridge: Cambridge U. Press, 1969. Pp. viii + 235.

Rev. (favorably) by John M. Bullitt in Scriblerian, 2 (1969),
21-22; (enthusiastically) by C.J. Rawson in RES, n.s. 21 (1970),
504-06; by Patrick Cruttwell in Essays in Criticism, 20 (1970),
479-84; (with other works) by Colin J. Horne in MLR, 67 (1972),
170-72; in review art. ("Recent Studies in the Restoration and
Eighteenth Century") by Marshall Waingrow in SEL, 10 (1970),
605-36; (with reservations) by Pierre Danchin in English Studies,
54 (1973), 293-94; in review art. ("Images of Swift: A Review of
Some Recent Criticism") by Robert W. Uphaus in Eire-Ireland, 6,
no. 3 (Fall, 1971), 16-22; (with reservations) by Phillip Harth in
ECS, 4 (1971), 484-85; in review art. ("The State of the Dean") by
Robert Martin Adams in Hudson Review, 23 (1970), 578-84.

Challenging widespread assumptions about personae and satiric form,
Donoghue emphasizes Swift's characteristic discontinuity and
instability, his use of false perspectives, of paradoxes not "for
any of our modern reasons," but "to deflate the pretensions of
others." Therefore, of the Tale (an example of "plural form"): "We
should not assume ... that the words are primarily designed to carry
the voice of a single identifiable speaker. We are reading words on
a page; implying rather things being said than a voice saying them."
Of Gulliver's Travels: "the digressions and the collapsing sentences
are subject to the author's whim and to nothing else"; "it is
irrelevant ... to talk of Gulliver's character; he has no character,
he is a cipher." In Swift's poems, "like 'The Beasts' Confession'
and 'On Poetry: A Rhapsody' [sic]he curbs the same themes which, in
prose, drive him to violence." (Donoghue gives octosyllabic couplets
great credit as restrainers of the "enemies of day and mind.")
Donoghue suggests that Swift's tradition sanctioned this cavalier

way of treating words. But Swift himself was a unique master of
"riddance and negation," and of prudent ignorance.

287. Donoghue, Denis (ed.). Swift Revisited. Cork: The Mercier Press;
     Hatboro, Pa.: Folklore Associates, 1968. Pp. 89.

     Rev. by Clive T. Probyn in Scriblerian, 1 (1969), 12-13.

     "As a contribution to the Swift tercentenary celebrations, Radio
     Telefis Eireann arranged this series of Thomas Davis Lectures. The
     aim of the lectures was to convey a personal response to Swift's
     major work, and at least to imply the presence of his work as a
     whole. There was no attempt to 'cover everything,' or even to deal
     in detail with the inescapable works." Contains the following items:
     Roger McHugh, "The Life of Jonathan Swift"; Matthew Hodgart,
     "Gulliver's Travels"; Mark Kinkead-Weekes, "The Dean and the
     Drapier"; John Holloway, "Dean of St. Patrick's: A View from the
     Letters"; Denis Donoghue, "Swift as Poet."

288. Donoghue, Denis. "A Very Special Case." New York Review of Books,
     12, January 16, 1969, pp. 10-12.

     Reviews the following: John Middleton Murry, Jonathan Swift: A
     Critical Biography; Irvin Ehrenpreis, Swift: The Man, His Works, and
     the Age, vol. 2; Nigel Dennis, Jonathan Swift; Susie I. Tucker,
     Protean Shape: A Study in Eighteenth-Century Vocabulary and Usage.
     Donoghue comments that Swift's works are often "not ironic at all"
     and ought not to be searched for strict coherence. Also: "Swift is
     concerned with public order, not with private conscience."

289. Dooley, D.J. "Image and Point of View in Swift." PLL, 6 (1970),
     125-35.

     See Dooley's letter concerning this essay in Scriblerian, 3
     (1970), 82.

     Though this essay re-insists that Swift's exact relationship to his
     work and to his central character is never easy to determine, its
     main thrust is in favor of reading Swift's images as expressing his
     own point of view.

290. Dubashinsky, J.A. Pamflety Swifta. Riga: Zvaigzne, 1968.

     Noted by Leonid M. Arinshtein in Scriblerian, 2 (1970), 39-40;
     rev. (favorably) by V.A. Kharitonov in Voprosy Literatury, July,
     1969, pp. 234-36.

291. Dutu, Alexandru. "Swift." Secolul XX, 163 (1974), 21-22.

     Very brief survey of life and works in Romanian.

292. Ehrenpreis, Irvin. "Lecture on a Master Mind: Jonathan Swift."
     Proceedings of the British Academy, 54 (1968), 149-63. London:
     Oxford U. Press, 1970.

     Rev. by Colin J. Horne in MLR, 67 (1972), 170-72; by Philip
     Roberts in N&Q, 218 (1973), 430-31.

     Because, for Swift, "morality, religion, and politics are
     inseparable," he has sometimes been mis-perceived as narrow-minded
     or short-sighted. However, Swift's "moral energy" consistently
     transcended the mere material developments of his time.

293. Ehrenpreis, Irvin. "Letters of Advice to Young Spinsters." Pp.
     245-69 of Stuart and Georgian Moments. Edited by Earl Miner.
     Berkeley: U. of California Press, 1972.

     Orig. pub. Los Angeles: William Andrews Clark Memorial Library,
     1969.

     Swift's attitudes on the education of females and the status of
     unmarried women set him apart from his contemporaries: he believed a
     woman's intellectual and moral character should be developed as
     fully as possible; and he assumed that women who never marry remain
     complete human beings, requiring no special justification. Evidence
     is drawn mostly from Swift's letters to Stella and Vanessa.

294. Ehrenpreis, Irvin. Literary Meaning and Augustan Values.
     Charlottesville: U. of Virginia Press, 1974. Pp. vii + 119.

     Rev. (with reservations) by Eric Rothstein in Scriblerian, 7
     (1974), 34-35; in review art. ("Order and Misrule:
     Eighteenth-Century Literature in the 1970's") by C.J. Rawson in
     ELH, 42 (1975), 471-505; in review art. ("Exuberant Mixtures: Some
     Recent Studies in the Eighteenth Century") by Patricia Carr
     Brückmann in University of Toronto Quarterly, 46 (1976), 83-91;
     (with other works) by Martin Price in Sewanee Review, 85 (1977),
     639-51.

     A collection of essays calling for the re-anchoring of "style to
     meaning and of literary value to both" and disparaging the
     identification of Dryden, Swift, and Pope "with modern allusiveness
     and subversiveness." Two sections are particularly relevant to Swift
     studies: "Personae," pp. 49-60 (originally published in Restoration
     and Eighteenth-Century Literature: Essays in Honor of Alan Dugald
     McKillop, ed. Carroll Camden (U. of Chicago Press, 1963)), warns
     against automatic and overly ingenious applications of this concept.
     (See the discussion triggered by this essay, Item 240.) "The Styles
     of Gulliver's Travels," pp. 94-109, enthuses about the continuous
     stylistic changes and structural impurity of Book I while
     complaining about the tedium, heavy-handedness, and bleak uniformity
     of Book IV. The power and profundity of Gulliver's voyage to the
     Houyhnhnms, asserts Ehrenpreis, does not spring from conscious
     literary technique.

295. Ehrenpreis, Irvin. "Swift on Liberty." Pp. 59-73 of <u>Swift: Modern</u>
     <u>Judgements</u>. Edited by A. Norman Jeffares. London: Macmillan, 1969;
     Nashville, Tenn.: Aurora, 1970.

     Orig. pub. in <u>JHI</u>, 13 (1952).

     Explains many of Swift's political opinions, including how he
     reasoned his way from support of liberty to Tory partisanship.

296. Elkin, P.K. <u>The Augustan Defence of Satire</u>. New York and Oxford:
     Oxford U. Press, 1973. Pp. 235.

     Rev. (favorably) by Michael Cordner in <u>Scriblerian</u>, 6 (1974),
     91-92; (with another work) by William Kinsley in <u>Humanities</u>
     <u>Association Review</u>, 24, no. 4 (Fall 1973), 331-33.

     Explores the controversies about satire among Swift and his
     contemporaries.

297. Elliott, Robert C. "Swift's 'I'." <u>Yale Review</u>, 62 (1973), 372-91.

     Arguing against the romanticized notion of a Swift who implicates
     himself in the ludicrous tragedy of the human predicament, Elliott
     makes a vigorous case for Swift's use of, rather than identification
     with, the personae of his enemies: "when Swift fantasizes himself
     into the skin of one he hates, extraordinary energies are
     liberated.... But to impersonate the enemy, and even at some level
     of one's being to have sympathy with him, is not ... automatically
     to take on the enemy's guilt or to admit complicity in his acts."
     <u>Contra</u> Ehrenpreis, Donoghue, Carnochan, and Stout.

298. Elliott, Robert C. "Swift's Satire: Rules of the Game." <u>ELH</u>, 41
     (1974), 413-28.

     Swift's satire consistently provides "positives" as well as victims,
     though both categories may be obscurely defined on occasion. Another
     rule of Swift's game: though the major figures Swift creates are
     hardly <u>characters</u> in our ordinary sense, it is precisely our idea of
     character that controls our reponses to the works. Elliott goes on
     to argue in a general way that Swift's satirical attacks on satire
     exclude Swift himself--or else, paradoxically, they actually
     <u>reinforce</u> the satirical effect.

299. Falle, George. "Divinity and Wit: Swift's Attempted Reconciliation."
     <u>University of Toronto Quarterly</u>, 46 (1976), 14-30.

     The argument here, that "Swift uses his wit as a means of
     intensifying the complexity of the perennial problems that confront
     the Christian world, and this practice serves in turn to enhance the
     order of divine providence," is not always sensitive to the very
     critical questions it should be addressing. For example, <u>do</u> readers

of A Tale of a Tub automatically recognize the "integrity of the
satirist's perspective"? Are there no dangers in implicating the
reader in important questions without answering those questions?

300. Falle, George. "Swift's Writings and a Variety of Commentators."
University of Toronto Quarterly, 34 (1965), 294-312.

A review essay, offering opinions of: The Correspondence of Jonathan
Swift, ed. Sir Harold Williams (1963); A Bibliography of the
Writings of Jonathan Swift, ed. Herman Teerink and Arthur H. Scouten
(1963); Edward W. Rosenheim, Jr., Swift and the Satirist's Art
(1963); Oliver W. Ferguson, Jonathan Swift and Ireland (1962);
Milton Voigt, Swift and the Twentieth Century (1964); Swift: A
Collection of Critical Essays, ed. Ernest Tuveson (1964).

301. Feinberg, Leonard. Introduction to Satire. Ames: Iowa State U.
Press, 1967. Pp. ix + 293.

Rev. (severely) by John D. Erickson in Comparative Literature, 21
(1969), 366-69.

Contains brief and scattered remarks on Swift's satiric technique.

302. Flanagan, Thomas. "A Discourse by Swift, A Play by Yeats."
University Review (Dublin), 5 (1968), 9-22.

Includes an account of Yeats's opinions about Swift, especially
about A Discourse of the Contests and Dissensions.

303. Fletcher, John. "From 'Gentle Reader' to 'Gentle Skimmer'; Or, Does
It Help to Read Swift as if He Were Samuel Beckett?" Angol
Filológiai Tanulmányok, 12 (1979), 49-59.

The answer is "Yes" in this pro-Rawson essay. Both writers sabotage
the reader's expectations; both create compelling myths about human
nature.

304. Fluchère, Henri. "Satire et mystification." Europe, 463 (1967),
82-93.

Not merely agents of black humor, Swift's personae are actually
instruments of salvation through special shared acts of imagination.
Often radically ambiguous, Swift's irony may finally express no more
than mystification.

305. Foot, Michael. "Jonathan Swift." Essays by Divers Hands, 35 (1969),
55-66.

Addressed to a general audience, this defense of Swift explains his

popularity with liberal thinkers in terms of his defense of liberty,
his fight against pride and complacency, and his abhorrence of
indifference to inhumanity and war.

306. Fréchet, René. "Célébration du Tricentenaire de Swift à Dublin."
     ["The Dublin Celebration of Swift's Tricentenary."] Etudes
     Anglaises, 20 (1967), 217-18.

     An account of the celebration at Trinity College, Dublin.

307. Frost, William. "Religious and Philosophical Themes in Restoration
     and Eighteenth-Century Literature." Pp. 399-433 of History of
     Literature in the English Language. Vol. 4: Dryden to Johnson.
     Edited by Roger Lonsdale. (Sphere Books.) London: Barrie &
     Jenkins, 1971.

     Swift's rhetorical tactics and philosophical perspectives in the
     Tale, A Modest Proposal, and An Argument Against Abolishing
     Christianity are briefly compared to those of Dryden, Defoe, and
     Shaftesbury.

308. Frost, William. "The Irony of Swift and Gibbon: A Reply to F.R.
     Leavis." Essays in Criticism, 17 (1967), 41-47.

     Rept. (in part) as pp. 684-88 of The Writings of Jonathan Swift:
     Authoritative Texts, Backgrounds, Criticism. Edited by Robert A.
     Greenberg and William Bowman Piper. New York: Norton, 1973.

     Frost elevates Swift's intimidating and demoralizing irony over
     Gibbon's habituating and reassuring variety.

309. Fussell, Paul. The Rhetorical World of Augustan Humanism: Ethics and
     Imagery from Swift to Burke. London, Oxford, and New York: Oxford
     U. Press, 1965. Pp. xiv + 314.

     Rev. by Vincent M. Bevilacqua in Quarterly Journal of Speech, 52
     (1966), 302-03; by Aubrey Williams in ELN, 5 (1967-68), 59-62;
     (with another work) by Patricia Meyer Spacks in Critical
     Quarterly, 9 (1967), 91-93; (favorably) by James T. Boulton in
     N&Q, 211 (1966), 474-76; by Roger Lonsdale in RES, n.s. 18 (1967),
     76-78; (favorably) by S.W. Jackman in Burke Newsletter, 8
     (1966-67), 670-73; in review art. ("Recent Studies in the
     Restoration and Eighteenth Century") by Frederick W. Hilles in
     SEL, 6 (1966), 599-628; (favorably) by A. Dayle Wallace in
     Criticism, 9 (1967), 92-93; by R.G. Cox in British Journal of
     Aesthetics, 6 (1966), 307-09; (favorably) by Arthur Pollard in
     MLR, 63 (1968), 195-96.

     Fussell describes the ethical convictions of Swift (along with
     others) by examining his images of military tactics, architecture
     (as analogues of learning and government), clothing (in his habitual

satire of oversymbolizing), vermin (as evidence of the unredeemable squalor of the subhuman), and travel.

310. Garratt, Robert F. "'Aware of My Ancestor': Austin Clarke and the Legacy of Swift." Eire-Ireland, 11, no. 2 (Summer 1976), 92-103.

Garratt points out Clarke's conception of Swift as a "chuckling rhymster" and stresses that the satire of each "reduces and deflates man's vanity and arrogance."

311. Gilbert, Jack G. Jonathan Swift: Romantic and Cynic Moralist. Austin and London: U. of Texas Press, 1966. Pp. xi + 161.

Rev. by Paul Fussell, Jr. in MP, 65 (1967), 393-95; in review art. ("Recent Studies in the Restoration and Eighteenth Century") by Ronald H. Paulson in SEL, 7 (1967), 531-58; (severely) by C.J. Rawson in N&Q, 213 (1968), 228-29; (favorably) by Ricardo Quintana in Scriblerian, 1, no. 1 (Autumn 1968), 21-23.

Part One outlines "the general directions of the complex body of Swift's ethical opinions" by examining his debasement of human nature--its selfishness, inhumanity, intellectual folly, cowardice, and injustice; his admiration for virtue; and his "devotion to a heroic or romantic ideal" (here meaning respect for the dignity of human nature). Having outlined Swift's ethical opinions, Gilbert proceeds to find them mirrored in that "repository of what Swift regarded as ethical wisdom," Gulliver's Travels.

312. Golden, Morris. The Self Observed: Swift, Johnson, Wordsworth. Baltimore and London: Johns Hopkins U. Press, 1972. Pp. ix + 190.

Rev. by Harold E. Pagliaro in Scriblerian, 5 (1972), 43-44; (with other works) by Max F. Schulz in ECS, 7 (1974), 378-81; (unfavorably) by Colin J. Horne in Yearbook of English Studies, 5 (1975), 287-88; (unfavorably) by Thomas Atteridge in South Atlantic Quarterly, 72 (1973), 174-75; (with reservations) by C.J. Rawson in RES, n.s. 24 (1973), 250-51; (with reservations) by Robert E. Kelley in PQ, 52 (1973), 431.

Pp. 33-66 are on Swift. Swift's personae reflect his view of the self in the world, taking two characteristic forms: the mad conformist-individualist or the civilized, humane figure who speaks for values. Golden also points to the "mutual illumination" between these personae and an implied general self representing the common ground shared with worthy readers of all times. Swift's habitual ways of depicting himself--as grave priest, slightly absurd poet, and humane observer--mirror his fascination with complexity and with the assumptions on which the striving self is ordinarily based.

313. Goldgar, Bertrand A. "Satires on Man and 'The Dignity of Human Nature'." PMLA, 80 (1965), 535-41.

A general discussion, <u>contra</u> Rosenheim, of the appropriateness of calling attacks on human nature "satires," with a survey of some reasons for their generally hostile reception.

314. Gordon, Robert C. "Jonathan Swift and the Modern Art of War." <u>Bulletin of Research in the Humanities</u>, 83 (1980), 187-202.

Swift's connection between systems and inhumanity to man explains his hatred of the new military professionalism. With Bolingbroke, Swift attributed the destructive technology of new warfare to the same source as the Caesaristic technology of new ministerial forms of government. Gulliver's own military victories are old-fashioned and comparatively humane: he is a military amateur, engaging in naval battle, who accomplishes that military ideal, a bloodless victory.

315. Greene, Donald. "Swift: Some Caveats." Pp. 341-58 of <u>Studies in the Eighteenth Century</u>. Vol. 2. Edited by R.F. Brissenden. Canberra: Australian National U. Press; Toronto: U. of Toronto Press, 1973.

A vigorous call for caution: too many recent studies are reductive and misrepresent Swift as "the reactionary Tory, the extreme High Churchman, the hater of modern science."

316. Greene, Donald. "The Via Media in an Age of Revolution: Anglicanism in the 18th Century." Pp. 297-320 of <u>The Varied Pattern: Studies in the 18th Century</u>. Edited by Peter Hughes and David Williams. (Publications of the MacMaster U. Association for 18th-Century Studies, 1.) Toronto: A.M. Hakkert, 1971.

Includes a vigorous defense of Swift's orthodox Anglicanism, using texts most often employed to disprove the same point: <u>A Tale of a Tub</u>, Section VI; <u>Gulliver's Travels</u>, Book IV; "The Day of Judgement" (which Greene reads as satire of sectarian partisanship); and <u>Verses on the Death of Dr. Swift</u> (as an orthodox analysis of the deadly sin of envy).

317. Grenfell, Ian. "Swiftian Anecdotes." Pp. 147-50 of <u>American Notes and Queries: Supplement</u>. Vol. 1: Studies in English and American Literature. Edited by John L. Cutler and Lawrence S. Thompson. Troy, N.Y.: Whitson Publishing Co., 1978.

<u>Lloyd's Evening Post</u> for 9-11 April 1759 printed a small collection of Swiftian anecdotes—four never reprinted—concerning King William, Swift's pride, Dr. Delany, and Swift's ill-nature.

318. Gunny, Ahmad. <u>Voltaire and English Literature: A Study of English Literary Influences on Voltaire</u>. (Studies on Voltaire and the Eighteenth Century, 177.) Oxford: Voltaire Foundation, 1979. Pp. 309.

Rev. (with another work) by O.R. Taylor in MLR, 76 (1981), 186-88.

Pp. 244-70 are "The Influence of Swift and Sterne on Voltaire," for the most part merely documenting Voltaire's admiration for Swift, but with some discussion of Voltaire's borrowings in theme and technique from A Tale of a Tub and Gulliver's Travels.

319. Halewood, William H. "Young William Temple and Young Jonathan Swift." CLA Journal, 10 (1966), 105-13.

The temper of a satirist, a joyous playfulness, a pessimistic view of human nature--these qualities of Temple's youthful work induce Halewood to see a "spiritual kinship" with the young Swift.

320. Hall, Basil. "'An Inverted Hypocrite': Swift the Churchman." Pp. 38-68 of The World of Jonathan Swift: Essays for the Tercentenary. Edited by Brian Vickers. Cambridge, Ma.: Harvard U. Press; Oxford: Basil Blackwell, 1968.

Argues for the sensibleness of Swift's insistence on decent limitations in religion, for the sake of order. Swift's "inverted hypocrisy" springs from his conviction that "we are commanded to hide, even from ourselves, those [virtues] we really have."

321. Hamm, Victor M. "Burke and Swift." Thought, 48 (1973), 107-19.

Mostly a list of references to Swift in Burke's correspondence, with hints about "broader and deeper affinities" of temperament, education, birth, politics, and career. Denis Donoghue's stylistic comparison is quoted approvingly, and "common political wisdom" (the ideals of balance and tradition) is claimed for the two.

322. Harrington, John P. "Swift Through Le Fanu and Joyce." Mosaic, 12, no. 3 (Spring, 1979), 49-58.

"The metaphors Swift, Le Fanu and Joyce use, though they differ in being comical, melodramatic and sexual, respectively, all reiterate the sense of loss and victimization as integral of Anglo-Irish sensibility in the eighteenth as in the twentieth-century."

323. Hartley, Lodwick. "'Swiftly-Sterneward': The Question of Sterne's Influence on Joyce." Studies in the Literary Imagination, 3 (1970), 37-47.

Swift exerted far more influence on Joyce than did Sterne.

324. Hogan, J.J. "Bicentenary of Jonathan Swift 1667-1745." Pp. 47-58 of Swift: Modern Judgements. Edited by A. Norman Jeffares. London: Macmillan, 1969; Nashville, Tenn.: Aurora, 1970.

Orig. pub. in Studies, 34 (1945).

Simplified dicta on Swift's "grasp of the common world," his "philosophy of life," view of politics, reason, religion, Ireland, life, and creative energy. No mention of works.

325. Horsley, Lee Sonsteng. "'Of All Fictions the Most Simple': Swift's Shared Imagery." Yearbook of English Studies, 5 (1975), 98-108.

A survey of some of Swift's favorite images and metaphors.

326. Hunter, J. Paul. "'Peace' and the Augustans: Some Implications of Didactic Method and Literary Form." Pp. 161-89 of Studies in Change and Revolution: Aspects of English Intellectual History 1640-1800. Menston, Yorkshire: Scolar Press, 1972.

Pp. 172-81 discuss Swift and Defoe as representing "very nearly the poles of thought on practically every major issue in the first half of the century."

327. Hunting, Robert. Jonathan Swift. (Twayne's English Authors Series, 42.) New York: Twayne Publishers, 1967. Pp. 149.

Rev. by George Mayhew in Scriblerian, 1, no. 1 (Autumn 1968), 26-27.

A limited introduction to Swift's "best prose and poetry," including, in addition to A Tale of a Tub and Gulliver's Travels, Journal to Stella, the Proposal for Correcting the English Tongue, "Description of a City Shower," A Modest Proposal, and just a few others.

328. Irwin, W.R. "Swift and the Novelists." PQ, 45 (1966), 102-13.

Surveys several novels in which Swift appears by reference or as a character, with particular attention to T.H. White 's Mistress Masham's Repose and Walter de la Mare's Memoirs of a Midget.

329. Jarrell, Mackie L. "'Jack and the Dane': Swift Traditions in Ireland." Pp. 311-41 of Fair Liberty Was All His Cry: A Tercentenary Tribute to Jonathan Swift 1667-1745. Edited by A. Norman Jeffares. London: Macmillan; New York: St. Martin's Press, 1967.

Orig. pub. in Journal of American Folklore, 77 (1964), 99-117.

Fictional anecdotes about Swift and a witty servant, along with other traditions, document the affection for Swift among the Irish people.

330. Jeffares, A. Norman (ed.). Fair Liberty Was All His Cry: A
Tercentenary Tribute to Jonathan Swift 1667-1745. London:
Macmillan; New York: St. Martin's Press, 1967. Pp. xxi + 410;
illustrations.

Rev. (with another work) by Francis Doherty in RES, n.s. 19
(1968), 200-02; (with another work) by Bonamy Dobrée in Critical
Quarterly, 11 (1969), 288; (favorably) by Bertrand A. Goldgar in
South Atlantic Quarterly, 67 (1968), 571-72; by James H. Sims in
Southern Humanities Review, 3 (1969), 104-05.

Contains the following: D. Nichol Smith, "Jonathan Swift: Some
Observations"; T.G. Wilson, "Swift's Personality"; Bonamy Dobrée,
"The Jocose Dean" Herbert Davis, "Swift's View of Poetry"; A.L.
Rowse, "Swift as Poet"; Virginia Woolf, "Swift's Journal to Stella";
F.R. Leavis, "The Irony of Swift"; Kathleen M. Williams, "'Animal
Rationis Capax.' A Study of Certain Aspects of Swift's Imagery";
J.C. Beckett, "Swift as an Ecclesiastical Statesman"; George Orwell,
"Politics vs. Literature: An Examination of Gulliver's Travels";
W.B. Yeats, "Introduction to Words upon the Window-Pane"; Irvin
Ehrenpreis, "The Origins of Gulliver's Travels"; Marjorie Nicolson
and Nora M. Mohler, "The Scientific Background of Swift's 'Voyage to
Laputa'"; Marjorie W. Buckley, "Key to the Language of the
Houyhnhnms in Gulliver's Travels"; Vivian Mercier, "Swift and the
Gaelic Tradition"; George P. Mayhew, "Jonathan Swift's Hoax of 1722
upon Ebenezor Elliston"; Mackie L. Jarrell, "'Jack and the Dane':
Swift Traditions in Ireland"; Ricardo Quintana, "A Modest Appraisal:
Swift Scholarship and Criticism, 1945-65"; Claire Lamont, "A
Checklist of Critical and Biographical Writings on Jonathan Swift,
1945-65."

331. Jeffares, A. Norman. Jonathan Swift. (Writers & Their Work Series.)
Harlow, Essex: Longman for the British Council, 1976. Pp. 56.

An introductory survey of life and some works.

332. Jeffares, A. Norman (ed.). Swift: Modern Judgements. (Modern
Judgements Series.) London: Macmillan, 1969; Nashville, Tenn.:
Aurora Publishers, 1970. Pp. 279.

Contains the following: A. Norman Jeffares, "Introduction"; J.J.
Hogan, "Bicentenary of Jonathan Swift 1667-1745"; Bonamy Dobrée,
"The Jocose Dean"; Irvin Ehrenpreis, "Swift on Liberty"; Louis A.
Landa, "Swift's Economic Views and Mercantilism"; J.W. Johnson,
"Swift's Historical Outlook"; F.R. Leavis, "The Irony of Swift";
A.L. Rowse, "Swift as Poet"; Herbert Davis, "Literary Satire in A
Tale of a Tub"; Virginia Woolf, "Swift's Journal to Stella"; W.B.
Ewald, Jr. "M.B., Drapier"; George Orwell, "Politics vs.
Literature"; Marjorie Nicolson and Nora M. Mohler, "The Scientific
Background of 'Voyage to Laputa'"; Kathleen M. Williams, "Gulliver's
Voyage to the Houyhnhnms"; W.E. Yeomans, "The Houyhnhnm as Menippean
Horse."

333. Jeffares, A. Norman. "Teaching Anglo-Irish Literature." Hermathena, 129 (Winter, 1980), 17-22.

     Stresses the importance of the "politico-historical content" of Swift's Irish writings in a course on Anglo-Irish literature.

334. Johnson, Clifford R. Plots and Characters in the Fiction of Eighteenth-Century English Authors. Vol. 1: Swift, Defoe, and Richardson. Hamden, Ct.: Archon Books, Shoe String Press, 1977. Pp. xx + 270.
     Summarizes Gulliver's Travels, The Battle of the Books, A Tale of a Tub and The Mechanical Operation of the Spirit.

335. Johnson, Maurice. "T.S. Eliot on Satire, Swift, and Disgust." PLL, 5 (1969), 311-15.

     Eliot's declared preference for a literary tradition over a human background required an exception for Swift's satire, which could only be produced by "deep and intense emotion, terror, passion, bitter personal feeling, and tortured talent."

336. Johnston, Denis. "Swift of Dublin." Eire-Ireland, 3, no. 3 (Fall 1968), 38-50.

     Rev. by Clive T. Probyn in Scriblerian, 1, no. 2 (Spring 1969), 12.

     That Swift was a Tory and High Church Dean strikes Johnston as nearly hypocrisy. Because of his Irishness, Swift ought be regarded as "a prototype Separatist and Republican, an advocate of industrial Protection and of an Ireland, free and Gaelic."

337. Jonathan Swift: Tercentenary Essays. (U. of Tulsa Department of English Monograph Series, 3.) Tulsa: U. of Tulsa, 1967. Pp. 73.

     Includes the following essays: David French, "The Identity of C.M.P.G.N.S.T.N.S."; Philip Mahone Griffith, "Dr. Johnson's 'Diction of Common Life' and Swift's Directions to Servants"; Paul J. Ketrick, "Jonathan Swift: Great Wit or Blest Madman?"; Thomas F. Staley, "The Poet Joyce and the Shadow of Swift"; Winston Weathers, "A Technique of Irony in A Tale of a Tub"; Lester F. Zimmerman, "Lemuel Gulliver."

338. Kagarlitsky, Yu. "Jonathan Swift." Sovetskii Soyuz, November, 1967, p. 52.

     Noted in Scriblerian, 2 (1969), 39.

339. Kallen, Horace M. Liberty, Laughter, and Tears: Reflections on the Relations of Comedy and Tragedy to Human Freedom. DeKalb, Ill.: Northern Illinois U. Press, 1968. Pp. x + 402.

     Rev. by Van Meter Ames in Journal of Aesthetics and Art Criticism, 28 (1969), 262; (severely) in Scriblerian, 1, no. 2 (Spring 1969), 27.

     Pp. 143-75 ("Laughter and Tears of the English Enlightenment: Jonathan Swift") offhandedly scans Swift's life and works, then pronounces him "a sick soul," with a "sordid and bad-tempered" sense of life, plagued by the "misanthropy of a defeated man."

340. Kesterson, David B. "Swift and Music." TSLL, 11 (1969), 687-94.

     The claim here is that, in objecting to music's lack of good sense, Swift was valuing reason as a force governing the senses in a conventional eighteenth-century way. Certainly this is not the only possible interpretation of Swift's notorious inability to appreciate music (or architecture, for that matter).

341. Korshin, Paul J. "Johnson and Swift: A Study in the Genesis of Literary Opinion." PQ, 48 (1969), 464-78.

     Attributes Johnson's frequently negative literary opinions on Swift, as well as his comparative neglect of Swift's writings, not so much to his disapproval of Swift's life as to his "basic disagreement with Swift's conceptions of humanity and rationality as expressed chiefly in Gulliver's Travels."

342. Köster, P. "Swift, Arbuthnot and the Law." American Notes and Queries, 7 (1969), 83-84.

     A reply to Richard H. Passon, "Legal Satire in Gulliver from John Bull." American Notes and Queries, 5 (1967), 99-100.

     Repudiates Swift's indebtedness to Arbuthnot for satirical treatment of the law, since the Scriblerians and lots of other satirists found lawyers to be inviting targets. Swift himself indulged in legal satire both before John Bull was published and before he made the acquaintance of Arbuthnot.

343. Köster, Patricia. "Words and Numbers: A Quantitative Approach to Swift and Some Understrappers." Computers and the Humanities, 4 (1970), 289-306.

     Rept. (titled "Computer Stylistics: Swift and Some Contemporaries") as pp. 129-47 of The Computer in Literary and Linguistic Research, ed. R.A. Wisbey (Cambridge: Cambridge U. Press, 1971).

See the reply ("Comment on Mrs. Köster's Article") by Louis T. Milic in Computers and the Humanities, 4 (1970), 304-06.

Köster finds the method of Louis T. Milic (Item 365) inconclusive in distinguishing Swift from a quite homogeneous group of writers--in this case, possible authors of The Story of the St. Albans Ghost. In his reply, Milic points to procedural flaws on Köster's part.

344. Kropf, C.R. "Literary Persona and Role Theory." Enlightenment Essays, 5, no. 3/4 (Fall-Winter 1974), 14-25.

This intelligent essay argues against concepts of persona that either see the author obliterated by his creation or hold the historic author and his work accountable for the accuracy of all relevant historical and biographical data. Since the role a persona fills is created by readers' expectations, we must know these to know ourselves and to understand the literary work.

345. Kupersmith, William. "Vice and Folly in Neoclassical Satire." Genre, 11 (1978), 45-62.

Discusses Swift's avowed preference for Horatian satire (Intelligencer, No. 3, 1728).

346. Lamoine, Georges. "Swift, critique du Langage." Etudes Anglaises, 25 (1972), 132-46.

A survey of Swift's remarks on language and contemporary writers.

347. Landa, Louis A. Essays in Eighteenth-Century English Literature. Princeton: Princeton U. Press, 1980.

Includes the following previously published essays on Swift: "Jonathan Swift: 'Not the Gravest of Divines' (1967) (see above, Item 192); "Swift's Deanery Income," Pope and His Contemporaries: Essays Presented to George Sherburn, ed. James L. Clifford and Louis A. Landa (Oxford: Clarendon Press, 1949), pp. 159-70; "Jonathan Swift and Charity," JEGP, 44 (1945), 337-50; "Swift, the Mysteries, and Deism," Studies in English Literature, Department of English, The University of Texas, 1944 (Austin: U. of Texas Press, 1945), pp. 239-56; "Swift's Economic Views and Mercantilism," Journal of English Literary History, 10 (1943), 310-35; "A Modest Proposal and Populousness," MP, 40 (1942), 161-70.

348. Leavis, F.R. "The Irony of Swift." Pp. 116-30 of Fair Liberty Was All His Cry: A Tercentenary Tribute to Jonathan Swift 1667-1745. Edited by A. Norman Jeffares. London: Macmillan; New York: St. Martin's Press, 1967.

Orig. pub. in Determinations (1934). Rept. as pp. 121-134 of

Swift: Modern Judgements. Edited by A. Norman Jeffares. London: Macmillan, 1969; Nashville, Tenn.: Aurora, 1970; in Gulliver's Travels: An Authoritative Text. Edited by Robert A. Greenberg. New York: Norton, 1970; in Da Swift a Pound: Saggi di critica letteraria by F.R. Leavis. Translated by G. Singh. Torino: Einaudi, 1973. Pp. xxxi + 343.

This famous essay scarcely needs comment; its effect on criticism of Swift has been enormous. Leavis argues that even when Swift's peculiar emotional intensity is directed to the defense of something important to him, "the effect is essentially negative. The positive itself appears only negatively--a kind of skeletal presence, rigid enough, but without life or body; a necessary pre-condition, as it were, of directed negation. The intensity is purely destructive." The analysis of "A Digression Concerning Madness" is, by all odds, the most provocative ever written.

349. Lebedev, A.A. "Tradicii Swifta V Tvurchestve H. Wellsa." ["Swiftian Tradition in the Works of H. Wells."] Uchenye Zapiski Gorkovskogu Universiteta [Proceedings of the University of Gorkii], 160 (1973), 140-54.

Noted in Scriblerian, 6 (1974), 70.

350. Lee, Jae Num. Swift and Scatological Satire. Albuquerque: U. of New Mexico Press, 1971. Pp. 158.

Rev. (severely) by John Traugott in Scriblerian, 4 (1971), 22-23; (unfavorably) by Paul J. Korshin in ECS, 6 (1973), 399-400.

A rather näive effort to explain Swift's uses of scatology wholly in traditional terms.

351. Lockwood, Thomas. "The Augustan Author-Audience Relationship: Satiric vs. Comic Forms." ELH, 36 (1969), 648-58.

Sound rudimentary comments on moral versus social author-reader relationships, audience victimization, and the tragic quality in late Augustan writing.

352. Macaree, David. "Truth and Fiction in Memoirs of Captain John Creichton." Pp. 11-26 of Transactions of the Samuel Johnson Society of the Northwest. Vols. 5-6. Edited by Thomas R. Cleary. Victoria, B.C.: U. of Victoria Press, 1974.

Attributes the anti-Presbyterian bias of Creichton's memoirs to Swift's editorial hand.

353. Makoto, Iwata. "Swift's View of Religion." Rising Generation (Tokyo), 113 (1967), 772-74.

Noted in <u>Scriblerian</u>, 1, no. 1 (Autumn 1968), 7.

Practical about religious matters, Swift based his defense of the
Anglican church on the value of social stability; his antipathy to
religious controversy also derives from its danger to individuals as
well as to the state. The essay is in Japanese.

354. Maresca, Thomas E. "Language and Body in Augustan Poetic." <u>ELH</u>, 37
(1970), 374-88.

The corpuscular theory of the material nature and effect of language
created, for Swift and others, the alarming possibility that bad art
can call into being a chaotic, purely material world. Contains
references to <u>Gulliver's Travels</u>, Book III, and <u>A Tale of a Tub</u>.

355. Martynov, I.F. "English Literature and Eighteenth-Century Russian
Reviewers." Pp. 30-42 of <u>Oxford Slavonic Papers</u>. Vol. 4. Edited by
Robert Auty, J.L.I. Fennell, and J.S.G. Simmons, General Editor.
Oxford: Clarendon Press, 1971.

Both Swift's panegyrical odes and his satirical writings were
"unsympathetic" to the Russian poet and critic, N.M. Karamzin.

356. Maxwell, D.E.S. "Swift's Dark Grove: Yeats and the Anglo-Irish
Tradition." Pp. 18-32 of <u>W.B. Yeats 1865-1965: Centenary Essays</u>.
Edited by D.E.S. Maxwell and S.B. Bushrui. Ibadan: Ibadan U.
Press, 1965.

The lessons of Yeats's journey through "Swift's dark grove," more
covert in his poetry than in his philosophical writings, were
nonetheless profound. Yeats felt at home with Swift's denunciations
of unprincipled politicians and nerveless masses, with the idea of a
glorious past betrayed, and with the easy commerce of like-minded
people sharing an intellectual gracefulness that is mirrored in
Swift's poems. Maxwell even claims that Yeats found encouragement
for his Irish nationalism in Swift's commendations of Dublin and the
countryside around it.

357. Mayhew, George P. "Recent Swift Scholarship." Pp. 187-97 of <u>Jonathan
Swift 1667-1967: A Dublin Tercentenary Tribute</u>. Edited by Roger
McHugh and Philip Edwards. Dublin: Dolmen Press; London: Oxford U.
Press, 1967.

Discusses five major developments in Swift scholarship since 1926:
(1) textual editing; (2) biographical studies; (3) the revaluation
of <u>A Tale of a Tub</u>; (4) the debate over Book IV of <u>Gulliver's
Travels</u>; (5) new critical theories of research and evaluation.
Mayhew notes in 1967 that books and articles about Swift have
numbered "perhaps over 600 during the past 40 years" (compare the
number listed in this book for the past 15 years!).

358. McHugh, Roger. "The Woven Figure: Swift's Irish Context." University
     Review (Dublin), 4 (1967), 35-52.

     Relying on generalities that seem as true of English writers as of
     Irish (e.g., "Swift's digressive style in The Tale of a Tub ... is
     one way of being, as far as a writer can be, all-inclusive"), this
     essay provides no valuable insight into Swift's "Irish Context."

359. McHugh, Roger, and Philip Edwards (eds.). Jonathan Swift 1667-1967:
     A Dublin Tercentenary Tribute. Dublin: Dolmen Press, 1967; London:
     Oxford U. Press, 1968. Pp. xix + 231; plates. Rev. by C.J. Rawson
     in RES, n.s. 20 (1969), 93-94; (with another work) by Pierre
     Danchin in English Studies, 53 (1972), 166-70; by Colin J. Horne
     in MLR, 65 (1970), 390-91; (with factual corrections) in TLS, July
     4, 1968, p. 707 (see the reply by Austin Clarke, "Swift's Verse,"
     in TLS, August 8, 1968, p. 857); in Scriblerian, 1, no. 1 (Autumn
     1968), 8-11;

     Includes the following: Herbert Davis, "Introduction"; Herbert
     Davis, "Swift's Character"; Irvin Ehrenpreis, "Dr. S***t and the
     Hibernian Patriot"; Louis A. Landa, "Jonathan Swift: 'Not the
     Gravest of Divines'"; James Sutherland, "Forms and Methods in
     Swift's Satire"; Ricardo Quintana, "Gulliver's Travels: The Satiric
     Intent and Execution"; Austin Clarke, "The Poetry of Swift"; Vivian
     Mercier, "Swift's Humour"; J.N.P. Moore, "Swift's Philanthropy";
     J.G. Simms, "Ireland in the Age of Swift"; R.B. McDowell, "Swift as
     a Political Thinker"; George P. Mayhew, "Recent Swift Scholarship."

360. Mell, Donald C. "Swift, Jonathan." Pp. 636-53 of Macmillan
     Dictionary of Irish Literature. Edited by Robert Hogan. Westport,
     Ct. and London: Macmillan, 1979; 1980.

     Rev. in Scriblerian, 13 (1980), 18-19.

     A very useful short summary, well-balanced between life and works,
     reflecting better than most the critical concerns of the past
     decade, including Swift's poetry, the critical dispute over
     Gulliver's Travels, and a general salutary sense of Swift's
     contradictoriness. The Scriblerian review noted two factual errors.

361. Mercier, Vivian. "Swift and the Gaelic Tradition." Pp. 279-89 of
     Fair Liberty Was All His Cry: A Tercentenary Tribute to Jonathan
     Swift 1667-1745. Edited by A. Norman Jeffares. London: Macmillan;
     New York: St. Martin's Press, 1967.

     Orig. pub. in Review of English Literature, 3, no. 3 (July, 1962).

     There is a general resemblance, especially in self-righteousness and
     intemperateness, between Swift and Gaelic satire; specific
     influences of leprechaun stories may be seen in Lilliput and
     Brobdingnag; finally, Swift's presence is strong in subsequent

Gaelic writing: extended irony in a Gaelic poem is a sure sign of Swift's influence.

362. Mercier, Vivian. "Swift's Humour." Pp. 116-36 of <u>Jonathan Swift 1667-1967: A Dublin Tercentenary Tribute</u>. Edited by Roger McHugh and Philip Edwards. Dublin: Dolmen Press; London: Oxford U. Press, 1967.

Rept. (with additions) in <u>Tri-Quarterly</u>, 11 (1968), 125-43.

A survey of Swift's love of practical jokes and of his poetry, especially his "ungrammatical tirades of cook-maids and ladies' maids," poems "which bring the Latin classics up to date, compliments, raillery, the teasing of young women, and quizzical self-portraits. His vague and undifferentiated concept of humor leads Mercier to call the Stella poems failures of humor.

363. Mesjatseva, G. "Velikii satirik." ["The Great Satirist. The 300th Anniversary of the Birth of Jonathan Swift."] <u>Narodnoje Obrazovanije</u>, 10 (October 1967), 105-07.

Noted in <u>Scriblerian</u>, 2 (1969), 39.

364. Milburn, D. Judson. <u>The Age of Wit, 1650-1750</u>. New York: Macmillan; London: Collier-Macmillan, 1966. Pp. 348.

Rev. by Richard I. Cook in <u>MLQ</u>, 28 (1967), 111-13.

Pp. 141-52 are "The Truth of Wit in Jonathan Swift's <u>Gulliver's Travels</u>," a routine introduction to Swift's "overlapping ironies."

365. Milic, Louis Tonko. <u>A Quantitative Approach to the Style of Jonathan Swift</u>. (Studies in English Literature, 23.) The Hague and Paris: Mouton, 1967. Pp. 317 + Key.

Pp. 122-35 were originally published (in part) as "Unconscious Ordering in the Prose of Swift." Pp. 79-106 of <u>The Computer and Literary Style</u>. Edited by Jacob Leed. Kent, Ohio: Kent State U. Press, 1966; and reprinted ("Swift and Syntactical Connection") as pp. 266-80 of <u>Literary English Since Shakespeare</u>. Edited by George Watson. London, Oxford, and New York: Oxford U. Press, 1970; other parts were reprinted in altered form ("Connectives in Swift's Prose Style") as pp. 243-57 of <u>Linguistics and Literary Style</u>. Edited by Donald C. Freeman. New York: Holt, Rinehart and Winston, 1970; as "Rhetorical Choice and Stylistic Option" in <u>Literary Style: A Symposium</u>. Edited by Seymour Chatman. New York: Oxford U. Press, 1971.

Rev. (favorably) by Karl Kroeber in <u>Computers and the Humanities</u>, 1 (1966), 55-58; (with another work) by Josephine Miles in <u>Journal of Aesthetics and Art Criticism</u>, 26 (1968), 558-59; (with other

works) by Colin J. Horne in MLR, 64 (1969), 401-03; by Sally
Yeates Sedelow in Style, 3 (1969), 205-07.

Milic's premises are (1) that style reflects personality; (2) that
this is an unconscious process; (3) that in mature writers this
process is consistent. By analyzing texts into word-classes, he aims
to distinguish Swift's style from that of Macauley, Gibbon, Addison,
and Johnson (the controls he selected) by such quantitative matters
as the frequency of verbals versus finite verbs, etc. Among other
notable stylistic characteristics are Swift's fondness for series,
"an array of analogous syntactical units, numbering more than three,
in close proximity," and his use of "neutral connectives," which
give no clue of the nature of the relationship of the language units
they connect. This is a seminal work for the entire field of
quantitative stylistic analysis.

366. Misrahi, Victor. "Le retour du Doyen." Synthèses, 242-243
(July-August, 1966), 100-02.

Swift, haunter of Yeats, is every bit as relevant to us in 1966.

367. Miyazaki, Yoshizo. "Swift Studies in Japan." Studies in English
Literature (Tokyo), 43 (1967), 139-47.

A review, in Japanese, of twentieth-century Japanese Swift studies.

368. Mouravjev, V. "Swift in Russia." Trudy Vsesoynzhoi Biblioteki
Inostrannoi Literatury [Studies of the All-Union Library for
Foreign Literature, Moscow], 2 (1973), 126-42.

Noted in Scriblerian, 8 (1975), 8.

Interest in Swift ran high in Russia from his death until the
1830's. After a severe devaluing in the 1840s and 1850s, Swift's
reputation has been consistently high (nearly five million copies of
Gulliver's Travels sold).

369. Murray, Patrick. "Some Notes on the Interpretation of Swift's
Satires." Irish Ecclesiastical Record, 110 (1968), 158-172.

Examining Swift's satires on religion, Murray is nonplussed (and
probably offended) by Swift's seeming denial of positive norms.

370. Murray, Patrick. "Swift: The Sceptical Conformist." Studies, 58
(1969), 357-67.

Like most religious sceptics, Swift fortified himself behind
conformism and conservative politics, a mixture, as Murray
illustrates, that throughout history has been the rule rather than
the exception.

371. Nagy, Zoltan Abadi. "The Satirist as Projector: A New Approach to Jonathan Swift." Angol Filológiai Tanulmányok, 6 (1972), 5-46.

An uninspired treatment of a problem that deserves better: Swift himself seriously proposed projects about as often as he mocked projectors.

372. Nakano, Yoshio. Swift-ko. [Study of Swift.] Tokyo: Iwanami Shoten, 1969. Pp. 224.

373. Nemoianu, Virgil. "Cucerirea lui Swift." Seculol XX, 15, no. 2 (1972), 61-63.

374. Nersesova, M.A. Dzh. Svift. [Jonathan Swift. To Celebrate the 300th Anniversary of His Birth.] Moscow: Znanie, 1967.

Noted in Scriblerian, 2 (1969), 39.

Introduction for a general Russian audience.

375. New, Melvyn. Laurence Sterne as Satirist: A Reading of Tristram Shandy. Gainesville: U. of Florida Press, 1969. Pp. x + 209.

Rev. by Pierre Danchin in English Studies, 54 (1973), 514-16; by Robert L. Vales in Enlightenment Essays, 2 (1971), 61-63.

Pp. 12-20 are a discussion of Swift's sermons to identify "the set of norms an orthodox position in the Anglican church makes available to the satirist." Pp. 51-69 ("Sterne and Swiftian Satire") surveys Swift's personae, exuberance, scatology, rhetoric, and, most interesting, his irony as a trap for the reader.

376. Nichols, James W. Insinuation: The Tactics of English Satire. The Hague and Paris: Mouton, 1971. Pp. 142.

Rudimentary observations about Swift (especially Gulliver's Travels and A Modest Proposal) are scattered through an unremarkable outline of English satire.

377. Nokes, David. "'Hack at Tom Poley's': Swift's Use of Puns." Pp. 43-56 of The Art of Jonathan Swift. Edited by Clive T. Probyn. New York: Barnes & Noble; London: Vision Press, 1978.

Also pub. as pp. 43-56 of A Centenary Symposium, ed. Alice Shalvi (Jerusalem: Jerusalem Academic, 1976).

Swift's puns are acts of "incarnation," by which abstractions become tangible, revealing the doubleness beneath all sorts of apparently simple words and ideas. The rhetorical pressures that create the pun "make each word as much an area of moral struggle as a man's soul."

378. O'Connor, John. "Swift's Attitude Toward Women." <u>Notre Dame English Journal</u>, 2, no. 2 (Spring 1966-67), 13-22.

Did Swift's criticism of women go beyond their practices to revile woman herself as a physical being? No, argues this defense. Swift's attitude is part of his rigorous application of standards of equality between the sexes.

379. Okazaki, Yoshiaki. "Swift no fushi no shoso." ["Aspects of Swift's Satire."] <u>English Studies</u> (Nihon U.), 27 (1977), 1-13.

Noted by Zenzo Suzuki in <u>Scriblerian</u>, 11 (1978), 11-12.

"This is a comparative study of <u>A Tale of a Tub</u> and <u>Gulliver's Travels</u> as satire. Although the <u>Tale</u> has dazzling wit and powerful imagination, Mr. Okazaki argues that it lacks a sincere attitude to face up to the reality of good and bad.... On the other hand, Swift in the <u>Travels</u> restrains verbal energy of metaphor and describes men's weaknesses and ugliness with a disinterested and matter-of-fact tone." (Suzuki)

380. Pagetti, Carlo. <u>La Fortuna di Swift in Italia</u>. (Biblioteca di Studi Inglesi, 21.) Bari: Adriatica Editrice, 1971. Pp. 327.

Rev. by C.J. Rawson in <u>N&Q</u>, 219 (1977), 79-80; by Gilberto Pizzamiglio in <u>Lettere Italiane</u>, 25 (1973), 136-40; by Rosa Maria Colombo in <u>Nuova Antologia</u>, 515 (1972), 276-79.

Almost unknown in eighteenth-century Italy, Swift's writings withstood the nineteenth-century vagaries of Romantic repudiation, then discovery both by popularizers of <u>Gulliver's Travels</u> for children and by serious scholars. Though twentieth-century Italian interest in Swift has been substantial, Pagetti argues that <u>Gulliver's Travels</u> and Swift have not exerted their full influence. The volume includes a limited annotated bibliography (pp. 277-313).

381. Paulson, Ronald. <u>The Fictions of Satire</u>. Baltimore: Johns Hopkins U. Press, 1967. Pp. viii + 228.

Rev. by Lilla A. Heston in <u>Quarterly Journal of Speech</u>, 54 (1968), 305; in review art. ("The Muse of Satire: A Harlot's Progress") by Eric Rothstein in <u>MLQ</u>, 29 (1968), 222-29; (favorably) by George R. Levine in <u>Criticism</u>, 10 (1968), 256-58; (with another work) by A.B. Kernan in <u>JEGP</u>, 68 (1969), 182-86; (with reservations) by G.D. Josipovici in <u>RES</u>, n.s. 20 (1969), 389-90; (with another work) by Michael F. Shugrue in <u>Seventeenth-Century News</u>, 26 (1968), 75-76; in review art. ("Recent Studies in the Restoration and Eighteenth Century") by Frank Brady in <u>SEL</u>, 8 (1968), 551-72; (with reservations) by Colin J. Horne in <u>MLR</u>, 65 (1970), 388-90; (unfavorably) by John R. Clark in <u>Satire Newsletter</u>, 4, no. 1 (Fall 1968), 80-84.

Pp. 129-222 is "Swift: The Middleman and the Dean." Swift's version

of Tory satire makes its central element the plot or project, the
purpose of which is to implicate or catch the mindless crowd. A
positive norm appears outside the fiction in Swift's true
audience, those readers "with ordinary moral and intellectual
awareness" who can appreciate Swift's ironic structure. The civil
chaos that ensues from the project takes one of two forms: an
image of imminent destruction, or a perfect, orderly anti-utopia.
The evil agent is a prototypical liar, an ordinary man become
proud of his own weaknesses and anxious to impose them on others
(even Gulliver derives from this figure). Perhaps most telling,
Swift, unlike Dryden, eschews the intermediary of a normative
satiric commentator. The principal texts discussed are The
Drapier's Letters, the Tale, The Bickerstaff Papers, "The Life and
Genuine Character of Doctor Swift," and the Stella poems.

382. Probyn, Clive. Jonathan Swift: The Contemporary Background.
     (Literature in Context Series.) Manchester: Manchester U. Press,
     1978; New York: Barnes & Noble, 1979. Pp. viii + 219.

     Rev. in review art. ("Recent Studies in the Restoration and
     Eighteenth Century") by J. Paul Hunter in SEL, 20 (1980), 517-46;
     in review art. ("Uncertainties of Satire") by Patricia Meyer
     Spacks in MLQ, 40 (1979), 403-11; in review art. ("Gentle
     Readings: Recent Work on Swift") by William Kinsley in ECS, 15
     (1982), 442-53.

     Selections from the writings of Swift's contemporaries are grouped
     under the headings "Satire on Dissent and Enthusiasm"; "Ancients and
     Moderns"; "Church and State"; "Politics and Parties"; "The State of
     Ireland"; "Scientists and Satire"; "The Nature of Man." Probyn
     contributes an Introduction and prefaces to the sections.

383. Probyn, Clive T. (ed.). The Art of Jonathan Swift. New York: Barnes
     & Noble; London: Vision Press, 1978. Pp. 215; plates.

     Rev. (favorably) by Paula R. Backscheider in ECCB, n.s. 4 (1981),
     464-65; (with reservations) by Maurice Johnson in Scriblerian, 11
     (1978), 37-38; (favorably) by A.R. Humphreys in MLR, 75 (1980),
     626-27; (favorably) by C.J. Rawson in RES, n.s. 30 (1979), 86-88;
     (with another work) by Peter J. Schakel in JEGP, 79 (1980),
     124-27; in review art. ("Gentle Readings: Recent Work on Swift")
     by William Kinsley in ECS, 15 (1982), 442-53.

     Contains the following (noted separately): Clive T. Probyn,
     "Preface: Swift and the Reader's Role"; W.B. Carnochan, "The
     Consolations of Satire"; David Nokes, "'Hack at Tom Poley's':
     Swift's Use of Puns"; Clive T. Probyn, "Swift and the Human
     Predicament"; Angus Ross, "The Hibernian Patriot's Apprenticeship";
     J.A. Downie, "The Conduct of the Allies: THe Question of Influence";
     David Woolley, "Swift's Copy of Gulliver's Travels: the Armagh
     Gulliver, Hyde's Edition, and Swift's Earliest Corrections"; Pat
     Rogers, "Gulliver's Glasses"; Jenny Mezciems, "Gulliver and Other
     Heroes."

384. Probyn, Clive T. "Preface: Swift and the Reader's Role." Pp. 7-14 of
     The Art of Jonathan Swift. Edited by Clive T. Probyn. New York:
     Barnes & Noble; London: Vision Press, 1978.

     Swift uniquely exploited imprecisions of meaning to disorganize his
     readers, turning the "created author's self-conscious act of
     communication with the reader into an involuntary act of
     self-indictment and a revelation of private obsession."

385. Probyn, Clive T. "Swift and the Human Predicament." Pp. 57-80 of The
     Art of Jonathan Swift. Edited by Clive T. Probyn. New York: Barnes
     & Noble; London: Vision Press, 1978.

     A survey, following R.S. Crane ("Philosophy, Literature, and the
     History of Ideas"), of Swift's hatred of the mental habits of
     logical classification and their effects on human personality.
     Gulliver's misanthropy, for example, is the only logical conclusion
     for him, but he fails to see that the Houyhnhnms are homonyms for
     man--a most equivocal sort of identification.

386. Probyn, Clive. ["Thomas Twining on Swift and Pope."] Scriblerian, 8
     (1976), 125-26.

     Quotes Twining's perceptive 1783 defense of Swift.

387. Quinlan, Maurice J. "Swift's Use of Literalization as a Rhetorical
     Device." PMLA, 82 (1967), 516-21.

     Literalization of metaphor is "a type of ambivalence achieved by
     contrasting the metaphorical and the literal significance of a term,
     in order to reveal an ironic disparity between the two meanings." A
     number of examples are given, though the implications of this
     attitude toward metaphor are not exhausted.

388. Quintana, Ricardo. Two Augustans: John Locke and Jonathan Swift.
     Madison: U. of Wisconsin Press, 1978. Pp. vii + 148.

     Rev. by C.J. Rawson in RES, n.s. 30 (1979), 219-21; (with
     reservations) by W.B. Carnochan in ELN, 17 (1979-80), 148-49; John
     M. Hill in Scriblerian, 11 (1978), 130-31; (favorably and with
     another work) by Peter J. Schakel in JEGP, 79 (1980), 124-27.

     Addressed to a general audience, this long essay on Swift includes a
     biographical synopsis and a perceptive account of recent Swiftian
     criticism as well as a discussion of Swift as Anglican rationalist.

389. Rawson, C.J. "The Character of Swift's Satire." Pp. 17-75 of Focus:
     Swift. Edited by C.J. Rawson. London: Sphere Books, 1971.

     This is a thematic survey, with little comment on techniques. To begin with, Swift's satire rests on the premise that the human mind is by its nature restless and unsatisfied, irrational and subversive. In its collective forms, this perversity is equal to badness for Swift, hence the apparently cynical or paradoxical pragmatism of his thinking about politics and laws. By the same token, Swift constantly prefers in government men of sound moral principles over those with the refinements of expertise, and in religion he shows the relentless pressure of misdirected intensities in "modern" thinking. However, because Swift's repudiating mimicry of the mind's subversive restlessness is based on a profound understanding, his satire usually tends to subvert its own positives by irony or to both praise and blame the same things. These self-subverting attitudes extend to the question of authority itself and to lofty or sincere styles. Most of the material in this essay has subsequently been incorporated into Rawson's essays in Gulliver and the Gentle Reader; however, this essay, if Americans can get hold of it, would be an excellent concise introduction for undergraduates.

390. Rawson, C.J. (ed.). Focus: Swift. London: Sphere Books Ltd., 1971. Pp. 270.

    Rev. by Clive T. Probyn in Scriblerian, 4 (1971), 20-21.

    Includes the following essays (listed separately), all in introductory styles: C.J. Rawson, "Biographical Introduction"; C.J. Rawson, "The Character of Swift's Satire"; John Traugott, "A Tale of a Tub"; W. A. Speck, "The Examiner Examined: Swift's Tory Pamphleteering"; J.C. Beckett, "Swift and the Anglo-Irish Tradition"; Charles Peake, "The Coherence of Gulliver's Travels"; Irvin Ehrenpreis, "Swift's Letters"; Ian Watt, "The Ironic Tradition in Augustan Prose from Swift to Johnson"; John Traugott, "Swift, Our Contemporary."

391. Rawson, C.J. Gulliver and the Gentle Reader: Studies in Swift and Our Time. London and Boston: Routledge & Kegan Paul, 1973. Pp. x + 190.

    Rev. (favorably) by Colin J. Horne in MLR, 70 (1975), 155-57; (favorably) by Peter Dixon in Scriblerian, 6 (1974), 90-91; (with reservations) by Isobel Grundy in N&Q, 220 (1975), 369-71; (severely) by Pierre Danchin in English Studies, 57 (1976), 267-68; (with reservations) by Harry Miller Solomon in South Atlantic Quarterly, 74 (1975), 280-82; in review art. ("Exuberant Mixtures: Some Recent Studies in the Eighteenth Century") by Patricia Carr Brückmann in University of Toronto Quarterly, 46 (1976), 83-91; (severely and with another work) by Malcolm Kelsall in RES, n.s. 25 (1974), 472-75; (favorably) by W.B. Carnochan in JEGP, 73 (1974), 247-50; (favorably) by Colin J. Horne in MLR, 70 (1975), 155-57.

    Chapter one is a slightly altered version of "Gulliver and the Gentle Reader" (1968) (Item 1088); chapter two is a version of

"Order and Cruelty: A Reading of Swift (with some comments on Pope
and Johnson)" (1970) (Item 394); chapter three a version of "'Tis
Only Infinite Below" (1972) (Item 393). Chapter four ("Circles,
Catalogues and Conversations: Swift, with Reflections on Fielding,
Flaubert, Ionesco") argues that, unlike post-Romantic writers, whose
personal vision may turn a chaotic catalogue into an image of
coherence and order, Swift's lists tend to become "a vast
incriminating net" rather than a bountiful abundance. Moreover,
unlike Pope or Fielding, whose triumphant definitiveness conveys
reassurance, Swift's structures of "openness," his "satirical
catalogues," as well as his chains of infinite escalation or
regress," tend to become imprisoning infinitites. Swift's arch-list
maker, Simon Wagstaff, is discussed as a primary example. Chapter
five ("Catalogues, Corpses and Cannibals: Swift and Mailer, with
Reflections on Whitman, Conrad and Others") continues with Swift's
lists, their simultaneous ordered juxtapositions and chaotic and
inexhaustible numerousness, in Gulliver's Travels and A Tale of a
Tub.

392. Rawson, C.J. "Nature's Dance of Death. Part I: Urbanity and Strain
in Fielding, Swift, and Pope." ECS, 3 (1970), 307-38.

Rept. in Henry Fielding and the Augustan Ideal Under Stress:
"Nature's Dance of Death" and Other Studies. London and Boston:
Routledge & Kegan Paul, 1972. Pp. xiii + 266.

Sentiments of a Church-of-England Man is contrasted to what Rawson
refers to as "couplet-style" ("a mode of statement ... whose clear
outlines are unblurred by doubts and by the loose ends of an
introspective self-implication"). Swift's characteristic ironic
discourse "opens up damaging possibilities without defining their
limits"; the "headlong, anarchic quality of much of Swift's most
vital prose" mirrors his fundamental open-endedness. Most of the
points about Swift here are better developed in Gulliver and the
Gentle Reader (1973) (Item 391).

393. Rawson, C.J. "''Tis only infinite below': Speculations on Swift,
Wallace Stevens, R.D. Laing and Others." Essays in Criticism, 22
(1972), 161-81.

Rept. as pp. 60-83 of Gulliver and the Gentle Reader. London and
Boston: Routledge & Kegan Paul, 1973.

This account of "that interplay between configurations of
imprisoning circularity, or limitless (ad infinitum) escalation, and
of starkly polarized opposites" in Swift is provocative, though
rather sketchily illustrated. The comparison with modern writers for
once seems strained and not very helpful.

394. Rawson, Claude. "Order and Cruelty: A Reading of Swift (with some
comments on Pope and Johnson)." Essays in Criticism, 20 (1970),
24-56.

Rept. as pp. 33-59 of Gulliver and the Gentle Reader. London and
Boston: Routledge & Kegan Paul, 1973; (in part) in Swift:
Gulliver's Travels, A Casebook. London: Macmillan, 1974.

See the exchange among G.K. Holzknecht in Essays in Criticism, 20
(1970), 496-97; C.J. Rawson in Essays in Criticism, 21 (1971),
115-16; Philip Drew in Essays in Criticism, 21 (1971), 417-18.

One of the most influential works listed in this book, Rawson's
reader-response essay concentrates on those points at which Swift's
satire "suggests an impasse, a blocking of escape routes and saving
possibilities." There is a variety of cruelty in how readers are not
allowed to remain wholly unimplicated, even in the specific charges
of the satire. The exchange among Holzknecht, Rawson, and Drew,
centers on the "flay'd woman" passage in A Tale of a Tub.

395. Rensi, Emilia. "Jonathan Swift nel terzo centenario della sua
     nascita." ["The Tricentenary of Swift's Birth."] Volontà, Dec.,
     1967.

396. Revol, Enrique Luis. "Nuestro Contemporáneo Jonathan Swift."
     Revista de Literaturas Modernas, 8 (1969), 35-54.

     Rept. in Revista de Occidente, 24 (1969), 182-200.

     Another case, contra Greenacre and Orwell, for Swift's modernity.
     Gulliver's Travels, A Tale of a Tub and A Modest Proposal are the
     texts.

397. Richman, Jordan. "Johnson as a Swiftian Satirist." University of
     Dayton Review, 7, no. 2 (Spring 1971), 21-28.

     General similarities between Swift and Johnson are pointed to;
     Johnson's excluded Idler 22 is described as a Swiftian indictment of
     war.

398. Rodway, Allan. English Comedy: Its Role and Nature from Chaucer to
     the Present Day. Berkeley and Los Angeles: U. of California Press,
     1975. Pp. x + 288.

     Pp. 158-59 make a case for Books I and II as comedy, "whose delight
     comes not so much from anything that could be strictly called
     celebratory as from a related creative exuberance that allows us to
     see reality freed from the prison of habitual perception."

399. Rogers, Katharine M. The Troublesome Helpmate: A History of Misogyny
     in Literature. Seattle and London: U. of Washington Press, 1966.
     Pp. xvii + 288.

     Pp. 167-74 attack Swift as "almost completely negative" to women, as

practically unique in his apparent insistence that a superficially
beautiful female body really is disgusting even under its cosmetic
artifice. Swift's emphasis on the breast suggests an even greater
aversion to woman as mother than as sexual partner. After
administering this flailing, Rogers admits that Swift respected
women's minds and characters and defended their rights more than
most of his contemporaries.

400. Rogers, Pat. "Swift and the Idea of Authority." Pp. 25-37 of The
World of Jonathan Swift: Essays for the Tercentenary. Edited by
Brian Vickers. Cambridge, Ma.: Harvard U. Press; Oxford: Basil
Blackwell, 1968.

Stresses Swift's literal-minded belief in authority and the
positiveness of his thought, but then turns to consider the
"anti-satiric" qualities of his works: the lack of ideal
alternatives; the absence of sharp distinctions between inside and
outside; the toleration of cant, providing it has a good effect.

401. Rousseau, Andre Michel. L'Angleterre et Voltaire. (Studies on
Voltaire and the Eighteenth Century.) Oxford: Voltaire Foundation
at the Taylor Institution, 1976.

Rev. by G.S. Rousseau in MLN, 92 (1977), 854-56.

A very general survey of Voltaire's literary and personal
relationships with English writers, including Swift.

402. Said, Edward W. Beginnings: Intention and Method. New York: Basic
Books, 1975. Pp. xvii + 414.

Various scattered (often intriguing) remarks on Swift: Gulliver's
Travels is a "set of experiments in changing directions" (pp.
30-32); though in each new piece by Swift, a new voice emerges,
"there is nowhere any mistaking the Swiftian manner"; Verses on the
Death of Dr. Swift presents the "Swiftian motif" of a writer's
approaching career end provoking both opposition and attraction to
the subject matter of endings.

403. Said, Edward W. "Swift's Tory Anarchy." ECS, 3 (1969), 48-66.

Said describes this essay as "a preliminary investigation of how
Swift's work can be approached and characterized as the highly
dramatic encounter between the anarchy of resistance (agraphia) to
the written page, and the abiding tory order of the page." Swift's
"real" subject is, again and again, the act of writing itself, an
idea Said illustrates principally with A Tale of a Tub and Verses on
the Death of Dr. Swift.

404. Sams, Henry W. "An End to Writing About Swift." Essays in Criticism,
24 (1974), 275-85.

Replied to by Colin J. Horne ("Hazlitt on Swift") in Essays in Criticism, 25 (1975), 276-77.

That, despite a lack of new information, critical scribbling should go on furiously as ever is as it should be, according to Sams. "Maggots, as I understand them," he writes, "are one of nature's devices for reducing dead lions to fertile soil, from which all manner of new life may spring." Horne, in his reply, deplores mistaking Hazlitt for anything but an admirer of Swift.

405. Samuel, Irene. "Swift's Reading of Plato." SP, 73 (1976), 440-62.

The main thrust here is towards documenting that Swift did read and frequently refer to Socrates and Plato, but there are also insights into Plato's influence on Swift's political and religious thinking.

406. Schmidt, Johann N. Satire: Swift und Pope. (Sprache und Literatur, 101.) Stuttgart: W. Kohlhammer, 1977. Pp. 152.

Half of this book offers unremarkable views on satire; half offers unremarkable readings of Pope and Swift (A Tale of a Tub, Gulliver's Travels, A Modest Proposal).

407. Schmidt, Johann N. "Der Satiriker und die Sprache: Jonathan Swift und Karl Kraus." Pp. 477-86 of Grobritannien und Deutschland: Festschrift für John W.P. Bourke. Edited by Ortwin Kuhn. Munich: Wilhelm Goldmann, 1974.

Noted in Scriblerian, 8 (1976), 81-82.

Swift's satires, especially A Tale of a Tub and Polite Conversation, attack their victims by faithfully imitating empirical reality.

408. Schuhmann, Kuno, and Joachim Möller. Jonathan Swift. (Erträge der Forschung, 159.) Darmstadt: Wissenschaftliche Buchgesellschaft, 1981. Pp. ix + 245.

A thorough evaluation of 26 primary texts and 426 scholarly studies, including a good deal of English and American criticism from the last fifteen years. A few peculiar omissions mar the discussions, which are, nevertheless, nearly unrelenting. At least the equal of Milton Voigt's Swift and the Twentieth Century (1964).

409. Schulte, Edvige. "Defoe, Swift e l'Accademia inglese." Annali. (Instituto Orientale di Napoli) Sezione Germanica, 8 (1965), 201-20.

Standard remarks on the context of Polite Conversation and A Proposal for Correcting the English Tongue.

410. Scruggs, Charles. "'Sweetness and Light': The Basis of Swift's Views on Art and Criticism." Tennessee Studies in Literature, 18 (1973), 93-104.

Looks at parts of Battle of the Books, Swift's letters, A Proposal for Correcting the English Tongue, A Tale of a Tub and Gulliver's Travels, and arrives at the conclusion that Swift's aesthetic principles are the standard ones of Augustan humanism.

411. Selby, Hopewell. "'Never Finding Full Repast': Satire and Self-Extension in the Early Eighteenth Century." Pp. 217-47 of Probability, Time, and Space in Eighteenth-Century Literature. Edited by Paula R. Backscheider. New York: AMS Press, 1979.

Swift, more than Pope, was preoccupied with the human ambivalence toward the need for eating and its analogues with writing, creating, excreting, and sleeping.

412. Selby, Hopewell R. "The Cell and the Garret: Fictions of Confinement in Swift's Satires and Personal Writings." Pp. 133-56 of Studies in Eighteenth-Century Culture. Vol. 6. Edited by Ronald C. Rosbottom. Madison: U. of Wisconsin Press for the American Society for Eighteenth-Century Studies, 1977.

Although Swift is bent on destroying his satiric personae, imprisoning them and torturing them in a kind of solitary confinement, he writes about himself as a similarly trapped victim. These fictions of confinement express a fear that subjectivity can be ultimately both delusive and destructive. Some of Swift's favorite confinement images are spiders, prisons, snails, beds, and pulpits.

413. Selden, Raman. English Verse Satire 1590-1765. London: George Allen & Unwin, 1978. Pp. 193.

Rev. in review art. ("Recent Studies in the Restoration and Eighteenth Century") by Eric Rothstein in SEL, 19 (1979), 533-60.

Pp. 144-52 comprise dated remarks on Swift's "Hudibrastic" and "Juvenalian" verses, including Market Hill poems.

414. Sertoli, Giuseppe. "L'anatomia swiftiana." Nuova Corrente, 67 (1975), 276-312.

This thoughtful review article of Attilio Brilli (Items 260, 114) mentions other Italian works on Swift, including Item 156.

415. Severikova, N. "Jonathan Swift." Sredneje Speialnoje Obrazovanije, December, 1967, pp. 41-44.

Noted in Scriblerian, 2 (1970), 39.

416. Shamsuddoha, M. "Swift's Satire on Science." <u>Dacca University</u>
     <u>Studies</u>, 24 (1976), (Part A), 32-48.

     Stresses Swift's participation in the "tradition of anti-scientific
     humanism" which recognized the primacy of morality and distrusted
     the optimism of a naturalistic philosophy based upon the new
     science.

417. Shoichi, Shimpo. "On Swift's Misogyny." <u>Journal of English Studies</u>
     <u>of Waseda University</u> (Tokyo), 32 (1968), 56-66.

     Noted in <u>Scriblerian</u>, 1, no. 1 (Autumn 1968), 7.

     Swift's detailed descriptions of repulsive women (as in Book II)
     document his sexual obsessions and repressions. The essay is in
     Japanese.

418. Shuntaro, Ito. "Swift and Science in Eighteenth-Century England." In
     <u>Eighteenth Century English Studies: In Celebration of Professor</u>
     <u>Natsuo SHumuta's Sixty-first Birthday</u>. Tokyo: Kenyusha, 1971. Pp.
     328.

     Noted by Zenzo Suzuki in <u>Scriblerian</u>, 4 (1972), 61.

     In Japanese. "Swift criticized the dehumanization of man at the time
     when the progress of science began to threaten human happiness."
     (Suzuki)

419. Siebert, Donald T., Jr. "Masks and Masquerades: The Animus of
     Swift's Satire." <u>South Atlantic Quarterly</u>, 74 (1975), 435-45.

     Endorses the opinion of Irvin Ehrenpreis, that Swift and his masks
     are generally fused, and insists that the personality and attitudes
     of Swift himself are crucial to the meaning of his persona.

420. Sisson, C.H. "Yeats and Swift." <u>Agenda</u>, 9, no. 4-10, no. 1
     (Autumn-Winter, 1971-72), 34-38.

     Rept. as pp. 271-74 of <u>The Avoidance of Literature: Collected</u>
     <u>Essays</u>. Edited by Michael Schmidt. Manchester: Carcanet, 1978.

     A brief sketch of Yeats's failure to catch the spirit of Swift.

421. Smith, D. Nichol. "Jonathan Swift: Some Observations." Pp. 1-14 of
     <u>Fair Liberty Was All His Cry: A Tercentenary Tribute to Jonathan</u>
     <u>Swift 1667-1745</u>. Edited by A. Norman Jeffares. London: Macmillan;
     New York: St. Martin's Press, 1967.

     Orig. pub. in <u>Transactions of the Royal Society of Literature</u>, 14
     (1935).

Smith comments on several of the misunderstandings of Swift common in 1935.

422. Söderlind, Johannes. "Swift and Linguistics." English Studies, 51 (1970), 137-43.

This is a preliminary sketch of Swift's prescriptive and creative linguistics, stressing, in the former, Swift's criticism of affected phrases, conceited words, manglings, and abbreviations, and, in the latter, the sounds, orthography, morphology, and syntax of the "languages" of Journal to Stella and Gulliver's Travels.

423. Sokolyansky, M.G. "Johnathan [sic] Swift's Paradoxes." Radyansko Literaturoznavstvo (Kiiv), May, 1968, pp. 61-68.

Noted by Leonid M. Arinshtein in Scriblerian, 2 (1970), 39-40.

In Ukrainian.

424. Solomon, Petre. "Swift in Romanian." Romania Today, 10 (1967), 34.

425. Spacks, Patricia Meyer. "Uncertainties of Satire." MLQ, 40 (1979), 403-11.

A review article covering Edward A. Bloom and Lillian D. Bloom, Satire's Persuasive Voice; Clive T. Probyn, Jonathan Swift: The Contemporary Background; Peter J. Schakel, The Poetry of Jonathan Swift: Allusion and the Development of a Poetic Style.

426. Speck. W.A. (ed.). Swift. (Literature in Perspective Series.) London: Evans Brothers Limited, 1969; (Arco Literary Critiques.) New York: Arco Publishing, 1970. Pp. 143.

Rev. in Scriblerian, 2 (1969), 27.

Includes Chapters on "Life and Tracts for the Times," "Swift's Literary Techniques," "Swift's Poetry" (by Philip Roberts), "A Tale of a Tub," "Gulliver's Travels," "Epilogue: 'He served Human Liberty'," and a short Bibliography--all aimed at an audience of beginners.

427. Spence, Joseph. Observations, Anecdotes and Characters of Books and Men. Collected from Conversation. 2 Vols. Edited by James M. Osborn. Oxford: Clarendon Press, 1966.

In addition to frequent remarks about Swift, Vol. 2 contains an appendix on "Pope's Portrait of Swift" (p. 622).

428. Spiller, Michael R.G. "The Idol of the Stove: The Background to
     Swift's Criticism of Descartes." <u>RES</u>, n.s. 25 (1974), 15-24.

     In attacking Descartes, Swift did not merely follow the lead of
     Anglican rationalists, but aimed at the inner act of reduction.
     Swift was almost alone (except for Meric Casaubon) in also attacking
     Descartes's laziness, enthusiasm, connections with religious
     fanaticism, proselytizing, and introversion.

429. Starkman, Miriam K. "Swift's Rhetoric: The 'overfraught pinnace'?"
     <u>South Atlantic Quarterly</u>, 68 (1969), 188-97.

     Swift the moralist has been obscured by recent concern with Swift
     the rhetorical strategist, Starkman insists. Questions about meaning
     should be resolved by considerations of genre, i.e., the
     "situational construct that is historical and biographical" and by a
     notion of rhetoric "conceived in historical terms."

430. Steele, Peter. <u>Jonathan Swift: Preacher and Jester</u>. Oxford and New
     York: Oxford U. Press, 1979. Pp. ix + 252.

       Rev. (favorably) by Timothy Keegan in <u>JEGP</u>, 79 (1980), 127-29;
       (favorably) by C.J. Rawson in <u>RES</u>, n.s. 31 (1980), 83-85;
       (favorably) by R. Quintana in <u>MLR</u>, 75 (1980), 163-64; by Frank
       Brady in <u>Scriblerian</u>, 12 (1979), 41-42; in review art. ("Gentle
       Readings: Recent Work on Swift") by William Kinsley in <u>ECS</u>, 15
       (1982), 442-53.

     This finely written meditation on "apparently contradictory impulses
     in the work" of Swift is divided into chapters on Fools, Acting,
     Play, and The Grotesque and Dying Animal. The method is neither
     formalist nor poststructuralist analysis, but a kind of shrewd
     impressionism blended with phenomenology: "the interest and
     plausibility of Swift's writing, today at least, depends upon this
     sensed authoritative presence, rather than upon the array of
     oratorical devices through which it is deployed."

431. Sutherland, James. "Forms and Methods in Swift's Satire." Pp. 61-77
     of <u>Jonathan Swift 1667-1967: A Dublin Tercentenary Tribute</u>. Edited
     by Roger McHugh and Philip Edwards. Dublin: Dolmen Press; London:
     Oxford U. Press, 1967.

     A very general discussion of some satirical techniques—"direct and
     forthright denunciation," diminution, mock-panegyric, persona,
     parody, travesty, ridicule, infiltrating his reader's
     position—offered "for the convenience of the general reader." Texts
     discussed include "A Satirical Elegy," <u>Short Character of Wharton</u>,
     <u>The Bickerstaff Papers</u>, <u>Mr. Collins's Discourse</u>, <u>Battle of the
     Books</u>, and <u>Gulliver's Travels</u>.

432. Thacker, Christopher. "Swift and Voltaire." <u>Hermathena</u>, 104 (Spring,
     1967), 51-66.

This is less a study of influence than a report on Voltaire's admiration for Swift. Speculations about the personal relations between the two are inconclusive as to whether Swift and Voltaire ever met.

433. Thomas, L.H.C. "Swift in German Literature." Hermathena, 104 (Spring, 1967), 67-77.

Chronicles the admiration of nearly a dozen German writers, especially Herder and Goethe.

434. Thornburg, Thomas R. Swift and the Ciceronian Tradition. (Ball State Monograph, 28; Publication in English, 20.) Muncie: Ball State U., 1980. Pp. 28.

A survey of what is Ciceronian and/or Quintilian in Swift's prose, with special attention to An Argument Against Abolishing Christianity and A Modest Proposal. There is little attempt to discuss the significance of this for interpretation.

435. Timpe, Eugene F. "Swift as Railleur." JEGP, 69 (1970), 41-49.

This is a useful preliminary study, presenting Swift's definitions of raillery and delineating several techniques by which he created it. See also Items 264, 596.

436. Torchiana, Donald T. W.B. Yeats and Georgian Ireland. Evanston: Northwestern U. Press, 1966. Pp. xvi + 378.

Pp. 120-67 ("Imitate Him If You Dare") describe the two channels of Swift's intensity that Torchiana thinks haunted Yeats most: Swift's prophetic isolation, and his powerful devotion to justice.

437. Traugott, John. "In-House Hullaballoo." Scriblerian, 5 (1972), 73-75.

Briefly surveys the history of the concept of persona in Swift criticism and urges present critics to "a description of his affectiveness and of the personality behind it."

438. Traugott, John. "Swift, Our Contemporary." University Review (Dublin), 4 (1967), 11-34.

Rept. as pp. 239-64 of Focus: Swift. Edited by C.J. Rawson. London: Sphere Books, 1971.

The essay mostly concerns Orwell, Yeats, and Norman O. Brown, "theoreticians of history." Traugott finds Orwell (for all his complaints about Swift) less affirmative than Swift: "Orwell figures apocalyptic finality, Swift only the need for free intelligence to know our own motives." Yeats did not see Swift clearly: "For Yeats, Swift is a symbol of the arrogant free intellect" (but "Swift had no sympathy whatever with mystical nationalism, glory, heroes, or movements"). Traugott approves of Brown's theories generally, especially the remark that "Swift's ultimate horror in these [scatological] poems is at the thought that sublimation—that is to say, all civilized behaviour—is a lie and cannot survive confrontation with the truth."

439. Traugott, John L. "The Professor as Nibelung." <u>ECS</u>, 3 (1970), 532–43.

Flinging deterministic theological and historical scholarship to the ground, Traugott argues for accepting "our <u>intuitive</u> experience of the cast of mind of the writer," our reimagining "of the history he lived."

440. Traugott, John, Gardner D. Stout, Jr., et. al. "Sternian Realities: Excerpts from Seminars Chaired by John Traugott: 'New Directions in Sterne Criticism' and Gardner D. Stout, Jr.: 'Sterne and Swift'." Pp. 76–93 of <u>The Winged Skull: Papers from the Laurence Sterne Bicentenary Conference</u>. Edited by Arthur H. Cash and John M. Stedmond. Kent State U. Press, 1971; London: Methuen, 1972.

A mostly psycho-biographical discussion, by Claude Rawson, Jean-Jacques Mayoux, Helene Moglen, Traugott, and Stout, consistently distinguishing between Swift and Sterne.

441. Trowbridge, Hoyt. <u>From Dryden to Jane Austen: Essays on English Critics and Writers, 1660–1818</u>. Albuquerque: U. of New Mexico Press, 1977.

Rev. by Barry Roth in <u>ECS</u>, 12 (1978), 122–26; by Emerson R. Marks in <u>Scriblerian</u>, 10 (1978), 131–32; by Cecil Price in <u>N&Q</u>, 224 (1979), 254–55.

Pp. 81–123 is "Swift and Socrates." Swift's allusions to Socrates illuminate his attitude toward freethinkers and deists (their hatred of religion is actually fear that it will restrict their passions and vices), his position on the place of reason in religion and morality (even without divine assistance, reason can attain truth in both divinity and ethics), and his intentions in Book IV (hard school).

442. Tuveson, Ernest. "Swift: The View from within the Satire." Pp. 55–85 of <u>The Satirist's Art</u>. Edited by H. James Jensen and Malvin R. Zirker, Jr. Bloomington and London: Indiana U. Press, 1972.

Tuveson focuses on Swift's self-imposed task of "writing satire that for the first time is truly effective for the individual." In the <u>Argument Against Abolishing Christianity</u>, Swift himself speaks

openly with an ironic voice. His target is not restricted to
lukewarm or critical Christians; rather, his satirical conceit is
"like a searchlight," illuminating one murky group or faction after
another. In A Modest Proposal Swift also speaks in his own voice,
adopting the ironic mode "quite literally as a form of shock
treatment." Though Book IV of Gulliver's Travels, abstractly
paraphrased, says nothing either new or unique, Swift brings his
point home by evoking an intense emotional participation, rather
than cool and rational observation.

443. Uphaus, Robert W. "Images of Swift: A Review of Some Recent
     Crticism." Eire-Ireland, 6, no. 3 (Fall 1971), 16-22.

     Reviews Denis Donoghue, Jonathan Swift: A Critical Introduction;
     Martin Kallich, The Other End of the Egg; W.B. Carnochan Lemuel
     Gulliver's Mirror for Man; John R. Clark, Form and Frenzy in Swift's
     Tale of a Tub.

444. Uphaus, Robert W. The Impossible Observer: Reason and the Reader in
     Eighteenth-Century Prose. Lexington: University Press of Kentucky,
     1979. Pp. 160.

     Rev. by Dustin Griffin in MLQ, 41 (1980), 195-98; in review art.
     ("Recent Studies in the Restoration and Eighteenth Century") by J.
     Paul Hunter in SEL, 20 (1980), 517-46; (favorably) by Alistair M.
     Duckworth in South Atlantic Quarterly, 80 (1981), 237-39;
     (unfavorably) by Eric Rothstein in ECS, 13 (1980), 446-49; by Alan
     T. McKenzie in Western Humanities Review, 34 (1980), 271-73.

     Pp. 9-27, "Swift and the Problematical Nature of Meaning," stress
     the sheer variousness and successiveness of manifest fictions in
     Gulliver's Travels to argue that the function of Book III and the
     meaning of the Houyhnhnms are problematical by their natures. Like
     Gulliver's Travels, A Modest Proposal violates its readers'
     expectations by moving back and forth between the text's apparently
     self-referential system of meaning to the "open and problematical
     world of the reader's experiences and expectations."

445. Vakhrushev, V. "The Multifaced Laugh." Uchitelskaja Gazeta, Nov. 30,
     1969.

     Noted by Leonid Arinshtein in Scriblerian, 2 (1970), 39.

446. Vickers, Brian. "Swift and the Baconian Idol." Pp. 87-128 of The
     World of Jonathan Swift: Essays for the Tercentenary. Edited by
     Brian Vickers. Cambridge, Ma.: Harvard U. Press; Oxford: Basil
     Blackwell, 1968.

     Bacon stood for the new science, the prideful concept of virtù,
     and other things Swift detested and retaliated upon through parody
     of Bacon's opinions, attitudes, and style. Appendix A (pp. 121-24)

is "Possible Non-Ironic Borrowings from Bacon"; Appendix B (pp. 124-28) is "Possible Parodies of Bacon."

447. Vickers, Brian (ed.). The World of Jonathan Swift: Essays for the Tercentenary. Cambridge, Ma.: Harvard U. Press; Oxford: Basil Blackwell, 1968. Pp. x + 273.

Rev. (favorably) by Colin J. Horne in Journal of the Australasian Universities Language and Literature Association, 33 (1970), 124-26; (with another work) by Pierre Danchin in English Studies, 53 (1972), 166-70; (with reservations) by C.J. Rawson in RES, n.s. 21 (1970), 84-86.

Includes the following: Brian Vickers, "Introduction"; Pat Rogers, "Swift and the Idea of Authority"; Hugh Sykes Davies, "Irony and the English Tongue"; Herbert Davis, "Swift's Use of Irony"; Basil Hall, "'An Inverted Hypocrite': Swift the Churchman"; W.A. Speck, "From Principles to Practice: Swift's Party Politics"; Brian Vickers, "Swift and the Baconian Idol"; Roger Savage, "Swift's Fallen City: A Description of the Morning"; Geoffrey Hill, "Jonathan Swift: The Poetry of Reaction"; Irvin Ehrenpreis, "Swift and the Comedy of Evil"; Angus Ross, "The Social Circumstances of Several Remote Nations of the World"; Brian Vickers, "The Satiric Structure of Gulliver's Travels and More's Utopia"; John Holloway, "Dean of St. Patrick's: A View from the Letters."

448. Vozar, Lea Bertani. "Yeats, Swift, Irish Patriotism and 'Rationalistic Anti-intellectualism'." Massachusetts Studies in English, 3 (1972), 108-16.

Emphasizes Yeats's affinity for Swift's "contempt of the average man," his "cyclic theory of history," and asserts that both were "rationalistic anti-intellectuals."

449. Ward, David. Jonathan Swift: An Introductory Essay. London: Methuen; New York: Barnes & Noble, 1973. Pp. viii + 216.

Rev. by Colin J. Horne in MLR, 70 (1975), 153-55; (severely) by W.A. Speck in N&Q, 220 (1975), 513-14; (with reservations) by Clive T. Probyn in Scriblerian, 6 (1974), 93-94; (with another work) by Malcolm Kelsall in RES, n.s. 25 (1974), 472-75; by Pierre Danchin in English Studies, 57 (1976), 77-79.

Unremarkable readings of all the major works as attempts to help "people learn to see through their own lies." Scant notice is given of previous criticism.

450. Watson, Sheila. "Swift and Ovid: The Development of Metasatire." Humanities Association Bulletin, 38, no. 1 (Spring 1967), 5-13.

An unconvincing development of a potentially good thesis ("metasatire" is satire on Ovidian satire).

451. Watt, Ian. "The Ironic Tradition in Augustan Prose from Swift to
     Johnson." Pp. 216-38 of <u>Focus:</u> <u>Swift</u>. Edited by C.J. Rawson.
     London: Sphere Books, 1971.

     Orig. pub. Los Angeles: Clark Library, 1957. Rept. as pp. 161-88
     of <u>Stuart</u> <u>and</u> <u>Georgian</u> <u>Moments:</u> <u>Clark</u> <u>Library</u> <u>Seminar</u> <u>Papers</u> <u>on</u>
     <u>Seventeenth</u> <u>and</u> <u>Eighteenth</u> <u>Century</u> <u>English</u> <u>Literature</u>. Edited by
     Earl Miner. Berkeley, Los Angeles, London: U. of California Press,
     1972.

     Concerned mostly with Swift, this well-known essay defines his two
     major contributions to the ironic tradition--understatement and a
     cool, distant generality of diction--and makes an important
     statement about the concept of a double audience for irony.

452. Weinbrot, Howard D. <u>Augustus</u> <u>Caesar</u> <u>in</u> <u>"Augustan"</u> <u>England:</u> <u>The</u>
     <u>Decline</u> <u>of</u> <u>a</u> <u>Classical</u> <u>Norm</u>. Princeton: Princeton U. Press, 1978.
     Pp. xi + 270.

     Rev. (favorably) by Donald S. Taylor in <u>Comparative</u> <u>Literature</u>, 30
     (1978), 378-80.

     Pp. 249-52 are "Appendix II: Pope's 'To Augustus' (Lines 221-24) and
     the Response to Swift's Drapier." The passage evokes a number of
     Dublin broadsides which conjure up an image of Ireland's becoming
     "vocal and graphic in response to Swift's triumphant Drapier."

453. Weinbrot, Howard D. <u>The</u> <u>Formal</u> <u>Strain:</u> <u>Studies</u> <u>in</u> <u>Augustan</u> <u>Imitation</u>
     <u>and</u> <u>Satire</u>. Chicago: U. of Chicago Press, 1969. Pp. xi + 234.

     Rev. by Paul R. Corts in <u>Quarterly</u> <u>Journal</u> <u>of</u> <u>Speech</u>, 56 (1970),
     102-03; (with other works) by Frederick W. Hilles in <u>Yale</u> <u>Review</u>,
     59 (1969-70), 130-37; in review art. ("Recent Studies in the
     Restoration and Eighteenth Century") by Marshall Waingrow in <u>SEL</u>,
     10 (1970), 605-36; (favorably) by Rebecca Parkin in <u>ECS</u>, 4 (1971),
     492-94; (with reservations and with another work) by C.J. Rawson
     in <u>Yearbook</u> <u>of</u> <u>English</u> <u>Studies</u>, 1 (1971), 268-70; (severely) by
     Bertrand A. Goldgar in <u>JEGP</u>, 69 (1970), 308-10; (favorably) in
     <u>Antioch</u> <u>Review</u>, 29 (1969), 112.

     In this study of the backgrounds and conventions of the overlapping
     genres, imitation and formal satire, Swift's "partial imitations" of
     Horace are described (pp. 49-51); <u>Gulliver's</u> <u>Travels</u> (a "revelatory"
     satire) is distinguished from "Augustan formal verse satire," in
     which the presence of a clearly workable norm is portrayed (pp.
     86-92); and "On Reading Dr. Young's Satires, Called the Universal
     Passion" is discussed in relation to Young's satiric norms.

454. Weitzman, Arthur J. "Pseudonymous Publication as a Mode of Satire."
     <u>Satire</u> <u>Newsletter</u>, 4, no. 1 (Fall 1968), 12-18.

     "Whether it was the scholarly mockery of Bickerstaff's predictions of Partridge's imminent death or the mercantile projector's modest proposal to market children's flesh or a coffee-house wit's defense of nominal Christianity, Swift adapted or changed his mask to deceive his audience into thinking they were facing their own kind. Only slowly and imperceptibly does the intended victim realize the trap he has been caught in: that his comfortable opinions and untested beliefs have been subjected to the extremes of their own logical tendencies."

455. Welcher, Jeanne. "Swift-Hogarth Give and Take." Pp. 23-53 of
     Ventures in Research. Edited by Richard R. Griffith. New York:
     C.W. Post Center, 1975.

     Fractious argument for Swift's and Hogarth's "direct use of one another's images and style," "similar treatment of subjects and themes," and "commonality" of creative approach and metaphor.

456. Wendt, Allan. "Who's a Yahoo!" College English, 33 (1971), 317-23.

     Teaching "The Lady's Dressing Room" and Gulliver's Travels by means of "centering exercises" and games.

457. West, Alick. "Satire and Revolution." Angol és Amerikai Filológiai
     Tanulmányok, 1 (1971), 170-95.

     This essay talks about contradictions between Swift's "intention" and "effect," as if West had secret information about Swift's reasons for writing. But the question raised here has never fully been answered: Swift was a Whig who became a Tory. Why then does his satire seem so disturbing and liberating?

458. Willems, J.-P. "Swift Revisited." Revue des Langues Vivantes, 33
     (1967), 541-50.

     A review essay, praising Herbert Davis's Jonathan Swift: Essays on His Satire and Other Studies (Oxford, 1964).

459. Williams, Aubrey. "The Gloomy Dean." Sewanee Review, 74 (1966),
     551-54.

     A review essay, evaluating Milton Voigt, Swift and the Twentieth Century (1964), Phillip Harth, Swift and Anglican Rationalism (1961), Charles Allen Beaumont, Swift's Classical Rhetoric (1961).

460. Williams, Kathleen. "Jonathan Swift." Pp. 60-99 of History of
     Literature in the English Language. Vol. 4: Dryden to Johnson.
     Edited by Roger Lonsdale. (Sphere Books.) London: Barrie &
     Jenkins, 1971.

Carefully balanced consideration of biographical, religious, and historical contexts pinions this standard appraisal of A Tale of a Tub, Gulliver's Travels, Battle of the Books, An Argument Against Abolishing Christianity, The Conduct of the Allies, and A Modest Proposal. The continuity of Swift's satirical methods and the consistency of his Christian humanism are stressed.

461. Williams, Kathleen. Jonathan Swift. (Profiles in Literature Series.) London: Routledge & Kegan Paul; New York: Humanities Press, 1968. Pp. 111.

   Rev. by Clive T. Probyn in Scriblerian, 3 (1970), 5-6; in TLS, May, 23, 1968, p. 529.

   Extracts from Swift's works plus critical commentary on Satiric Use of Apparently Straightforward Narration, Description, Exposition, and Argument; Parody of a Style; Parody of a Form; Satiric Use of Imagery; Use of Contemporary Attitudes, Ideas, and Institutions for Satiric Purposes.

462. Williams, Kathleen (ed.). Swift: The Critical Heritage. (Critical Heritage Series.) London: Routledge & Kegan Paul; New York: Barnes & Noble, 1970. Pp. ix + 348.

   Rev. by Clive T. Probyn in Scriblerian, 3 (1970), 4-5; (with other works) by A.E. Dyson in Critical Quarterly, 12 (1970), 284, 286; by A. Norman Jeffares in Yearbook of English Studies, 1 (1971), 267; (with other works) by Philip Roberts in N&Q, 218 (1973), 430-31; by Oliver Ferguson in South Atlantic Quarterly, 70 (1971), 121-22; in TLS, Aug. 21, 1970, p. 930.

   Includes sixty-three selections, from 1704 to 1819, mostly on A Tale of a Tub and Gulliver's Travels.

463. Williams, Kathleen. "Restoration Themes in the Major Satires of Swift." RES, n.s. 16 (1965), 258-71.

   Concerning ideas about the nature of man and about the relations of language and reality, Swift establishes his own independent position, neither Ancient nor Modern.

464. Williams, Kathleen M. "'Animal Rationis Capax.' A Study of Certain Aspects of Swift's Imagery." Pp. 131-45 of Fair Liberty Was All His Cry: A Tercentenary Tribute to Jonathan Swift 1667-1745. Edited by A. Norman Jeffares. London: Macmillan; New York: St. Martin's Press, 1967.

   Orig. pub. in Journal of English Literary History, 21 (1954).

   Swift's stress on physical images indicate both an intense dislike of filth and infirmity and an unwillingness to ignore the body.

Similarly, his fight against deception "is conditioned by his feeling that only by compromise can we find place for the whole of our complicated reality."

465. Wolper, Roy S. "Swift's Enlightened Gulls." <u>SVEC</u>, 58 (1967), 1915-37.

The points about Swift's antagonism towards natural science, utilitarianism, and religious rationalism are familiar, but the examples come from a specific blood line: Swift's gulls (Simon Wagstaff, Bickerstaff, Descartes, Bentley, Tindal, Peter, etc.).

466. Yamaguchi, Katsumasa. "Overstatement to Understatement: Defoe-Swift Oboegaki." <u>Annual Reports of English and American Literature</u> (Osaka Shoin Women's College), 15 (1978), 54-67.

Noted by Zenzo Suzuki in <u>Scriblerian</u>, 13 (1981), 85.

According to Yamaguchi, "Defoe emphasizes overstatement or excessive expression; Swift leans towards understatement or controlled expression." (Suzuki)

467. Yeats, W.B. "The Words Upon the Window-Pane." Pp. 186-99 of <u>Fair Liberty Was All His Cry: A Tercentenary Tribute to Jonathan Swift 1667-1745</u>. Edited by A. Norman Jeffares. London: Macmillan; New York: St. Martin's Press, 1967.

Orig. pub. as "Introduction" to <u>Words Upon the Window-Pane</u> (1934).

Yeats's famous obsession ("Swift haunts me") with Swift's insistence upon liberty and with his general conservativism.

468. Zacharasiweicz, Waldemar. <u>Die Klimatheorie in der englischen Literatur and Literaturkritik von der Mitte des 16. bis zum frühen 18. Jahrhundert</u>. Wien and Stuttgart: Wilhelm Braumüller, 1977. Pp. xii + 666.

Rev. by Hermann J. Real in <u>Scriblerian</u>, 11 (1979), 94-95.

A study of the "idea that specific historical concepts and cultural phenomena are to be explained within the terms of the milieu in which they originated." (Real) Pp. 540-56 concern Swift.

See also Items 172, 596, 652, 728, 739, 781, 797, 872, 884, 976, 996.

SECTION 4

Poetry

469. Aden, John M. "Corinna and the Sterner Muse of Swift." <u>ELN</u>, 4
     (1966-67), 23-31.

     Stresses the doubleness of Swift's vision, "tragic and comic, or
     ridiculous and pathetic," which creates "a remarkable testament of
     the power of shaped reality to plead its own case and excite its own
     due measure of sympathy." An influential article.

470. Aden, John M. "Those Gaudy Tulips: Swift's 'Unprintables'." Pp.
     15-32 of <u>Quick Springs of Sense: Studies in the Eighteenth
     Century</u>. Edited by Larry S. Champion. Athens: U. of Georgia Press,
     1974.

     This assessment of the "poetical properties" of the scatological
     poems reaches (among others) the following conclusions: "The
     Progress of Beauty" works by "scaling down, by ambiguities, ironic
     pitfalls, and land mines, until we can call a slut a slut without
     loss of composure and realize that a second-hand rose by any other
     name will smell as rank"; the notorious impasse in the last lines of
     "The Lady's Dressing Room" is actually a call to simple
     clear-sightedness; "Strephon and Chloe" fails poetically, since its
     features of "burlesque epithalamium" tend to upstage its ultimate
     satiric tenor; "Cassinus and Peter" weaves together the comic
     threads of carpe diem, elegy, pastoral, scatology, and melodrama.

471. Anderson, G.L. "A Reply to Swift's 'Excellent New Song' (1711)."
     <u>PBSA</u>, 69 (1975), 237-40.

     The poetical reply, probably by John Oldmixon, in defense of
     Nottingham, is reprinted.

472. Anderson, Phillip B. "Transformations of 'Swift' and the Development
     of Swift's Satiric Vision in <u>Verses on the Death of Dr. Swift</u>."
     <u>Publications of the Arkansas Philological Association</u>, 6, no. 1
     (Spring 1980), 19-32.

     Reads the poem as transforming Swift through a series of roles: from
     witty conversationalist, to ailing man, to a revised version after
     his death, to the object of his friends' indifference, to an
     identification with his own works, and finally to the panegyric. The

concluding eulogy is complex: as myth, it is "a fatuous exercise in
moral oversimplification. The Spokesman for a society which no
longer reads 'Swift' can comfortably eulogize him." However, the
eulogy is also one last denial of the truth that is "Swift."
Studying the Verses as a series of transformations of Swift's
identity ought to be more provocative than the rather bland
conclusions of this essay suggest.

473. Bà, Paolo. "A Character, Panegiric, and Description of the Legion
Club di Jonathan Swift." Studi Urbinati di Storia Filosofia e
Letteratura, ser. B, 44, nos. 1-2 (1970), 54-75.

An application of Pope's classes of disordered figures—the
confusing, the magnifying, and the diminuting (Peri Bathous)—to a
rhetorical analysis of "The Legion Club." The schematic conclusion
insists on exclusive correlations between "confusing" and
"Character," "diminuting" and "Panegyric," and "magnifying" and
"Description."

474. Bà, Paolo. "Il Posto dei Dannati di Jonathan Swift." Il Lettore di
Provincia, 2, no. 4 (March 1971), 35-41.

Uses "The Place of the Damn'd" to introduce students to personae,
syllogism as a means of structuring "argument," and the rhetorical
function of italics, and other tradition figures of poetic invention
and rhetoric.

475. Barnett, Louise K. "Fictive Self-Portraiture in Swift's Poetry." Pp.
101-11 of Contemporary Studies of Swift's Poetry. Edited by John
Irwin Fischer and Donald C. Mell, Jr. With David M. Vieth as
Associate Editor. Newark, Del.: U. of Delaware Press, 1981.

"The abiding concern of Swift's poetry of fictive self-portraiture
is not to lead back to biography through the expression of a 'real
self,' but to refract and thus meditate upon the world's perceptions
and misperceptions of this self."

476. Barnett, Louise K. "The Mysterious Narrator: Another Look at The
Lady's Dressing Room." Concerning Poetry, 9, no. 2 (Fall 1976),
29-32.

Of the ending: "Rather than being a commendable attitude, the
narrator's tolerance of" the absence of sweetness and cleanliness
"is the sophisticated counterpart of Strephon's horrified rejection.
Neither wholesale condemnation nor blanket admiration is the proper
response, neither obsession with the inescapable bodily functions
nor complete disregard of them." In other words, all attitudes
presented by the poem are implicitly condemned.

477. Barnett, Louise K. "'Saying the Thing That is Not': Swift's
Metalinguistic Satire." Concerning Poetry, 12, no. 1 (Spring,
1979), 21-27.

In his poems against linguistic offenses, including "The Progress of
Beauty," "His Grace's Answer to Jonathan," "Quibbling Elegy on the
Worshipful Judge Boat," "The Salamander," "The Place of the Damn'd,"
and "On the Words Brother Protestants and Fellow Christians," Swift
expresses his commitment to reality, attacking the falsifying
relations of word and meaning.

478. Barnett, Louise K. "Swift's Poetry and the Critics." Review, 2
     (1980), 41-48.

     Reviews Nora Crow Jaffe, The Poet Swift (1976), John Irwin Fischer,
     On Swift's Poetry (1978), and Peter J. Schakel, The Poetry of
     Jonathan Swift: Allusion and the Development of a Poetic Style
     (1978).

479. Bleich, David. Subjective Criticism. Baltimore and London: Johns
     Hopkins U. Press, 1978, pp. 284-93.

     By way of conclusion to his affective theory, Bleich reprints a
     student's lengthy subjective response to "A Beautiful Young Nymph
     Going to Bed." He goes on to suggest that what seems "regular" about
     either Swift or the eighteenth century is only a function of our
     collective contemporary interests: "The question of whether Swift
     was an instance of or an exception to his culture becomes idle; if
     he lived in a specific culture, he was necessarily part of it. The
     various emphases in his literature are explainable as a synthesis of
     personal experiences each of which is common to only a part of his
     culture and some of which are completely idiosyncratic."

480. Blesch, Edwin J., Jr. "'A Species Hardly a Degree Above a Monkey':
     Jonathan Swift's Concept of Woman." Nassau Review, 3, no. 3
     (1977), 74-84.

     Proceeding from the utterly mistaken assumption that "most recent
     critics" believe that Swift's "deplorable poems about women"
     document his deteriorating mental condition, Blesch eschews critical
     analysis for wide-eyed "feminist" denunciation of Swift's "fear and
     hatred" of women's bodies as well as their foibles.

481. Borkat, Roberta F.S. "Swift, Shaw, and the Idealistic Swain."
     English Studies, 61 (1980), 498-506.

     Discussing "Strephon and Chloe," Borkat emphasizes the connection
     between the protagonist's self-contempt and his idealizing of Chloe.
     Swift's message, she concludes, is that "[t]o preserve the myth of
     perfection, complexity and truth must be covered with a veneer of
     specious beauty."

482. Borkat, Roberta Sarfatt. "The Cage of Custom." University of Dayton
     Review, 10, no. 3 (Summer 1974), 47-57.

In the Stella poems and <u>Cadenus and Vanessa</u>, Swift satirizes the emptiness of the code of "a docile mind in a chaste and beautiful body."

483. Briggs, Peter M. "Notes Toward a Teachable Definition of Satire." <u>Eighteenth-Century Life</u>, 5, no. 3 (Spring, 1979), 28-39.

"The Lady's Dressing Room" is read as presenting a "positive, though cautionary and sceptical, moral," about the need to see tulips and dung as complementary, not contradictory.

484. Brilli, Attilio. "Il vaso di Pandora. Sulle poesie escrementali di Swift." Pp. 156-79 of <u>La materialità del testo. Ricerca interdisciplinare sulle pratiche significanti</u>. (Il lavoro critico/semiotica, 11.) Verona: Bertani, 1977.

485. Calhoun, Douglas. "Swift's 'The Lady's Dressing Room'." <u>Discourse</u>, 13 (1970), 493-99.

The ending of "The Lady's Dressing Room" is read as an endorsement of sublimation--a reading anticipated by Donald Greene, "On Swift's 'Scatological' Poems" (Item 521).

486. Cartwright, Faith Wotton. "Jonathan Swift and the Psychoanalysts." <u>Revista de la Universidad de Costa Rica</u>, 39 (1974), 47-58.

Noted in <u>Scriblerian</u>, 10 (1978), 88.

"Swift's use of excrement, often alluded to by Freudians, is due not to any phobia but is 'sensationalism devised to bring us back to common sense' (italics added).... [Cartwright's] attack on the absurdities of psychoanalytic criticism goes over ground covered by, among others, Milton Voigt and Louis Landa." (<u>Scriblerian</u>)

487. Clark, John R. "Embodiment in Literature: Swift's Blasted Pocky Muse of Poetry." <u>Thalia</u>, 2, no. 3 (Winter, 1979-80), 23-33.

In this salutary counterstatement to books by Jaffe, Fischer, and Schakel, Clark decries their inability to get at the "voltage" of Swift's poetic force. His own alternative is to examine passages from a number of famous poems in which Swift's images and lines "burst into seminal topics besetting the human condition: disgrace, overwhelming foetor, ravishment, mortification, decay, and damnation." Tension, contradiction, kinetic energy, and "damnable bedevilment" are the qualities Clark values most highly in Swift's poems.

488. Clarke, Austin. "The Poetry of Swift." Pp. 94-115 of <u>Jonathan Swift 1667-1967: A Dublin Tercentenary Tribute</u>. Edited by Roger McHugh

and Philip Edwards. Dublin: Dolmen Press; London: Oxford U. Press, 1967.

An appreciative wander through Swift's verse with only one or two interesting insights ("I felt instantly that Swift had really remained provincial and that this much-despised limitation was his strength, the secret of his intensity.")

489. Cohen, Ralph. "The Augustan Mode in English Poetry." Pp. 171-92 of Studies in the Eighteenth Century: Papers Presented at the David Nichol Smith Memorial Seminar, Canberra, 1966. Edited by R.F. Brissenden. Canberra: Australian National U. Press; Toronto: U. of Toronto Press, 1968.

Orig. pub. in ECS, 1 (1967), 3-32.

"Description of a City Shower," "On Stella's Birthday 1719," "A Beautiful Young Nymph Going to Bed," and Verses on the Death of Dr. Swift exemplify Swift's characteristic serial or successive approach, his spatial images of process (specifically dismemberment), the harmony of his fragmentary images, his allusions, and his creation of a social role-playing observer.

490. Colum, Padraic. "Swift's Poetry." Dublin Magazine, 6, nos. 3-4 (Autumn/Winter, 1967), 5-13.

Rept. (with slight changes, and with a following exchange with the audience) as "The Poetry of Jonathan Swift." Proceedings of the American Academy of Arts and Letters and the National Institute of Arts and Letters, 2nd ser., 18 (1968), 3-19.

Attributes Swift's current unattractiveness as a poet to the romantic movement and to the fact that his themes are taken, not from the country, but from "the court and the street"; praises Swift for his ability to make readers join him in his praise or condemnation.

491. Cronin, Edward R. "A Panegyrick on the Dean." Revue des Langues Vivantes, 37 (1971), 524-34.

A bland description of the poem.

492. Davies, Paul C. "Rochester: Augustan and Explorer." Durham University Journal, 61 (1969), 59-64.

Hints at Rochester's affinities to Swift without actually ascribing influence. Also contains an extensive and hazy account of "The Lady's Dressing Room" as "reconciling" two views of woman (goddess and greasy whore).

493. Davis, Herbert. "Swift's View of Poetry." Pp. 62-97 of Fair Liberty
     Was All His Cry: A Tercentenary Tribute to Jonathan Swift
     1667-1745. Edited by A. Norman Jeffares. London: Macmillan; New
     York: St. Martin's Press, 1967.

     Orig. pub. in Studies in English, ed. Malcolm Wallace (1931).

     By contrast with Dryden and Pope, Swift took no professional pride
     in writing poetry and put little value on it generally. He wrote to
     influence public events or to advance his reputation. Many of his
     poems are motivated entirely by literary satire, an interpretation
     which enables Davis to make, among other things, an early defense of
     the scatological poems.

494. De Bhaldraithe, Tomás. "Fonóta do lucht Swiftiana." ["Notes for
     Swift Scholars."] Studia Hibernica, 14 (1974), 140-42.

     Reprints two Irish poems (from Mezentius on the Rack, 1734)
     satirizing Rev. Charles Carthy, whose translation of Horace was also
     attacked by friends of Swift and (de Bhaldraithe suspects) by Swift
     himself.

495. Donoghue, Denis. "Swift as Poet." Pp. 75-89 of Swift Revisited.
     Edited by Denis Donoghue. Cork: Mercier; Hatboro, Pa.: Folklore
     Associates, 1968.

     Contains some of the points in the chapter on Swift's poetry in
     Donoghue's book (Item 286), aimed at a general audience.

496. Downie, J.A. "Swift's Dismal." N&Q, 223 (1978), 43.

     Replying to A.J. Varney (Item 619), Downie points out that
     Nottingham was by no means an eloquent orator, and Swift does not
     play off an assumption of that eloquence in his satire. Rather,
     Swift was using an old formula to ridicule Nottingham's speech.

497. Ehrenpreis, Irvin. "Meaning: Implicit and Explicit." Pp. 117-55 of
     New Approaches to Eighteenth-Century Literature: Selected Papers
     from the English Institute. Edited by Phillip Harth. New York and
     London: Columbia U. Press, 1974.

     Pp. 150-53 are an argument, contra Barry Slepian (RES, n.s. 14
     (1963), 249-56), that the eulogy in Verses on the Death of Dr. Swift
     should be taken as straightforward.

498. England, A.B. Byron's Don Juan and Eighteenth-Century Literature: A
     Study of Some Rhetorical Continuities and Discontinuities.
     Lewisberg, Pa.: Bucknell U. Press, 1975. Pp. 197.

Rev. in Scriblerian, 9 (1976), 54.

Chapter two, "Byron, Swift, Butler, and Burlesque," studies Swift's poetry along the lines of England's earlier article (Item 501). (See below.)

499. England, A.B. Energy and Order in the Poetry of Swift. Lewisberg, Pa.: Bucknell U. Press, 1980. Pp. 241.

Rev. (with reservations) by Nora Crow Jaffe in Scriblerian, 13 (1981), 112-14; by Patricia Brückmann in University of Toronto Quarterly, 51 (1982), 419-20.

Stylistic analysis of various ways in which Swift flouts traditionally ordered poetic discourse: for example, the "apparent violation of orderly sequence by the force of spontaneous impulse," or "an anarchic inventiveness that expresses itself particularly through metaphor." England is also shrewdly aware of opposite tendencies in some of Swift's poems. And his conclusions never are lazily reached nor left unexamined. This is perhaps the most provocative writing on Swift's poetry to date.

500. England, A.B. "Rhetorical Order and Emotional Turbulence in Cadenus and Vanessa." PLL, 14 (1978), 116-23.

Rept. as pp. 69-78 of Contemporary Studies of Swift's Poetry. Edited by John Irwin Fischer and Donald C. Mell, Jr. With David M. Vieth as Associate Editor. Newark, Del.: U. of Delaware Press, 1981.

In the midst of the highly ordered rhetorical frameworks erected by the poem, Swift constantly implies the presence of unruly emotions, not to diminish those emotions by making them fall woefully short of the authoritative order implied by the poem's rhetoric, but to undermine the notion that neat structures and systems are adequate means of defining and containing the emotional experience.

501. England, A.B. "The Style of Don Juan and Augustan Poetry." Pp. 94-112 of Byron: A Symposium. Edited by John D. Jump. London: Macmillan; New York: Barnes & Noble, 1975.

Swift's distinctive version of the burlesque mode breaks down rather than enforces ordinary distinctions between physical and abstract words, constantly undermining hierarchies. One of his major tendencies is to enumerate miscellaneous specifics without providing coherent patterns, which England illustrates in "A Description of a City Shower."

502. England, A.B. "The Subversion of Logic in Some Poems by Swift." SEL, 15 (1975), 409-18.

In "The Description of a Salamander," "The Fable of Midas," "The Virtues of Sid Hamet the Magician's Rod," and "A Serious Poems upon William Wood," techniques of formal logic are actually devices by which Swift lures his readers into ironic complexities beyond the logician's scope.

503. England, A.B. "Swift's 'An Elegy on Mr. Partrige' and Cowley's 'On the Death of Mr. Crashaw'." N&Q, 218 (1973), 412-13.

Swift's changing attitude towards Cowley--an interesting index of his development as a poet--is further illuminated by this "imitation."

504. England, A. B. "World Without Order: Some Thoughts on the Poetry of Swift." Essays in Criticism, 16 (1966), 32-43.

England's thesis is that Swift insists upon a "shifting inconclusiveness" to generate the special disconcertment of his satire. The poems he discusses to illustrate this are "The Lady's Dressing Room," "Verses Wrote in a Lady's Ivory Table-Book," "On Dreams," "A Description of the Morning," "On Poetry: A Rapsody," and "Mrs. Harris's Petition."

505. Fabricant, Carole. "The Garden As City: Swift's Landscape of Alienation." ELH, 42 (1975), 531-55.

This detailed discussion of the Market Hill poems assumes that Swift's images of the landscape are meant to reveal some of his most profound judgments on confusion, collapse, and estrangement.

506. Fetting, Hans F. "Swift's Verses on the Death of Dr. Swift, 189-192." Explicator, 26, no. 9 (May 1968), Item £75.

Walpole's question in line 191 ("Why is he dead without his shoes?") is a turn on the usual English proverb meaning to die a sudden death. However, Motteux and Gay used the expression in the sense of being hanged.

507. Fischer, John I. "Apparent Contraries: A Reading of Swift's 'A Description of a City Shower'." Tennessee Studies in Literature, 19 (1974), 21-34.

The poem creates for readers much the same problem faced by the poet described in them: the meaning of events grows less distinct than our expectations. The monumental and the insignificant, the tragic and the comic "blur together in a haze which obscures their significance even as it bestows upon the event itelf a preternatural clarity." Meaning must finally be sought "in Swift's own vibrant consciousness of the finally mysterious autonomy of life"--a consciousness "in every way the reverse of that habit of mind" which drive men to seek certainty in the story of Noah.

508. Fischer, John Irwin. "The Dean <u>Contra</u> Heathens: Swift's The Day of
     Judgement." <u>Revue</u> <u>des</u> <u>Langues</u> <u>Vivantes</u>, 43 (1977), 592-97.

     This is an interesting, but not conclusive, attempt to mediate
     between reading the poem as specific satire on dissenters and seeing
     it as a general attack on human nature.

509. Fischer, John Irwin. "Faith, Hope, and Charity in Swift's Poems to
     Stella." <u>PLL</u>, 14 (1978), 123-29.

     Rept. as pp. 79-86 of <u>Contemporary</u> <u>Studies</u> <u>of</u> <u>Swift's</u> <u>Poetry</u>.
     Edited by John Irwin Fischer and Donald C. Mell, Jr. With David M.
     Vieth as Associate Editor. Newark, Del.: U. of Delaware Press,
     1981.

     A concise, but rich, reading of the Stella poems as versions of
     Christian consolation.

510. Fischer, John Irwin. "How to Die: <u>Verses</u> <u>on</u> <u>the</u> <u>Death</u> <u>of</u> <u>Dr.</u> <u>Swift</u>."
     <u>RES</u>, n.s. 21 (1970), 422-41.

     Fischer's conclusion is that "Neither the panegyric, then, nor the
     whole of the <u>Verses</u> should be understood as a praise of Swift's
     stoic fortitude in the face of adversities, but rather as a praise
     of his ability, through trust in God, to translate these adversities
     to positive goods." He reaches it by stressing that Swift proceeded
     from the traditional Christian ethic that "the love we have for our
     friend is founded in our own self-love," and by recognizing that the
     language of the concluding eulogy alludes frequently to Scripture.
     Swift presents himself as a sincere model in the eulogy by drawing
     from all the adversities of his life his own true good.

511. Fischer, John Irwin. <u>On</u> <u>Swift's</u> <u>Poetry</u>. Gainesville: U. of Florida
     Press, 1978. Pp. viii + 207.

     Rev. (with another work) by Kenneth J. Wagner in <u>University</u> <u>of</u>
     <u>Toronto</u> <u>Quarterly</u>, 48 (1978-79), 182-85; (with another work) by
     Peter J. Schakel in <u>Scriblerian</u>, 10 (1978), 122-24; in review art.
     ("Embodiment in Literature: Swift's Blasted Pocky Muse of Poetry")
     by John R. Clark in <u>Thalia</u>, 2, no. 3 (Winter, 1979-80), 23-33; in
     review art. ("Swift's Poetry and the Critics") by Louise K.
     Barnett in <u>Review</u>, 2 (1980), 41-48; (favorably, and with another
     work) by Richard Rodino in <u>ECCB</u>, n.s. 4 (1981), 460-62;
     (favorably) by Francis Doherty in <u>RES</u>, n.s. 30 (1979), 353-55;
     (with another work) by Merritt Eugene Lawlis in <u>JEGP</u>, 80 (1981),
     138-40; by Clive T. Probyn in <u>TLS</u>, Nov. 17, 1978, p. 1334; by
     James L. Tyne, S.J., in <u>Thought:</u> <u>A</u> <u>Review</u> <u>of</u> <u>Culture</u> <u>and</u> <u>Idea</u>, 54
     (1979), 111-12; in review art. ("Gentle Readings: Recent Work on
     Swift") by William Kinsley in <u>ECS</u>, 15 (1982), 442-53.

     This is a highly selective study, analyzing relatively few poems at
     considerable length. Fischer leaves out poems about which he feels

he has nothing new to add, including the scatological poems, but
finds an amount to say about some poems (twenty-three pages about
"Vanbrug's House," for example) that may surprise some readers.
However, for all the length of his individual analyses, Fischer's
book is more than a series of close readings. His argument is that
"Swift's lifelong task was to temper his hubristic sense of
righteousness with a standard of judgment larger than himself." By
the same token, though, there is nothing dogmatic about the
argument; detail is never for the sake of scholarly show, but
conveys some of the feeling of a learned, tentative, deliberative
reading. If there is a failing, it is that Fischer sometimes loses
the sheer fun of reading Swift.

512. Fischer, John Irwin. "The Uses of Virtue: Swift's Last Poem to
     Stella." Pp. 201-09 of Essays in Honor of Esmond Linworth Marilla.
     Edited by Thomas Austin Kirby and William John Olive. Baton Rouge:
     Louisiana State U. Press, 1970.

     The strategy of Swift's last Stella poem is determined by his view
     of faith: faith is apparent to the virtuous man, and therefore the
     assent to faith must be made, not through assertion or argument, but
     through the practice of virtue. Therefore the poem employs such
     tactics as making Stella "a type of the very providential care which
     is in doubt" and offering Swift himself as an object for Stella's
     pity, which provides her both with a model of practical virtue and
     an occasion for the exercise of her own virtue.

513. Fischer, John Irwin, and Donald C. Mell, Jr. (eds.). Contemporary
     Studies of Swift's Poetry. With David M. Vieth as Associate
     Editor. Newark: U. of Delaware Press, 1981. Pp. 215.

     Includes the following essays (listed separately): John Irwin
     Fischer, "Introduction: 'All ... Manifestly Deduceable'"; David
     Sheehan, "Swift on High Pindaric Stilts"; Donna G. Fricke, "Swift
     and the Tradition of Informal Satiric Poetry"; Arthur H. Scouten,
     "Swift's Poetry and the Gentle Reader"; David M. Vieth, "Metaphors
     and Metamorphoses: Basic Techniques in the Middle Period of Swift's
     Poetry, 1698-1719"; A.B. England, "Rhetorical Order and Emotional
     Turbulence in 'Cadenus and Vanessa'"; John Irwin Fischer, "Faith,
     Hope, and Charity in Swift's Poems to Stella"; Richard H. Rodino,
     "Notes on the Developing Motives and Structures of Swift's Poetry";
     Louise K. Barnett, "Fictive Self-Portraiture in Swift's Poetry";
     James Woolley, "Autobiography in Swift's Verses on His Death";
     Donald C. Mell, Jr. "Imagination and Satiric Mimesis in Swift's
     Poetry: An Exploratory Discussion"; Peter J. Schakel, "Swift's
     Remedy for Love: The 'Scatological' Poems"; Nora Crow Jaffe, "Swift
     and the 'agreeable young Lady, but extremely lean'"; Thomas B.
     Gilmore, Jr. "Freud, Swift, and Narcissism: A Psychological Reading
     of 'Strephon and Chloe'"; Robert W. Uphaus, "Swift's Irony
     Reconsidered"; Aubrey L. Williams, "'A vile Encomium': That
     'Panegyric on the Reverend D--n S--t'"; James Woolley, "Arbuckle's
     'Panegyric' and Swift's Scrub Libel: The Documentary Evidence."

514. Fisher, Alan S. "Swift's Verse Portraits: A Study of His Originality
     as an Augustan Satirist." <u>SEL</u>, 14 (1974), 343-56.

     From the premise that every literary portrait is a metaphor, Fisher
     shows that Swift's portrait satire works by showing us the world in
     terms of process, not essence, by assuming that devaluation is
     truth, and by positing irreverent critical intelligence as the
     closest thing to a true ideal. Even scepticism is rendered
     sceptically. All the portraits entertain the reader with a jest,
     usually playing off a standard formula to reach unexpected
     consequences. Fisher moves to Swift's satire as a whole, arguing
     that "we are left with a sense that life forces us to pick our way
     through diverse paths of wrongness," and though complacency will not
     do, neither do we get a sense that anything we can do will help. And
     yet, Swift never entirely ignores the possibility of reform.
     Analyses of "Vanbrug's House," "The Salamander," and Swift's
     "Satirical Elegy" on Marlborough illustrate these points.

515. Fox, Jeffrey R. "Swift's 'Scatological' Poems: The Hidden Norm."
     <u>Thoth</u>, 15 (1975), 3-13.

     The conclusions of this essay are similar to those of John Aden
     (Item 420).

516. Fricke, Donna G. "Jonathan Swift's Early Odes and the Conversion to
     Satire." <u>Enlightenment</u> Essays, 5, no. 2 (Summer 1974), 3-17.

     Underplaying the satiric qualities of the odes, Fricke points out
     that the high emotional content of Swift's youthful writing made the
     pindaric at least theoretically an appropriate mode and she argues
     that Swift fully understood the nature and tradition of the ode.

517. Fricke, Donna G. "Swift and the Tradition of Informal Satiric
     Poetry." Pp. 36-45 of <u>Contemporary</u> Studies of Swift's Poetry.
     Edited by John Irwin Fischer and Donald C. Mell, Jr. With David M.
     Vieth as Associate Editor. Newark, Del.: U. of Delaware Press,
     1981.

     Fricke reminds us that Swift's poetry was not a rhetorical revolt,
     but rather belongs to a different literary tradition from that of
     Dryden and Pope--a more indigenous English form of octosyllabic
     couplets, colloquial tones, and, often, negative vision.

518. Fricke, Donna G. "Swift, Hogarth, and the Sister Arts."
     <u>Eighteenth-Century</u> Life, 2 (1975), 29-33.

     Emphasizing Hogarth's understanding of Swift's "excremental" and
     "grotesque" visions, Fricke describes general similarities (but not
     dissimilarities) between the works of Hogarth and Swift, especially
     "A Beautiful Young Nymph" and the "Progress" poems and <u>A Harlot's
     Progress</u>.

519. Gilmore, Thomas B., Jr. "The Comedy of Swift's Scatological Poems."
     PMLA, 91 (1976), 33-43.

     See the exchange among Donald Greene ("Neither as a Christian
     clergyman, nor as someone familiar with the elements of classical
     and Renaissance literary theory, would Swift have conceded that
     there is any justification for comic satire ... except
     'didacticism'"), Peter J. Schakel ("the scatological poems show us
     a more human Swift, fallible, uncertain, struggling--trying to
     work through his feelings, but not succeeding entirely") and
     Gilmore in the "Forum" section of PMLA, 91 (1976), 464-67.

     Stressing the "nonsatiric comedy" of Swift's scatological poems,
     Gilmore asserts that "Corinna's daily resurrections link her with
     Falstaff," and that the narrator of "The Lady's Dressing Room"
     represents true maturity compared to Strephon's overwrought
     reactions, among other controversial statements.

520. Gilmore, Thomas B., Jr. "Freud and Swift: A Psychological Reading of
     Strephon and Chloe." PLL, 14 (1978), 147-51.

     Rept. (as "Freud, Swift, and Narcissism: A Psychological Reading
     of 'Strephon and Chloe'") as pp. 159-68 of Contemporary Studies of
     Swift's Poetry. Edited by John Irwin Fischer and Donald C. Mell,
     Jr. With David M. Vieth as Associate Editor. Newark, Del.: U. of
     Delaware Press, 1981.

     Arguing that Strephon's "rouzer" provides a liberating and
     pleasurable experience for the reader, Gilmore sees a later passage
     (11. 203-18) as surprising readers by exposing the lovers' seemingly
     "innocent if infantile sexuality" as "a symptom of anal fixation or
     eroticism resulting from narcissism." Gilmore's focus on readers'
     psychology, rather than Swift's own "neuroses," seems less morbid
     and more useful than most psychological criticism of Swift.

521. Greene, Donald. "On Swift's 'Scatological' Poems." Sewanee Review,
     75 (1967), 672-89.

     Stressing Swift's orthodox Christian condemnation of ego-bolstering
     illusions, Greene argues that the poems present Swift's comic
     acceptance of imperfect reality: "If Swift makes much frank mention
     of the human excremental function, it is in order to discount its
     importance and satirize those who think it is important, in the hope
     that those obsessed by its importance may come to revise their
     values." An important answer to Norman O. Brown.

522. Gubar, Susan. "The Female Monster in Augustan Satire." Signs:
     Journal of Women in Culture and Society, 3 (1977-78), 380-94.

     See the exchange between Ellen Pollak ("Comment on Susan Gubar's
     'The Female Monster in Augustan Satire'") and Gubar ("Reply to

Pollak") in Signs: Journal of Women in Culture and Society, 3 (1978), 728-33.

Focusing on the scatological poems, this essay rejects the arguments of both Norman O. Brown and Donald Greene, as well as various rhetorical readings of Swift's satire, to assert that "Swift describes his own inability to accept the ambiguities and contradictions of the human condition, portraying his failure in the figure of the repulsive female." Gubar's own responses are curiously close in spirit to those of Middleton Murry and Orwell. Pollak distinguishes Swift from his contemporaries by his deliberate use of anti-feminine images to reveal the inadequacy of his society's view of women.

523. Haas, Rudolf. "Swift's Description of a City Shower als satirische Sozialkritik." Pp. 164-68 of Theorie und Praxis der Interpretation: Modellanalysen englischer und amerikanischer Texte. Berlin: Erich Schmidt, 1977.

524. Hagstrum, Jean H. "Verbal and Visual Caricature in the Age of Dryden, Swift and Pope." Pp. 173-95 of England in the Restoration and Early Eighteenth Century: Essays on Culture and Society. Edited by H.T. Swedenberg, Jr. Berkeley, Los Angeles, London: U. of California Press, 1972.

Swift's use of what Hagstrum calls "emblematic caricature"--shorthand allegory, animal grotesquerie, fierce reductiveness--is illustrated by "Ode to the King," verses to Lady Acheson, "Description of a Salamander," and other poems.

525. Halsband, Robert. "'The Lady's Dressing Room' Explicated by a Contemporary." Pp. 225-31 of The Augustan Milieu: Essays Presented to Louis A. Landa . Edited by Henry Knight Miller, Eric Rothstein, and G.S. Rousseau. Oxford: Clarendon Press, 1970.

Reprints the attack on Swift's coarseness and obscenity in "The Dean's Provocation For Writing The Lady's Dressing Room" (1734) by Lady Mary Wortley Montagu.

526. Harris, Kathryn Montgomery. "'Occasions So Few': Satire As a Strategy of Praise in Swift's Early Odes." MLQ, 31 (1970), 22-37.

Swift characteristically praises the heroes of his odes for surviving in an evil world, but he alters the traditional proportions of praise and blame to focus on the satiric target. This source of the odes' comparative failure is nevertheless a primary link between them and his mature work.

527. Heinemann, M. "Swift's 'Corinna' Again." N&Q, 217 (1972), 218-21.

"Corinna" is neither Mrs. Manley nor Mrs. Haywood, but "a composite

description of the woman writers, reputedly licentious, who work for
Curll."

528. Hill, Geoffrey. "Jonathan Swift: The Poetry of Reaction." Pp.
     195-212 of The World of Jonathan Swift: Essays for the
     Tercentenary. Edited by Brian Vickers. Cambridge, Ma.: Harvard U.
     Press; Oxford: Basil Blackwell, 1968.

     Emphasizes the co-existences of extreme tendencies in Swift and the
     close connection in his work between public and private issues.
     Swift abhorred the anarchic in theory, but it kindled a poetical
     fire in him.

529. Hirai, Takashi. "Philemon to Baucis no henbo." ["The Metamorphosis
     of Philemon and Baucis."] English and English-American Literature
     (Yamaguchi U.), 12 (1977), 17-32.

     Noted in Scriblerian, 11 (1979), 97.

     A comparison of Dryden's and Swift's versions.

530. Horne, C.J. "'From a Fable Form A Truth': A Consideration of the
     Fable in Swift's Poetry." Pp. 193-204 of Studies in the Eighteenth
     Century: Papers Presented at the David Nichol Smith Memorial
     Seminar, Canberra 1966. Edited by R.F. Brissenden. Canberra:
     Australian National U. Press; Toronto: U. of Toronto Press, 1968.

     Very general remarks on Swift's versions of Ovidian and Aesopian
     fables, with special attention to "Baucis and Philemon," "The Fable
     of Midas," "The Faggott," "The Bubble," and "The Beasts Confession."

531. Horne, Colin J. "Swift's Comic Poetry." Pp. 51-67 of Augustan
     Worlds: New Essays in Eighteenth-Century Literature in Honour of
     A.R. Humphreys. Edited by J.C. Hilson, M.M.B Jones, and J.R.
     Watson. New York: Barnes & Noble; Leicester: U. of Leicester
     Press, 1978.

     Directs attention to poems and passages of poems that are comic "in
     the more popular sense of that term as being funny." No attempt is
     made to show how comedy functions as merely one element in a complex
     mixture in poems such as "A Beautiful Young Nymph" and Verses on the
     Death of Dr. Swift.

532. Hunter, J. Paul. Occasional Form: Henry Fielding and the Chains of
     Circumstance. Baltimore and London: Johns Hopkins U. Press, 1975.
     Pp. xiv + 263.

     Pp. 36-40 describe Fielding's debts in The Tragedy of Tragedies. to
     "City Shower," "Description of the Morning," and Gulliver's Travels.

533. Irwin, W.R. "Swift the Verse Man." PQ, 54 (1975), 222-38.

This study of the "methods of light verse" stresses tricks of style, representations of the mechanical, rehearsal of details, exploitation of occasions, incisive declaration, and detachment of performer from performance.

534. Jaffe, Nora Crow. The Poet Swift. Hanover: University Press of New England, 1977. Pp. x + 190.

Rev. in review art. ("Swift's Poetry and the Critics") by Louise K. Barnett in Review, 2 (1980), 41-48; (with reservations) by Maurice Johnson in ECS, 11 (1978), 410-13; (with reservations) by John M. Aden in South Atlantic Quarterly, 77 (1978), 384-85; in review art. ("Embodiment in Literature: Swift's Blasted Pocky Muse of Poetry") by John R. Clark in Thalia, 2, no. 3 (Winter, 1979-80), 23-33; in review art. ("Recent Studies in the Restoration and Eighteenth Century") by G.S. Rousseau in SEL, 18 (1978), 553-93; (with another work) by Peter J. Schakel in Scriblerian, 10 (1978), 122-24; (with another work) by Kenneth J. Wagner in University of Toronto Quarterly, 48 (1978-79), 182-85; by Colin J. Horne in MLR, 75 (1980), 852-54; (favorably, and with another work) by Richard Rodino in ECCB, n.s. 4 (1981), 460-62; (with other works) by Max Byrd in Yale Review, 67 (1977-78), 424-30; (with another work) by Merritt Eugene Lawlis in JEGP, 80 (1981), 138-40; by Claude Rawson in TLS, Feb. 10, 1978, p. 165.

The first chapter of The Poet Swift seems based on some widely held and questionable assumptions about Swift's poetry: that it is a more or less homogeneous batch, sui generis, that it did not evolve much, if at all, during the course of Swift's career, and that it cannot be read as one reads other poetry. Furthermore, in a book dated 1977, Jaffe ignores quite a lot of the really good critical work of the early 1970's, though in a short preface she sums up as best she can a scholarly situation that is changing too quickly and substantially for anyone to have much of an overview. The value of an introductory study such as this lies in the quality of its analysis, and in The Poet Swift, close readings of individual poems are the strongest features, with special attention to poems poetry, the early odes, the two "Description" poems, poems Stella, the excremental poems, verses of daily social life, poems of anger (mostly political). Always intelligible, generally graceful, Jaffe does the best job yet of describing a "biographical presence" that Maurice Johnson predicted would but key to Swift's poetry.

535. Jaffe, Nora Crow. "Swift and the 'agreeable young L extremely lean'." PLL, 14 (1978), 129-37.

Rept. as pp. 149-58 of Contemporary Studies of Swift Poetry. Edited by John Irwin Fischer and Donald C. Mell, Jr. With David M. Vieth as Associate Editor. Newark, Del.: U. of Delare Press, 1981.

Reading "Death" as a stand-in for Swift himself in his relation to
Lady Acheson, or "Life," Jaffe finds "Death and Daphne" (1730) to be
Swift's clearest statement about the tutorial relationships he
adopted with Vanessa, Stella, and Lady Acheson herself.

536. Jefferson, D.W. "The Poetry of Age." Pp. 121-137 of Focus: Swift.
     Edited by C.J. Rawson. London: Sphere Books, 1971.

     Quite a general introduction, mentioning Swift's frequent
     adaptation, then perversion, of a classical model to enhance a
     personal or contemporary subject, his use of a mythological setting
     furnished with traditional images and inherited concepts, and the
     increased personal element in his later poetry.

537. Johnson, Maurice. "Swift's Poetry Reconsidered." Pp. 233-48 of
     English Writers of the Eighteenth Century. Edited by John H.
     Middendorf. New York and London: Columbia U. Press, 1971.

     Johnson calls attention to several important patterns in Swift's
     verse: mutually exclusive opposites; item by item deflation; comedy
     of continuity by means of a seemingly undiscriminating continuum of
     items. However, his primary purpose is to plead for attention to the
     "biographical presence" that "one strongly feels but cannot quite
     account for in much of Swift's poetry."

538. Jones, Gareth. "Swift's Cadenus and Vanessa: A Question of
     'Positives'." Essays in Criticism, 20 (1970), 424-40.

     Rev. (favorably) in Scriblerian, 3 (1970), 58-59.

     This is a close reading of the poem, which concludes that Swift's
     purpose is "to compel us, by tempting us ever and again to rest
     thankful in the easy certainties of judgment, and then subverting
     those certainties, not merely to contemplate but to live the
     difficulties of our predicament." A very influential essay.

39. Jump, John D. Burlesque. (Critical Idiom Series.) London: Methuen;
    New York: Barnes & Noble, 1972. Pp. x + 77.

    Briefly discusses Baucis and Philemon as an example of travesty.

5.
    Kelly, Ann Cline. "A Rowlands-Butler-Swift Parallel." N&Q, 219
    (1974), 101-02.

    ift's imitation of "Hoc Erat in Votis" echoes both Hudibras, III,
    1277-78, and Samuel Rowlands's Good Newes and Bad Newes (1622).

541. Kl, Julie B. "The Art of Apology: 'An Epistle to Dr. Arbuthnot'
     a 'Verses on the Death of Dr. Swift'." Costerus, 8 (1973),
     77 7.

A reading of the Verses as a conventional "neoclassical" apologia in the tradition of Horace, Juvenal, and Persius. The richness with which Slepian, Waingrow, Scouten and Hume have taught us to read the poem is conspicuously missing.

542. Loffredo, Irene. "Minus amant qui acute vident. Elementi rinascimentali negli 'unprintable poems' di Jonathan Swift." Pp. 196-205 of La materialità del testo. Ricerca interdisciplinare sulle pratiche significanti. (Il lavoro critico/semiotica, 11.) Verona: Bertani, 1977.

543. Manousos, Anthony. "Swiftian Scatology and Lockian Psychology." Gypsy Scholar, 7 (1980), 15-25.

The Strephon poems illustrate Locke's point that linking independent ideas will lead to delusions. The essay is not well enough focused on Locke to be as helpful as the title suggests.

544. Mell, Donald C. "Elegiac Design and Satiric Intention in 'Verses on the Death of Dr. Swift'." Concerning Poetry, 6, no. 2 (Fall 1973), 15-24.

Rept. as pp. 53-62 of A Poetics of the Augustan Elegy: Studies of Poems by Dryden, Pope, Prior, Swift, Gray, and Johnson. Amsterdam: Rodopi, 1974 (distributed through Forest Grove, Ore.: International Scholarly Books Services, 1976). Pp. 116.

By maintaining a fragile balance between traditional elegiac features and the conventions of satire, Swift expresses his confidence in the "redemptive or restorative" aspects of art itself.

545. Mell, Donald C., Jr. "Imagination and Satiric Mimesis in Swift's Poetry: An Exploratory Discussion." Pp. 123-35 of Contemporary Studies of Swift's Poetry. Edited by John Irwin Fischer and Donald C. Mell, Jr. With David M. Vieth as Associate Editor. Newark, Del.: U. of Delaware Press, 1981.

Mell argues that Swift's distrust of the imaginative idealizations of art is "actually not anti-poetic but pro-poetic, and represents an indirect expression of a belief in art's moral force."

546. Moskovit, Leonard A. "Pope and the Tradition of the Neoclassical Imitation." SEL, 8 (1968), 445-62.

"Part of the Seventh Epistle of the First Book of Horace Imitated" gives Swift a classically authoritative basis for treating humorously what might otherwise be seen as deception or ingratitude; "Toland's Invitation to Dismal," on the other hand, creates an ironic disparity between the base and ludicrous activities of the persons attacked and the noble and civilized activities alluded to.

547. Motto, Anna Lydia, and John R. Clark. "Idyllic Slumming 'Midst Urban
     Hordes: the Satiric Epos in Theocritus and Swift." Classical
     Bulletin, 47 (1971), 39-44.

     A discussion of "A Description of a City Shower" for classroom use,
     focusing on "Swift's brilliance in turning the traditional
     references to the Trojan War most fully on their ear."

548. Munker, Dona F. "That Paultry Burlesque Stile: Seventeenth-Century
     Poetry and Augustan 'Low Seriousness'." Seventeenth-Century News,
     33 (1975), 14-22.

     Contains a good discussion of the difficulties of "The Lady's
     Dressing Room" together with the unnecessary plea that Swift's
     "down-to-earth" verses be regarded as a "valid" development in
     English poetry.

549. Naumov, Nicifor. "Poezija Dzonatana Swifta." ["The Poetry of
     Jonathan Swift."] Anali Filoloskoq Faulteta (Belgrade U.), 7
     (1967), 401-32.

     Naumov buttresses his claims for the importance of Swift's poetry by
     analyses of Verses on the Death of Dr. Swift, Cadenus and Vanessa,
     the Stella poems, "On Poetry: A Rapsody," Baucis and Philemon, and
     "Mrs. Harris's Petition." Includes a summary of the essay in
     English.

550. Nemoianu, Virgil. "Swift Printu Stiluri." ["Swift Among the
     Styles."] Seculol XX, 9 (1967), 195-99.

551. Nemoianu, Virgil. "Swift şi istoria rimei engleze." ["Swift and the
     History of English Rhyme."] Revista de istorie şi teorie literara
     (Bucarest), 16 (1967), 441-48.

     Taking off from the work of Quintana and Price, Nemoianu classifies
     Swift's verse as follows: odes, realistic descriptive poems, and
     political polemics. In all his poetry, Swift's constant goal is to
     impose rationalistic order on the anarchy of reality.

552. Nussbaum, Felicity. "Juvenal, Swift, and The Folly of Love." ECS, 9
     (1976), 540-52.

     This examination of "the tradition of satires directed at women as a
     context for reading Swift's 'A Beautiful Young Nymph Going to Bed'"
     leads to the conclusion that Swift's contribution to the tradition
     is to "allow" sympathy for Corinna's plight. However, though Swift
     does not indict the entire sex, he does associate "the loss of
     reason--madness--with most women, and he warns against the perils of
     the imagination."

An idea "similar" to Betty fleeing her master's bed is present in Richard Blackmore's Prince Arthur.

566. Real, Hermann J. ["Puppy Water in the Eighteenth Century."] Scriblerian, 11 (1979), 145.

Noting additional references to cosmetic terms such as "puppy water," Real suggests that "we either have to discard the notion of Swift's excremental vision altogether or to declare the whole lot insane."

567. Real, Hermann. "A Recipe for Puppy Water." Scriblerian, 7 (1975), 121-22.

Reprints the recipe for "To make Pig, or Puppidog, Water for the Face" from Mundus Muliebris: Or, the Ladies Dressing-Room Unlock'd (London, 1690).

568. Real, Hermann J. "Swift's 'A Satirical Elegy on the Death of a Late Famous General'." Explicator, 36, no. 2 (Winter, 1978), 26-27.

Real excuses Swift for speaking ill of the dead since a sentence in the Journal to Stella suggests that Swift (echoing Samuel Butler in "Upon Modern Critics"?) thought of Marlborough as no ordinary satiric victim but as the devil himself!

569. Real, Hermann J., and Heinz J. Vienken. [Correspondence.] Scriblerian, 13 (1980), 51.

Corroborates Frances Harris's pregnancy (see Item 572) by references to seventeenth-century connections between money and sex.

570. Rees, Christine. "Gay, Swift, and the Nymphs of Drury-Lane." Essays in Criticism, 23 (1973), 1-21.

This brief history of the fiction of the "'nymph' whose beauty is satirically defined by the conflicting principles of art and nature" sheds some light on "The Lady's Dressing Room," "The Progress of Beauty" and "A Beautiful Young Nymph Going to Bed." (Particularly useful is Rees's little history of tulip imagery in connection with the final line of "The Lady's Dressing Room.") In distinguishing Swift from Gay, she stresses the former's attack on the "fictions of poetry."

571. Reichard, Hugo M. "The Self-Praise Abounding in Swift's Verses." Tennessee Studies in Literature, 18 (1973), 105-12.

Reichard argues that self-praise suffuses the entire poem but is "variously concealed and cushioned by a range of expedients and consequences" until the eulogy. He concludes that as Swift buoys

himself up, "so he contrives stealthily to hold humanity's head
above water," in a "much-tempered compliment to human nature."

572. Reynolds, Richard. "Swift's 'Humble Petition' from a Pregnant
     Frances Harris?" Scriblerian, 5 (1972), 38-39.

     Yes, argues this article, by pointing to a few plays on words and by
     references to Frances Harris's "narrative and tone," her situation
     and her ambition. See also Item 569.

573. Risk, May H. "'Bradley the taylor'." Hermathena, 108 (Spring 1969),
     18-23.

     In "The Yahoo's Overthrow," there is a reference to Richard Bradley
     who, though obscure, was "indeed a byword for religious
     eccentricity."

574. Roberts, Philip. "Swift, Queen Anne, and The Windsor Prophecy." PQ,
     49 (1970), 254-58.

     New evidence from the diary of Sir David Hamilton, physician to the
     Queen, indicates how much in the dark Swift was in supposing that
     The Windsor Prophecy could produce anything but more trouble for
     Swift himself.

575. Rodino, Richard H. "Blasphemy or Blessing? Swift's 'Scatological'
     Poems." PLL, 14 (1978), 152-70.

     Swift's poems about women from 1696-1730 work through normative
     "Augustan" structures of definition and consolidation, but the
     unprintable poems of 1730-33 (along with "The Progress of Beauty,"
     1719) force readers to choose between being fools or knaves. In the
     "Lady's Dressing Room," for example, we are the butts of a serious
     joke, nearly embracing "gaudy Tulips rais'd from Dung" as a
     "blessing." "The Progress of Beauty" manipulates readers into
     expecting some middle ground resolution of its problems, then
     presents them with the speaker's inhuman cheerfulness at the
     spectacle of a diseased woman. "Vexatious" writing is "moral" only
     by the extent to which it allows the reader some motive, however
     tenuous, to resist its own extreme indifference to moral reform and
     to seek a way out of the impasse.

576. Rodino, Richard H. "Notes on the Developing Motives and Structures
     of Swift's Poetry." Pp. 87-100 of Contemporary Studies of Swift's
     Poetry. Edited by John Irwin Fischer and Donald C. Mell, Jr. With
     David M. Vieth as Associate Editor. Newark, Del.: U. of Delaware
     Press, 1981.

     The deteriorating relations between symbol and idea in Swift's early
     odes are replaced by normative Augustan structures in the period

1698-1714, including the inclusiveness of a middle ground of
compromise, the exclusiveness of normative comparisons, and the
serial structure (e.g., "The Author Upon Himself," "A Description of
the Morning") of an empirical epistemology. Between 1730 and 1733,
however, Swift's motives were more radical and urgent; his
characteristic structures involve deliberate fraudulence and
entrapment of the audience.

577. Rodino, Richard H. "Robert Gould and Swift's 'The Day of
Judgement'." N&Q, 224 (1979), 549.

The likely source of ll. 15-16 of Swift's "greatest poem" ("You who
in different Sects have shamm'd, / And come to see each other
damn'd") is Gould's A Satyr against Man (London, 1709. 2 Vols.).
Also, Swift's famous self-description, "He lash'd the Vice but
spar'd the Name," appears in almost exactly the same form in Gould's
"Advertisement" to the same volume.

578. Rodino, Richard Hodge. "The Private Sense of Cadenus and Vanessa."
Concerning Poetry, 11, no. 2 (Fall, 1978), 41-47.

Read as a private document between Swift and Vanessa, the poem
creates a series of impasses beween extremes of conduct. Through its
"serial process" of ironic oppositions and to-and-fro movements, the
poem is open-ended, accurately describing a relationship that defies
logical or even wholly rational explication.

579. Rosenheim, Edward W. "Swift's Ode to Sancroft: Another Look." MP, 73
(1976), S24-S39.

Rosenheim looks at the poem, not as a dutiful tribute to an outlawed
prelate, but as a partisan and polemical document, addressed to a
specific, heated controversy between King William and the nonjurors.

580. Rothstein, Eric. "Jonathan Swift as Jupiter: 'Baucis and Philemon'."
Pp. 205-24 of The Augustan Milieu: Essays Presented to Louis A.
Landa . Edited by Henry Knight Miller, Eric Rothstein, and G.S.
Rousseau. Oxford: Clarendon, 1970.

Defends the revisions Swift made in "Baucis and Philemon" on
Addison's advice by insisting that they integrate the entire work in
the name of a multi-part "intention": (1) contemporary (Christian)
application of the myth; (2) defining of spiritual identity through
material change; (3) Providential justice.

581. Rowse, A.L. "Swift as Poet." Pp. 98-106 of Fair Liberty Was All His
Cry: A Tercentenary Tribute to Jonathan Swift 1667-1745. Edited by
A. Norman Jeffares. London: Macmillan; New York: St. Martin's
Press, 1967.

Orig. pub. (as "Jonathan Swift") in The English Spirit (1945).
Rept. as pp. 135-42 of Swift: Modern Judgements. Edited by A.
Norman Jeffares. London: Macmillan, 1969; Nashville, Tenn.:
Aurora, 1970; as pp. 170-78 of The English Spirit. 2nd. ed.
(Revised and reset.) London: Macmillan, 1966; rev. ed., New York:
Funk & Wagnalls, 1967.

Asserts that Swift's self-expression and development of themes are
both more complete and mature in his poetry than in his prose.
Though there is a lack of variety in tone, this is a function of
Swift pursuing his "chief emotion," intellectual passion, rather
than romantic inspiration.

582. San Juan, E., Jr. "The Anti-Poetry of Jonathan Swift." PQ, 44
(1965), 387-96.

The "anti-poetic" element in Swift's verse, in its concentration on
masses of detail, represents a "unifying sensibility," which
counteracted the "eighteenth-century tendency to narrow the language
of poetry and its range of subject matter." A well-meaning essay
that represents the best that 1965 could say of Swift's poetry,
rather than the opening of new avenues of appreciation.

583. Savage, Roger. "Swift's Fallen City: A Description of the Morning."
Pp. 171-94 of The World of Jonathan Swift: Essays for the
Tercentenary. Edited by Brian Vickers. Cambridge, Ma.: Harvard U.
Press; Oxford: Basil Blackwell, 1968.

Both the realistic present and the classical ideal are weighed and
found wanting in "A Description of the Morning," argues Savage in
this much-cited analysis. "City Shower" is also discussed.

584. Schakel, Peter J. The Poetry of Jonathan Swift: Allusion and the
Development of a Poetic Style. Madison and London: U. of Wisconsin
Press, 1978. Pp. x + 218.

Rev. (with reservations) by Dustin Griffin in JEGP, 78 (1979),
554-56; (favorably) by Francis Doherty in RES, n.s. 31 (1980),
469-70; (with another work) by Carole Fabricant in Criticism, 21
(1979), 369-74; in review art. ("Uncertainties of Satire") by
Patricia Meyer Spacks in MLQ, 40 (1979), 403-11; (favorably) by
Richard H. Rodino in Scriblerian, 12 (1979), 42-44; in review art.
("Embodiment in Literature: Swift's Blasted Pocky Muse of Poetry")
by John R. Clark in Thalia, 2, no. 3 (Winter, 1979-80), 23-33; in
review art. ("Gentle Readings: Recent Work on Swift") by William
Kinsley in ECS, 15 (1982), 442-53.

The better part of Schakel's aims is reached in good order: an
exploration of the ways Christian, classical, and contemporary
allusions modify or reinforce other designs in Swift's poems. Less
satisfying is the "development" Schakel plots out for Swift as poet
beginning with a conventional reading of the early odes. Chapter two

proposes to compare the two versions of "Vanbrug's House," which leads to some rather obvious points about "development," but also to some interesting connections among the poem, the Battle of the Books, and the Orpheus myth. His source-hunting enables Schakel to read Cadenus and Vanessa, in light of allusions to Virgil and Ovid, as a more toughminded presentation than has previously been thought; to interpret "A Beautiful Young Nymph" as an imitation of Ovid and therefore a failed comedy; to broaden our sense of the motives of "Verses on the Death of Dr. Swift," by the light of allusions to Opposition rhetoric; and to enrich "The Legion Club" by recognizing the full extent of biblical and classical allusions. Schakel's interpretations are provocative, and his scholarship is thorough and accurate.

585. Schakel, Peter J. "The Politics of Opposition in 'Verses on the Death of Dr. Swift'." MLQ, 35 (1974), 246-56.

Recognizing allusions which identify the eulogist as a member of the Tory Opposition helps Schakel to see the poem's theme of "private Ends" extended to an attack on all political parties and factions. The eulogist "uses Swift's death as the occasion, not for an unselfish bestowal of the praise Swift's life deserves, but for a speech which invokes Swift's image and accomplishments in order to advance the eulogist's continuing campaign against the Whig party."

586. Schakel, Peter J. "Swift's 'dapper Clerk' and the Matrix of Allusions in 'Cadenus and Vanessa'." Criticism, 17 (1975), 246-61.

Allusions to The Art of Love and to The Aeneid make the poem more than a personal statement of a private situation. It is an "examination of the universal human need for self-acceptance and self-sacrifice in love."

587. Schakel, Peter J. "Swift's Remedy for Love: The 'Scatological' Poems." PLL, 14 (1978), 137-47.

Rept. as pp. 136-48 of Contemporary Studies of Swift's Poetry. Edited by John Irwin Fischer and Donald C. Mell, Jr. With David M. Vieth as Associate Editor. Newark: U. of Delaware Press, 1981.

Because he assumes from the epigraph of "A Beautiful Young Nymph Going to Bed" that Swift must have been trying to write Ovidian comedies, Schakel finds the scatological poems to be revealing failures, disclosing "a fallible, uncertain, struggling Swift, trying to work through unwanted feelings, but not succeeding entirely."

588. Schakel, Peter J. "Swift's Verses Wrote in a Lady's Ivory Table-Book." Explicator, 28, no. 9 (May 1970), Item #83.

This is generally a sound reading of how the casual manner of the poem develops a complex satire. However, Schakel's assumption that the "Verses" referred to in the title are Swift's own poem, rather than the rhymed scribblings of fashionable men and women quoted in the poem, leads to a questionable interpretation of the ending.

589. Schakel, Peter J. "Virgil and the Dean: Christian and Classical Allusion in The Legion Club." SP, 70 (1973), 427-38.

Rept. (somewhat shortened) in The Poetry of Jonathan Swift: Allusion and the Development of a Poetic Style (1978) (Item 584).

Swift's allusions to Virgil and to the Bible work together, infusing his satirical poem with a universal standard by which he can damn corrupt legislators.

590. Scouten, Arthur H. "Swift's Poetry and the Gentle Reader." Pp. 46-55 of Contemporary Studies of Swift's Poetry. Edited by John Irwin Fischer and Donald C. Mell, Jr. With David M. Vieth as Associate Editor. Newark, Del.: U. of Delaware Press, 1981.

Scouten points out the need to distinguish between poems Swift intended for the general public and those which were designed for a specific, private audience. He goes on to warn against ignoring the playfulness of Swift's mind, overpraising minor, playful pieces, and using poems with cryptic and private references as the basis for serious analysis of Swift's verse.

591. Scouten, Arthur H., and Robert D. Hume. "Pope and Swift: Text and Interpretation of Swift's Verses on His Death." PQ, 52 (1973), 205-31.

Rev. in Scriblerian, 6 (1973), 80.

In a very influential essay, Scouten and Hume establish that only recently has the authentic text been subject to critical scrutiny. They read the eulogy as ironical, its praise burlesqued just enough that "the reader should be too delighted by the multiple ironies to resist the apologia."

592. Scruggs, Charles. "Swift's Views on Language: The Basis of His Attack on Poetic Diction." TSLL, 13 (1972), 581-92.

Defends Swift's criticism of poetical cliches and abstractions, his desire to "fix" the language against dishonesty, his insistence on simplicity, and his invigoration of old words in new contexts.

593. Sena, John F. "Swift as Moral Physician: Scatology and the Tradition of Love Melancholy." JEGP, 76 (1977), 346-62.

Ovid, Lucretius, Avicenna, Bernardus of Gordon, and other writers on the subject of "love melancholy" (considered a serious, debilitating disorder) advised a look at a <u>vetula</u>, or old hag, whose "ugly appearance and 'foul dispositions'" could shock a young man from his obsession with the female body. Or else they advised the lover to take a close look at his mistress's artifices or underlying ugliness. Viewed in the context of these traditional cures, Swift's poems "The Lady's Dressing Room" and "A Beautiful Young Nymph" do "not seem unusually savage or severe."

594. Sheehan, David. "The Ironist in Rochester's 'A Letter from Artemisia in the Town to Chloe in the Country'." <u>Tennessee</u> <u>Studies</u> <u>in</u> <u>Literature</u>, 25 (1980), 72-83.

Rochester's "Letter" is similar to "The Lady's Dressing Room" both in its lack of a positive norm and in the theme it treats.

595. Sheehan, David. "Swift on High Pindaric Stilts." Pp. 25-35 of <u>Contemporary</u> <u>Studies</u> <u>of</u> <u>Swift's</u> <u>Poetry</u>. Edited by John Irwin Fischer and Donald C. Mell, Jr. With David M. Vieth as Associate Editor. Newark, Del.: U. of Delaware Press, 1981.

Argues that what some critics see as a struggle between Swift's personal satiric consciousness and the panegyrical intention of the pindaric form is in fact part of a development in the seventeenth century that saw the pindaric turned to satiric as well as panegyrical ends. Examples come from Jonson, Cotton, Oldham, Butler, and Otway.

596. Sheehan, David. "Swift, Voiture, and the Spectrum of Raillery." <u>PLL</u>, 14 (1978), 171-88.

From Voiture, a much more skillful railleur than has been thought, Swift learned "a spectrum of rallying modes, ranging from simple praise-by-blame to a sharp raillery in which praise and blame coexist in a delicate balance, compliment poised on the edge of satire." Examples of several types may be found in the Stella poems. See also Items 264, 435.

597. Sherbo, Arthur. "Mundus Muliebris." <u>Scriblerian</u>, 11 (1978), 45-46.

"The Fop-Dictionary," appended to Mary Evelyn's poem, "Mundus Muliebris," defines a number of terms used by Swift in "The Lady's Dressing Room" and elsewhere, including the recipe for "Puppy Water."

598. Shipps, Anthony W. "A Probable Source." <u>N&Q</u>, 218 (1973), 262.

Swift's "Daphne," ll. 43-48, was quoted in Elwin's review of the <u>Newcomes</u>.

599. Sisson, C.H. "The Early Poems of Jonathan Swift." Books and Bookmen, 18, no. 8 (May 1973), 54-56.

A patronizing account of Swift's early odes, emphasizing the dissociation from Sir William Temple that they suggest.

600. Sisson, C.H. "The Poetry of Jonathan Swift." The Avoidance of Literature: Collected Essays. Edited by Michael Schmidt. Manchester: Carcanet, 1978, pp. 501-07.

This reprint (with slight changes) of Sisson's introduction to Jonathan Swift: Selected Poems (Item 146) is biographical but uneventful.

601. Solomon, Harry. "Swift's 'Poeta De Tristibus'." Pp. 140-46 of American Notes and Queries: Supplement. Vol. 1: Studies in English and American Literature. Edited by John L. Cutler and Lawrence S. Thompson. Troy, N.Y.: Whitson Publishing Co., 1978.

The anonymous lament "Poeta De Tristibus" may be alluded to in "To Congreve," "Mrs. Harris's Petition," "Vanbrug's House," "Verses on the Death of Dr. Swift," and other poems, since Swift felt a special identification with this ludicrously unsuccessful poet.

602. Solomon, Harry M. "'Difficult Beauty': Tom D'Urfey and the Context of Swift's 'The Lady's Dressing Room'." SEL, 19 (1979), 431-44.

D'Urfey's "Paid for Peeping" seems to be "exactly the facile and sexually suggestive idealization which Swift seems to have abhorred," though the parallels presented between it and Swift's "The Lady's Dressing Room" are too general to suggest anything but a common ancestry.

603. Solomon, Miller. "'To Steal a Hint Was Never Known': The Sodom Apple Motif and Swift's 'A Beautiful Young Nymph Going to Bed'." Tennessee Studies in Literature, 22 (1977), 105-16.

Argues that "not only was Swift working in a clearly defined popular English poetic tradition in 'A Beautiful Young Nymph' but that his process of composition was almost certainly directly influenced by several specific poems in that tradition." Influence, as opposed to parallelism, is by no means established.

604. Staley, Thomas F. "The Poet Joyce and the Shadow of Swift." Pp. 39-52 of Jonathan Swift: Tercentenary Essays. (U. of Tulsa Department of English Monograph Series, 3.) Tulsa: U. of Tulsa, 1967.

A blurry comparison of Joyce's "Holy Office" with ideas about Swift's verse.

605. Steensma, Robert C. "Swift's Apologia: 'Verses on the Death of Dr. Swift'." <u>Proceedings of the Utah Academy of Sciences, Arts and Letters</u>, 42 (1965), 23-28.

Although Swift "somewhat idealizes himself," he intends the eulogy in <u>Verses</u> to be taken quite literally. This reading is similar to that of Marshall Waingrow (Item 624), but lacks the directness with which Waingrow rises to the challenge of Barry Slepian's ironical reading (<u>RES</u>, n.s. 14 (1963), 249-56).

606. Trickett, Rachel. <u>The Honest Muse: A Study in Augustan Verse</u>. Oxford: Clarendon Press, 1967. Pp. ix + 309.

Rev. (favorably) by Kathleen Williams in <u>RES</u>, n.s. 19 (1968), 323-25; (with reservations) by Paul Fussell in <u>MP</u>, 66 (1968), 373-76; (with other works) by Clarence Tracy in <u>MLR</u>, 64 (1969), 880-82; by Paul J. Korshin in <u>Scriblerian</u>, 2 (1969), 23; by Terence Wright in <u>N&Q</u>, 213 (1968), 319-20.

Describes the "Description" poems (pp. 121-26), <u>Cadenus and Vanessa</u>, "Baucis and Philemon," the Stella poems, and "Description of an Irish Feast" as Swift's reversals of Restoration conventions, including the coldness of the coquette, the falseness of fashionable love, the honesty and innocence of the country, its consequent boorishness, and the contemporary state of poetry.

607. Tyne, James L., S.J. "Gulliver's Maker and Gullibility." <u>Criticism</u>, 7 (1965), 151-67.

In "Cassinus and Peter," "The Lady's Dressing Room," and "Strephon and Chloe," as in <u>Gulliver's Travels</u>, "Idealization, the expectation of the impossible from human nature or from life, is followed by Frustration, the chagrin which occurs when the impossible is not forthcoming, which in turn culminates in Demoralization, the complete disintegration of the rational personality in the face of a reality that is so frightfully different from what one had expected."

608. Tyne, James L., S.J. "'Only a Man of Rhimes': Swift's Bridled Pegasus." <u>PLL</u>, 14 (1978), 189-204.

Rhime, sense, and often an intricate counterpoint of sound and sense, are the elements of Swift's verse. This is an introductory-level discussion.

609. Tyne, James L., S.J. "Swift and Stella: The Love Poems." <u>Tennessee Studies in Literature</u>, 19 (1974), 35-47.

The title notwithstanding, this essay spends most of its time showing how the Stella poems are <u>not</u> love poems in any usual sense. Understanding Swift's verses to Stella as genuine love poetry remains an important challenge.

610. Tyne, James L., S.J. "Swift's Mock Panegyrics in 'On Poetry: A Rapsody." <u>PLL</u>, 10 (1974), 279-86.

A discussion of how the "panegyrics" on George Augustus and on Walpole develop their devastating satire: by reminding us of what Virgil and Horace said of their Augustus, in the first case; by serving the purposes of "both parody and satire with equal brilliance," in the second.

611. Tyne, James L., S.J. "Terrestrial and Transcendental Man as Viewed by Swift and Byron." <u>Enlightenment Essays</u>, 8 (1977), 22-37.

A search for similarities in the views and satires of Swift and Byron: their insistence on the realistic truth, their dislike of physicality, their apprehensiveness about threats to spirituality.

612. Tyne, James L., S.J. "Vanessa and the Houyhnhnms: A Reading of 'Cadenus and Vanessa'." <u>SEL</u>, 11 (1971), 517-34.

Vanessa's "moral integrity, her inflexible adherence to principle, her refusal to dabble in either the foolish or the frivolous, and her blunt honesty" link her with the inhuman perfection of the Houyhnhnms: "the reader is reminded that he cannot transcend this tainted world of our [sic] and still live in it."

613. Uphaus, Robert W. "From Panegyric to Satire: Swift's Early Odes and <u>A Tale of a Tub</u>." <u>TSLL</u>, 13 (1971), 55-70.

Seeing <u>A Tale of a Tub</u> as "a parody with the persona as victim," Uphaus argues that it profits from what Swift learned in his failed pindaric odes. The odes were abortive "not just because they were uncongenial and derivative in form but because, being that, they became miscellaneous, incoherent, and ultimately private," as though the satiric anarchy of the Tale teller's inventiveness were the fruit of Swift's own wayward attempts at ingenuity.

614. Uphaus, Robert W. "Swift's Irony Reconsidered." Pp. 169-77 of <u>Contemporary Studies of Swift's Poetry</u>. Edited by John Irwin Fischer and Donald C. Mell, Jr. With David M. Vieth as Associate Editor. Newark, Del.: U. of Delaware Press, 1981.

Agreeing with F.R. Leavis that the powerfulness of Swift's prose writings comes from his willingness to thrust readers back onto their own resources, Uphaus nevertheless sharply distinguishes Swift's later poems, claiming that Swift's biographical presence replaces the ironic contrasts of his earlier prose works.

615. Uphaus, Robert W. "Swift's Poetry: The Making of Meaning." <u>ECS</u>, 5 (1972), 569-86.

Defends Swift against "anti-poetry" labels by stressing his attempt
to preserve the distinction between genuine poetry and derivative
scribbling, his alliance with, rather than against, the traditional
uses of poetry. Poetical conventions behind "Verses wrote on a
Lady's Ivory Table-Book," "The Description of a Salamander," "A
Satirical Elegy," "Stella's Birthday, 1727," "A Beautiful Young
Nymph Going to Bed," and "On Poetry: A Rapsody" are mentioned.

616. Uphaus, Robert W. "Swift's Stella and Fidelity to Experience."
     Dublin Magazine, 8, no. 3 (Spring 1970), 31-42.

     Rept. (as "Swift's Stella Poems and Fidelity to Experience") in
     Eire-Ireland, 5, no. 3 (Autumn 1970), 40-52.

     This is a thematic survey, which concludes that Swift urges "the
     primacy of experience as the ultimate source of judgment."
     Resolution in the Stella poems is founded on "the vitality of
     separating and sifting out self-knowledge (on which virtue is based)
     from the temptations of self-deception."

617. Uphaus, Robert W. "Swift's 'Whole Character': The Delany Poems and
     'Verses on the Death of Dr. Swift'." MLQ, 34 (1973), 406-16.

     Taking Maurice Johnson's hint about the "biographical presence" in
     Swift's poetry, Uphaus asserts that the Delany poems and Swift's
     verses on his own death "abruptly depart from the uses of irony we
     have come to expect from Swift," so that Swift can work towards
     autobiographical self-revelation. These poems establish "vaguely
     theoretical pronouncements," that are made concrete by Swift's
     personal conviction. A very provocative, though not entirely
     convincing argument, in the face of a continuing critical debate
     over Swift's use of irony in the "Verses."

618. Vance, John A. "As Much for Swift as They Are for Stella." Gypsy
     Scholar, 5 (1978), 87-95.

     The birthday poems seen as the expression and resolution of Swift's
     own mental anguish, adding to the usual view that they were meant to
     console Stella.

619. Varney, A.J. "Swift's Dismal and Otway's Antonio." N&Q, 222 (1977),
     224-25.

     See the reply by J.A. Downie (Item 496).

     The influence must be taken on the basis of "satiric congruity,"
     since the one verbal parallel is slight.

620. Vieth, David M. "Fiat Lux: Logos versus Chaos in Swift's 'A
     Description of the Morning'." PLL, 8 (1972), 302-07.

A parody of the divine fiat of Creation, "A Description of the
Morning" intimates order and positive significance, but "meaningful
order is so little evident that a full aesthetic response requires
the reader to search for it." The reader is therefore pushed into
unusually strenuous participation in the poem.

621. Vieth, David M. "Introduction to A Symposium on Women in Swift's
     Poems: Vanessa, Stella, Lady Acheson, and Celia." PLL, 14 (1978),
     115-16.

     An introduction to papers presented at the first (of three) MLA
     Special Sessions on Swift's poetry.

622. Vieth, David M. "Metaphors and Metamorphoses: Basic Techniques in
     the Middle Period of Swift's Poetry, 1698-1719." Pp. 56-68 of
     Contemporary Studies of Swift's Poetry. Edited by John Irwin
     Fischer and Donald C. Mell, Jr. With David M. Vieth as Associate
     Editor. Newark, Del.: U. of Delaware Press, 1981.

     The two techniques, mock-Ovidian metamorphosis and extended,
     unorthodox metaphor, both involve "in intention at least, a
     eucharistic transformation of the bread and wine of life into the
     body and blood of art, which may be triumphantly successful on the
     part of the poet, or hilariously unsuccessful on the part of his
     subjects, or--ideally--both at once."

623. Vieth, David M. "The Mystery of Personal Identity: Swift's Verses on
     His Own Death." Pp. 245-62 of The Author in His Work: Essays on a
     Problem in Criticism. Edited by Louis L. Martz and Aubrey
     Williams. Introduction by Patricia Meyer Spacks. New Haven: Yale
     U. Press, 1978.

     This thorough and illuminating overview of critical opinions on the
     Verses concludes that its contradictory pictures of Swift finally
     express that identity is mysterious or secret.

624. Waingrow, Marshall. "Verses on the Death of Dr. Swift." SEL, 5
     (1965), 513-18.

     Countering Barry Slepian's reading of the eulogy as intentional
     self-irony (RES, n.s. 14 (1963), 249-56), Waingrow's well-known
     reading sees Swift sincerely offering himself as a model of moral
     perception and behavior.

625. Waller, Charles T. "Swift's Apologia Pro Satura Sua." Satire
     Newsletter, 10, no. 1 (Fall 1972), 19-24.

     Points out that "An Epistle to a Lady" plays off the tradition of
     Horace's adversarius and, in a rather old-fashioned way, shows off
     some of the "excellences" of the poem.

626. Waller, Charles Thomas. "Swift's Poems on the Wood's Halfpence Affair." <u>South</u> <u>Atlantic</u> <u>Bulletin</u>, 34, no. 2 (March 1969), 1-3.

Merely a summary description.

627. Watanabe, Koji. "<u>The</u> <u>Lady's</u> <u>Dressing</u> <u>Room</u>." <u>English</u> <u>Quarterly</u> (Kyoto), 11 (1974), 229-45.

Noted by Zenzo Suzuki in <u>Scriblerian</u>, 8 (1976), 83-84.

In Japanese. A naive attempt to identify the "pocky quean" with Queen Caroline. If "Statira" is correctly read in place of "Satira," this sort of speculation need never come up. See David Vieth (Item 94).

628. Williams, Aubrey. "Swift and the Poetry of Allusion: 'The Journal'." Pp. 227-43 of <u>Literary</u> <u>Theory</u> <u>and</u> <u>Structure:</u> <u>Essays</u> <u>in</u> <u>Honor</u> <u>of</u> <u>William</u> <u>K.</u> <u>Wimsatt</u>. Edited by Frank Brady, John Palmer, and Martin Price. New Haven and London: Yale U. Press, 1973.

Sketches the occasion of this seemingly slight and familial poem, discusses its allusions to Lucretius and to contemporary politics, and places "The Journal" in relation to the tradition of Lucretian/Epicurian rural poems.

629. Wimsatt, William K. "Rhetoric and Poems: The Example of Swift." Pp. 229-44 of <u>The</u> <u>Author</u> <u>in</u> <u>his</u> <u>Work:</u> <u>Essays</u> <u>on</u> <u>a</u> <u>Problem</u> <u>in</u> <u>Criticism</u>. Edited by Louis L. Martz and Aubrey Williams. Introduction by Patricia Meyer Spacks. New Haven: Yale U. Press, 1978.

This is principally a study of how Swift used the short couplet: "to invert all those rules enunciated by classical authorities on the heroic of the sublime."

630. Woolley, James. "Autobiography in Swift's Verses on His Death." Pp. 112-22 of <u>Contemporary</u> <u>Studies</u> <u>of</u> <u>Swift's</u> <u>Poetry</u>. Edited by John Irwin Fischer and Donald C. Mell, Jr. With David M. Vieth as Associate Editor. Newark, Del.: U. of Delaware Press, 1981.

Comparing the seemingly self-aggrandizing conclusion of the poem with statements in Swift's letters, Woolley concludes that "the eulogy as a whole is far closer to a serious representation of Swift than is sometimes supposed," an accurate presentation of "the righteous sense of self-identity from which much of Swift's satire springs." This is a provocative essay, which does however ignore the likelihood that Swift, of all writers, would be very sensitive to the various ways a tone of voice may function in different contexts. A statement intended to strike a friend and correspondent as a serious expression of Swift's personal values might well be used for utterly different effects in a public poem.

631. Woolley, James. "Friends and Enemies in <u>Verses on the Death of Dr.</u>
     <u>Swift</u>." Pp. 205-32 of <u>Studies in Eighteenth-Century Culture</u>. Vol.
     8. Edited by Roseann Runte. Madison: U. of Wisconsin Press for the
     American Society for Eighteenth-Century Studies, 1979.

     The idea of friendship gives the <u>Verses</u> a loosely defined unity that
     explains Swift's treatment of Queen Caroline and Mrs. Howard
     (betrayers of friendship), his depiction of his closest friends, and
     the ostensible weakness of the concluding eulogy. The "letdown" of
     the eulogy is appropriate to a poem in which Swift analyzes
     unsatisfactory alternatives to the recognition and esteem he
     expected from his friends.

632. Yamaguchi, Katsumasa. "<u>Verses on the Death of Dr. Swift</u> ni tsuite."
     ["An Essay on <u>Verses on the Death of Dr. Swift</u>."] <u>Annual Reports</u>
     <u>of English and American Literature</u> (Osaka Shoin Women's College),
     14 (1977), 1-15.

     Noted by Zenzo Suzuki in <u>Scriblerian</u>, 11 (1978), 12.

     Suggests (a bit late in the game) that the eulogy ought to read as
     irony.

     See also Items 2, 20, 22, 23, 26, 28, 33, 35, 51, 52, 55, 64, 74,
     86, 90, 96, 98, 100, 103, 104, 132, 168, 172, 248, 263, 264, 266,
     267, 268, 286, 316, 340, 355, 356, 362, 381, 402, 403, 430, 431,
     453, 456, 701, 707, 722, 781, 808, 854, 897, 1004, 1121.

SECTION 5

Prose Writings

A. The Battle of the Books

633. Ahrends, Günter. "Swifts Battle of the Books und die Querelle des Anciens et des Modernes. Pp. 217-36 of Englische und amerikanische Literaturtheorie: Studien zu ihrer historischen Entwicklung. Edited by Rüdiger Ahrens and Erwin Wolff. Vol I: Renaisance, Klassizismus und Romantik. Heidelberg: Carl Winter, 1978.

A general account of the conflict of ancient and modern literature and literary criticism.

634. Ahrends, Günter. "Theorie der Dichtung und der literarischen Kritik in Swifts Battle of the Books." Germanisch-Romanische Monatsschrift, 18 (1968), 360-80.

An overview of the Ancients-Moderns dispute, which finds Swift endorsing a balance between invention and judgment that might be called "imitation."

635. Borkat, Roberta F. Sarfatt. "The Spider and the Bee: Jonathan Swift's Reversal of Tradition in The Battle of the Books." Eighteenth-Century Life, 3 (1976), 44-46.

Since the spider was traditionally associated with medieval rationalist philosophers, the bee frequently represented the Moderns, especially followers of Bacon. Swift's reversal of the traditional emblems gives a special power to his satire.

636. Estall, H.M. "The Snows of Yesteryear." Humanities Association Review, 26 (1975), 1-9.

Swift, Henry Adams, and C.P. Snow are compared on the duality of humanities and science. A useful reminder that Swift's terms are not necessarily those of the 19th or 20th centuries.

637. Folkenflik, Robert. "Some Allusions to Dryden in The Battle of the Books." Revue des Langues Vivantes, 40 (1974), 355-58.

"The Lady in a Lobster" and "Mouse under a Canopy of State" link
Swift, in satire of Dryden, with (of all people) Shadwell.

638. Irving, William Henry. "Boccalini and Swift." ECS, 7 (1973-74),
     143-60.

     Boccalini's Advertisements from Parnassus may have influenced the
     general idea of Battle of the Books. From Boccalini's Rosicrucian
     manifestoes, Swift may have borrowed the subtitle of A Tale of a
     Tub. Furthermore, the two writers share a "paradoxical hovering
     between hope and despair on the possibility of social reform" and
     "the insistence on the deceptiveness of appearances."

639. Real, Hermann J. "Die Biene und die Spinne in Swifts 'Battle of the
     Books'." Germanish-Romanische Monatsschrift, 23 (1973), 169-77.

     After a brief survey of the bee as metaphor for creativity, Real
     suggests that Aesop's stress on the bee's usefulness is most
     relevant to Swift's Battle, which here is seen as a clash between
     uselessness and usefulness.

640. Real, Hermann J. "A Hitherto Unrecorded Meaning of 'Event'." N&Q,
     215 (1970), 423-24.

     In Lucretius (De Rerum Natura), eventa is used in the sense of
     "accident." This usage evidently entered English vocabulary via
     seventeenth-century translators, in time for Swift to have Jupiter
     describe certain inferior deities as "Accidents or Events."

641. Real, Hermann J. "Swifts 'Battle of the Books': ein
     Forschungsbericht." Archiv das Studium der Neueren Spraqchen und
     Literaaturen, 210 (1973), 75-85.

     Surveys recent scholarship on the Battle and poses the remaining
     questions concerning textual problems, composition, publication,
     reception, organization, the relation of author and persona and
     generic classification.

642. Real, Hermann J. "Swifts Battle of the Books: Satire oder Burleske?"
     Anglia, 90 (1972), 349-54.

     Reviews the critical debates to classify "Bücherschlact" as parody,
     travesty, allegory, mock heroic, lampoon, and concludes that "Battle
     of the Books" is a unified satire which uses burlesque as its
     instrument to skewer "theses."

643. Real, Hermann J. "'That Malignant Deity': An Interpretation of
     Criticism in Swift's Battle of the Books." PQ, 52 (1973), 760-66.

     Swift's goddess Criticism, read in light of the theory of humours and the conception of the <u>vir bonus</u>, is seen to suffer from morbid melancholy and to represent a complete inversion of the ideal of <u>vir bonus iudicandi peritus</u>.

644. Vourgaft, E.M. "<u>The Battle of the Books</u> and the Formation of Swift's Aesthetics." <u>Nauchnyje Doklady Literaturovedov Povolzhja</u> (Ulyanovsk), 1968, pp. 267-81.

Noted by Leonid M. Arinshtein in <u>Scriblerian</u>, 2 (1970), 39.

"Miss Vourgaft sees Swift with his strong democratic sympathies veering away from neoclassicism (exemplified by Steele), and turning towards realistic aesthetics akin in spirit to those of the French 'bourlesque' novel (Scarron)." (Arinshtein)

645. Wickham, John F. "The Emergence of Swiftian Satire in <u>The Battle of the Books</u>." Pp. 82-90 of <u>Transactions of the Samuel Johnson Society of the Northwest</u>. Vols. 5-6. Edited by Thomas R. Cleary. Victoria, B.C.: U. of Victoria Press, 1974.

The indirection and distancing characteristic of "Swiftian satire" are seen as stemming from Pindaric style, "Never advancing in a direct Line, but wheeling with incredible Agility and Force."

See also Items 7, 172, 237, 410, 431, 460, 467, 687.

B. <u>A Tale of a Tub</u>

646. Adams, Robert M. "In Search of Baron Somers." Pp. 165-202 of <u>Culture and Politics</u>. Edited by Perez Zagorin. Berkeley: U. of California Press, 1980.

Somers, the dedicatee of the <u>Tale</u>, the sneerer at King William III, is a central figure in the <u>Tale</u>, argues Adams, reinforcing his conviction that the work is a heap of scraps and patches "from the great paper-storms of the seventeenth century."

647. Adams, Robert M. "The Mood of the Church and <u>A Tale of a Tub</u>." Pp. 71-99 of <u>England in the Restoration and Early Eighteenth Century: Essays on Culture and Society</u>. Edited by H.T. Swedenberg, Jr. Berkeley, Los Angeles, London: U. of California Press, 1972.

The <u>Tale</u>'s immediate circumstances were the currents of passion and interest swirling through the late seventeenth-century British church: fears about plutocracy, monomanias, the controversy over moderation, the economic and social grievances of the established clergy, the Locke-Stillingfleet controversy, worries about worldliness.

648. Anselment, Raymond A. "Betwixt Jest and Earnest": Marprelate, Milton, Marvell, Swift and the Decorum of Religious Ridicule. Toronto: U. of Toronto Press, 1979. Pp. x + 203.

Rev. by H.A. Marshall in N&Q, 226 (1981), 192; by P.G. Stanwood in JEGP, 80 (1981), 253-55; (favorably) by James Egan in Seventeenth-Century News, 39 (1981), 12-14.

In four separate studies, Anselment demonstrates the equipose "Betwixt Jest and Earnest" evident in the religious satires of Marprelate, Milton, Marvell and Swift. arguments, In this sanatized version of the Tale, Swift invites his readers to recognize the satirist's own limitations and to laugh at those who lack the largeness of mind to appreciate the narrowness of their vision. The Tale is "decorous," "useful and diverting" to those who have the wit and taste "to avoid compartmentalizing the humor and the seriousness."

649. Anselment, Raymond A. "A Tale of a Tub: Swift and the 'Men of Tast'." HLQ, 37 (1974), 265-82.

Points to similarities between the Tale and Marvell's The Rehearsal Transpros'd, though without firmly establishing direct influence; of special importance is Marvell's Samuel Parker--like Swift's "Modern," an enthusiast, "the antithesis of the man of taste."

650. Beam, Marjorie. "'The Reach and Wit of the Inventor': Swift's Tale of a Tub and Hamlet." University of Toronto Quarterly, 46 (1976), 1-13.

Assuming without question that the tale-teller is a coherent fictional persona, Beam describes him as "a frustrated, bitter little Hamlet: like Hamlet, very self-conscious about his own suffering and the spiritual purity which it implies; like him, an alienated observer of a society which he regards as both obtuse and corrupt." Both Hamlet and tale-teller parody and ridicule conventions, fashions, and genres, but "the satirical vision has lost its princely prerogatives."

651. Bradham, Jo Allen. "Pope's An Epistle to Dr. Arbuthnot, 104-106." Explicator, 26 (February 1968), Item #50.

The slavering serpent in the Tale was alluded to by Pope in the lines referred to above.

652. Brunetti, Giuseppe. "Swift e la Satira della Scienza." English Miscellany, 24 (1973-74), 59-104.

Demonstrates that the common target of Swift's satire of science
from A Tale of a Tub through Gulliver's Travels is the failure of
natural philosophy to distinguish clearly between epistome and doxa
and to appreciate the economic and political consequences of the
zeal for "conjecture and dubious propositions." Mostly concerned
with the Tale.

653. Canavan, Thomas L. "Robert Burton, Jonathan Swift, and the Tradition
of Anti-Puritan Invective." JHI, 34 (1973), 227-42.

The anti-Puritan tradition of Causaubon, Burton, More, from which
Swift proceeded, saw the political and social threats of enthusiasm
(they suspected that enthusiasm was likely to result in the wrongful
exercise of individual liberty) as even more insidious than the
theological controversies.

654. Carnochan, W.B. "Notes on Swift's Proverb Lore." Yearbook of English
Studies, 6 (1976), 63-69.

A great many of Swift's so-called "literary allusions" in A Tale of
a Tub are actually drawn from a common stream of proverbial wisdom.
The significance of Swift's own devoted use of proverbs on our
understanding his attack on them in Polite Conversation was
developed much more completely by David Hamilton (Item 812).

655. Carnochan, W.B. "Swift's Tale: On Satire, Negation, and the Uses of
Irony." ECS, 5 (1971), 122-44.

Carnochan's first premise is that the Tale aspires to the condition
of nothingness: "It is a fantasia on a theme. It is about words, the
materials of which it is made. Words, the Aeolists say, are only
wind. So the Tale is very much like nothing and returns to nothing
like the other productions of modern wit." His second premise, that
"satire typically ... tries to ... obliterate its subjects," leads
to paradox: how can the satirist talk of non-being without
incorporating being, speak of nothing without attributing something?
Carnochan proposes that irony resolves the paradox, through the
admission of the truth of both opposites: "Irony fuses what we can
only say consecutively."

656. Clark, John R. Form and Frenzy in Swift's Tale of a Tub. Ithaca and
London: Cornell U. Press, 1970. Pp. xvi + 237.

Rev. (in an important counterstatement) by Gardner D. Stout, Jr.
in JEGP, 71 (1972), 135-40; (favorably) by Pierre Danchin in
English Studies, 55 (1974), 561-63; (favorably) by Peter Thorpe in
Criticism, 12 (1970), 361-63; (favorably) by C.J. Rawson in RES,
n.s. 22 (1971), 214-16; (favorably) by Ruth L. Basenbach in
Enlightenment Essays, 1 (1970), 214-16; (severely) by Miriam K.
Starkman in Scriblerian, 3 (1970), 21-22; by Eberhard Kreutzer in
Archiv für das Studium der Neuren Sprachen, 208 (1972), 386-87;

in review art. ("Images of Swift: A Review of Some Recent
Criticism") by Robert W. Uphaus in <u>Eire-Ireland</u>, 6, no. 3 (Fall
1971), 16-22; (favorably) by David P. French in
<u>Seventeenth-Century</u> <u>News</u>, 28 (1970), 68, 70; in review art. ("The
State of the Dean") by Robert Martin Adams in <u>Hudson</u> <u>Review</u>, 23
(1970), 578-84.

A <u>Tale</u> <u>of</u> <u>a</u> <u>Tub</u> is a work of mimetic art, with a clear pattern of
action, and a complex organic form sustained by the continuity of
its characters, episodes, thought, diction, and scenes. The vexing
debates about the relationship of the digressions and the fable, the
protean qualities of the persona and even about multiple authorship
are squarely faced, if not fully resolved.

657. Clark, John R. "Further <u>Iliads</u> in Swift's Nut-Shell." <u>PQ</u>, 51 (1972),
945-50.

Concerning A <u>Tale</u> <u>of</u> <u>a</u> <u>Tub</u>'s reference, in Section VII, to "an <u>Iliad</u>
in a <u>Nut-shell</u>," Clark shows that the phrase was originally
honorific, meaning something vast and meaningful contained in
miniature. By the seventeenth century, however, when the rage for
the curious and the miniscule produced actual nutshells containing
complete transcriptions of the <u>Iliad</u>, the phrase became satirical.

658. Clark, John R. "Swift's Knaves and Fools in the Tradition: Rhetoric
Versus Poetic in A <u>Tale</u> <u>of</u> <u>a</u> <u>Tub</u>, Section IX." <u>SP</u>, 66 (1969),
777-96.

Contains a valuable survey of the tradition of humours and
characters, which Swift knew, and which identified both credulity
and curiosity as defects. Clark also attempts to explain why this
passage does not simply induce readers to find for themselves a
viable middle ground: "despite the brotherhood of credulity and
curiosity in so many ways, these two still remain isolated, the
poles of Cartesian dualism: mind and matter." Clark's claim that the
<u>Tale</u> is "poetry," rather than "rhetoric," and therefore presents a
whole, without revealing the author's opinions or trying to vex the
reader, is provocative but hardly squares with how the work was
actually read, in the eighteenth century and since.

659. Clifford, Gay. <u>The</u> <u>Transformations</u> <u>of</u> <u>Allegory</u>. (Concepts of
Literature.) London and Boston: Routledge & Kegan Paul, 1974. Pp.
viii + 132.

Swift, particularly in the <u>Tale</u>, provides key transitions in the
development of allegory, responding to that pressure to give "form
to the ideal and the abstract" which has always prompted
allegory—but instead writing a deliberate parody.

660. Cohen, Ralph. "On the Interrelations of Eighteenth-Century Literary
Forms." Pp. 33-78 of <u>New</u> <u>Approaches</u> <u>to</u> <u>Eighteenth-Century</u>

Literature: Selected Papers from the English Institute. Edited by
Phillip Harth. New York and London: Columbia U. Press, 1974.

Pp. 68-74 discuss A Tale of a Tub. Swift's use of multiple
authorship and digressions represents "the factionalism of society
and the dangers of this division."

661. A Complete Key to the 'Tale of a Tub', 1710. (Scolar Students'
     Facsimiles.) Menston, Yorkshire: Scolar Press, 1970.

662. Crider, J.R. "Swift's A Tale of a Tub, Section X." Explicator, 28,
     no. 7 (March 1970), Item #62.

The reference to "the famous Troglodyte Philosopher" in Section X,
Paragraph 3, evokes Bacon's idols of the cave--delusions about
nature caused by the eccentricities of each individual thinker.

663. Davis, Herbert. "Literary Satire in A Tale of a Tub." Pp. 143-61 of
     Swift: Modern Judgements. Edited by A. Norman Jeffares. London:
     Macmillan, 1969; Nashville, Tenn.: Aurora, 1970.

Orig. pub. in Jonathan Swift (1964).

For Davis, the enabling paradox of the Tale is that it is "a product
of the seventeenth century, entirely characteristic in form and
manner, and at the same time a repudiation and criticism of all the
most vigorous literary fashions of the previous sixty years."

664. DePorte, Michael V. "Digressions and Madness in A Tale of a Tub and
     Tristram Shandy." HLQ, 34 (1970-71), 43-57.

Seeing the taleteller as insane, by the definition of Hobbes and
others, helps to explain the Tale's disjointed and haphazard
structure as well as the narrator's occasional "lapses" into
lucidity.

665. DePorte, Michael V. Nightmares and Hobbyhorses: Swift, Sterne, and
     Augustan Ideas of Madness. San Marino: The Huntington Library,
     1974. Pp. xi + 164.

    Rev. (favorably) by David Fairer in N&Q, 223 (1978), 560-62;
    (favorably) by Lodwick Hartley in South Atlantic Quarterly, 75
    (1976), 136-37; (severely) by T.R. Steiner in JEGP, 74 (1975),
    245-47; (favorably) by John F. Sena in Scriblerian, 7 (1974),
    38-40; (with another work) by Patricia Meyer Spacks in MP, 73
    (1976), 305-10; in review art. ("Exuberant Mixtures: Some Recent
    Studies in the Eighteenth Century") by Patricia Carr Brückmann in
    University of Toronto Quarterly, 46 (1976), 83-91.

This three-part study begins by scrutinizing eighteenth-century

theories of psychology and insanity before proceeding to analyses of
the *Tale* and *Tristram Shandy*. According to Hobbes's definition, the
taleteller is a madman, accounting for his obsessive digressions,
and narrative peculiarities, as well as his lucid intervals. Where
Swift is out to reveal civilized norms which can define madness as
perverse, Sterne is not so sure that madness is not an inevitable,
"natural" response to experience.

666. Evans, James E. "The English Lineage of Diedrich Knickerbocker."
     Early American Literature, 10 (1975), 3-13.

     Makes a tenuous connection between Knickerbocker and the *Tale,* based
     on such observations as "Not as ... consistently ironic as the
     Tubbian hack, Knickerbocker provides a cheerful muddle for the
     reader to solve," and Knickerbocker requires an inquisitive reader
     "looking over the shoulder of the narrator to discern the ironies of
     Knickerbocker's rhetoric, to make discriminations of the kind
     Swift's reader must make in *A Tale of a Tub*."

667. Fisher, Alan S. "An End to the Renaissance: Erasmus, Hobbes, and *A
     Tale of a Tub*." *HLQ*, 38 (1974), 1-20.

     Finding Swift's satire more rueful than grim, even giving a "sense
     of *having* fun," Fisher sees the *Tale*'s paradoxes in the tradition of
     Erasmus's efforts to see things whole, to dissolve seeming opposites
     into one another. This is Swift's way of resisting or subverting the
     "end of the Renaissance" most thoroughly embodied in Hobbes's
     mechanistic systems. A provocative essay.

668. Hammond, Eugene R. "A Swiftian Borrowing from Erasmus' *Colloquies* in
     A Tale of a Tub." *N&Q*, 225 (1980), 32-33.

     In both, myths of the relics of Mary's milk and Christ's cross (also
     the supposed flight to Europe of Mary's house) are mocked for being
     outrageously exaggerated.

669. Hayman, John G. "Shaftesbury and the Search for a Persona." *SEL*, 10
     (1970), 491-504.

     Shaftesbury's persona in *Miscellaneous Reflections* resembles Swift's
     tale-teller in some general ways, but his concern with coherence of
     character "may well have checked the free development of a confused
     persona" similar to Swift's.

670. Hoilman, Dennis R. "Pope's *An Essay on Man*, IV, 195-196." *PQ*, 50
     (1971), 308-09.

     A borrowing by Pope from the *Tale,* Section XI.

671. Hopkins, Robert H. "The Personation of Hobbism in Swift's *Tale of a Tub* and *Mechanical Operation of the Spirit*." PQ, 45 (1966), 372-78.

In Section IX, Swift uses Hobbes's discussion of uncontrolled fancy in *Leviathan* as a structural principle and a narrative technique in order to satirize abuses of religion and learning and Hobbism itself. The tale-teller's treatise on Aeolism in Section VIII is both a satire of enthusiasm and a satire of Hobbist literalism.

672. Hunkler, Margaret. "'Tale of a Tub' Source." *American Notes and Queries*, 9 (1970), 8.

A reply to Karl S. Nagel (Item 689).

If the butcher from "Rub a dub dub/Three men in a tub" can be identified with Swift's Jack, why can't Peter be the baker (bread for mass) and Martin the candlestick maker ("the true source of religion and light")?

673. Iwasaki, Yasuo. "A Tale of a Tub ni okeru guzo no image." ["The Idol Image in *A Tale of a Tub*."] *Studies in English Literature* (Tokyo), 55 (1978), 15-30.

Noted by Zenzo Suzuki in *Scriblerian*, 12 (1979), 11.

"Opposed in their philosophical principles, Peter and Jack in Swift's *Tale*, Mr. Iwasaki points out, nonetheless agree in idol-worshipping and a belief in the philosophy of deception. ... The 'idol image in the *Tale*,' Mr. Iwasaki concludes, is derived from 'the ancient Christian tradition and the modern Baconian one'." (Suzuki)

674. Josipovici, Gabriel. *The World and the Book: A Study in Modern Fiction*. London: Macmillan, 1971. Pp. xvii + 318.

Rev. by Clive T. Probyn in *Scriblerian*, 4 (1972), 59-60.

An example of the "process" anti-novel, the *Tale* is "a desperate burlesque designed to keep madness at bay only by the frenzy of its own activity."

675. Kallich, Martin. "Swift and the Archetypes of Hate: *A Tale of a Tub*." Pp. 43-67 of *Studies in Eighteenth-Century Culture*. Vol. 4. Edited by Harold Pagliaro. Madison: U. of Wisconsin Press for the American Society for Eighteenth-Century Studies, 1975.

Though Swift had little love of Puritan typological practice and thought, and rejected all archetypal symbols associated with mysterious and sublime emotion, he made good use himself of "archetypes." Here "archetypes" evidently refers to almost any use

of image, metaphor, or symbol. Though the title refers to
"archetypes of hate," the essay concerns itself primarily with
images of madness and sexual depravity.

676. Kauvar, Elaine M. "Swift's Clothing Philosophy in A Tale of a Tub
and Joyce's 'Grace'." James Joyce Quarterly, 5 (1968), 162-65.

Stresses the worship of the surface of things and the reversal of
body and soul in Swift's "clothing religion" as the basis of Joyce's
irony in "Grace."

677. Kim, Hwal. "Jonathan Swift's Paradox in A Tale of a Tub." English
Language and Literature (Seoul), 43 (1972), 73-100.

Treating the Tale as "mimetic art per se," Kim describes satire as
the mimesis of paradox and finds a repetitive pattern of "Icarean
Flight" in the Tale: rising and falling, swelling and collapsing,
attempting and retreating. He goes on to distinguish the Modern's
use of rhetorical paradox, satirized by Swift, and Swift's own use
of satiric paradox.

678. Kinahan, Frank. "The Melancholy of Anatomy: Voice and Theme in A
Tale of a Tub." JEGP, 69 (1970), 278-91.

Argues against pinpointing the personae of the Tale, since to reduce
the voices to a finite number "is to isolate them; and the whole
technique of the Tale revolves around the fact that its several
voices do not exist in isolation." Statements that might appear to
be distinguishably by the author and by the tale-teller in actuality
"exist in a state of interaction rather than isolation," playing
against the moderns' solipsistic efforts to reduce everything to a
state of order.

679. Koon, William. "Swift on Language: An Approach to A Tale of a Tub."
Style, 10 (1976), 28-40.

The unsurprising thesis here is that the Tale contains a satire on
corrupt language and its perversions of understanding and pride.

680. Korkowski, Eugene. "The Second Tale of a Tub: A Link from Swift to
Sterne?" Studies in the Novel, 6 (1974), 470-74.

Written by George Duckett and Sir Thomas Burnet, A Second Tale of a
Tub (1715), a satire on the Tories and on Swift himself, contains a
"shaggy-dog-nose-allegory" that may have inspired a part of Tristram
Shandy.

681. Korkowski, Eugene. "Swift's Tub: Traditional Emblem and Proverbial
Enigma." Eighteenth-Century Life, 4 (1978), 100-03.

This concise, packed essay surveys a good many emblematic appearances of the tub, including two paintings by Peter Breughel the Elder which depict tubs as, respectively, an analogue for man's moral predicament and a profitless waste of time, an emblem for senseless war in Lucian, via Rabelais, and for threats to civil order in the Guy Fawkes casks of gunpowder. In all cases, the tub is a symbol of all objects of materialistic human curiosity.

682. Korkowski, Eugene Bud. "With An Eye to the Bunghole: Figures of Containment in A Tale of a Tub." SEL, 15 (1975), 391-408.

The tub itself is one of many images of containment and surface, depth and height, diversification and reductiveness in the Tale, working to satirize unaided reason.

683. Korshin, Paul J. "Swift and Typological Narrative in A Tale of a Tub." Pp. 67-91 of The Interpretation of Narrative: Theory and Practice. Edited by Morton W. Bloomfield. (Harvard English Studies, 1.) Cambridge, Mass.: Harvard U. Press, 1970.

Rept. as pp. 279-302 of Studies in the Eighteenth Century. Vol. 2. Edited by R.F. Brissenden. Canberra: Australian National U. Press; Toronto: U. of Toronto Press, 1973.

Swift's "typological narrative" in Section VII of the Tale is "based on the creation of an absurd, mock-mysterious correspondence between the works of the ancients and the productions of his contemporaries," which also associates pretended inspiration in scholarship and secular learning with similar pretenses in religion. The essay includes a brief survey of the intellectual context of Biblical typology when Swift was writing the Tale.

684. Lengler, Rainer. "Desunt Caetera: Swifts Tonnenmärchen als Fragment." Germanish-Romanishe Monatsschrift, 17 (1967), 181-93.

Remarks on the disjunctiveness of the Tale.

685. Levine, Jay Arnold. "The Design of A Tale of a Tub (With a Digression on a Mad Modern Critic)." ELH, 33 (1966), 198-227.

Rept. (in part) as pp. 712-15 of Item 125.

The taleteller is modeled after "Bentleyan" critics of sacred scripture, whose pride and arrogance, and disordered personality, cause his defense of religion to disintegrate. The "Mad Modern Critic" is Nabokov's Dr. Charles Kinbote (Pale Fire) who, in quite general ways, resembles Swift's taleteller.

686. Linderman, Deborah. "Self-Transforming Ironies in Swift's Tale of a Tub." Comparative Literature Studies, 16 (1979), 69-78.

This argument for the foundational and brilliant ambiguity of the
Tale ("a negativity of unstabilized ironies") leads to the
conclusion that Swift unconsciously allowed his language to corrode
the spirituality he valued.

687. Maresca, Thomas E. *Epic to Novel*. Columbus: Ohio State U. Press,
     1974. Pp. 238.

   Rev. (with reservations) by John M. Aden in *South Atlantic
   Quarterly*, 75 (1976), 267; (favorably) by Thomas R. Edwards in
   Scriblerian, 8 (1975), 37-38; in review art. ("Recent Studies in
   the Restoration and Eighteenth Century") by Ronald Paulson in *SEL*,
   16 (1976), 517-44; in review art. ("Exuberant Mixtures: Some
   Recent Studies in the Eighteenth Century") by Patricia Carr
   Brückmann in *University of Toronto Quarterly*, 46 (1976), 83-91;
   (severely) in review art. ("Order and Misrule: Eighteenth-Century
   English Literature in the 1970's") by C.J. Rawson in *ELH*, 42
   (1975), 471-505; (with reservations) by Douglas Brooks in *MLR*, 72
   (1977), 150-51.

   Pp. 135-78 diffusedly discuss the *Tale*, *Battle of the Books*, and
   Mechanical Operation of the Spirit as satires on "the peculiarly
   modern temperament that substitutes theorizing about life for living
   it." *Gulliver's Travels*, giving us "the hero as synechdoche rather
   than exemplar," points the way to a new kind of prose epic, which
   explores "the existence and dimensions of the human spirit and the
   possibility of freeing it from the bind of matter."

688. Mechanic, Leslie. "Food Imagery and Gluttony in *A Tale of a Tub*."
     Eighteenth-Century Life, 5, no. 4 (Summer, 1979), 14-28.

   A lack of temperance and discrimination in diet is Swift's
   deflationary metaphor for the abandonment of rationally tempered
   thought and behavior among religious bodies and members of the body
   of the arts and sciences. See also Item 411.

689. Nagel, Karl S. "Source for *A Tale of a Tub*." *American Notes and
     Queries*, 6 (1967), 22-23.

   See the reply by Margaret Hunkler (Item 672).

   Somewhere in the back of Swift's mind may have been the child's
   rhyme "Rub a dub dub / Three men in a tub." Nagel suggests that the
   butcher is analogous to the dissenters of Swift's time "who were
   butchering and dismembering Christianity"; the candlestick maker may
   represent the Roman Catholics' concern with ceremony; the baker, who
   produces the staff of life, symbolizes the Church of England,
   "offering true doctrine, nourishment for the soul as is bread for
   the body."

690. Nelson, Cary. "Form and Claustrophobia: Intestinal Space in A Tale
    of a Tub." Pp. 105-25 of The Incarnate Word: Literature as Verbal
    Space. Urbana, Chicago, and London: U. of Illinois Press, 1973.

    Stresses the "genuine threat" the Tale makes against its readers:
    "Whether we accept Swift's dark vision or reject it ... our response
    will be violent enough to destroy our security." The real source of
    our shock is Swift's "anal vision of eschatology"; the final horror
    is a vision of the mystical body of Christ reduced to self-infecting
    process.

691. Nugel, Bernfried, and Peter Freimark. "Swift's Treatment of Rabbi
    Jehuda Hannasi in A Tale of a Tub." N&Q, 218 (1973), 3-4.

    A rather lengthy explanation of one brief reference in the Tale.

692. Oka, Teruo. "Gift and Vessel: Terms of Satire." English Quarterly,
    (Kyoto), 6 (1968), 37-52.

    Noted in Scriblerian, 1, no. 2 (Spring 1969), 12.

    In Japanese. In the Tale and Mechanical Operation of the Spirit,
    Swift uses the Puritan catchword, "gift," to describe empty
    holding-forth.

693. Omasreiter, Ria. "Die kritischen Essays Swifts: die Paradoxie als
    Mittel der Gesellschaftskritik." ["Swift's Critical Essays:
    Paradox as the Tool of the Social Critic."] Anglia, 93 (1975),
    361-90.

    Argues that A Tale of a Tub and A Modest Proposal not only satirize
    the specialists, the virtuosi critics and projectors, but
    "paradoxically" they demonstrate the "true" functions of criticism.
    Setting down narrow rules, assaulting individual adversaries,
    satirizing character types, and creating systematic social, literary
    or economic theories are not, for Swift, the concerns of the critic.
    The discipline of the ideal critic is the "commonwealth of
    learning"; in theory and in practice, he is a bulwark and cultivator
    of traditional commonwealth values.

694. O'Neill, John H. "Rochester's 'Imperfect Enjoyment': 'The True Veine
    of Satyre' in Sexual Poetry." Tennessee Studies in Literature, 25
    (1980), 57-71.

    Notes that for Swift, at least in the Tale, the obscene wit of the
    Restoration "epitomizes the modern deviation from the common
    elements of the classical tradition," a claim possibly in need of
    modification in light of Swift's admiration of the occasionally
    "obscene" wit of such classical writers as Juvenal and Catullus.

695. Pinkus, Philip. Swift's Vision of Evil: A Comparative Study of A
     Tale of a Tub and Gulliver's Travels. Vol. 1: A Tale of a Tub.
     (English Literary Studies Monograph Series, 3.) Victoria, British
     Columbia: U. of Victoria, 1975. Pp. 138.

     Rev. (severely) by C.J. Rawson in MLR, 73 (1978), 884-85; by
     Patricia Köster in Scriblerian, 8 (1976), 79-80.

     The Tale is what Pinkus calls a "satire of contempt." Its imagery is
     predominantly mechanical and reveals Swift's confident assumption
     that human reason offers normative values, deviations from which are
     largely acts of stupidity and madness. Evil "is an absence of virtue
     more than an active malevolence." Chapters on "The Nature of
     Satire," 'The Satiric Focus," "The Demonic," "Structure and Unity,"
     "Grub Street," "The Digressions," and "The Pattern of Imagery" ring
     the changes of this theme.

696. Probyn, Clive T. "The Odyssey of Homer's Iliad in a Nut-Shell." N&Q,
     219 (1974), 47-48.

     Two new occurrences of the phrase are noted, one
     seventeenth-century, one eighteenth-century.

697. Pullen, Charles. "The Role of the Reader of Eighteenth-Century
     Literature and Swift's A Tale of a Tub." English Studies in
     Canada, 1 (1975), 280-89.

     The key to Swift's satire is his refusal to tell his readers "how to
     judge the victim."

698. Quilligan, Maureen. The Language of Allegory. Ithaca: Cornell U.
     Press, 1979. Pp. 312.

     Rev. by William J. Kennedy in MLN, 95 (1980), 1425-27.

     Pp. 134-55 is an analysis of the reader's role in A Tale of a Tub
     and Nabokov's Pale Fire. The question the Tale asks is: what is the
     proper relationship between reader and text? Swift's answer is that
     to interpret as vigorously as his narrator is to be insane. "At the
     same time that it satirizes allegoresis, A Tale of a Tub anatomizes
     the causes of the end of an allegorical age."

699. Quintana, Ricardo. "Two Paragraphs in A Tale of a Tub, Section IX."
     MP, 73 (1975), 15-31.

     An attempt to attribute sources for the famous "fool among knaves"
     passage: Bacon and Descartes, for the most part.

700. Rogers, Pat. "Form in A Tale of a Tub." Essays in Criticism, 22
     (1972), 142-60.

The <u>Tale</u> is neither an example of formlessness nor a coherent demonstration of literary folly. Rather, it demonstrates excess of empty forms; its structure "is one of inorganic, over-developed, <u>useless</u> 'form'." Rogers goes on to argue against the notion that the putative author is himself an object of satire (<u>contra</u> Wayne C. Booth).

701. Rogers, Pat. <u>Grub</u> <u>Street</u>: <u>Studies</u> <u>in</u> <u>a</u> <u>Subculture</u>. London: Methuen, 1972. Pp. 430.

Rev. by Edward A. Bloom in <u>Yearbook</u> <u>of</u> <u>English</u> <u>Studies</u>, 4 (1974), 296-99; by Graham Midgley in <u>RES</u>, n.s. 24 (1973), 342-44; (with reservations) by Aubrey Williams in <u>MP</u>, 72 (1975), 324-27; (favorably) by Douglas Brooks in <u>Critical</u> <u>Quarterly</u>, 14 (1972), 286; (with reservations) by James T. Boulton in <u>N&Q</u>, 219 (1974), 278-80; (unfavorably) by Aubrey Williams in <u>MP</u>, 72 (1975), 324-27; (with reservations) by Pierre Danchin in <u>English</u> <u>Studies</u>, 56 (1975), 163-65; (with reservations) by John A. Hay in <u>Journal</u> <u>of</u> <u>the</u> <u>Australasian</u> <u>Universities</u> <u>Language</u> <u>and</u> <u>Literature</u> <u>Association</u>, 41 (1974), 91-92.

Pp. 218-76, "Swift and the Scribblers," trace Swift's many references to Grub Street, to show how, throughout his career, Swift used it as a powerful satiric fiction. Rogers pays particular attention to <u>A</u> <u>Tale</u> <u>of</u> <u>a</u> <u>Tub</u>, the <u>Journal</u> <u>to</u> <u>Stella</u>, and the "Description" and other poems--mostly just to pick out references to Grub Street.

702. Roscelli, William John. "<u>A</u> <u>Tale</u> <u>of</u> <u>a</u> <u>Tub</u> and the 'Cavils of the Sour'." <u>JEGP</u>, 64 (1965), 41-56.

An attempt to show that Swift does not always successfully discriminate between the corruption he wishes to ridicule and the belief of which it is a corruption. As a result, he does frequently appear to scoff at divine power and at faith, just as his contemporary critics charged.

703. Schaeffer, Neil. "'Them That Speak, and Them That Hear': The Audience as Target in Swift's <u>Tale</u> <u>of</u> <u>a</u> <u>Tub</u>." <u>Enlightenment</u> <u>Essays</u>, 4, no. 2 (Summer 1973), 25-35.

Proceeds from the orthodox reader-response assumption that subjects are less important than ways of proceeding to propose that Swift provokes sensible readers of the <u>Tale</u> into dissociating themselves from an implied group of foolish readers. This approach seems on an important track, but the insistence here on a clear distinction between sensible and foolish readers of the <u>Tale</u> is less advanced than the insights of Henry W. Sams and C.J. Rawson, not mentioned in this essay.

704. Scruggs, Charles. "George Orwell and Jonathan Swift: A Literary
     Relationship." South Atlantic Quarterly, 76 (1977), 177-89.

     Points out very general correspondences between A Tale of a Tub and
     Animal Farm.

705. Scruggs, Charles. "Swift's Use of Lucretius in A Tale of a Tub."
     TSLL, 15 (1973), 39-49.

     Swift not only attacked Lucretius, but he also used De Rerum Natura
     for his artistic purposes: the tale-teller derives his "world view"
     from Epicureanism; and echoes of De Rerum Natura "give structure to
     a world where chaos and change are the primary realities."

706. Seidel, Michael. Satiric Inheritance: Rabelais to Sterne. Princeton:
     Princeton U. Press, 1979. Pp. xiv + 283.

     Rev. in review art. ("Satire or Sense: A Truer Mix") by John M.
     Aden in Sewanee Review, 89 (1981), 441-47; in Yale Review, 69
     (1979-80), no. 3, vi, xi, xii; in review art. ("Recent Studies in
     the Restoration and Eighteenth Century") by J. Paul Hunter in SEL,
     20 (1980), 517-46.

     Pursuing his thesis that satire is subversion of succession and
     inheritance, Seidel (pp. 169-200) sees the subject of the Tale as
     "the inability to transmit donated value across historical and
     generational boundaries," both through its form and in its story.
     Gulliver, hero of a story about degeneration, is like no one so much
     as the taleteller (pp. 201-25).

707. Seijas, Joaquin Rojo. "Temas de 'A Tale of a Tub' en las Primeras
     Odas de Swift." Cuadernos de Filologia, June, 1972, pp. 17-26.

     The important transition from panegyrical odes to the Tale is
     discussed much better by Robert W. Uphaus (Item 613).

708. Smith, Frederik N. "The Epistemology of Fictional Failure: Swift's
     Tale of a Tub and Beckett's Watt." TSLL, 15 (1974), 649-72.

     Claiming not only similarities between the two works but also
     Swift's direct influence on Watt, Smith sees both as "attempts at
     fictional meaning that must fail because they have at their cores
     unconquerable nonmeanings." (During the course of the essay we are
     not always certain whether Swift's or the tale-teller's "attempt at
     meaning" is being described.)

709. Smith, Frederik N. Language and Reality in Swift's A Tale of a Tub.
     Columbus: Ohio State U. Press, 1979. Pp. 172.

     Rev. (favorably) by Ann Cline Kelly in Scriblerian, 14 (1982),

116-17; (with reservations) in review art. ("Gentle Readings: Recent Work on Swift") by William Kinsley in ECS, 15 (1982), 442-53.

In this stylistic analysis, the Hack's convoluted verbosity is constantly undercut by Swift's own concrete matter-of-factness. The empirical, physical reality suggested by the Tale's imagery is the only ballast for its high-flying intellectualism. The meaning or effect of this double style is changeful, from repudiation of the Hack's emptiness, to a sneer at the lowness of concrete reality itself. But in the final telling, Swift's partial identification with the mad Hack proves that Swift did not care to write about modern insanity from the safe position of modern sanity. "The responsibility for distinguishing between sanity and insanity, truth and error, is in the Tale turned over to us."

710. Smith, Winston. "Simon Suggs and the Satiric Tradition." Pp. 49-56 of Essays in Honor of Richebourg Gaillard McWilliams. Birmingham, Ala.: Birmingham-Southern College, 1970.

Swift's satire, particularly the Tale's attack on religious enthusiasm, seems to have inspired the nineteenth-century American humorist Johnson Jones Hooper in Some Adventures of Captain Simon Suggs.

711. Stout, Gardner D., Jr. "Satire and Self-Expression in Swift's Tale of a Tub." Pp. 323-39 of Studies in the Eighteenth Century. Vol. 2. Edited by R.F. Brissenden. Canberra: Australian National U. Press; Toronto: U. of Toronto Press, 1973.

An influential argument, contra prevailing theories of persona, that "Swift's vivid parodies and personations are often reflective embodiments of repressed aspects of his own personality as the Tale's author."

712. Stout, Gardner D., Jr. "Speaker and Satiric Vision in Swift's Tale of a Tub." ECS, 3 (1969), 175-99.

The speaking voice in the Tale is best heard as Swift himself, mimicking and parodying the ideas and rhetoric of hacks, pedants, and apologists for the moderns. Because Swift's genuine tones and attitudes tend to merge with those of his victims, the motives and ends of Swift's own satire are constantly called into question. This approach, along the lines recommended by Irvin Ehrenpreis, and contra the widespread persona readings of the Tale, has stirred up more than a little healthy controversy.

713. Traugott, John. "A Tale of a Tub." Pp. 76-120 of Focus: Swift. Edited by C.J. Rawson. London: Sphere Books, 1971.

Accountable neither by persona theory nor by scholarly

paraphernalia, the "mad voices" of the Tale may be discovered in the
mind of any man, particularly in Swift's own radically imagining
mind. A long analysis of Swift at Moor Park explains how his
snobbish defensiveness about Sir William Temple led to subversively
accurate mimicry of vulgarian types offensive to him. Sections
follow on Swift's use of "the zany licence of the fool," on his
imagery, and on "The Digression Concerning Madness," in the last of
which Traugott answers F.R. Leavis's criticism by relishing Swift's
"potpourri of attitudes." Written in an introductory style, though
full of sharp opinions.

714. Turner, Richard C. "Burbank and Grub-Street: A Note on T.S. Eliot
     and Swift." English Studies, 52 (1971), 347-48.

     Eliot adapted the line, "clipt his Wings, pared his Nails," from the
     Tale to "put himself in the tradition with Swift as those who see
     the forces that corrupt civilization."

715. Vieth, David M. "Divided Consciousness: The Trauma and Triumph of
     Restoration Culture." Tennessee Studies in Literature, 22 (1977),
     46-62.

     The Tale is one example of "reversible meaning," for the traditional
     norms by which we condemn the taleteller are less "real" than the
     immediacy of the speaker's perceptions, fantasies, and metaphors.

716. Vieth, David M. "Toward an Anti-Aristotelian Poetic: Rochester's
     Satyr Against Mankind and Artemisia to Chloe, with Notes on
     Swift's Tale of a Tub and Gulliver's Travels." Language and Style,
     5 (1972), 123-45.

     An example of "anti-Aristotelian" structure, the Tale exhibits both
     a "centrifugal effect that leaves a gap at its center and renders
     its boundaries indefinite or unstable," and also a "centripetal"
     effect, in that commentors who sound too much like "W. Wotton"
     become themselves targets of the satire they are reading.

717. Von Koppenfels, Werner. "Swifts Tale of a Tub und die Tradition
     satirischer Metaphorik." ["Swift's Tale of a Tub and the Tradition
     of Satiric Metaphor."] Deutxche Vierteljahrs Schrift für
     Literaturwissenschaft un Geistesgeschichte, 51 (1977), 27-54.

     Recalls the metaphoric use of clothing, aeolism, and the barrel/tub
     in the satires of Rabelais, Ben Jonson, and lesser figures and
     unpersuasively presents these metaphors as the key structural
     components of the Tale.

718. Washington, Eugene. "Swift and Ramus." Proceedings of the Utah
     Academy of Sciences, Arts & Letters, 53 (1976), 30-32.

The taleteller's slips of memory, amorality, and disjunctive
narrative style resemble a Ramist orator.

719. Weathers, Winston. "A Technique of Irony in A Tale of a Tub." Pp.
       53-60 of Jonathan Swift: Tercentenary Essays. (U. of Tulsa
       Department of English Monograph Series, 3.) Tulsa: U. of Tulsa,
       1967.

       Rept. as pp. 176-83 of Rhetorical Analyses of Literary Works.
       Edited by Edward P.J. Corbett. New York: Oxford U. Press, 1969.

       Because Weathers assumes that Swift believed "his meaning depended
       upon a conventional use of words that were well established in the
       social order," believed "in a normal audience, an audience of
       readers who were like unto himself," and "believed in a normal level
       of denotative meaning," he has no trouble finding "precise and
       definite meaning" in the Tale. An analysis of Section V, paragraph
       1, leads to the conclusion that Swift is (always) either mocking his
       persona or ruefully endorsing what the persona has unwittingly said.

720. Weygant, Peter S. "Three Kinds of Reply to A Tale of a Tub." Library
       Chronicle, 36 (1970), 47-62.

       To wit: (1) derivative titles, with little substantial connection;
       (2) direct attacks; (3) imitations (second parts and parodies).

       See also Items 1, 7, 29, 32, 59, 65, 172, 248, 265, 267, 271, 280,
       286, 298, 299, 307, 316, 318, 348, 354, 357, 358, 379, 381, 391,
       394, 396, 403, 406, 407, 410, 430, 460, 463, 613, 638, 722, 904,
       907, 996, 1000, 1100.

C. The Mechanical Operation of the Spirit

721. Crider, J.R. "Dissenting Sex: Swift's 'History of Fanaticism'." SEL,
       18 (1978), 491-508.

       Crider glosses the "History" in great detail, fortifying Ronald
       Paulson's contention (Theme and Structure in Swift's Tale of a Tub,
       1960) that Swift was decisively influenced by Irenaeus, showing how
       Swift uses the general condemnation of Gnosticism to satirize later
       enthusiastic sects and to link them with extreme antinomianism and
       individualism.

722. Kernan, Alvin B. The Plot of Satire. New Haven: Yale U. Press, 1965.
       Pp. vii + 227.

Rev. (favorably) by Ernest J. Lovell, Jr. in MP, 64 (1966),
380-82; (with another work) by Ronald Paulson in JEGP, 65 (1966),
602-04; (with reservations) by Philip Pinkus in PQ, 45 (1966),
518-20; by Charles Witke in Comparative Literature, 18 (1966),
277-79; (favorably) by G.K. Hunter in N&Q, 211 (1966), 395;
(favorably) by P.K. Elkin in Journal of the Australasian
Universities Language and Literature Association, 28 (1967),
248-49.

Pp. 51-65 ("The Diminishing Tendency: The Mechanical Operation of
the Spirit") discuss the target of The Mechanical Operation not only
as English Dissent and the new science, but the tendency of men to
reduce life, thought, and action to things and mechanisms. Two marks
of Swift's style are the use of images drawn from machinery and the
mock-solemn arrangement of argument into stiff, pseudological
patterns. There are also a few references to A Tale of a Tub, Verses
on the Death of Dr. Swift, and A Modest Proposal.

723. Probyn, Clive T. "Swift's Anatomy of the Brain: The Hexagonal Bite
of Poetry." N&Q, 219 (1974), 250-51.

William Wotton's Reflections Upon Ancient and Modern Learning
(1694), chapter 17, is the source of Swift's anatomy of the brain.

See also Items 172, 671, 687, 692, 1062.

D. Political Writings

724. Backscheider, Paula R. "The First Blow Is Half the Battle: Swift's
Conduct of the Allies." Pp. 47-55 of Newsletters to Newspapers:
Eighteenth-Century Journalism. Edited by Donavan H. Bond and W.
Reynolds McLeod. Morgantown, W.V.: West Virginia U. School of
Journalism, 1977.

The rhetorical devices of The Conduct of the Allies are evidence of
a satire disguised as "a simple political essay."

725. Béranger, Jean. Les Hommes de lettres et la politique en Angleterre
de la révolution de 1688 à la Mort de George Ier. (Université de
Paris, Faculté des lettres et sciences humaines.) Bordeaux:
Biscaye Freres, 1968. Pp. 658.

Rev. by C. DeWitt Eldridge in Scriblerian, 1, no. 2 (Spring,
1969), 6; in review art. ("Augustan Politics and Men of Letters")
by Ricardo Quintana in Études Anglaises, 22 (1969), 387-92.

Perhaps the most thorough comparison of Defoe and Swift, as working journalists, men of letters, political animals, yet written.

726. Cook, Richard I. *Jonathan Swift as a Tory Pamphleteer*. Seattle and London: U. of Washington Press, 1967. Pp. xxxiv + 157.

Rev. (favorably) by James J. Stathis in *Georgia Review*, 23 (1969), 110-11; by C.J. Rawson in *RES*, n.s. 20 (1969), 230-32; (with reservations) by Phillip Harth in *MLQ*, 29 (1968), 493-95; (with reservations) by Pierre Danchin in *English Studies*, 52 (1971), 272-74; (favorably) by Samuel N. Bogorad in *Eire-Ireland*, 9, no. 1 (Spring 1974), 153-55; by A.J. Sambrook in *Scriblerian*, 1, no. 1 (Autumn 1968), 23-24; (with other works) by Maurice Johnson in *Satire Newsletter*, 5 (1968), 175-78; by Phillipp Wolff-Windegg in *Erasmus*, 21 (1969), 32-34; (with other works) in *TLS*, July 4, 1968, p. 707.

Prior to 1710 Swift frequently wrote with no clear sense of audience and with something less than urgency about the dangers of religious and intellectual corruption. But from 1710-1714, the audience he conceived for his Tory tracts was most often the country squirearchy. Cook goes on to examine Swift's applications of classical rhetoric and of various satiric devices in these political writings, including ways of naming, allegories, imagery, and polemical characters. Comparison with Defoe's political tracts leads to further distinctions as to audience and manner. Finally, Cook argues that Swift's Tory writings constitute a valid writing of history--"less a straightforward record of fact than an instructive dramatic narration of a climactic moment in the national life."

727. Cook, Richard I. "'Mr. *Examiner*' and 'Mr. *Review*': The Tory Apologetics of Swift and Defoe." *HLQ*, 29 (1965), 127-46.

After an interesting review of the exchange of insults between Swift and Defoe, Cook distinguishes the audiences of the two journals. Knowing his readers were basically hostile to the Tories, Defoe exploits his own personality for rhetorical effect, offering himself as a man of native wit and practical experience in whom readers can feel a personal interest. Swift, on the other hand, seems to assume that it is his status as a well-educated gentleman that entitles him to a hearing. Cook's main example is the responses of the two journalists to the furor created by the Tories' dismissal of Malborough as general of the Allied armies.

728. Dalsimer, Adele M. "Yeats's Unchanging Swift." *Eire-Ireland*, 9, no. 2 (Summer 1974), 65-89.

Partly a discussion of what Yeats learned about intellectual liberty and the threat of the Many from *A Discourse on the Contests and Dissensions of the Commons and Nobles in Athens and Rome*; also a survey of what Yeats thought were the personal resemblances between himself and Swift. Most of what Yeats thought about Swift came from Richard King's *Swift in Ireland* (1895).

729. Dammers, Richard H. "Swift, Steele, and the Palatines: A Case of
     Political Principle." Ball State University Forum, 18, no. 3
     (Summer 1977), 17-22.

     Discusses the background to Examiner, No. 4, 7 June 1711, without
     providing new evidence.

730. Dickinson, H.T. "The October Club." HLQ, 33 (1970), 155-73.

     Tells the history of the Tory extremist group, founded in 1710 to
     pressure Harley against the Whigs; a list of the members is
     appended. The effect of the group on Swift's political writing for
     Harley is not analyzed.

731. Downie, J.A. "The Conduct of the Allies: The Question of Influence."
     Pp. 108-28 of The Art of Jonathan Swift. Edited by Clive T.
     Probyn. New York: Barnes & Noble; London: Vision Press, 1978.

     After a brief discussion of the circumstances of The Conduct of the
     Allies and a review of the work itself, Downie repeats the usual
     mention of St. John as a source of Swift's ideas, but goes further
     to suggest considerable influence by Oxford. The assumption that
     Oxford's attitude to the "conspiracy thesis" was fundamentally
     different from that of Swift and St. John is laid to rest;
     similarities between Harley's 1708 attack on the Godolphin ministry
     and the passages in Swift's work are presented; and, finally,
     details in The Conduct that could have come from no one but Harley
     are unearthed.

732. Downie, J.A. Robert Harley and the Press: Propaganda and Public
     Opinion in the Age of Swift and Defoe. Cambridge: Cambridge U.
     Press, 1979. Pp. xii + 232.

     Pp. 131-48 are "Swift, Defoe, and the Peace Campaign." An economical
     comparison of the different audiences and purposes of the
     propagandist writings of Swift and Defoe. Swift's Examiner essays
     appealed to both ministerial supporters and to the "political
     nation" at large (the landed gentry and provincial clergymen);
     Defoe, meanwhile, had the sticky job of addressing the dissident
     Whigs. Recruited to "moderate" the tone of the Examiner, Swift
     eventually sounded more like St. John than Harley wanted to hear.
     Downie's analysis of Swift's involuntary resignation of the Examiner
     post is especially good; along the way, he presents brief
     discussions of The Conduct of the Allies, An Excellent New Song, and
     Some Remarks on the Barrier Treaty.

733. Ehrenpreis, Irvin. Acts of Implication: Suggestion and Covert
     Meaning in the Works of Dryden, Swift, Pope, and Austen. (The
     Bechman Lectures, Berkeley, 1978.) Berkeley, Los Angeles, and
     London: U. of California Press, 1980. Pp. x + 158.

Chapter 2, "Swift: The Examiner and the Drapier" (pp. 51-82), discusses the political aims of those works and traces the development of Swift's "methods of implication," including antithesis, ironical metaphors, similes, personifications, metonymy, synecdoche, and allegories. Where The Drapier's Letters define a true concept of heroism, the Examiner merely attacks a false one.

734. Evans, James E. "Swift's Partisan Pen: The Example of Lord Wharton." Enlightenment Essays, 6 (1975), 13-21.

A stock analysis of Swift's satirical devices in attacking Wharton (Examiner essays and A Short Character of Wharton), with special emphasis on the understatement and obliqueness necessitated by legal prohibitions.

735. Horne, Colin J. "The Roles of Swift and Marlborough in The Vanity of Human Wishes." MP, 73 (1976), 280-83.

In lines 175-190 of his poem, Johnson adapted Swift's depiction of Marlborough in The Conduct of the Allies and Examiner, No. 16.

736. Horsley, L.S. "Rogues or Honest Gentlemen: The Public Characters of Queen Anne Journalists." TSLL, 18 (1976), 198-228.

This study of how a "public character" is created in the journalism of Defoe, Tutchin, and Swift, distinguishes Swift by his aloofness, confidence, and authority.

737. Horsley, Lee. "Vox Populi in the Political Literature of 1710." HLQ, 38 (1975), 335-53.

This study of Tory mobs and propaganda during the Sacheverell controversy discusses the way Swift's Examiner essays appropriate the arguments of Whig defectors to argue, in contrast to High Church complete opposition to the theory of vox populi, vox Dei, that the people's voice now supported the Tories.

738. Köster, Patricia. "Means and Meaning: Translation as a Polemic Weapon." Classical News and Views (Ottawa), 14 (1970), 13-20.

Includes a brief discussion of Swift's use of Cicero's attack on Verres to satirize Wharton.

739. Kramnick, Isaac. Bolingbroke and His Circle: The Politics of Nostalgia in the Age of Walpole. (Harvard Political Studies.) Cambridge, Ma.: Harvard U. Press, 1968. Pp. xiii + 321.

Rev. (favorably) by J.H. Plumb in Scriblerian, 2 (1969), 20-21; (favorably) by Richard I. Cook in ELN, 7 (1969), 143-45; in TLS, Apr. 10, 1969, p. 379.

"The Savage Indignation of Dean Swift" (pp. 206-17) is a general
survey of Swift's political opinions, with stress on his ideal of a
"hierarchical ordering of society and nature according to the
divinely ordered chain of being," and on his criticism of the new
financial order in England.

740. Lein, Clayton. "Rhetoric and Allegory in Swift's Examiner 14." SEL,
    17 (1977), 407-17.

    Rev. in review art. ("Augustan Literature") by William Kupersmith
    in PQ, 57 (1978), 473-91.

    From a discussion of the essay's rhetorical organization, especially
    the speaker's distinct religious character, the polarization
    implicit everywhere, and the emblem "Veritas filia temporis," Lein
    describes an implicit allegory justifying the Tory ascendency.

741. McDowell, R.B. "Swift as a Political Thinker." Pp. 176-86 of
    Jonathan Swift 1667-1967: A Dublin Tercentenary Tribute. Edited by
    Roger McHugh and Philip Edwards. Dublin: Dolmen Press; London:
    Oxford U. Press, 1967.

    Describes the importance to Swift of a national church, his attacks
    on trade restrictions (The Story of the Injured Lady) and on the
    authority of England to enslave Ireland, combining these points with
    a running account of Swift's own political fortunes. For a more
    analytical treatment, see W.A. Speck (Item 752).

742. McKenzie, Alan T. "Proper Words in Proper Places: Syntax and
    Substantive in The Conduct of the Allies." ECS, 1 (1968), 253-60.

    Swift's stylistic effectiveness is largely created by the middle
    degree of abstraction of his substantives.

743. Müllenbrock, Heinz-Joachim. Whigs Kontra Tories: Studien zum
    Einfluth der Politik aug die englische Literatur des frühen 18.
    Jahrdunderts. Heidelberg: Carl Winter, 1974. Pp. 345.

    Includes several pages of scholarly comments on the Examiner in its
    context.

744. Patterson, Emily H. "Swift's Marginalia in Burnet's History of His
    Own Time." Enlightenment Essays, 3 (1972), 47-54.

    In his "last comments upon his religion and politics," Swift attacks
    Burnet's softness towards Dissent, his Whiggish partisanship in
    accounts of the Prince of Wale's birth, his alliance with William of
    Orange, his role in the Revolution, and his opposition to the Treaty
    of Utrecht negotiations. He also criticized Burnet's sloppy rhetoric
    and lack of objectivity. Some things never change.

745. Quinlan, Maurice J. "The Prosecution of Swift's Public Spirit of the Whigs." TSLL, 9 (1967), 167-84.

Stresses the personal recrimination motivating the prosecution.

746. Rogers, Pat. "Dying of a Hundred Good Symptoms." N&Q, 214 (1969), 195.

Identifies The Conduct of the Allies as a possible antecedent for Pope's famous remark about "dying of a hundred good symptoms."

747. Rogers, Pat. "Swift and Bolingbroke on Faction." Journal of British Studies, 9, no. 2 (May 1970), 71-101.

A detailed glossing of the word Bolingbroke and Swift identified with the root of all evil: "faction."

748. Rogers, Pat. "Swift and Cicero: The Character of Verres." Quarterly Journal of Speech, 61 (1975), 71-75.

Swift's use of Cicero in his fourth contribution to the Examiner shows that he did not think of periodical writing as necessarily topical, opportunistic, occasional, and that he expected his readers to be ready to pick up detailed classical allusions and to respond to political debate in the form of oratory. Includes comparisons of passages by Swift and by Cicero.

749. Rosenheim, Edward, Jr. "The Text and Context of Swift's Contests and Dissentions." MP, 66 (1968), 59-74.

This is a very detailed review of the Frank H. Ellis edition. Rosenheim denies that Contests and Dissentions is satiric and urges Swift critics to keep this particular minor text in its subordinate place.

750. Snyder, Henry L. "Arthur Maynwaring and the Whig Press, 1710-12." Pp. 120-36 of Literatur als Kritik des Lebens: Festschrift zum 65. Geburtstag von Ludwig Borinski. Edited by R. Haas, H. Müllenbrock, and C. Uhlig. Heidelberg: Quelle und Meyer, 1975.

Provides useful information about the press wars in which The Examiner and The Conduct of the Allies took part.

751. Speck, W.A. "The Examiner Examined: Swift's Tory Pamphleteering." Pp. 138-154 of Focus: Swift. Edited by C.J. Rawson. London: Sphere Books, 1971.

As much an introduction to the political period of Swift's life as an analysis of his journalistic writing, this essay nevertheless manages to be both concise and detailed.

752. Speck, W.A. "Swift's Politics." University Review (Dublin), 4
     (1967), 53-71.

     Rept. (as "From Principles to Practice: Swift's Party Politics")
     as pp. 69-86 of Item 447.

     Identifying three major issues separating Whigs and Tories in
     Swift's time--(1) the origin of government; (2) the position of the
     Church of England in society; (3) England's role in Europe--Speck
     provides a masterful analysis of Swift's political opinions,
     delivering him once and for all of the taint of mere place-seeking.
     Swift believed, with Hobbes, that sovereign power was in the
     legislature, thus his advocacy of a balanced constitution and even a
     contract theory. Consequently, Swift thought the Church could
     provide a "moral police force" to encourage virtue and discourage
     vice in this kind of state. Throughout, Speck emphasizes that Swift
     must be seen, not as adopting the moderate positions of both parties
     on particular issues, but as consistently taking extreme positions
     on the real issues.

753. Wilson, T.G. "Swift: The Prince of Journalists." Dublin Magazine, 6,
     nos. 3-4 (Autumn/Winter 1967), 46-73.

     The story of Swift's journalism career in England, with little
     analysis of his style or political thinking.

     See also Items 31, 158, 172, 175, 282, 302, 343, 460, 467, 842,
     866, 985.

E. Historical Writings

754. Johnson, James William. The Formation of English Neoclassical
     Thought. Princeton: Princeton U. Press, 1967. Pp. 63-68.

     Discusses the influence of Greco-Roman historiography on Swift's
     "increasing pessimism," from Contests and Dissentions (1701) to The
     Drapier's Letters (1724) and to letters of 1737.

755. Johnson, James William. "Swift's Historical Outlook." Journal of
     British Studies, 4, no. 2 (May, 1965), 52-77.

     Rept. as pp. 96-120 of Item 332.

     This challenging essay describes Swift's belief in classical
     uniformitarianism, Christian egalitarianism, Decline, Time, Climate,
     and Luxury, then goes on to argue that the body of historiography

that gave Swift his concepts also provided him with theses to
prevent fatalism and despair. Johnson ignores the vast difference in
Swift's attitudes during what Johnson calls the "last ten years of
his life," but which might well be seen as the last _twenty_ years of
Swift's life.

756. Jones, Myrddin. "A Living Treasury of Knowledge and Wisdom: Some
Comments on Swift's Attitude to the Writing of History." Durham
University Journal, 67 (1974), 180-88.

Rev. in review art. ("Studies in Augustan Literature") by William
Kupersmith in PQ, 55 (1976), 533-52.

The emphasis here on Swift's eventual loss of faith in history at
least starts to balance J.W. Johnson's persuasive claims for Swift's
historical optimism (see Item 755).

757. Seijas, Joaquin Rojo. "Swift y La Revolucion de 1688-89." Filologia
Moderna, 10 (1970), 113-30.

The title is misleading. This is a general review of Swift's
historical and political views culled from English and American
scholarship. J.W. Johnson does it better (Item 755).

758. Vance, John A. "A Most Deliberate Omission Concerning Harley."
Scriblerian, 11 (1978), 44-45.

After his dashed hopes for an English deanery, Swift altered a
sentence in his History of the Four Last Years which made allowances
for Harley's inattention to the welfare of "particular Persons."

759. Watt, Ian. "Two Historical Aspects of the Augustan Tradition." Pp.
67-88 of Studies in the Eighteenth Century: Papers Presented at
the David Nichol Smith Memorial Seminar, Canberra 1966. Edited by
R.F. Brissenden. Canberra: Australian National U. Press; Toronto:
U. of Toronto Press, 1968.

Describes the influence of landed interests and surveys attitudes
towards the Roman parallel including Swift's view: a "process
whereby moral decay led remorselessly to political collapse."

See also Item 172.

F. The Drapier's Letters and Irish Tracts

760. Abernethy, P.L. "The Identity of Hawthorne's Major Molineux."
     American Transcendental Quarterly, 31 (1976), 5-8.

     A principal source of Hawthorne's Major Molineux was probably
     Swift's ironic account of the execution in effigy of William Wood,
     though William Molyneux in some ways more closely resembles
     Hawthorne's character in being a man caught between two factions.

761. Beckett, J.C. "Swift and the Anglo-Irish Tradition." Pp. 155-70 of
     Focus: Swift. Edited by C.J. Rawson. London: Sphere Books, 1971.

     Introduction to Swift's complex attitudes as compassionate colonial,
     with fairly detailed attention to the circumstances of his various
     Irish writings.

762. Bertelsen, Lance. "Ireland, Temple, and the Origins of the Drapier."
     PLL, 13 (1977), 413-19.

     The figure of the Drapier symbolically represents precise knowledge
     of public fashion and caprice, evokes Swift's boycott scheme, and
     reminds readers of the ruined Irish industry. In addition, Sir
     William Temple had used the term "drape" to mean "jeer or satirize."

763. Coughlin, Matthew N. "'This Deluge of Brass': Rhetoric in the First
     and Fourth Drapier Letters." Eire-Ireland, 11, no. 2 (Summer
     1976), 77-91.

     Letter One is written in the five-part form of a classical oration,
     arguing by "half-truths, hypothetical examples, maxims and
     innuendoes" for a boycott based on economics, playing on his
     audience's fears by suggesting the direst consequences. One of its
     most important functions is to establish the good character and
     rapport of the Drapier. Letter Four modifies the classical form and
     works by Digressions, principally, rather than Narration, to appeal
     to nationalism.

764. Ehrenpreis, Irvin. "Dr. S***t and the Hibernian Patriot." Pp. 24-37
     of Jonathan Swift 1667-1967: A Dublin Tercentenary Tribute. Edited
     by Roger McHugh and Philip Edwards. Dublin: Dolmen Press; London:
     Oxford U. Press, 1967.

     Compares Swift's Irish writings with the political rhetoric of his
     London years, to the great advantage of the former. Ehrenpreis
     concludes that Swift's apparent disdain for Ireland "belongs in the
     rhetorical category, so much practised by him, of love expressed
     through insult."

765. Ewald, W.B., Jr. "M.B., Drapier." Pp. 170-91 of <u>Swift: Modern</u>
     <u>Judgements</u>. Edited by A. Norman Jeffares. London: Macmillan, 1969;
     Nashville, Tenn.: Aurora, 1970.

     Orig. pub. in <u>The Masks of Jonathan Swift</u> (1954).

     In an essay of broad illumination, Ewald stresses the fitness of the
     Drapier persona for Swift's arguments, especially his various "forms
     of humility."

766. Guskin, Phyllis J. "Intentional Accidentals: Typography and Audience
     in Swift's <u>Drapier's Letters</u>." <u>Eighteenth-Century Life</u>, 6, n.s. 1
     (1980), 80-101.

     This study of italicized and capitalized words and phrases in <u>The</u>
     <u>Drapier's Letters</u> should provide a valuable warning that
     typographical features in all eighteenth-century printed texts may
     be purposeful, persuasive devices. In <u>The Drapier's Letters</u>
     particularly, Swift used capitals and italics primarily to thrust
     his sarcasm and invective in even the slowest reader's face.

767. Kinkead-Weekes, Mark. "The Dean and the Drapier." Pp. 41-55 of <u>Swift</u>
     <u>Revisited</u>. Edited by Denis Donoghue. Cork: Mercier; Hatboro, Pa.:
     Folklore Associates, 1968.

     A summary of Swift's Irish career, for a general audience.

768. Kuczynski, Jürgen. "Defoe, Pope und Swift." Pp. 9-40 of <u>Gestalten</u>
     <u>und Werke: soziologische Studien zur Englischsprachigen und</u>
     <u>französischen Literatur</u>. Berlin and Weimar: Aufbau-Verlag, 1971.

     Noted by Hermann J. Real in <u>Scriblerian</u>, 8 (1976), 81.

     "Swift's Irish tracts mirror the strident social injustices of life
     in an English colony." (Real)

769. Lein, Clayton D. "Jonathan Swift and the Population of Ireland."
     <u>ECS</u>, 8 (1975), 431-53.

     The figure of 1,500,000 given in the second <u>Drapier's Letter</u> and in
     <u>A Modest Proposal</u> was low by probably at least 1,000,000. That Swift
     and his friends actively, and apparently sincerely, countered
     attempts to correct these figures is due to their insistence on
     Ireland's poverty: according to mercantilist theory, large numbers
     of people inherently created wealth.

770. Macaree, David. "Reason and Passion Harmonized: <u>The Drapier's</u>
     <u>Letters</u> and the Language of Political Protest." <u>Canadian Journal</u>
     <u>of Irish Studies</u>, 2, no. 2 (December 1976), 47-60.

     A sketch of the Wood's coinage affair is followed by a few examples

of The Drapier's Letters' influence on Irish and American political
writers, particularly John Dickinson's Letters from a Farmer in
Pennsylvania (1767). Swift's lesson of peaceful persuasion was
mastered, then unfortunately put aside.

771. Rawson, C.J. "The Injured Lady and the Drapier: A Reading of Swift's
     Irish Tract." Philological Society Transactions, 3 (1980), 15-43.

     Rawson continues his efforts to find a coherent vision in Swift's
     writings by ascribing similarities between the themes and "energies
     of style" of the Drapier's Letters and other Irish tracts and those
     of A Tale of a Tub, Swift's poetry, and Gulliver's Travels
     (especially Book III). Of course, the Irish tracts seem to place
     their blame more concretely and precisely (on English tyranny and
     Irish folly) than the Travels or A Modest Proposal, never quite
     reaching the extreme scepticism or indeterminacy of Swift's most
     disturbing works. Nonetheless, the Drapier himself is reminiscent of
     the Political Projectors of Book III, and the Irish writings
     generally share "that unsettling sense of a general blurring of
     values that makes good and bad, satirist and villain, tyrant and
     tyrannised partake of the same folly."

772. Ross, Angus. "The Hibernian Patriot's Apprenticeship." Pp. 83-107 of
     The Art of Jonathan Swift. Edited by Clive T. Probyn. New York:
     Barnes & Noble; London: Vision Press, 1978.

     Also pub. as pp. 83-107 of A Centenary Symposium, ed. Alice Shalvi
     (Jerusalem: Jerusalem Academic, 1976).

     The "double vision" imparted by Swift's Anglo-Irish experiences
     colors four Irish tracts he wrote before 1714, as well as his
     theories of language and style.

773. Schmidt, Johann N. "Die Fiktionen des Tuchhändlers." Pp. 107-30 of
     Of Private Vices and Publick Benefits: Beiträge zur englischen
     Literatur des frühen 18. Jahrhunderts. Edited by Johann N.
     Schmidt. (Anglo-American Forum, 11.) Frankfurt: Peter Lang, 1979.

     Analyzes rhetorical techniques by which Swift created an ideal
     speaker in The Drapier's Letters and an ideal reader, whom his
     audience was persuaded to become. The discussion treats imagery,
     diction, irony, and persona.

774. Simms, J.G. "Dean Swift and the Currency Problem." Occasional Papers
     of the Numismatic Society of Irreland, 20 (1978), 8-18 + 1 pl.

775. Tanaka, Mitsuo. "Swift's Immodest Proposals After the Drapier."
     Doshisha Literature, 29 (1979), 1-24.

     A bland and general survey of A Short View of the State of Ireland
     and A Modest Proposal.

776. Thomas, W.K. "The Bickerstaff Caper." Dalhousie Review, 49 (1969), 346-60.

    A readable account of the literary demolishing of John Partridge; the rub, as Thomas tells it, lies in the renewed success the Bickerstaff publicity created for Partridge's almanac.

777. Treadwell, J.M. "Swift, William Wood, and the Factual Basis of Satire." Journal of British Studies, 15, no. 2 (Spring 1976), 76-91.

    Describes Wood's career, showing him as in reality the arch-projector Swift depicted: "Rapacious, Obscure, Ignominious."

    See also Items 56, 60, 101, 268, 282, 381, 431, 454 465, 733, 741, 846, 856, 875.

G. A Modest Proposal

778. Alkon, Paul K. "Defoe's Argument in The Shortest Way with the Dissenters." MP, 73 (1976), S12-S23.

    Alkon argues that The Shortest Way presents insurmountable rhetorical difficulties to readers striving to establish their own superiority to the speaker. He (provocatively) sees A Modest Proposal as a direct contrast: "no one has any trouble defining his own intentions in relation to those of the speaker."

779. Bernard, F. V. "Swift's Maxim on Populousness: A Possible Source." N&Q, 210 (1965), 18.

    The notion that people are the riches of a nation was also used in essays by Sir William Temple ("Of Popular Discontents" and "An Essay Upon the Advancement of Trade in Ireland").

780. Bogel, Frederic V. "Irony, Inference, and Critical Uncertainty." Yale Review, 69 (1979-80), 503-19.

    This theoretical discussion of the relations between readers and ironical personae arrives at the conclusion that all irony gives readers the experience of uncertainty. The essay is especially good on the consequences for readers trying to distinguish themselves from speakers who are fools or knaves. The main example from Swift is A Modest Proposal.

781. Booth, Wayne C. A Rhetoric of Irony. Chicago: U. of Chicago Press,
     1974. Pp. xiv + 292.

     Rev. by Gloria Cigman in RES, n.s. 27 (1976), 361-63; in
     Scriblerian, 7 (1975), 113-14; in review art. ("You Must Be
     Joking") by Mark Roberts in Essays in Criticism, 26 (1976), 83-90;
     by Terry Heller in Arizona Quarterly, 31 (1975), 367-69;
     (severely) by George McFadden in Journal of Aesthetics and Art
     Criticism, 33 (1975), 361-63; (with reservations) by H.D. Kelling
     in ELN, 13 (1975), 232-38; (another work) by Robert Buffington in
     Sewanee Review, 83 (1975), xxxiv-xl; by Paul Newell Campbell in
     The Quarterly Journal of Speech, 60 (1974), 511; (with
     reservations) by Philip Stevick in Comparative Literature, 28
     (1976), 277-79.

     Pp. 101-23 discuss Swift. Booth gives a very detailed analysis of
     the "controlled inconsistencies" of A Modest Proposal,
     distinguishing three voices: a calm but indignant rationalist; a mad
     proposer of cannibalism; and Swift's own voice, devoid of irony.
     However, the complex interweavings of these voices forces each
     reader into an "active battle to reconstruct the genuine values from
     the grotesque mixture of sane, half-sane, and mad." Readers derive
     their building materials from the innumerable assumptions they make
     about how Swift himself would believe about the matters raised in
     the essay. In addition, Booth analyzes the structure of a letter
     from Bathurst to Swift and briefly comments on the relevance of
     ironical readings of the eulogy in Verses on the Death of Dr. Swift.

782. Borkat, Roberta Sarfatt. "Moral Mathematics in Jonathan Swift's
     Modest Proposal." Eighteenth-Century Life, 1 (1975), 64-67.

     A Modest Proposal makes a covert "argument in favor of charity and
     respect for human life" through the ghastly implications of the
     proposer's arithmetic.

783. Brilli, Attilio. "La Modesta Proposta di Swift fra Satira e
     Ideologia." ["Swift's Modest Proposal: Between Satire and
     Ideology."] Pp. 283-89 of Critical Dimensions: English, German and
     Comparative Literature Essays in Honour of Aurelio Zaneo. Edited
     by Mario Curreli and Alberto Martino. Cuneo: SASTE, 1978.

     General remarks on the influence of Swift's humanism ("moral
     intelligence") on A Modest Proposal.

784. Brown, Thomas. "Ellipsis in 'The Modest Proposal'." CEA Critic, 38,
     no. 1 (November 1975), 14-16.

     By "ellipsing" "all words and phrases connected with the processing
     of children for food," Swift exacerbates his readers' anxiety,
     forcing them to "mentally commit the necessary murder" as a
     preliminary to provoking their terrified renunciation of the scheme.

785. Carpenter, Andrew. "Two Possible Sources for Swift's 'A Modest Proposal'." Irish Booklore, 2 (1972), 147-48.

   The idea of children harvested for food was also hinted in: (1) William King's Some Observations on the Taxes paid by Ireland to Support the Government; and (2) a speech by Anthony Dopping against the proposed repeal of the Act of Settlement.

786. Celati, Gianni. "La Quête Demoniaca." Caffé, July, 1968, pp. 48-62.

   A study of symbolism and the use of the imagination in A Modest Proposal.

787. Clark, John R. "Initiation Rite: Swift's Modest Proposal, Sentence 1." American Notes and Queries, 14 (1975), 20-21.

   The opening sentence is deliberately ambiguous and cunningly periodic, according to Clark.

788. Conrad, Robert C. "The Relationship of Heinrich Böll's Satire 'The Thrower-Away' to Jonathan Swift's 'A Modest Proposal'." Michigan Academician, 10 (1977), 37-46.

   Böll may not actually have been influenced by Swift, but their satires share a few general satiric impulses, including realistic description combined with outrageous exaggeration.

789. Corbett, Edward P.J. "A Method of Analyzing Prose Style with a Demonstration Analysis of Swift's Modest Proposal." Pp. 81-98 of Contemporary Essays on Style: Rhetoric, Linguistics, and Criticism. Edited by Glen A. Love and Michael Payne. Glenview, Ill.: Scott, Foresman and Co., 1969.

   Orig. pub. as pp. 106-24 of Reflections on High School English: NDEA Institute Lectures 1965. Edited by Gary Tate. Tulsa: U. of Tulsa Press, 1966; rept. as pp. 294-312 of Teaching Freshman Composition. New York, 1967.

   Findings: the average sentence in A Modest Proposal is almost 50% longer than in other writings by Swift--we are listening, not to the master of concise statement, but to a persona who is "so infatuated with the sound of his own words, that he rambles on at inordinate length"; frequent use of parentheses, absolute constructions, and compounding elements "betray a man who is unusually concerned for the accuracy of his statements and for the image he is projecting"; so does the projector's polysyllabic diction and mathematical and mercantile terminology; animal metaphors and the diminution trope of litotes points up the inhumanity of Anglo-Irish landlords; emotional impact is enhanced by deliberate underplaying of emotions and by repetition of key words and phrases. An appendix offers lists of repeated words, animal imagery, monosyllabism, outdated idioms, as well as statistics on words, sentences, and paragraphs.

790. Gilmore, Thomas B., Jr. "Swift's Modest Proposal: A Possible
     Source." PQ, 47 (1968), 590-92.

     Elaborates on Oliver Ferguson's suggestion of a parallel with Sir
     William Temple's "Essay Upon the Advancement of Trade in Ireland"
     (1673).

791. Gilmore, Thomas B. "On Teaching A Modest Proposal." English Record,
     23, no. 2 (Winter 1972), 47-51.

     Gilmore outlines several possible approaches to A Modest Proposal:
     by way of its satiric objects, either the persona, or the English,
     or Swift himself (since only an idealistic fool could imagine the
     Irish capable of acting in a humane, sensible way); in terms of
     three levels of irony, including the "pre-ironic" (supposing that
     this is the work of a madman, Thackeray-fashion), the "ironic"
     (patronizing the madness of the persona), and the "post-ironic"
     (accepting the impossibility of alternatives--"Nothing in the
     Proposal mitigates its harshness").

792. Greany, H.T. "Satiric Masks: Swift and Pope." Satire Newsletter, 3
     (1966), 154-59.

     Swift's and Pope's voices are often not personae but rather
     masks--attitudes, posturings--which allow the emergence of a "second
     voice" not in keeping with the principal attitude. A Modest Proposal
     is the chief example.

793. Hozeski, Bruce W. "A Mathematical Error in Jonathan Swift's A Modest
     Proposal." American Notes and Queries, 15 (1976), 53-55.

     The correct calculation reveals a satire on affluence: the 1000
     wealthiest families would actually eat 91,250 of the 100,000
     available infants in a year.

794. Jacobs, Edward Craney. "Echoes of Micah in Swift's Modest Proposal."
     Eire-Ireland, 13, no. 3 (Fall, 1978), 49-53.

     The "echoes" cited of the Book of Micah's metaphor of butchery and
     cannibalism, its prophesy of God's retribution against the rich, and
     its attack on animosities and factions are actually only general
     parallels.

795. Lockwood, Thomas. "Swift's Modest Proposal: An Interpretation." PLL,
     10 (1974), 254-67.

     Rev. (with reservations) in Scriblerian, 7 (1974), 16-17.

     Taking his hint from Irvin Ehrenpreis's 1963 assertion that Swift is
     speaking in his own voice, Lockwood argues that what is monstrous

about A Modest Proposal is "not the putative author but his putative audience," which must first of all be forced to admit that no one cares. The conclusions this essay reaches are stimulating; however, it offers little textual evidence in support of its major premise.

796. Macey, Samuel L. "The Persona in A Modest Proposal." Lock Haven Review, 10 (1968), 17-24.

Swift offers us his own "positive proposals" in a negative framework by having the projector dismiss them as impractical.

797. Manlove, C.N. Literature and Reality: 1600-1800. London: Macmillan; New York: St. Martin's Press, 1978. Pp. x + 238.

Pp. 114-24 see Swift, in A Modest Proposal and An Argument Against Abolishing Christianity, as being "comprehensive in his treatment of reality." He presents no norms, takes no sides, but rather pulls the ground from under his readers' feet. "What each man may learn from Swift's satire, each man may learn: the object is to force him into questioning himself, not to resent fixed values."

798. Meek, Jay. "Swift's A Modest Proposal, Paragraph 10." Explicator, 33, no. 2 (October 1974), Item #11.

The calculation in paragraph 10 is in error.

799. Miyazaki, Yoshizo. "Swift no Katarikuchi: A Modest Proposal o Yomu." ["Swift's Style of Talking."] Eigo Seinen (Tokyo), 124 (1978), 379-81.

Naïve treatment of A Modest Proposal as Swift's own direct suggestions.

800. Muecke, D.C. The Compass of Irony. London: Methuen, 1967. Pp. 73-74, 83-86.

A Modest Proposal illustrates many ironic strategies: Pretended Advice; Irony Displayed; Misrepresentation; Innuendo; Internal Contradiction; Parody; Praising in Order to Blame; Understatement; Overstatement.

801. Patterson, Emily. "Swift, Voltaire and the Cannibals." Enlightenment Essays, 6 (1975), 3-12.

Claims that both Voltaire (Candide) and Swift (A Modest Proposal), evidently suffering from "judgments of primitivism," offered defenses of cannibalism.

802. Pendexter, R.S., Jr. "Pregnant Wit in A Modest Proposal." American
     Notes and Queries, 17 (1979), 71-73.

     The proposer's figure of 120,000 annual births is miscalculated.

803. Pullen, Charles. "Eighteenth-Century Madness, Swift, and A Modest
     Proposal." Dalhousie Review, 58 (1978), 53-62.

     The proposer is a madman of a special variety, by virtue of reason
     that aspires to more than common sense. The essay itself is an
     "aborted" satire, since the author "so blatantly admits the failure
     of his weapons to make for a change of heart or policy"--most
     horrifying is "the lack of satiric rebuttal."

804. Rawson, Claude. "A Reading of A Modest Proposal." Pp. 29-50 of
     Augustan Worlds: New Essays on Eighteenth-Century Literature in
     Honour of A.R. Humphreys. Edited by J.C. Hilson, M.M.B. Jones, and
     J.R. Watson. New York: Barnes & Noble; Leicester: U. of Leicester
     Press, 1978.

     Beginning with an intriguing reminder that Swift genuinely despised
     beggars, Rawson points to the "explosive mixture" of compassion and
     contempt in A Modest Proposal and suggests that we are not listening
     to a simple ironic persona. At some points, the irony stops working
     in reverse and instead parallels Swift's own feelings.

805. Rogal, Samuel J. "The Timelessness of 'A Modest Proposal'." English
     Record, 18, no. 4 (April 1968), 48-53.

     Because Swift controls his passion by irony, by parody of human
     types, and by distancing his persona, A Modest Proposal demonstrates
     the worthlessness of furious, and speciously engaged, rhetoric.
     Swift gives the essay a classical form so that "the sharp sting of
     his insinuations would appear reasonably ethical to his
     contemporaries." The appeal of A Modest Proposal is therefore
     "timeless," transcending its immediate circumstances.

806. Smith, Charles K. "Toward a 'Participatory Rhetoric': Teaching
     Swift's Modest Proposal." College English, 30 (1968), 135-50.

     Advises teachers to assign original satires using Swift's rhetorical
     techniques to attack a contemporary social wrong.

807. Spacks, Patricia Meyer. "Some Reflections on Satire." Genre, 1
     (1968), 13-30.

     Rept. as pp. 360-78 of Satire: Modern Essays in Criticism. Edited
     by Ronald Paulson. Englewood Cliffs: Prentice-Hall, 1971.

     A valuable reading of A Modest Proposal as repeatedly establishing and then subverting the illusion that readers can safely share a point of view with the author superior to that of the Proposer. "If we take his essay seriously, allow ourselves to be affected by it, we are left in a state of profound uneasiness, recognizing our involvement in the evil to which we have earlier felt superior."

808. Thomson, Philip. The Grotesque. (Critical Idiom, 24.) London: Methuen, 1972.

"A Beautiful Young Nymph" is an example of the grotesque overwhelming the satiric point. A Modest Proposal horrifies its readers, making them temporarily uncertain of their responses--conflicting with the standard response to irony.

809. Tilton, John W. "Swift among the Cannibals." Satire Newsletter, 7 (1970), 153-57.

Describes the furor among citizens of Johnstown, Pa., when a parody of A Modest Proposal was printed in their town newspaper, 7 Aug. 1965.

810. Tilton, John W. "The Two 'Modest Proposals': A Dual Approach to Swift's Irony." Bucknell Review, 14, no. 3 (December 1966), 78-88.

Attacks critics who hear Swift's voice breaking through the persona (or who hear no persona at all, per Irvin Ehrenpreis) as "in effect reading scholarly notes to the 'Proposal' rather than the work itself." As an alternative, Tilton recommends distinguishing an imaginative re-creation of the original impact of the essay from analysis based on twentieth-century information and technique. Without making a thorough demonstration of his case, he claims that "nothing but the twentieth-century scholar's trained ear prevents our accepting every word in the 'Proposal' as the utterance of an Irish economist."

811. Uphaus, Robert W. "Gulliver's Travels, A Modest Proposal, and the Problematical Nature of Meaning." PLL, 10 (1974), 268-78.

Swift "breaks and extends the frame of reference of his manifest fictions to establish a larger, more problematical connection with the reader's own experiences." He aims at no one effect but rather seeks to violate the reader's expectations of coherent meaning. The main example is from A Modest Proposal.

812. Willson, Robert F., Jr. "A Modest Proposal: Swift's Persona as Absentee." Ball State University Forum, 17, no. 4 (Autumn 1976), 3-11.

The argument that the persona is an archetypal absentee landlord is thorough and ingenious, though not necessarily convincing. But it

does point up the shortcomings of seeing the persona as a
representative propagandist, a blind scientist, Swift himself, or a
self-deceived enthusiast.

See also Items 268, 276, 307, 376, 392, 396, 406, 430, 434, 444,
460, 653, 693, 722, 769, 775, 860, 1148.

H. Polite Conversation

813. Bliss, Alan. "Irish Proverbs in Swift's Polite Conversation." Irish
     University Review, 9 (1979), 23-30.

     Rept. as pp. 23-30 of Image and Illusion: A Festscrift for Roger
     McHugh. Edited by M. Harmon. Dublin, 1980.

     A number of expressions in Polite Conversation parallel those in an
     Irish manuscript of about 1670, suggesting that Swift was drawing
     from a fund of orally transmitted proverbs.

814. Hamilton, David. "Swift, Wagstaff, and the Composition of Polite
     Conversation." HLQ, 30 (1966), 281-95.

     First Hamilton shows that the irony in Wagstaff's introduction
     derives from the way he is "almost right" about opinions that were
     Swift's own—though he belabors those opinions and blunders into
     drawing absurd conclusions from them. Then Hamilton uses this
     notion, that Swift was "capable of sharing part of the ground
     occupied by those whom he ridiculed," to explain how this satire on
     empiricism and proverbial lore could have been written empirically
     by a man who collected proverbs all his life.

815. Kelly, Anne Cline. "Swift's Polite Conversation: An Eschatological
     Vision." SP, 73 (1976), 204-24.

     Rev. (favorably) in review art. ("Augustan Studies in 1976") by
     William Kupersmith in PQ, 56 (1977), 470-97.

     Swift exploits two antithetical trends in "courtesy literature": the
     humanistic ideal of good conversation as the basis of society serves
     as a norm, while the mechanical "cookbook" attitude towards
     conversation is satirized for its anti-social forces.

816. Mayhew, George. "Some Dramatizations of Swift's Polite Conversation
     (1738)." PQ, 44 (1965), 51-72.

     A complete account of the little that is known about several stage
     adaptations of Polite Conversation in Dublin and London from 1738 to
     1749.

817. Stewart, Susan. "The Pickpocket: A Study in Tradition and Allusion." MLN, 95 (1980), 1127-54.

By exaggerating and diminishing features of the allusive process, Polite Conversation attacks "the bourgeois quantification of the literary," affirming the autonomy and transcendence of the literary.

818. Stytsyna, S.H. "A Study of J. Swift's Phraseological Heritage." Sbornik Nauchnyh Trduov Moskovskogo Pedagogicheskogo Instituta Inostrannyh Yazykov [Studies of the Moscow Pedagogical Institute of Foreign Languages], 67 (1972), 201-14.

Noted in Scriblerian, 6 (1973), 4-5.

A study of Polite Conversation's idioms in three aspects: linguistic, stylistic, and aesthetic. (See also Item 819.)

819. Stytsyna, S. H. "Stylistic Use of Phraseological Units for Satire and Humour, Based on Swift's Works." Sbornik Nauchnyh Trudov Moskovskogo Pedagogicheskogo Instituta Inostrannyh Yazykov [Studies of the Moscow Pedagogical Institute of Foreign Languages], 70 (1972), 141-48.

Noted in Scriblerian, 6 (1973), 4-5.

Continues the study of idioms in Polite Conversation. (See Item 818.)

See also Items 407, 409, 654.

I. Correspondence

820. Abernethy, Cecil. "Addison and Swift: A Note on Style and Manners." Pp. 1-8 of Essays in Honor of Richebourg Gaillard McWilliams. Birmingham, Ala.: Birmingham-Southern College, 1970.

Mostly just a summary of Swift's relations with Addison, through the lens of Journal to Stella.

821. Crawford, Fred D. "Journals to Stella." Shaw Review, 18 (1975), 93-109.

This is a very detailed analysis of similarities between Swift's letters to Stella and Shaw's to Ellen Terry and to Mrs. Patrick Campbell: playfulness, exaggeration, deromanticizing of sex by ironic references to bodily functions and frailties, sexual banter, disparaging remarks about others' physical appearance, gossip, feigned detachment, doggerel verses, an inclination to instruct, the pretence that the correspondents are men, trivial inconveniences balancing a sense of self-importance.

822. Davidow, Lawrence Lee. "Pope's Verse Epistles: Friendship and the Private Sphere of Life." HLQ, 40 (1977), 151-70.

In the course of this discussion of how Pope uses the norm of private friendship as a standard for public and literary actions, Swift's distinction between Pope's prose letters and his verse epistles is pointed out.

823. Davis, Herbert. "The Correspondence of the Augustans." Pp. 1-13 of The Familiar Letter in the Eighteenth Century. Edited by Howard Anderson, Philip B. Daghlian, and Irvin Ehrenpreis. Lawrence and London: U. Press of Kansas, 1966, 1968.

Orig. pub. as pp. 181-97 of The Seventeenth Century: Studies in the History of English Thought and Literature from Bacon to Pope. Stanford: Stanford U. Press; London: Oxford U. Press, 1951. Reissued 1965. Reprinted 1969. Rept. as pp. 195-212 of Essays in English Literature from the Renaissance to the Victorian Age Presented to A.S.P. Woodhouse. Edited by Millar MacLure and F.W. Watt. Toronto: U. of Toronto Press, 1964.

Mostly concerning Swift, this essay wanders from Swift's expectation of his letters' publication to his use of irony and raillery, with final mention of his use of invective to hurt his correspondent.

824. Ehrenpreis, Irvin. "Swift's Letters." Pp. 197-215 of Focus: Swift. Edited by C.J. Rawson. London: Sphere Books, 1971.

The features of Swift's finest epistolary prose are his use of an intimate manner with the recipient and a detached tone toward the people or events discussed. Modern literary readers enjoy a double pleasure from Swift's letters: the mild excitement of an act of espionage, and the further excitement of hearing directly about an interesting but more or less concealed incident. Moreover, Swift's gifts for impersonation and aphorism, and for playing tricks upon loved and trusted friends, create frameworks for his characteristic deadpanned accounts of events.

825. Elias, A.C., Jr. "Stella's Writing-Master." Scriblerian, 9 (1977), 134-39.

The similarity of Stella's handwriting to that of Swift, in a transcript of a letter by Temple, provides evidence of Swift's tutelage of Stella.

826. England, A.B. "Private and Public Rhetoric in the <u>Journal</u> <u>to</u>
     <u>Stella</u>." <u>Essays</u> <u>in</u> <u>Criticism</u>, 22 (1972), 131-41.

   The tension between Swift's preoccupation with his public duties and
   his private personality is conveyed by a style "designed to give the
   impression that he communicates everything which passes through his
   mind as he is in the process of writing." This impression, however,
   is actually a created illusion. In fact, argues England, Swift is
   not merely engaged in reporting particulars, he is making a comment
   upon those particulars, "as they present themselves to him from
   moment to moment, on the <u>process</u> by which they will eventually
   become sequences." This last point is not documented beyond a doubt.

827. Ferguson, Oliver W. "'Nature and Friendship': The Personal Letters
     of Jonathan Swift." Pp. 14-33 of <u>The</u> <u>Familiar</u> <u>Letter</u> <u>in</u> <u>the</u>
     <u>Eighteenth</u> <u>Century</u>. Edited by Howard Anderson, Philip B. Daghlian
     and Irvin Ehrenpreis. Lawrence and London: U. Press of Kansas,
     1966, 1968.

   Emphasizing Swift's epistolary air of spontaneity, his allusiveness,
   raillery, and roleplaying, this essay sensibly demonstrates that
   letter-writing was always for Swift a "literary activity."

828. Holloway, John. "Dean of St. Patrick's: A View from the Letters."
     Pp. 258-68 of <u>The</u> <u>World</u> <u>of</u> <u>Jonathan</u> <u>Swift:</u> <u>Essays</u> <u>for</u> <u>the</u>
     <u>Tercentenary</u>. Edited by Brian Vickers. Cambridge, Ma.: Harvard U.
     Press; Oxford: Basil Blackwell, 1968.

   Rept. as pp. 57-74 of <u>Swift</u> <u>Revisited</u>. Edited by Denis Donoghue.
   Cork: Mercier; Hatboro, Pa.: Folklore Associates, 1968.

   Claiming that Swift's letters restore the rich epistolary immediacy
   and detail that had been lost since Ben Jonson, Holloway sketches
   Swift's final years through the letters. For a general audience,
   with emphasis on Swift's friendships, his raillery, and his
   simplicity.

829. Ong, Walter J., S.J. "The Writer's Audience is Always a Fiction."
     <u>PMLA</u>, 90 (1975), 9-21.

   In the course of describing fictionalized readers, Ong remarks that
   "No one today can capture exactly the fiction in Swift's <u>Journal</u> <u>to</u>
   <u>Stella</u>, though it is informative to try to reconstruct it as fully
   as possible, for the relationships of children to oldsters and even
   of man to woman have subtly altered, as have also a vast mesh of
   other social relationships which the <u>Journal</u> <u>to</u> <u>Stella</u> involves.

830. Seymour-Smith, Martin. <u>Poets</u> <u>Through</u> <u>Their</u> <u>Letters</u>. Vol. 1. London:
     Constable, 1969. Pp. 464.

   Pp. 157-205 stitches together remarks on Swift's life with
   quotations from his correspondence.

831. Smith, Frederik N. "Dramatic Elements in Swift's *Journal to Stella*."
     ECS, 1 (1968), 332-52.

     The three "dramatic worlds" of the *Journal to Stella* are Swift in
     dialogue with other characters, Swift in the act of writing, and
     Swift in relationship to his correspondent MD. Smith concludes that
     Swift was instinctively and spontaneously dramatic, even in his most
     artful works.

832. Smith, Frederik N. "Swift's Correspondence: The 'Dramatic' Style and
     the Assumption of Roles." *SEL*, 14 (1974), 357-71.

     The extreme looseness of Swift's syntax in correspondence indicates
     his primary interest in the sounds of speaking voices. The pose of
     pretended haughtiness is Swift's favorite.

833. Stillman, Claudia Ruth. "Swift in Wonderland: The Language of Dream
     in the *Journal to Stella*." *Literature and Psychology*, 25 (1975),
     108-16.

     The argument here is that the *Journal to Stella* exhibits a
     condensation of experience, an unlikely juxtaposition of things and
     events, shifts of identity, an atmosphere of omniscience and
     omnipresence, and a compression or confusion of sense, all of which
     "resemble the apparent absurdity of dreams." Just what this
     connection with dreams signifies, and why a verbal release from
     tension is most appropriately compared with a dream in the first
     place, is not explained.

834. Thompson, Paul V. "Suppressed Names in Swift's Letters, 1735." *N&Q*,
     216 (1971), 52-55.

     Restores Sir Walter Scott's "Corrigenda et Addenda" to letters of
     1735 between Swift and Mrs. Martha Whiteway.

835. Thompson, Paul V. "Swift's 'Poor Mr. Davis'." *N&Q*, 213 (1968),
     205-06.

     Argues for Peter Davis (d. 1698), rather than John Davis, as the
     friend lamented in Swift's letter of 13 January 1699.

836. Ulman, Craig Hawkins. *Satire and the Correspondence of Swift*.
     Cambridge, Ma.: Harvard U. Press, 1973. Pp. 53.

     A demonstration (by an undergraduate) that satiric masks and other
     literary devices permeate Swift's correspondence. Predictably,
     satire "does not govern entire letters; it appears in short
     flashes."

837. Whitley, E.M. "Contextual Analysis and Swift's Little Language of the Journal to Stella." Pp. 475-500 of In Memory of J.R. Firth. Edited by C.E. Bazell, J.C. Catford, M.A.K. Halliday, and R.H. Robins. London: Longmans, 1966.

A linguistic analysis of the little language addressing two questions: (1) the nature of the "mystic letters," "cyphers," or "odd combinations of letters," their identification with persons, the translation meanings given them by editors, and other related difficulties; (2) the nature of the little language as a whole, its place in the total text and its function, which is primarily to create the sound of an intensely personal, private speaking voice.

838. Woolf, Virginia. "Swift's Journal to Stella." Pp. 107-15 of Fair Liberty Was All His Cry: A Tercentenary Tribute to Jonathan Swift 1667-1745. Edited by A. Norman Jeffares. London: Macmillan; New York: St. Martin's Press, 1967.

Orig. pub. in The Common Reader, 2nd ser. (1935); rept. as pp. 162-69 of Swift: Modern Judgements. Edited by A. Norman Jeffares. London: Macmillan, 1969; Nashville, Tenn.: Aurora, 1970.

Stresses the privateness of the Journal to Stella as an escape from disguises thrust upon Swift by the public world.

See also Items 9, 19, 69, 73, 78, 79, 81, 93, 97, 172, 249, 293, 422, 568, 701, 781, 1060.

J. Miscellaneous Prose Writings

839. Arita, Masaya. "Swift no sekkyo." ["Swift's Sermons."] English Language and Literature (Chuo U.), 19 (1979), 55-82.

Noted by Zenzo Suzuki in Scriblerian, 12 (1980), 168-69.

"From his sermons Mr. Arita tries to reveal Swift's faith. But he goes no further than to indicate the conflict Swift felt between the political realism of the Church of England and his inner faith." (Suzuki)

840. Bandiera, Laura. "La 'Letter to a Young Gentleman' di Swift e l'omiletica anglicana del primo Settecento." Spicilegio Moderno: Saggi e Ricerche di Letterature e Lingue Straniere, 8 (1977), 174-89.

Wholeheartedly accepting the "Letter to a Young Gentleman" as Swift's, Bandiera goes on to find Swift repudiating the emotions for logic and reason. A naïve analysis.

841. Beckett, J.C. "Swift as an Ecclesiastical Statesman." Pp. 146-65 of
     Fair Liberty Was All His Cry: A Tercentenary Tribute to Jonathan
     Swift 1667-1745. Edited by A. Norman Jeffares. London: Macmillan;
     New York: St. Martin's Press, 1967.

     Orig. pub. as pp. 135-52 of Essays in British and Irish History in
     Honour of James Eadie Todd. Edited by H.A. Cronne, T.W. Moody, and
     D.B. Quinn. London, 1949.

     This is an overview of Swift's career as an ecclesiastical
     statesman, based largely on opinions expressed in Sentiments of a
     Church of England Man, stressing the permanence of his contribution
     to Anglican thought on the relations of Church and State.

842. Brown, Lloyd W. "The Person of Quality in the Eighteenth Century:
     Aspects of Swift's Social Satire." Dalhousie Review, 48 (1968),
     171-84.

     Three basic features of Swift's social satire are: the ironic
     juxtaposition of the ideal and the real; criticism of the
     aristocracy's lack of moral leadership; and the use of the person of
     quality as a satiric persona in developing these themes. The person
     of quality, "an unvarying symbol of the moral and intellectual
     shortcomings of the upper classes," is a specially useful instrument
     of Swift's ironic insight, being simultaneously a realistic analyst
     of social evils and the embodiment of many of these evils. The texts
     discussed are "An Argument," "The Advancement of Religion," and "A
     Letter to a Young Gentleman."

843. Coetzee, J.M. "The Agentless Sentence as a Rhetorical Device."
     Language and Style, 13 (1980), 26-34.

     The "vast preponderance of short passives over passives with
     expressed agents" makes the process of reading the Argument Against
     Abolishing Christianity largely a task of attributing the correct
     agents to the passive verbs. Though the text "is not finally
     ambiguous," it is cryptic and reveals Swift's concept of agentless
     passives as rhetorical rather than grammatical.

844. Cruttwell, Patrick. "Swift, Miss Porter, and the 'Dialect of the
     Tribe'." Shenandoah, 17, no. 4 (Summer 1966), 27-38.

     This summary, for a general audience, of Swift's attitudes in
     Proposal for Correcting the English Tongue locates his contradictory
     impulses in his "compulsive anxiety to rid himself of the filth of
     living."

845. Daw, C.P. "The Occasion of Swift's Excellency of Christianity." HLQ,
     41 (1978), 251-59.

     Because its "uncommon allusiveness" suggests an academic

congregation, and because Daw finds its light imagery reminiscent of the liturgy of the Epiphany season, this sermon may have been delivered to fulfill a requirement for Swift's Doctor of Divinity degree, at Trinity College, Dublin, shortly before February, 1702.

846. Daw, C.P. "Swift's 'Strange Sermon'." HLQ, 38 (1975), 225-36.

Rev. (severely) in review art. ("Studies in Augustan Literature") by William Kupersmith in PQ, 55 (1976), 533-52.

Relying on Orrery's 1752 description of Swift's sermons, Daw argues that Mutual Subjection is the "strange sermon" Bishop Evans complained about to Archbishop Wake on 28 February 1718.

847. Griffith, Philip Mahone. "Dr. Johnson's 'Diction of Common Life' and Swift's Directions to Servants." Pp. 10-30 of Jonathan Swift: Tercentenary Essays. (U. of Tulsa Department of English Monograph Series, 3.) Tulsa: U. of Tulsa, 1967.

Johnson's numerous dictionary quotations from Directions to Servants show its attractiveness to him as a repository of the diction of common life.

848. Irwin, Archibald B. "Swift as Translator of the French of Sir William Temple and His Correspondents." SEL, 6 (1966), 483-98.

This minute analysis of the style of Swift's French translations points to his concentration upon the fundamental sense of the originals, his comfortableness with the Latinate vocabulary, precision, and balance of the original language, and the extent to which Swift imposes his own succinct, antithetical style on the original letters.

849. Iwasaki, Yasuo. "Martinus Scriblerus: His Character as a Satirist." Bulletin of the Department of Commerce (Doshisha U., Kyoto), Special Issue (December 1968), 422-38.

Noted in Scriblerian, 2 (1970), 43.

Martinus is a complex satirical device, an object of ridicule himself, but also a penetrating satirist.

850. Johnson, Maurice. "A Note on Swift's Meditation upon a Broom-Stick and A Tale of a Tub." Library Chronicle, 37 (1971), 136-42.

The three-part structure of the Meditation sets up the concluding attack on man's pride in his own perversions of nature.

851. Kaiho, Masao. "Swift and Deism." Studies in English Literature (Tokyo), 48 (1972), 217-29.

A mechanical and overly simplified attempt to show Swift's attitudes towards Deism by the light of his sermons.

852. Kay, John. "The Hypocrisy of Jonathan Swift: Swift's Project Reconsidered." University of Toronto Quarterly, 44 (1975), 213-23.

The argument, that the Project is a disguised attack on the Whigs, is based on hearing Swift's own voice speaking directly to his purpose. It is fortified by references to a certain tolerance of hypocrisy in the writings of contemporary Anglican divines.

853. Kelly, Ann Cline. "Why Did Swift Sign His Name to A Proposal for Correcting ... the English Tongue?" Neophilologus, 63 (1979), 469-80.

Answer: to defend himself against accusations that he was Harley's tool, that he was a hack, that he was a follower, rather than a leader, that he was unable to be fully serious, that his motives were mercenary. All these defenses were willfully misconstrued by Swift's enemies, of course.

854. Lawson, E. Roy. "Jonathan Swift's Counsel to Clergymen." Pp. 29-36 of Increase in Learning: Essays in Honor of James G. Van Buren. Edited by Robert J. Owens, Jr. and Barbara E. Hamm. Manhattan, Kan.: Manhattan Christian College, 1979.

In his poems, Swift took his own advice about effective preaching (in "To a Young Gentleman Lately Enter'd into Holy Orders"). As a result, even the 'Unprintables' are "not pornographic but compassionate," if rather unsettling. More on the advice to clergymen than on the poetry.

855. Malek, James S. "Swift's Vindication of Lord Carteret: Authorial Intention and Historical Context." Rocky Mountain Review of Language and Literature, 29 (1975), 10-23.

Swift's persona, a chuckleheaded Whig who praises Carteret for the wrong reasons, enables the Vindication both to attack the Whigs and to compliment Carteret as the only exception.

856. Mayhew, George P. "Jonathan Swift's Hoax of 1722 Upon Ebenezor Elliston." Pp. 290-310 of Fair Liberty Was All His Cry: A Tercentenary Tribute to Jonathan Swift 1667-1745. Edited by A. Norman Jeffares. London: Macmillan; New York: St. Martin's Press, 1967.

Orig. pub. in Bulletin of the John Rylands Library, 44, no. 2 (March, 1962).

Swift's hoax on the soon-to-be-executed burglar is recounted, with the added suggestions that this active resistance to corruption helped lead Swift to the Drapier Papers, and that the interest exhibited here in the psychology of the criminal mind is exploited through the similarities between great men and criminals in Gulliver's Travels.

857. Meyers, Jeffrey. "The Sermons of Swift and Johnson." Personalist, 47 (1966), 61-80.

The opinions of Swift and Johnson on crucial Christian topics are compared, though no claims of literary influence are made.

858. Miyazaki, Yoshizo. "Swift no An Argument against Abolishing Christianity no kakidashi o megutte." ["On the First Paragraph of Swift's Argument against Abolishing Christianity."] Journal of the Faculty of Letters (Kobe U.), 7 (1978), 115-38.

Noted by Zenzo Suzuki in Scriblerian, 11 (1978), 11.

The "unexpected twist and frustration of expectation, according to Mr. Miyazaki, is Swift's forcible method of satire.... Mr. Miyazaki's paper reminds us of the recent phenomenological approach to literature by Wolfgang Iser and other 'affectivists'." (Suzuki)

859. New, Melvyn. "Sterne and Swift: Sermons and Satire." MLQ, 30 (1969), 198-211.

Advances the challenging argument that the sermons of both Swift and Sterne (often seen as representing an unimpassioned orthodoxy and a superficial or nominal Christianity, respectively) proceed from the same orthodox Anglican view of man's weaknesses as their satirical writings. Since man is not only susceptible, but indeed inclined, to sin, morality is never to be separated from religion, wisdom from revelation. Abuses of reason, at the heart of all religious, social, political, and literary aberrations, are the target of the sermons and the satires of both.

860. Nokes, David. "Swift and the Beggars." Essays in Criticism, 26 (1976), 218-35.

Warning that modern liberal principles may prejudice our understanding of Swift's irony, Nokes illustrates that Swift's "sermons demonstrate many of Swift's positive beliefs, and they are not of a kind to warm the hearts of humanitarians." Indeed, he shows that many of Swift's presumedly genuine opinions closely resemble the assertions of the modest proposer!

861. Orr, L. Anderson. "Proper Words in Proper Places: The Prayers of Swift and Johnson." Enlightenment Essays, 5, no. 2 (Summer, 1974), 26-32.

From the remarkable assumption that the prayers of Swift's sixtieth year must somehow represent his "settled" attitudes towards prayer, the style of Swift's prayers is found to suggest "an absence of stress, an intimate and confident pastoral presence, and even the nearness of God."

862. Peterson, Leland D. "Swift's Project: A Religious and Political Satire." PMLA, 82 (1967), 54-63.

See the exchange between Phillip Harth and Peterson ("Swift's Project: Tract or Travesty?") in PMLA, 84 (1969), 336-43; and between Jan R. Van Meter and Peterson ("On Peterson on Swift") in PMLA, 86 (1971), 1017-25; see also the reply by Donald Greene ("Swift's Project Continued") in the "Forum" section of PMLA, 87 (1972), 520.

A survey of the attitudes of Swift and other divines towards hypocrisy leads Peterson to read the Project as essentially ironic and satiric, "self-defeating in the extreme." The main targets of satire are "reformers and reforming societies, projectors, nominal Christianity, and the Whig Junto." Harth argues that Swift was not promoting hypocrisy but rather the encouragement of virtue and religion by the force of good example. Van Meter argues against the ironic persona Peterson claims to see and criticizes Peterson's use of evidence. Greene reminds us of La Rochefoucauld's maxim, "L'hypocrisie est un hommage que le vice rend à la vertu."

863. Philmus, Robert M. "Swift's 'Lost' Answer to Tindal." TSLL, 22 (1980), 369-93.

The argument here is that the Argument Against Abolishing Christianity is primarily an attack against Matthew Tindal's The Rights of the Christian Church (1706), presenting the design of the latter as a wholly imaginary project that no one would or could seriously entertain. However, "by exploiting the logically paradoxical relationship between the 'nominal' and the 'real,' Swift convincingly defends the apparently indefensible." Therefore, Philmus declares himself on the side of those who see Swift genuinely endorsing the necessity of "nominal Christianity."

864. Rao, E. Nageswara. "The Rhetoric of Unreason: Swift on the English Language." Osmania Journal of English Studies, 11 (1974-75), 37-45.

This paraphrase of A Proposal for Correcting the English Tongue concludes: "It is surprising that many of the finest products of the Age of Reason had failed to observe that language has a process of growth and decay like any other living organism."

865. Rawson, C.J. "Correspondence to the Editor." RES, n.s. 16 (1965), 406-07.

A line in A Modest Defence of a Late Poem By an Unknown Author, Call'd, The Lady's Dressing Room (1732), referring to the voiding of giant worms, recalls a 1716 letter of Gay to Parnell.

866. Richman, Jordan P. "The Political Sermons of Johnson and Swift." New Rambler, 10 (Spring 1971), 27-41.

Though generally similar in their views on the duties of a Christian in society and in their political conservatism, Johnson and Swift wrote for different audiences, accounting for the difference in their tones. Swift wrote for a particular group of readers on more or less specific occasions; Johnson's calmer mood derives from addressing a more universal audience.

867. Robertson, Mary F. "Swift's Argument: The Fact and the Fiction of Fighting with Beasts." MP, 74 (1976), 124-41.

Rev. (favorably) in Scriblerian, 9 (1977), 102-03; (with reservations) in review art. ("Augustan Studies in 1976") by William Kupersmith in PQ, 56 (1977), 470-97.

A long argument that Swift was capable of sincerely endorsing nominal Christianity is succeeded by the claim that the speaker, rather than being an impersonation, is actually a "mock encomium," an ironic stance taken by Swift himself. These points lead to the conclusion that the Argument is "both a mock-persuasive satire and at the same time a real example of his advocated rhetorical approach to free-thinkers and factionalists."

868. Rosenheim, E.W., Jr. "Swift and the Martyred Monarch." PQ, 54 (1975), 178-94.

Swift's contribution to the numerous political and polemical January 30th sermons on the martyrdom of Charles I was exceptional in stressing the "good uses" to which the story may be put in present circumstances.

869. Sams, Henry W. "Jonathan Swift's Proposal Concerning the English Language: A Reconsideration." SP, extra ser., 4 (January 1967), 76-87. (Essays in English Literature of the Classical Period Presented to Dougald MacMillan.) Edited by Daniel W. Patterson and Albrecht B. Strauss.

In addition to being a partisan tract, the Proposal may have been part of Swift's plans to become Historiographer Royal.

870. Stathis, James J. "Diminution in the Pulpit: Swift's Sermon Upon the Martyrdom of King Charles I." Tennessee Studies in Literature, 12 (1967), 51-55.

Points to Swift's attack on the characters and actions of the Puritans in hopes of preventing disunity among Anglicans.

871. Steensma, Robert C. "A Legal Proverb in Defoe, Swift, and Shenstone." Proverbium, 10 (1968), 248.

The expression "Laws are like Cobwebs" in "Tritical Essay" (1707) is not original with Swift.

872. Strang, Barbara. "Swift and the English Language: A Study in Principles and Practice." Pp. 1947-59 of To Honor Roman Jakobson: Essays on the Occasion of His Seventieth Birthday, 11 October 1966. (Janua Linguarum, Series Maior, 33.) Vol. 3. The Hague and Paris: Mouton, 1967.

This diffuse essay, "partly syntactical, partly stylistic," begins with a long account of Swift's attitudes toward language in A Proposal for Correcting ... the English Tongue, then moves on to mention his usage in such matters as "tho'," "whether," particles, demonstratives, the accidence and syntax of verbs, placing of adverbs and particles, and restrictions in lexical innovation.

873. Watanabe, Koji. "Swift's Image of Boyle." In Essays Presented to Shiko Murakami on the Occasion of His Retirement from Osaka University. Tokyo: Eihosha, 1974. Pp. 496.

Noted by Zenzo Suzuki in Scriblerian, 7 (1974), 83-84.

Internal evidence for reading A Meditation upon a Broom-Stick as partly a parody of Boyle's Occasional Reflections upon Several Subjects (1664). "Mr. Watanabe convincingly illuminates that for Swift, when he wrote his Meditation, Boyle was not a pious moralist, but a silly man." (Suzuki)

874. Weitzman, Arthur J. "A Spider's Poison: Wit in Swift's Letter of Advice to a Young Poet." Ariel (Canada), 4, no. 1 (January 1973), 24-34.

Proposing that the Letter of Advice to a Young Poet is "a satire on Swift's own wayward tendencies as a witty satirist," Weitzman argues that only Swift could have had in 1721 such "withering insight" into his own literary ambitions, not to mention the "audacity" to pen such a satire.

875. Yamaguchi, Katsumasa. "On Swift's Directions to Servants." Studies in Foreign Literatures (Ritsumeikan U.), 27 (1973), 1-17.

Noted by Zenzo Suzuki in Scriblerian, 6 (1974), 73.

The essay is in Japanese. "Swift's repeated instruction concerning the use of candles in <u>Directions to Servants</u> parallels the sentence from his sermon on <u>Causes of the Wretched Condition of Ireland</u>." (Suzuki)

See also Items 11, 12, 25, 50, 88, 172, 180, 198, 208, 243, 282, 307, 369, 392, 409, 410, 431, 434, 442, 460, 465, 797.

SECTION 6

Gulliver's Travels

876. Abernathy, Peter L., and Michael C. Stoune. "Swift, Telemann, and Gulliver's Travels." Eighteenth-Century Life, 3 (1977), 71-76.

Telemann's Gulliver Suite renders some of Swift's humor, though not his satire, in four appropriate movements.

877. Abrams, Fred. "Swift's Concealed Double Signature." American Notes and Queries, 12 (1973), 26-27.

An unintentionally amusing search for anagrams of Swift's name concealed in the text of Gulliver's Travels.

878. Allison, Alexander W. "Concerning Houyhnhnm Reason." Sewanee Review, 76 (1968), 480-92.

Though it claims to steer "an appropriate middle course" between "pro- and anti-Houyhnhnm positions," this essay becomes just another standard "soft-school" reading, because to see the Houyhnhnms as "faintly ridiculous throughout" is inevitably to remove some of the weight of Swift's satire from human nature.

879. André, Robert. "Les instruments d'Optique du Doyen." La Nouvelle Revue Française, 14 (1966), 677-88.

A brief discussion of optical effects in Gulliver's Travels is succeeded by a brief discussion of Swift's attitudes toward women.

880. Asselineau, Roger. "Satire et humour noir." Europe, 463 (1967), 77-82.

Swift's life, devoted to vexation rather than diversion, was inevitably tragic. His satire in Gulliver's Travels, however, fits Bergson's definition in Le Rire of a humorist.

881. Audisio, Felicita. "Il grottesco e i Viaggi di Gulliver." ["Gulliver's Travels and the Grotesque."] Bimestre, 4 (1972), 15-21.

882. Aytür, Ünal. "Houyhnhnm'lar Ülkesine Seyahat." ["Voyage to the
     Land of the Houyhnhnms."] Bati Dil ve Edebiyatlari Arastirmalari
     Dergisi [Journal of Modern Languages and Literatures], 1 (1969),
     63-68.

     Noted by Necla Aytür in Scriblerian, 6 (1973), 5.

     "Swift's point is that man is not rational but only rationis capax,
     and instead of benefiting from this capacity, man gives way to his
     passions, becoming thus a Yahoo-like creature." (Aytür)

883. Banks, Loy Otis. "Moral Perspective in Gulliver's Travels and
     Candide: Broadsword and Rapier?" Forum, 4, no. 7 (Summer, 1965),
     4-8.

     A useful, if not strikingly new, list of distinctions between the
     two satires: Gulliver is disillusioned from the start, Candide is a
     callow ingenue; Gulliver travels alone, Candide always in company;
     Gulliver visits grotesque worlds, Candide the familiar Western
     landscape; Gulliver observes both inferior and superior beings,
     Candide meets only knaves and dupes; all in all, Voltaire appears to
     be trying mankind in civil court, Swift in criminal court.

884. Barbé, Sheila. "Langue et langage dans la prose de Swift." Europe,
     463 (1967), 108-19.

     After repeating old chestnuts about Swift's love for stability in
     language, Barbe looks over the prose of Gulliver's Travels and
     finds--a love of stability in language, which is somehow modern
     rather than typically Augustan.

885. Barker, Rosalind A. "A Case for Religious Interpretation in Part III
     of Gulliver's Travels." Pp. 101-13 of A Festschrift for Professor
     Marguerite Roberts. Richmond, 1976.

     This essay proposes several norms of Christian behavior (mostly
     culled from Swift's sermons) and, not finding them embodied in
     Gulliver or many of the characters he meets, pronounces Book III a
     satire on religion.

886. Beauchamp, Gorman. "Gulliver's Return to the Cave: Plato's Republic
     and Book IV of Gulliver's Travels." Michigan Academician, 7
     (1974), 201-09.

     In the course of elaborating on R.S. Crane's interpretation of Book
     IV as an allusion to Plato's Allegory of the Cave, this essay blames
     Gulliver for abdicating the philospher's duty to enlighten those to
     whom he returns. (Yet, didn't Gulliver try to "mend the world
     wonderfully" by a book titled Travels into Several Remote Nations of
     the World?)

887. Beck, A. "Gulliver au Pays des Linguistes." <u>Les Langues Modernes</u>, 64 (1970), 279-80.

A Gulliverian satire on the teaching of foreign languages.

888. Beltic, Augustina. "Lumile lilliputane in vizunea lui Swift si Wells." ["The Vision of Lilliputian Worlds in Swift and Wells."] <u>Analele Stiintifice ale Universitatii Ias</u>, 20 (1974), 133-37.

Noted by Virgil Nemoianu in <u>Scriblerian</u>, 9 (1977), 92.

"Not claiming any direct influence of Swift upon Wells, Ms. Beltic merely points out parallels." (Nemoianu)

889. Benrekassa, Georges. "Le Statut du narrateur dans quelques textes dits Utopiques." <u>Revue des Sciences Humaines</u>, n.s. 39 (1974), 379-95.

890. Bentman, Raymond. "Satiric Structure and Tone in the Conclusion of <u>Gulliver's Travels</u>." <u>SEL</u>, 11 (1971), 535-48.

Rev. in <u>Scriblerian</u>, 4 (1971), 69.

Beginning with a complaint about misleading theories that see satire as clearly distinguishing good and evil, Bentman suggests that, on the contrary, Gulliver's raging and inconsistent behavior at the end demonstrates the futility of attempting to live by pure ideals. Therefore, the modern critical debate over whether the Houyhnhnms are ideal is itself an example of the singleness of vision Swift denounces.

891. Boas, Ralph P., Jr. "1724 Lilliputians." <u>American Notes and Queries</u>, 6 (1968), 115-16.

The second edition emends Book I, chapter 3, to read food for 1728 Lilliputians, rather than the original miscalculation of 1724. Boas feels the error was intended by Swift as a satire on the "excellent" mathematics of the Lilliputians.

892. Bony, Alain. "'Call Me Gulliver'." <u>Poétique</u>, 14 (1973), 197-209.

A post-Saussurean analysis, in which the "character" of Gulliver has no objective reality independent of the reader's own illusions and needs. The author, however, persists in creating the illusion that he is somewhere in control. A further insight is Pedro de Mendez's role as "false reader," outside Gulliver's frame of reference, and thereby able to help re-educate Gulliver on his road to recovery.

893. Borkat, Roberta Sarfatt. "Pride, Progress, and Swift's Struldbruggs." <u>Durham University Journal</u>, 68 (1976), 126-34.

The obvious claim here is that the Struldbruggs, Swift's "final
attack on the theory of progress," unify Book III as a satire on the
intellect and its capacity for progress.

894. Boulton, James T. "Arbitrary Power: An Eighteenth-Century
     Obsession." Studies in Burke and His Time, 9 (1968), 905-26.

     In Books II and III, Swift satirizes both the established theory of
     absolutism and the general human predilection for surrendering
     freedom.

895. Brady, Frank (ed.). Twentieth Century Interpretations of Gulliver's
     Travels. (Twentieth-Century Interpretations Series.) Englewood
     Cliffs, N.J.: Prentice-Hall, 1968. Pp. 118.

     Includes the following: Frank Brady, "Introduction"; Milton Voigt,
     "The Sources of Gulliver's Travels"; T.O. Wedel, "On the
     Philosophical Background of Gulliver's Travels"; Henry W. Sams,
     "Swift's Satire of the Second Person"; Robert C. Elliott, "The
     Satirist Satirized"; E.W. Rosenheim, "The Satiric Victim"; Kathleen
     Williams, "Gulliver in Laputa"; Samuel H. Monk, "The Pride of Lemuel
     Gulliver"; R.S. Crane, "The Houyhnhnms, the Yahoos, and the History
     of Ideas"; Martin Price, "Swift: Order and Obligation"; "Viewpoints"
     by Various Critics.

896. Brady, Frank. "Vexations and Diversions: Three Problems in
     Gulliver's Travels." MP, 75 (1978), 346-67.

     The three problems of interpretation--(1) the use of jokes; (2) the
     topic of degeneration; and (3) Swift's techniques in Book Four--all
     derive from critics' searches for consistency in Gulliver's Travels.
     Brady warns that "the assumption of fixed significance is equally
     natural and fatal." Book Four's "meanings (it has no one meaning)
     derive not from giving its elements fixed attributes but only from
     viewing these elements in a series of relations." This is salutary
     advice; but Brady's claim that only "a few critics have rejected the
     common either/or approach to the Houyhnhnms and the Yahoos" is not a
     fair representation of the last ten years' work; moreover, some of
     the critical positions he appears to repudiate (for example,
     "Swift's entrapment of the reader in his satiric attack") turn out
     to have a paper-thin difference from Brady's own opinions (e.g.,
     "behind Gulliver's sober narrative lie the shifting riddles of
     Erasmus's Folly. Gulliver leaves 'the judicious Reader to his own
     Remarks and Applications' (4.12.292). And Swift laughs in his
     face.").

897. Brezianu, Andrei. "Swift şi Cantemir sau Gulliver şi Licorna."
     ["Swift and Cantemir or Gulliver and the Unicorn."] Secolul XX,
     154-55, (1973), 39-53.

     Compares the definition of man in "The Beasts Confession" and

A vastly influential critique of the "historical" hypothesis on which much modern interpretation of Book IV is founded (a defense of the orthodox conception of human nature). Crane offers the alternative "historical explanation" that the aim of the last voyage is to "discredit" the common and sacred formula, Homo est animal rationale, of logic textbooks.

916. Crawford, Fred D. "Shaw Among the Houyhnhnms." Shaw Review, 19 (1976), 102-19.

Soft-school comments on Book IV by a Shaw enthusiast.

917. Crewe, J.V. "Further Travels with Gulliver." Theoria, 29 (1967), 51-66.

There is a pro-technology bias lurking here, in the apologies for Swift's supposed shortsightedness about the worth of technological progress. The official conclusion of this essay is, however, that "Swift's scepticism is a necessary corrective to the modern belief that all research is praiseworthy and self-justifying."

918. Dalnekoff, Donna Isaacs. "A Familiar Stranger: The Outsider of Eighteenth-Century Satire." Neophilologus, 57 (1973), 121-34.

Gulliver as satiric ingenu has affinities with Berkeley's theories of perception. Since our sense of space is founded only on experience, any change of experience can lead to new forms of space, optical, tactile, and kinesthetic, possessing equal validity; truth, necessity, and objectivity have only relative meaning. This is analogous to the problems of understanding of the satiric outsider.

919. Delastre, Pierre. "Un Chapitre Ajouté aux Aventures de Gulliver." Europe, 463 (1967), 152-67.

920. Dervin, Daniel A. "Breast Fantasy in Barthelme, Swift, and Philip Roth: Creativity and Psychoanalytic Structure." American Imago, 33 (1976), 102-22.

Book Two is discussed as one example of breast fantasies related to the "Family Romance" fantasy, by which children reconstruct their origins and do battle against father figures. Breast-fantasy "subordinates oceanic feeling, mystical fusion, and the Family Romance to the soundly traditional ends of satire."

921. Dickinson, H.T. "The Popularity of Gulliver's Travels and Robinson Crusoe." N&Q, 212 (1967), 172.

A letter (29 November 1726) from Anne Liddell to her kinsman testifies to the immediate popularity of Gulliver's Travels.

922. Dixsaut, Jean. "Le Sanglier du Parnasse." Les Langues Modernes, 62
     (1968), 500-02.

     Parallels between Gulliver and Ulysses lead to the conclusion that
     Swift almost incidentally invented a modern, degraded, version of
     the great epic.

923. Douglas, Lloyd. The Worlds of Lemuel Gulliver. (Oklahoma State U.
     Monographs, Humanities Series, 11.) Oklahoma State U. Press, 1968.
     Pp. 19.

     Gulliver appears in at least six personae: the simple adventurer of
     Book I; the socially aware traveller of Book II; the "detached
     foreigner observer" of Book III; the naive disciple of Book IV; the
     unhappy misanthrope at the end of Book IV; and the assertive
     missionary of the Letter to Sympson.

924. Downie, J.A. "Political Characterization in Gulliver's Travels."
     Yearbook of English Studies, 7 (1977), 108-20.

     An argument, contra Arthur E. Case, that Gulliver's adventures in
     Lilliput are only general, never specific, allusions to the
     political histories of Oxford and Bolingbroke. On the other hand,
     Downie argues, Book Two does contain a serious indictment of
     Walpole's administration--"the most potent and deliberate Swiftian
     satire on topical politics."

925. Dubashinsky, J.A. "Gulliver [sic] Travels in Ages." Literaturnaja
     Gazeta, Nov. 29, 1967.

     Noted by Leonid M. Arinshtein in Scriblerian, 2 (1970), 39.

926. Dubashinsky, J.A. "Inner and Outer Development in Gulliver's
     Travels." Voprosy Syuzhetoslozhenija (Rigas "Zvaigzne"), 1969, pp.
     119-44.

     Noted by Leonid M. Arinshtein in Scriblerian, 2 (1970), 40.

927. Dubashinsky, J.A. "Zanr 'putesestvij Gullivera'." ["Gulliver's
     Travels as Genre."] Filologiceskie, 13 (1970), 44-56.

928. Dupas, Jean-Claude. "Le Discours dans Les Voyages de Gulliver:
     misanthropie ou distance critique?" Pp. 85-94 of Individu et
     Société en Angleterre et dans les colonies américaines aux XVIIe
     et XVIIIe siécles. Paris: Paris III and Saint-Etienne, [1977].

     Rev. by Guy Laprevotte in Scriblerian, 10 (1978), 88-89.

"While rightly insisting on Swift's ironic detachment, Mr. Dupas plays down the implicit and explicit moral condemnation in order to controvert or qualify any belief in Swift's misanthropy." (Laprevotte)

929. Dussinger, John A. "'Christian' vs. 'Hollander': Swift's Satire on the Dutch East India Traders." N&Q, 211 (1966), 209-12.

Engelbert Kaempfer's remarks on Dutch traders (probably a reference to John Baptista Tavernier's A Collection of Several Relations & Treatises (1680)) parallels the Hollander-Christian disjunction in Book III.

930. Duthie, Elizabeth. "Gulliver Art." Scriblerian, 10 (1978), 127-31.

"[Sawrey] Gilpin's Houyhnhnms are not only more attractive visually than Gulliver is. Because of their expressions, their gracefulness, and their placing in the composition, they are also morally superior." Progressively reducing Gulliver in stature, Gilpin's three illustrations are "romantic," in that they emphasize natural virtue and sublimity. But they also limit the complexity of Swift's vision by underplaying the sheer reasonableness of the Houyhnhnms.

931. Dyson, A.E. The Crazy Fabric: Essays in Irony. London and Toronto: Macmillan, 1965. Pp. xiv + 233.

Rept. as pp. 672-84 of Item 125; in Gulliver's Travels: An Authoritative Text. Edited by Robert A. Greenberg. New York: Norton, 1970; (as "La Metamorfosi dell'Ironià") in Caffé, Oct.-Dec., 1967, pp. 107-117.

Rev. by G.D. Josipovici in RES, n.s. 17 (1966), 106-08; (favorably) by Juliet Sutton in Dalhousie Review, 46 (1966), 391-93; by R.C. Stephens in MLR, 61 (1966), 126-27.

Pp. 1-13 are "Swift: The Metamorphosis of Irony." In this 1959 essay (Essays and Studies, 1958), Dyson refers to Swift's "technique of betrayal" in Gulliver's Travels, his ironical attacks "upon states of mind which might, or might not, be alterable," his alterations of perspective that transform his satire into "a savage exploration of the world's essential unmendability"--"Swift is publicly torturing both himself and the species to which he belongs."

932. Eagleton, Terry. "Ecriture and Eighteenth Century Fiction." Pp. 55-58 of Literature, Society, and the Sociology of Literature. (Proceedings of the Conference Held at the University of Essex July 1976.) Edited by Francis Barker, John Coombes, Peter Hulme, David Musselwhite, and Richard Osborne. Colchester, Eng.: U. of Essex, 1977.

The final paragraph is an interesting discussion of Gulliver's

<u>Travels</u> in Derridean terms: "To deconstruct the reader, reducing him from positioned subject to a function of polyphonic discourses: this is the <u>ideological</u> intervention accomplished by all of Swift's writings."

933. Easthope, A.K. "The Disappearance of Gulliver: Character and Persona at the End of the 'Travels'." <u>Southern</u> <u>Review</u> (Adelaide), 2 (1967), 261-66.

Gulliver's character is a trap: the reader laughs too easily, only to find Gulliver melting "back into the verbal world he came from."

934. Ehrenpreis, Irvin. "The Origins of <u>Gulliver's</u> <u>Travels</u>." Pp. 200-25 of <u>Fair</u> <u>Liberty</u> <u>Was</u> <u>All</u> <u>His</u> <u>Cry:</u> <u>A</u> <u>Tercentenary</u> <u>Tribute</u> <u>to</u> <u>Jonathan</u> <u>Swift</u> <u>1667-1745.</u> Edited by A. Norman Jeffares. London: Macmillan; New York: St. Martin's Press, 1967.

Orig. pub. in <u>PMLA</u> (1957).

Comparing <u>Gulliver's</u> <u>Travels</u> with Swift's political writings of 1708-1715, Ehrenpreis unearths continuous references to Bolingbroke in Book One and to Sir William Temple in Book Two. The Houyhnhnms are an attack on the deistic doctrines Bolingbroke espoused in correspondence with Swift, while the Laputans are modeled after Thomas Sheridan, their city after his country property, Quilca. Ehrenpreis's conclusion is that approaches to Swift's satire which emphasize manipulation of ideas or the techniques of fiction usually are misleading. "Swift's imagination worked in terms of people."

935. Ehrmann, Jacques. "Le dedans et le dehors." <u>Poétique</u>, 9 (1972), 31-40.

Structuralist analysis of the strain between the inside and the outside, between nature and culture, in Swift's satire. In Book IV, chapter vi, Swift satirizes medical treatment for perverting the natural order of the body. The thrust strikes home against Swift's own satire, too, for moral as well as physical disease is the natural condition of man. Swift's excremental vision is also sign of an obsession with death, which his satire seeks to thwart by timely induction of vomiting.

936. Elliott, Robert C. <u>The</u> <u>Shape</u> <u>of</u> <u>Utopia:</u> <u>Studies</u> <u>in</u> <u>a</u> <u>Literary</u> <u>Genre.</u> Chicago and London: U. of Chicago Press, 1970. Pp. xii + 158.

Rev. (with another work) by Joanna Russ in <u>College</u> <u>English</u>, 33 (1971), 368-72; in <u>Antioch</u> <u>Review</u>, 31 (1971), 288; by Margaret Schlaugh in <u>MLR</u>, 67 (1972), 391-92; by Alvin Kernan in <u>ELN</u>, 9 (1972), 238-40; (favorably) by J. Grady in <u>N&Q</u>, 218 (1973), 80.

Pp. 50-67, "Swift's Utopias," argue that Houyhnhnmland is an impossible utopia for man, since Swift was "a utopian without illusions." Perhaps the more limited excellences of Brobdingnag could be aimed for by mere human commitment.

937. Ewald, William Bragg. "Jonathan Swifts 'Gulliver's Travels'." Interpretationen, 7 (1970), 261-85.

Emphasizes the integration of the voyages, the manifest issues of the satire, with the developing persona of Gulliver—similar to and less accessible than the discussion in The Masks of Jonathan Swift (1954).

938. Fabian, Bernhard. "Gulliver's Travels als Satire." Poetica, 3 (1970), 421-34.

Examines the development of paradox in satire to explain the complexity of Gulliver's Travels.

939. Fetrow, Fred M. "Swift's Gulliver's Travels." Explicator, 35, no. 3 (Spring, 1977), 29-31.

Gulliver's deteriorating self-knowledge is documented by the changing nature and number of the souvenirs he brings back from his voyages.

940. Fitzgerald, Robert P. "The Allegory of Luggnagg and the Struldbruggs in Gulliver's Travels." SP, 65 (1968), 657-76.

The claim here, that Luggnagg allegorically represents the France of Louis XIV, the Struldbruggs the French Academy ("that enduring institution whose members are still called 'the Immortals'"), is buttressed by discussion of the Academy's history, general reputation, Statutes and Regulations, work in progress, and by a few specific details of description. From this argument, Fitzgerald concludes that Swift is alluding to his own proposal for an English Academy, drawing upon the reception to his Proposal for Correcting ... the English Tongue for his presentation of Gulliver's reaction to the idea of Immortality.

941. Fitzgerald, Robert P. "The Structure of Gulliver's Travels." SP, 71 (1974), 247-63.

The continuing vitality of Gulliver's Travels is the result of its "structure": in each book (to a lesser degree, in the third) we are shown an individual in the process of adapting to a society, "with concomitant difficulties, successes, misunderstandings, and disappointments on both sides." In each case, the equivocal value of a society parallels the equivocal value of knowledge—a theme nearly always retained in selections from the Travels or simplified versions of it.

942. Forrester, Kent. "They Shoot Horses Don't They? Gulliver and the
     Houyhnhnms." <u>Kentucky Philological Association Bulletin</u>, (1974),
     27-31.

     Hard-school interpretation--Gulliver is not a novelistic character;
     the Houyhnhnms are not the objects of Swift's satire--for the
     general reader.

943. Fortunati, Vita. <u>La Letteratura Utopica Inglese. (Morfologia e
     Grammatica di un Genere Letterario).</u> (Il Portico Biblioteca di
     Lettere e Arti, 68. Sezione: Letteratura Straniera.) Ravenna:
     Longo Editore, 1979. Pp. 223.

     Pp. 89-118 ("Le Caratteristiche Dell'Utopismo Negativo") are an
     unstartling survey of how Swift turns utopian materials to satirical
     ends, including: (1) "La tecnica del 'realismo fantastico' nella
     descrizione del 'viaggio' nei 'Gulliver's Travels'"; (2) "Gulliver e
     lo 'straniamento'"; (3) "L'antiutopia politica: Lilliput e
     Brobdingnag"; (4) "L'antiutopia culturale: Laputa e Lagado"; (5)
     "Gulliver in Houyhnhnmsland ['sic]: i limiti di un Utopia."

944. Freeman, James A. "Sources of 'Tile, Stone, Brook' in 'Gulliver's
     Travels' II.7." <u>Scriblerian</u>, 2 (1970), 67-68.

     The Brobdingnagian "treatise of decay," with its citation of deaths
     by tile, stone, and brook, may be referring to Pyrrhus, Goliath, and
     Frederic Barbarossa: each was a "military champion, inspired wonder
     in commentators, and died a trivial, inglorious death."

945. Frese, Jerry. "Swift's Houyhnhnms and Utopian Law." <u>Hartford Studies
     in Literature</u>, 9 (1977), 187-95.

     "Utopian law," which ignores "man's value-creating capacity, his
     moral sense, his conscience," is therefore suitable only for such
     "equestrian computers" as the Houyhnhnms. "Human law," on the other
     hand, is scaled appropriately for man's middle state. Standard
     soft-school ideas given a new twist by a legal expert.

946. Gallagher, Fergal. "Swift's <u>Yahoo</u>: A Possible Source." <u>Scriblerian</u>,
     9 (1977), 146-47.

     From "You Whore," a Dublin expression.

947. Gaucheron, Jacques. "Mon cousin Swift, mon copain Gulliver." <u>Europe</u>,
     463 (1967), 3-16.

     Influential in France, perhaps even more than in England, <u>Gulliver's
     Travels</u> remains contemporary in its expression of alienation.

948. Gill, James E. "Beast Over Man: Theriophilic Paradox in Gulliver's
     'Voyage to the Country of the Houyhnhnms'." SP, 67 (1970), 532-49.

     Swift made narrative fact from the central premises of theriophily:
     (1) the hostility of all creatures (including man) to man; (2) man's
     physical inferiority to animals; (3) the moral inferiority of humans
     to beasts; (4) the peculiar evilness of human society; and (5) the
     weakness of human reason. Like most theriophilic works, the fourth
     voyage is fraught with paradoxes: the Yahoos' physical and moral
     superiority to Europeans, the Houyhnhnms' more inclusive, yet more
     restricted, reason, etc.

949. Gill, James E. "Discovery and Alienation, Nature and Reason in
     Gulliver's Travels, Parts I-III." Tennessee Studies in Literature,
     22 (1977), 85-104.

     A difficultly written attempt to show exactly how Gulliver's fourth
     voyage is the culmination of his three earlier alienating
     experiences. "Just as the mind is capable of 'creating' realities
     which it simultaneously recognizes as distortions of 'reality,' so
     the abuses of mind revealed through situation and language in
     Gulliver's first three voyages cooperate with parallel sumptuary
     themes in order to reveal the subtle, often self-defeating efforts
     of men to conceal, to transcend, and ultimately to fulfill the
     intrinsic limitations of human nature."

950. Gill, James E. "Man and Yahoo: Dialectic and Symbolism in Gulliver's
     'Voyage to the Country of the Houyhnhnms'." Pp. 67-90 of The Dress
     of Words: Essays on Restoration and Eighteenth Century Literature
     in Honor of Richmond P. Bond. Edited by Robert B. White, Jr. (U.
     of Kansas Publications, Library Series, 42.) Lawrence, Kansas: U.
     of Kansas Libraries, 1978.

     This study of the symbolic significance of the Yahoo also
     illuminates the perpetual critical disagreement over Book IV. The
     "dominant narrative process" of Book IV invites a straightforward
     and devastating equaling of man with Yahoo. The reader is blocked
     from this simple meaning, however, by a "dialectic" of definition
     and redefinition. The theriophilic tradition that civilized man is
     worse than the Yahoo provides the broadest complication, further
     developed by Gulliver's problems in using alien terms and concepts
     to describe Europe to his Master Houyhnhnm, and by the reader's
     awareness of problems in the narrative point of view. The eternal
     teasing of Book IV is partly created, therefore, by the reader's
     continual temptation to assign simple symbolic meaning to the Yahoos
     and by the text's simultaneous thwarting of that desire.

951. "Gilpin and Gulliver." Preview (Magazine of the City of York Art
     Gallery), 79 (July 1967).

     An account of different versions of Gilpin's paintings.

952. Gingerich, Owen. "The Satellites of Mars: Prediction and Discovery."
     Journal for the History of Astronomy, 1 (1970), 109-15.

     Partially debunks the uncanniness of Swift's prediction of the two
     Mars satellites by showing that his choice of planetary diameters
     very nearly also matches corresponding distances for known moons of
     Jupiter and Saturn. Gingerich attributes the coincidence to a lucky
     guess combined with accurate use of Kepler's harmonic law; the same
     attribution was made in 1937 by Marjorie Nicolson and Nora M. Mohler
     (Item 1050).

953. Goldgar, Bertrand A. "A Contemporary Reaction to Gulliver's
     Travels." Scriblerian, 5 (1972), 1-3.

     Reprints a critique of Gulliver's Travels written in 1727 by James
     Hume--interesting because of the author's (evidently genuine) shock
     and outrage: "... it may be of great benefit to the publick to
     Gibbet up such offenders under feign'd names."

954. Goldgar, Bertrand A. "Gulliver's Travels and the Opposition to
     Walpole." Pp. 155-73 of The Augustan Milieu: Essays Presented to
     Louis A. Landa. Edited by Henry Knight Miller, Eric Rothstein, and
     G.S. Rousseau. Oxford: Clarendon Press, 1970.

     The history of how the Opposition turned Gulliver's Travels to their
     own uses: as "particular reflections" of anti-Walpole sentiment; as
     a general satire that inevitably had contemporary political
     implications; and for the purposes of summary, quotation, and
     imitation.

955. Goldgar, Bertrand A. Walpole and the Wits: The Relation of Politics
     to Literature, 1722-1742. Lincoln and London: U. of Nebraska
     Press, 1976. Pp. x + 256.

     Rev. (favorably) by Howard Erskine-Hill in RES, n.s. 30 (1979),
     90-94; (with reservations) by Robert Halsband in JEGP, 76 (1977),
     552-54; (favorably) by Robert James Merrett in Dalhousie Review,
     58 (1978), 175-77; (favorably) by Howard D. Weinbrot in ECS, 11
     (1977-78), 263-68; (favorably) by G.L. Anderson in Scriblerian, 10
     (1977), 47.

     Surveys "belles-lettres" written in opposition to Walpole's
     ministry, with special focus on Gulliver's Travels and Swift's late
     poems. See F.P. Lock (Item 1022) for fuller treatment and
     counter-argument.

956. Gravil, Richard (ed.). Swift: Gulliver's Travels: A Casebook.
     (Casebook Series.) London: Macmillan, 1974. Pp. 256.

     Rev. (with another work) by Colin J. Horne in Yearbook of English
     Studies, 6 (1976), 275-78; by Clive T. Probyn in Scriblerian, 7
     (1974), 44.

Includes contemporary criticism, Romantic and Victorian views, and
the following modern essays: C.H. Firth, "The Political Significance
of Gulliver's Travels"; T.O. Wedel, "On the Philosophical Background
of Gulliver's Travels"; John H. Ross, "The Final Comedy of Lemuel
Gulliver"; Herbert Davis, "Moral Satire"; Kathleen Williams,
"Gulliver's Voyage to the Houyhnhnms"; R.S. Crane, "The Rationale of
the the Fourth Voyage"; A.E. Dyson, "Swift: The Metamorphosis of
Irony"; Kathleen Williams, "The Fantasy World of Laputa"; Philip
Pinkus, "Sin and Satire in Swift"; W.E. Yeomans, "The Houyhnhnms as
Menippean Horse"; M.M. Kelsall, "Iterum Houyhnhnms: Swift's
Sextumvirate and the Horses"; Claude Rawson, from "Order and
Cruelty: A Reading of Swift (with some comments on Pope and
Johnson)."

957. Greenacre, Phyllis. Emotional Growth: Psychoanalytic Studies of the
Gifted and a Great Variety of Other Individuals. 2 vols. New York:
International Universities Press, 1971. Pp. 863.

Reprints essays on Swift and Gulliver's Travels originally published
in Swift and Carroll (1955).

958. Greene, Donald. "The Education of Lemuel Gulliver." Pp. 3–20 of The
Varied Pattern: Studies in the Eighteenth Century. Edited by Peter
Hughes and David Williams. (Publications of the McMaster
University Association for Eighteenth-Century Studies, 1.)
Toronto: A.M. Hakkert Ltd., 1971.

Classic hard school insistence on Gulliver's plausibility and the
consequent shock to readers: Swift wants us to identify with
Gulliver so completely that "we live through the same experiences he
does and undergo the same painful process of re-education that he
does." Greene combines this view with the opinion that Swift is
thereby urging a "perennial Christian program," devastating some
cherished values of modern western civilization but endorsing
Christian humility and endurance.

959. Griffith, Philip Mahone. "Swift's Munodi and Bolingbroke, A Firmer
Identification." South Central Bulletin, 36 (1976), 145–46.

Reviews Swift's correspondence with Bolingbroke for further evidence
that the latter fits the character of Book III's Lord Munodi.

960. Grubb, Daniel S. "Another Gulliver?" Studies in the Humanities, 4,
no. 1 (March 1974), 3–9.

This comparison of scatology and sexuality in Gulliver's Travels and
in Saul Bellow's Mr. Sammler's Planet concludes that
twentieth-century American society and eighteenth-century English
society both reflect economic instability, technological revolution,
and a breakdown in conventional morality and formalized religion.
The characters, Gulliver and Mr. Sammler, share a sense of man's
bestiality—from which each is able to detach himself.

961. Gulliver, Lemuel. A New Voyage to the Country of the Houyhnhnms:
     Being the Fifth Part of the Travels into Several Remote Parts of
     the World. Edited with Notes by Matthew Hodgart, M.A. New York:
     Putnam, 1970. Pp. 91.

     Rev. by Robert D. Hume in Scriblerian, 3 (1970), 23; in review
     art. ("The State of the Dean") by Robert Martin Adams in Hudson
     Review, 23 (1970), 578-84.

     Gulliver returns to the Houyhnhnms only to find even their
     perfection perishable. Yahoos gain the upper hand; Gulliver is left
     (once more?) virtually insane.

962. Guskin, Phyllis J. "'A very remarkable Book': Abel Boyer's View of
     Gulliver's Travels." SP, 72 (1975), 439-53.

     The close reading of Gulliver's Travels by a contemporary of Swift
     reveals his understanding of the satiric strategy of persona, his
     rather prurient disgust at the "filth" in Swift's style and fiction,
     and his appreciation of both the specific political and the general
     moral satire.

963. Haefner, Gerhard. "Der Kaiser von Lilliput: Eine Studie zur
     Erzähltechnik Swifts in 'Gulliver's Travels'." ["The King of
     Lilliput: A Study of Swift's Narrative Technique in Gulliver's
     Travels."] Die Neueren Sprachen, n.s. 20 (1971), 206-15.

     Not a study of narrative technique, this essay focuses on one
     passage of description to show how Swift's satire of the Emperor of
     Lilliput parodies descriptive formulas.

964. Halewood, William H. "Gulliver's Travels I, vi." ELH, 33 (1966),
     422-33.

     Swift may have given Lilliput its seemingly incongruous utopian
     moment (the brief idealized account may have been borrowed from
     Plutarch's "Life of Lycurgus") to stiffen a "preacherly" pattern of
     symmetrical moral oppositions.

965. Halewood, William H. "Plutarch in Houyhnhnmland: A Neglected Source
     for Gulliver's Fourth Voyage." PQ, 44 (1965), 185-94.

     Parallels between Book IV and Plutarch's "Life of Lycurgus" lead
     Halewood tentatively to suggest that the Houyhnhnms may not be
     excessively rational but rather represent an actual condition of
     man.

966. Halewood, William H., and Marvin Levich. "Houyhnhnm Est Animal
     Rationale." JHI, 26 (1965), 273-81.

     Suggesting that Swift's principal source for a rational definition of man was contemporary cliché, this essay asserts that "Swift fully approved of the Houyhnhnm life of reason and conceived of it as fully possible for man" without bothering to analyze most disputed details of Book IV.

967. Harth, Phillip. "The Problem of Political Allegory in Gulliver's Travels." MP, 73 (1976), S40-S47.

Since Sir Charles Firth, allegorical interpretations of Book I have been a prop of complacency: it has been speciously easy to deflect Swift's satire onto real persons and events. Book I is not a partisan satire of English politics in the early eighteenth century; it is rather (in Swift's words) "a series of observations on the imperfections, the follies, and the vices of man."

968. Hartman, Jay H. "Gulliver's Travels: An Oblique Approach to Christianity." Cresset (Valparaiso), 43, no. 3 (January 1980), 9-13.

969. Hasan, Shuaib Bin. "A Critique of Gulliver's Voyage to Lilliput." Explorations, 7, no. 1 (Summer, 1980), 67-83.

Loaded with howlers, this routine examination of Book One insists upon its "delightful humour and fun."

970. Hassall, Anthony J. "Discontinuities in Gulliver's Travels." Sydney Studies in English, 5 (1979-80), 3-14.

Begins with the promising assertion that Swift puts the reader into a position similar to Gulliver's—blundering about, getting his bearings, learning the language; ends with a fairly standard "hard school" reading of Book IV.

971. Havens, George R. "Some Notes on Candide." MLN, 88 (1973), 841-47.

Implies that Swift, as well as Rabelais, influenced Voltaire's use of enumerations.

972. Heilman, Robert B. "Gulliver and Hardy's Tess: Houyhnhnms, Yahoos, and Ambiguities." Southern Review, 6 (1970), 277-301.

Suggesting that the relations of Gulliver, the Yahoos, and the Houyhnhnms may shed light on the triangle of Tess, Alec d'Urberville, and Angel Clare, Heilman emphasizes that Swift's "fictional imagination" interfered with and qualified his satirical indignation. He then proposes that English literary history can be divided into two antithetical movements lasting about a century each: total denial of the Yahoos as a mirror of human reality, as with Thackeray; and total acceptance of them, as with D.H. Lawrence.

973. Herman, Judith B. "Swift and Aristotle on Vocation." <u>American Notes</u>
     <u>and Queries</u>, 15 (1977), 67-68.

     Book IV's attack on modern professionals is paralleled by
     Aristotle's <u>Politics</u>.

974. Hill, John M. "Corpuscular Fundament: Swift and the Mechanical
     Philosophy." <u>Enlightenment Essays</u>, 6, no. 1 (Spring 1975), 37-49.

     Swift's satire on the Academy of Lagado "is not mere vituperation or
     caught within the ideological confines of orthodox reaction. He has
     analyzed Boyle's corpuscular science and found its flaws." These
     include the use of analogy as a basis for experimentation and (Boyle
     himself objecting) the imitation of seemingly random combinations in
     nature.

975. Hodgart, Matthew. "Gulliver's Travels." Pp. 25-39 of <u>Swift</u>
     <u>Revisited</u>. Edited by Denis Donoghue. Cork: Mercier; Hatboro, Pa.:
     Folklore Associates, 1968.

     For a general audience, with emphasis on <u>Gulliver's Travels</u> as a
     failed ethical and political satire.

976. Hodgart, Matthew. <u>Satire</u>. New York and Toronto: McGraw-Hill, 1969.
     Pp. 255.

     Includes the usual number of references to Swift in the course of
     unremarkable generalizations about satire. Pp. 67-71 discuss the
     attack on politics in <u>Gulliver's Travels</u> as "the doctrine of
     anarchy.... which finally came true in the concentration camps of
     thirty years ago."

977. Holly, Grant. "Travel and Translation: Textuality in 'Gulliver's
     Travels'." <u>Criticism</u>, 21 (1979), 134-52.

     "The essay on <u>Gulliver's Travels</u> which follows is divided into two
     parts. The first attempts to show the way in which Swift's text
     makes signifying its subject, by implying a vast textuality which
     incorporates the reader and which, therefore, he can participate in
     but is no longer free to comment on. As a way of avoiding the
     hypostasizing of signifying as the signified of the text, the second
     part of the essay attempts to indicate the problematic of
     differencing along which signifying plays without fear of falling
     into sense or significance." Challenging post-structuralism.

978. Hoskins, Robert V., III. "Swift, Dickens, and the Horses in <u>The End</u>
     <u>of the Road</u>." <u>James Madison Journal</u>, 37 (1979), 18-32.

     Like Gulliver, Jake Horner is attracted to an ideal (the Morgans) he
     cannot hope to emulate. (But Jake is ultimately disenchanted with

the Morgans.) Unlike Gulliver's Travels, The End of the Road ends
with "a haunting ambiguity."

979. Idol, John L., Jr. "Thomas Wolfe and Jonathan Swift." South Carolina
     Review, 8, no. 1 (November 1975), 43-54.

     Wolfe was evidently indebted to Swift's use of fantasy elememts in
     Gulliver's Travels and to his presumed ability to evade "the burden
     of subjectivity."

980. Irlen, Harvey Stuart. "Gulliver's Cousin Sympson." South Atlantic
     Bulletin, 36, no. 2 (March 1971), 21-23.

     Nothing new.

981. Izumi, Hajime. "Swift to Godwin: Houyhnhnms no futatsu no so."
     ["Swift and Godwin: Dual Aspects of the Houyhnhnms."] Studies in
     English Literature, 53 (1976), 27-42.

     Noted by Zenzo Suzuki in Scriblerian, 9 (1977), 92.

     "Mr. Izumi convincingly argues that Godwin who believed in 'a
     rational creature' without qualification failed to notice Swift's
     dual aspects of reason in Part IV." (Suzuki)

982. Jacobson, Richard. "A Biblical Allusion in 'Gulliver's Travels'."
     N&Q, 215 (1970), 286-87.

     The picture of Lilliputians carrying Gulliver's watch on a pole
     recalls the Book of Numbers, chapter 13, which "contains the kernal
     of the play upon comparative proportion in the first two books of
     Gulliver's Travels."

983. Jansen, F.J. Billeskov. "Gulliver's rejser: En Studie i
     Tendensromanens Aestetik." ["Gulliver's Travels: A Study of the
     Aesthetic Structure of a Tendency Novel."] Pp. 140-51 of
     Romanproblemer. [Critical Problems of the Novel] (Festskrift til
     Hans Sørensen.) Odense, 1968.

     Noted by Adina Forsgren in Scriblerian, 2 (1969), 4.

     "Swift's book is a roman àux idées with a definite aesthetic
     structure, a system of concentric circles, each having its affinity
     with a literary genre. The outer circle is the realistic
     framework.... The second circle is the world of
     adventure.... 'Statsbeskrivelsen,' the description of a state, a
     genre practised by Holberg, among others, is the third ring of the
     system, and the fourth is that of Swift's criticism of English and
     European civilization.... The inmost circle is finally said to be
     represented by Swift's personal disgust at mankind as mirrored in
     the picture of the Yahoos." (Forsgren)

984. Johnson, Maurice, Muneharu Kitagaki, and Philip Williams. Gulliver's
     Travels and Japan: A New Reading. (Moonlight Series, 4.) Kyoto,
     Japan: Amherst House, Doshisha University, 1977. Pp. xii + 50;
     plates.

     In no sense a "new reading," this monograph presents some likely
     sources of and analogues to Book III, together with a few
     speculations about the importance of Japan as a "framing device" in
     that Book. It makes some expert, but unilluminating, suggestions
     about the source of the "literary machine" (and about Plate 5, Part
     3).

985. Jones, Myrddin. "Swift, Harrington and Corruption in England." PQ,
     53 (1974), 59-70.

     The political philosophy of James Harrington--that the balance of
     power always reflects the balance of property and that abuses in
     government are caused by political power in the hands of those who
     do not own the land--is at the foundation of Book II. Swift also
     endorsed Harington's thinking in Contests and Dissensions.

986. Kallich, Martin (intro.). A Letter from a Clergyman to His Friend,
     with an Account of the Travels of Captain Lemuel Gulliver (1726).
     (Augustan Reprint Society, 143.) Los Angeles: William Andrews
     Clark Memorial Library, 1970. Pp. xii + 22.

     Evidence of the pained shock of some early readers: "In this long
     tedious Part the Reader loses all that might have been engaging to
     him in the three former; the Capacity and Character given there of
     Brutes, are so unnatural; and especially the great Preheminence
     asserted of them, to the most virtuous and noble of humane Nature,
     is so monstrously aburd and unjust, that 'tis with the utmost Pain
     a generous Mind must indure the Recital; a Man grows sick at the
     shocking Things inserted there; his Gorge rises; he is not able to
     conceal his Resentment; and closes the Book with Detestation and
     Disappointment."

987. Kallich, Martin. The Other End of the Egg: Religious Satire in
     "Gulliver's Travels". Bridgeport, Ct.: Conference on British
     Studies at the University of Bridgeport, 1970. Pp. ix + 119.

     Rev. by Ricardo Quintana in Scriblerian, 3 (1970), 25-26;
     (severely) by Phillip Harth in MP, 69 (1971), 165-69; in review
     art. ("Images of Swift: A Review of Some Recent Criticism") by
     Robert W. Uphaus in Eire-Ireland, 6, no. 3 (Fall 1971), 16-22.

     Religion as the key to all of Gulliver's Travels is the thesis of
     this tendentious study. Kallich's notion of religion is broad enough
     to allow him to find it in every human concern, and occasionally he
     emphasizes small details out of proportion. The satire in Book III,
     for instance, aims to tell us that "when in its excesses science
     denies reason and religion, it simply fosters absurd idolatry. Thus

in Laputa Swift indicts superstitious scientists who suffer from a kind of moral and religious paralysis." Book IV, accordingly, is little more than an attack on deism.

988. Keesey, Donald. "The Distorted Image: Swift's Yahoos and the Critics." PLL, 15 (1979), 320-32.

A useful survey of recent criticism of Book IV combined with a salutary correction of critics who see man as ultimately in a viable middle state between Houyhnhnms and Yahoos.

989. Kelling, H.D. "Gulliver's Travels IV, Once More." Scholia Satyrica, 2, no. 2 (Spring/Summer 1976), 3-12.

Kelling attacks the usefulness of either "hard" or "soft" schools of interpretation, since the Houyhnhnms and the Yahoos are metaphors (unwittingly "literalized" by Gulliver), making Swift's own opinion of them indeterminable. "A critic can only explain the text of Gulliver's Travels in such a way that readers can find their own meanings ... and react in a way which cannot be adequately described by words such as comic, tragic, or satiric."

990. Kelly, Ann Cline. "After Eden: Gulliver's (Linguistic) Travels." ELH, 45 (1978), 33-54.

Kelly reviews Gulliver's encounters with language to conclude that Swift dissented from the prevailing contemporary idea that language reform could foster an improvement in governance. Since Swift believed, on the contrary, that "divisiveness and obscurity are generated by people, not by the words they employ," his recommendation--implicit in Gulliver's Travels, explicit in other works--is the exercise of lively, disinterested conversation to draw people together in common sense.

991. Kelly, Ann Cline. "Swift's Explorations of Slavery in Houyhnhnmland and Ireland." PMLA, 91 (1976), 846-55.

Though "no direct evidence can be found in Book IV to support this view," if we imagine that the Yahoos were once as rational as Gulliver (or even as rational as the Houyhnhnms) and have been brutalized through years of slavery, the parallels between Ireland and Houyhnhnmland "are highly provocative." Kelly briefly reviews Swift's comments on Irish "slavery" then compares them to occurrences in Book IV. A tendentious exercise.

992. Kelsall, M.M. "Iterum Houyhnhnm: Swift's Sextumvirate and the Horses." Essays in Criticism, 19 (1969), 35-45.

Rept. as pp. 212-22 of Swift: Gulliver's Travels: A Casebook. Edited by Richard Gravil. London: Macmillan, 1974.

This "hard school" defense of the Houyhnhnms as an ideal of conduct argues that the six heroes mentioned in Book III, vii--the "one ideal picture in the Travels which even the most sophisticated critics would find difficult to read ironically"--resemble the Houyhnhnms in crucial ways. In fact, "in their determination that reason shall dominate the emotions and the flesh, Swift's heroes can be more extreme than the horses."

993. Kennedy, R.F. "Swift and Suetonius." N&Q, 214 (1969), 340-41.

Chapter 7 of Gulliver's Voyage to Lilliput alludes to Suetonius's life of Domitian, broadening the fiction beyond specific political satire.

994. Kenner, Hugh. "The Gulliver Game." Spectrum (U. of California, Santa Barbara), 8, no. 3 (Summer, 1966), 114-28.

Rept. (with changes) in pp. 100-42 of The Counterfeiters: An Historical Comedy. Bloomington and London: Indiana U. Press, 1968; (in part) as pp. 422-31 of Jonathan Swift: A Critical Anthology. Edited by Denis Donoghue. Harmondsworth and Baltimore: Penguin Books, 1971.

Gulliver, the Compleat Empiricist, is an ultimate modern man--"carrier and incarnation of the values we really value: notably accuracy, cleanliness, and the power to adjust." He has not a clue of what the past has to teach and so is the worst possible answerer of the question "What is man?," an inadequacy only exacerbated when Gulliver learns the Houyhnhnms' rational language, "the earliest form of Fortran." Oddest of all, generations of readers have identified both Yahoos and Gulliver with man, though the "Yahoo is not human at all; Gulliver is not human enough." An interesting collection of opinions without a serious attempt at documentation.

995. Kenner, Hugh. Joyce's Voices. (A Quantum Book.) Berkeley, Los Angeles, London: U. of California Press, 1978. Pp. xiii + 120.

Pp. 2-5 are a restatement of Kenner's main point in "The Gulliver Game" (see below): Swift's game is to have Gulliver "apply the empiric method to the whole conduct of his intellectual life, in a way we should find deliciously absurd."

996. Kiernan, Colin. "Swift and Science." Historical Journal, 14 (1971), 709-22.

For the anti-Newtonian Swift, catastrophism, not uniformity, was the norm; he sought to avoid the extremes of Newtonian and Paracelsian organic science. In this, Swift's science was "the handmaiden of his religion," working from man outwards to the natural world.

997. Kitagaki, Soji. "Gulliver in Japan." Main Currents (Kyoto), Special Issue, December, 1968, pp. 89-106.

Noted in Scriblerian, 1, no. 2 (Spring 1969), 11.

Book III, chapter xi, is read as a satire on Dutch sailors' perplexity over the crucifix-trampling ceremony. The name Shimoda may be a inversion for Xamoschi, a small coastal city in southeast Japan. The essay is in Japanese.

998. Knowles, A.S., Jr. "Defoe, Swift, and Fielding: Notes on the Retirement Theme." Pp. 121-36 of Quick Springs of Sense: Studies in the Eighteenth Century. Edited by Larry S. Champion. Athens: U. of Georgia Press, 1974.

If the Houyhnhnms are taken as a genuine ideal, Book IV may be read as a form of retirement literature. Knowles persuasively argues that because Swift is working so clearly within the tradition "that reaches back to the Sabine farm of Horace," it is highly questionable that the Houyhnhnms are the objects of satire.

999. Koroban, V. "Gulliver's Travels." Nistru (Kishinev), July, 1968, pp. 126-37.

Noted by Leonid M. Arinshtein in Scriblerian, 2 (1970), 39-40.

In Moldavian.

1000. Korshin, Paul J. "The Intellectual Context of Swift's Flying Island." PQ, 50 (1971), 630-46.

A survey of prototypes of flying machines previous to Laputa leads to the conclusion that Swift was well acquainted "with the large body of contemporary mystical and psuedo-scientific speculation," and that he based his satire consistently on actual experiments. Swift attacks not only the debasement of religion in scientific works, but also the scientific mysticism commonly found in theological writings. Book III therefore has more in common with A Tale of a Tub than with the remainder of Gulliver's Travels, both in its attack upon unacceptable learning and in its apparently poor organization, which parodies the shapelessness so typical of pseudo-scientific compilations.

1001. Kosok, Heinz. Lemuel Gullivers deutsche Kinder: Weltliteratur als Jugendbuch. (Wuppertaler Hochschulreden, 8.) Wuppertal: Peter Hammer, 1976. Pp. 28.

Lists and discusses fifteen adaptations of Gulliver's Travels currently available for German children.

1002. Köster, Patricia. "Notes Upon Notes: Gulliver and the
       Pepper-Water-Worms." <u>Scriblerian</u>, 2 (1969), 29-30.

   A reply to Alan T. McKenzie, "Gulliver and the
   Pepper-Water-Worms," <u>Scriblerian</u>, 1, no. 1 (Autumn 1968), 32.

   The "animalcules" discovered by van Leeuwenhoek were also mentioned
   in 1715 by William Browne.

1003. Kozo, Fukamachi. "A Reconsideration of the Houyhnhnms." <u>Studies in
       English Literature</u> (Yamagata English Literary Society, Japan), 12
       (1968), 1-14.

   Noted in <u>Scriblerian</u>, 1, no. 1 (Autumn 1968), 7.

   Garden variety soft-school argument: Swift's main attack is on
   free-thinkers and self-complacent philosophers, through ridicule of
   Gulliver himself; Pedro de Mendez is a rebuke to Gulliver's loony
   misanthropy. The essay is in Japanese.

1004. Krieger, Murray. <u>The Classic Vision: The Retreat from Extremity in
       Modern Literature</u>. Baltimore and London: Johns Hopkins U. Press,
       1971. Pp. xiv + 376.

   Rev. by M.K. Spears in <u>ELN</u>, 10 (1973), 310-13.

   Pp. 255-69 discuss Swift whose acceptance of "the human barnyard" in
   <u>Gulliver's Travels</u> and "The Lady's Dressing Room" is one of
   Krieger's four types of "retreat from extremity" characteristic of
   the classic vision.

1005. Kuwabara, Hiroaki. "<u>Gulliver's Travels</u>--Its Fascination." <u>Studies in
       Foreign Literature</u> (Ritsumeikan U., Kyoto), 21 (1971), 1-18.

   Noted by Zenzo Suzuki in <u>Scriblerian</u>, 4 (1971), 10.

   "Mr. Kuwabara tries to relate his argument to Northrop Frye's theory
   of satire as presented in <u>The Anatomy of Criticism</u>, and Mr. Kuwabara
   contends that the <u>Travels</u> fulfills its satiric function as
   'Morality' and 'fantasy,' notwithstanding Swift's failure to
   continue the comic irony in his later works." (Suzuki) The essay is
   in Japanese.

1006. LaCasce, Steward. "The Fall of Gulliver's Master." <u>Essays in
       Criticism</u>, 20 (1970), 327-33.

   After Gulliver provides his Master's first knowledge of evil, the
   Houyhnhnm loses his ideal manner of thinking, being stricken with
   doubts, making mistakes, learning to prevaricate, and so on. In the
   end, the Master Houyhnhnm is even willing to disobey reason itself.
   These observations lead to the conclusion, <u>contra</u> hard school, that

the "Houyhnhnms may indeed represent some kind of rational ideal,
but certainly not one that is useful for man to emulate."

1007. LaCasce, Steward. "Gulliver's Fourth Voyage: A New Look at the
      Critical Debate." Satire Newsletter, 8, no. 1 (Fall 1970), 5-7.

      Clifford's "hard and soft" schools of interpretation are convenient
      but obscure fundamental differences between criticism based on
      "philosophic" assumptions concerning the nature of man and criticism
      based on "theological" assumptions. The former sees Book IV in terms
      of the classical dichotomy of mind and matter; resolution is either
      through stoic resignation or by a via media fashioned through
      natural philosophy. The latter treats the Yahoos in terms of the
      passions corrupted by the prior condition of sin, the Houyhnhnms in
      relation to Christian ideals; resolution is possible in terms of
      compassion and even hope.

1008. LaCasce, Steward. "Swift on Medical Extremism." JHI, 31 (1970),
      599-606.

      Swift favored a moderate position in relation to the Ancients'
      insistence on letting nature take its course and the Moderns'
      Paracelsian mysticism and iatrochemistry. Though the Houyhnhnm ideal
      temperate regimen seems derived from classical practice, Swift does
      satirize extreme belief in the theory of contraries, with its cures
      of repletion and depletion, which derived from Hippocrates's Nature
      of Man.

1009. Lamoine, Georges. "Notes on Religion in Gulliver's Travels."
      Caliban, 10 (1973), 23-33.

      Includes a categorical list of all religious words in Gulliver's
      Travels as well as several remarkably naive assumptions about satire
      and religion.

1010. Landa, Louis. "The Dismal Science in Houyhnhnmland." Novel, 13
      (1979), 38-49.

      The Houyhnhnms' simple agrarian society rebukes the
      eighteenth-century English economy, consumer-oriented, luxurious,
      riddled with service trades. The unwarranted intricacy of
      mercantilist economies "had in it an element of the
      absurd ... comparable or parallel to the intellectual intricacy that
      he was averse to in philosophical and theological systems."

1011. Lapraz, Françoise. "Les Métamorphoses de la mort dan les Voyages de
      Gulliver (1726)." Pp. 133-47 of Hommage à Emile Gasquet
      (1920-1977). (Annales de la Faculté des lettres et Sciences
      Humaines de Nice, 34.) Paris: Les Belles Lettres, 1978.

      Primarily a summary of Gulliver's encounter with the Struldbruggs, along with some mention of nearly every reference to death and war in the Travels. Unlike the Houyhnhnms, man can never quite put death out of mind, but must face up to his legacy of sin.

1012. Lawlis, Merritt. "Swift's Uses of Narrative: The Third Chapter of the Voyage to Lilliput." JEGP, 72 (1973), 1-16.

Chapter iii of Book I illustrates the essential qualities of Gulliver's Travels: diversity, inconsistency, playfulness, and ambiguity. Swift lashes at a thousand victims, but the stance from which he does so is never clear. "Despite all his affinities with early eighteenth-century England, Swift seems also to have been a maverick, free from his own century."

1013. Lawry, Jon S. "Dr. Lemuel Gulliver and 'The Thing Which Was Not'." JEGP, 67 (1968), 212-34.

A fine sketch of Gulliver's "three faces": he gulls others, principally his readers; he is himself gulled by other people and places, constantly mistaking their worth; and he gulls himself into his final prideful delusions.

1014. Leigh, David Joseph. "Wollaston and Swift: A Source for the Houyhnhnms." Philosophy and Literature, 4 (1980), 92-106.

In the Houyhnhnms, Swift was attacking William Wollaston's exaggerated claims for "reason" in The Religion of Nature Delineated (1722). Seen in the light of Wollaston, Houyhnhnmland takes on new meaning, Leigh claims. Wollaston's moral theory provided Swift with a rational norm for judging English irrationalities, a rationalistic model for criticizing Gulliver's own conversion to a form of deism, and an intellectual pivot for a series of ironic plays on truth and falsehood that have fueled the ongoing debate about Book IV's meaning. Among other evidence, Leigh cites Wollaston's phrase for vice as "doing the thing that is not," along with general correspondences in the areas of vice and falsehood, in the relation between sensation and reason, in the insistence upon ambition as the cause of war, in the hesitancy toward marriage and affection.

1015. Leighton, J.M. "What's in a Name?" Standpunte, 27, no. 1 (October, 1973), 55-60.

Contains a list of named characters in Gulliver's Travels and the unconvincing argument that characters with proper names provide a positive "balance" to the "uniform maliciousness of the 'society' figures." It is hard to see how this is true of the King of Brobdingnag, for example.

1016. LeMire, E.D. "Irony in Erewhon." Humanities Association Bulletin, 16, no. 2 (Fall 1965), 27-36.

Identifies three "phases" of irony in Gulliver's Travels--relying on

Northrop Frye. The third phase is "something quite different from the normal reformative satire."

1017. Lenfest, David S. "Gessner's Illustration for the Fourth Part of
Gulliver's Travels." Scriblerian, 3 (1970), 34-35.

Reproduces Gessner's depiction of Gulliver attacked by the female
Yahoo for a 1761 German translation.

1018. Lenfest, David S. "Grandville's Gulliver." Satire Newsletter, 10,
no. 2 (Spring 1973), 12-24.

J.J. Grandville's four hundred plates for Gulliver's Travels (1838)
depict Gulliver himself in a "fantastic grotesque" mode (in Wolfgang
Kayser's terms), failing to perceive Gulliver as a butt of Swift's
satire, but accurately conveying most satirical implications of the
text. In depicting particular ironic fantasies, Grandville is more
imaginative, portraying "the concrete and physical aspects of ironic
metaphors that depend upon the opposition of these solid qualities
with very abstract ones."

1019. Lenfest, David S. "LeFebvre's Illustrations of Gulliver's Travels."
Bulletin of the New York Public Library, 76 (1972), 199-208.

Reproduces ten illustrations by LeFebvre (1797) and stresses their
shrewd analysis of Gulliver's pride.

1020. Leonard, David Charles. "Swift, Whiston, and the Comet." ELN, 16
(1979), 284-87.

The probable source for the Laputans' dread of comets is William
Whiston's A New Theory of the Earth (1696), which attributed the
Creation of the World, the Deluge, and the coming End to a periodic
comet.

1021. Link, L.J. "A Straight Look at Swift: Book I of Gulliver's Travels."
Thought Currents in English Literature (Aoyama Gakuin U.), 42
(1969), 1-8.

Noted in Scriblerian, 4 (1972), 60-61.

"Mr. Link argues that the basic assumptions about human nature are
as bitter here [in Book I] as they are in the following three
parts."

1022. Lock, F.P. The Politics of Gulliver's Travels. New York: Oxford U.
Press, 1980. Pp. ix + 156.

Rev. by Carole Fabricant in JEGP, 80 (1981), 419-23; in review art. ("Gentle Readings: Recent Work on Swift") by William Kinsley in ECS, 15 (1982), 442-53.

The original political impulses of Gulliver's Travels were neither narrowly partisan nor exclusively aimed at the contemporary histories of England and Ireland. Rather, Swift broadly addresses the "perennial political disease of which Whiggery was only a contemporary manifestation." The argument is based on close attention to general political thought and relevant history, reconsideration of the Motte and Faulkner texts, and a critique of conventional allegorical readings.

1023. MacAndrew, M. Elizabeth. "A Splacknuck and a Dung-Beetle: Realism and Probability in Swift and Kafka." College English, 31 (1970), 376-91.

Because Swift's literalized satiric metaphors outrage probability, he must employ special realism of technique to overcome the basic improbability of his fantasies. Reading Book II, we never "enter into" Gulliver and "learn what it feels like" to be a Splacknuck. However, the scenes portrayed are thoroughly "authentic"--a quality much referred to in this essay but sketchily illustrated.

1024. Manganelli, Giorgio. "Il Segreto del Gulliver è la Sproporzione Totale." Il Giorno, Oct. 25, 1967.

1025. Marnat, Marcel. "Le tricheur de Blefuscu." Preuves, 182 (April, 1966), 70-73.

A review of Emile Pons's edition of Swift gives rise to a quick discussion of Swift's modern "contradictions."

1026. McKee, John B. Literary Irony and the Literary Audience. Amsterdam: Rodopi, 1974. Pp. iv + 114.

Pp. 30-53 are "The Speaker as Victim: Context Witholding in Gulliver's Travels." Ostensibly a study of how readers are victimized by Swift's texts, this chapter practically turns into a soft school attack on Gulliver.

1027. McKenzie, Alan T. "'The Lamentation of Glumdalclitch for the Loss of Grildrig. A Pastoral': What We Have Been Missing." TSLL, 12 (1971), 583-94.

This claim for the excellence of the Scriblerians' "Verses Explanatory" to Gulliver's Travels presents "a few essential verbal parallels, some generic considerations, and several obscure references and an inside joke."

1028. McKenzie, Alan T. "Lemuel Gulliver and Pepper-Water-Worms."
      Scriblerian, 1, no. 1 (Autumn 1968), 31-32.

    See the reply by Patricia Köster ("Notes Upon Notes: Gulliver and
the Pepper-Water-Worms") in Scriblerian, 2 (1969), 29-30.

    "Pepper-Water-Worms" is an allusion to Anthony van Leeuwenhoek's
famous "Letter on the Protozoa" (1667), describing minute
"animalcules" discovered in an infusion of whole pepper into well
water.

1029. McManmon, John J. "The Problem of a Religious Interpretation of
      Gulliver's Fourth Voyage." JHI, 27 (1966), 59-72.

    A salutary corrective to careless generalizations about Christian
doctrine, this essay disputes that the pessimism of Gulliver's
Travels is rooted in universal Christian assumptions about fallen
human nature. It goes on to challenge the supposed affinities
between Swift's religious writings, particularly his sermons, and
the Travels and to question whether Swift's priesthood had to find
its way into his writings.

1030. McTurk, R.W. "Swift, Laxness, and the Eskimos." Scandinavica,
      (1972), supplement, pp. 45-62.

    Noted in Scriblerian, 5 (1973), 78.

Gulliver's Travels proves useful in understanding the Icelandic
novelist Halldór Laxness's Gerpla.

1031. Mehl, Dieter. Der englische Roman bis zum Ende des 18. Jahrhunderts.
      (Studienreihe Englisch, 28.) Düsseldorf, Bern, and Munich: August
      Bagel and Francke Verlag, 1977. Pp. 208.

    Pp. 85-92 is a discussion of Gulliver's Travels as novel.

1032. Merle, Robert. "L'amère et profonde sagesse de Swift." Europe, 463
      (1967), 47-76.

    The political meaning of Gulliver's Travels derives from Swift's
obsession with political freedom in England and Ireland. Moreover,
even in Book II, Swift's satire is primarily political, rather than
moral.

1033. Merton, Robert C. "The 'Motionless' Motion of Swift's Flying
      Island." JHI, 27 (1966), 275-77.

    One interpretation of how the "motionless" island moves involves a
satire on the Laputans. Perhaps Swift is suggesting that the same
theories that set the island afloat would also inevitably bring it
crashing down.

1034. Mezciems, Jenny. "Gulliver and Other Heroes." Pp. 189-208 of The Art
      of Jonathan Swift. Edited by Clive T. Probyn. New York: Barnes &
      Noble; London: Vision Press, 1978.

      Also pub. as pp. 189-208 of A Centenary Symposium, ed. Alice
      Shalvi (Jerusalem: Jerusalem Academic, 1976).

      This study of Swift's allusions to heroes works by comparisons with
      Defoe, Pope, and Rabelais to find that "ambiguity about time,
      history, and theoretical systems" make Swift's ideas about heroes
      "hard to evaluate or to place on a meaningful scale." The essay
      moves to the reader's relation to Gulliver and concludes that
      Gulliver mirrors, not so much ourselves, as our wish for illusions
      about ourselves.

1035. Mezciems, Jenny. "The Unity of Swift's Voyage to Laputa: Structure
      as Meaning in Utopian Fiction." MLR, 72 (1977), 1-21.

      By stimulating, then denying, our desire for unity and order, Swift
      catches us between two illusions "so that we may recognize and
      distinguish them." Gulliver's illusion of progress is superimposed
      on the circular voyage structure; the fragmentation of Book III
      highlights the expectations fostered by utopian fiction that "the
      accumulation of experience should express its meaning in some
      organized structure of pattern, in life as in fiction." This essay
      makes some good points about Plato, More, and Rabelais.

1036. Milhauser, Milton. "Dr. Newton and Mr. Hyde: Scientists in Fiction
      from Swift to Stevenson." Nineteenth-Century Fiction, 28 (1973),
      287-304.

      Swift's attitude in Book III, sceptical of Newton, generally
      contemptuous of scientific absurdities, is exceptional in the
      eighteenth century.

1037. Miller, Tom. "Gulliver and the Moons of Mars." Illustrated London
      News, 265 (1977), 57-58.

      For a sounder explanation of Swift's uncanny "guess" about Mars's
      moons, see Marjorie Nicolson and Nora M. Mohler (Item 1050), and
      Owen Gingerich (Item 952).

1038. Miura, Ken. "Gulliver's Travels to Robinson Crusoe." Journal of the
      Faculty of Liberal Arts (Chukyo U.), 19 (1978), 35-50.

      Noted by Zenzo Suzuki in Scriblerian, 11 (1978), 11.

      "Mr. Miura hardly distinguishes between the writer and his persona,
      and satire and spiritual autobiography." (Suzuki)

1039. Montgomery, Marion. "The Prophetic Poet and the Loss of Middle
      Earth." Georgia Review, 33 (1979), 66-83.

> Contains interesting passing observations on Gulliver's Travels, for
> example, "In the figure of Gulliver, Swift escapes somewhat from
> that threatening cold rationalism; by his art he turns the new
> realism in Western thought upon the imagination's province of the
> oulandish, with a devastating ironic effect at the expense of
> rationalistic distortions of the world and of man's nature" (pp.
> 72-73).

1040. Mood, John J.L. "Gulliver and the Lestrygonians: A Heterodox View of
      the Social Relevance of Literature." Midwest Quarterly, 16 (1975),
      409-24.

> A rather tired, post-Brownian, argument for the relevance of Swift's
> "excremental vision."

1041. Morris, John N. "Wishes as Horses: A Word for the Houyhnhnms." Yale
      Review, 62 (1972-73), 354-71.

> This discussion of the history of responses to Book IV identifies
> three primary types before going on to record its own "hard-school"
> response. Arguing that "The sanity of the Houyhnhnms is
> insufficiently childish for our tastes," Morris concludes that
> Swift's principal purpose is to provoke rather than to instruct. "It
> is not in what he says that the meaning of the book finally declares
> itself, but in what we say in response to it."

1042. Morrissey, L.J. Gulliver's Progress. Hamden, Ct.: Archon Books
      (Shoestring Press), 1978. Pp. 199.

> Rev. (severely) by W.B. Carnochan in Scriblerian, 11 (1978), 134;
> (severely) by Jenny Mezciems in RES, n.s. 30 (1979), 474-76;
> (severely) by Phillip Harth in ECS, 12 (1979), 403-05.

> The keys to Gulliver's Travels, according to Morrissey, are the
> lectionary readings specified in the Book of Common Prayer for the
> dates assigned to Gulliver's adventures. The continuity of religious
> meaning that results from this investigation seems arbitrary and not
> infrequently reductive.

1043. Moss, William M. "Mounting Evidence in Book IV." Southern Humanities
      Review, 8 (1974), 191-94.

> A leaden spoof: If Gulliver is Swift, then the Yahoos symbolize
> Christ and the Houyhnhnms represent Esther Vanhomrigh. The
> autobiographical drama that is Gulliver's Travels therefore depicts
> Swift's success at "mounting" Vanessa and his subsequent choice of
> church over love.

1044. Mouravjev, V. Puteshestivie s Gulliverom: 1699-1970. Moscow: Kniga, 1972. Pp. 207.

    Includes bibliographical materials.

1045. Munro, John M. "Book III of Gulliver's Travels Once More." English Studies, 49 (1968), 429-36.

    Book III is essential to the structural unity of Gulliver's Travels, not so much because of Gulliver's development as a character, but because of the symmetry of the entire work, the second half of which shows the futility of man renouncing fleshliness for disembodied reason.

1046. Murray, P.J.M. "Countries of the Mind: The Travellers of Swift and Nashe." Words (Victoria U.: Wai-te-ata Press), 3 (1971), 46-61.

    Noted by Jeremy Commons in Scriblerian, 4 (1972), 54.

    "In this comparison of Gulliver's Travels and The Unfortunate Traveller Mr. Murray concludes that "More, Swift, Johnson, Edmund Spenser ... well knew the true location of the countries and happenings they described, but Nashe ... only in glimpses saw that a fictional traveller might bring back news about familiar, and also usually neglected areas of the mind." (Commons)

1047. Napier, Elizabeth R. "Swift's 'Trampling Upon the Crucifix': A Parallel." N&Q, 224 (1979), 544-48.

    In George Psalmanaazar's Description of Formosa (1704), the Dutch traders are also implicated in crucifix-trampling. In a later note ("Swift, Kaempfer, and Psalmanaazar: Further Remarks on 'Trampling Upon the Crucifix'," N&Q, 28 (1981), 226), Napier suggests that Swift might have combined information from both Psalmanaazar and Kaempfer.

1048. Nath, Vishwanadha Hari Hara. "The Wisdom of the Ancients Is the Folly of the Moderns: A Reading of Gulliver's Travels, Book III." Publications of the Arkansas Philological Association, 6, no. 2 (Fall, 1980), 61-76.

    Relying on commonplace ideas about the Ancients and Moderns quarrel, this essay concludes that "the various themes of the book are synthesized by the larger theme of the confrontation between Ancients and Moderns." Moreover, not only is Book III itself thematically unified, it foreshadows and prepares for the duality of reason and passion in the Houyhnhnms and Yahoos.

1049. Neumeyer, Peter F. "Franz Kafka and Jonathan Swift: A Symbiosis." Dalhousie Review, 45 (1965), 60-65.

Kafka evidently took Gulliver at face value and attributed
Lilliputian ideas about economy and children-rearing to Swift--ideas
that "ran close to the torrent of his own passions."

1050. Nicolson, Marjorie, and Nora M. Mohler. "The Scientific Background
      of Swift's 'Voyage to Laputa'." Pp. 226-69 of Fair Liberty Was All
      His Cry: A Tercentenary Tribute to Jonathan Swift 1667-1745.
      Edited by A. Norman Jeffares. London: Macmillan; New York: St.
      Martin's Press, 1967.

      Orig. pub. in Annals of Science, 2 (1937); rept. as pp. 210-246 of
      Item 332.

This very well-known study demonstrates the extensiveness of Swift's
borrowings from contemporary science. A number of specific sources
are identified.

1051. Nordon, Pierre. "L'effet de glissement dans Gulliver's Travels." Les
      Langues Modernes, 62 (1968), 496-99.

Gulliver is a sort of anti-Crusoe, regressing through his voyages to
degradation, whereas Robinson progresses to earn his reward. The
reader participates in the disgusting developments of Book IV but
also retains some distance from the satiric victims--and this is the
source of the work's positive effect.

1052. Novak, Maximilian E. "The Wild Man Comes to Tea." Pp. 183-221 of The
      Wild Man Within. Edited by Edward Dudley and Maximilian E. Novak.
      Pittsburgh, 1972.

Exploring eighteenth-century speculations about wild men, Novak
finds three principal archetypes--"Wild Man, natural man, and
philosophic natural man." Yahoos seem most like the Wild Man, while
the savages at the end of Book IV resemble natural man. Gulliver
himself might be seen as a parody on the "natural man" as
philosopher.

1053. Novarr, David. "Swift's Relation with Dryden, and Gulliver's Annus
      Mirabilis." English Studies, 47 (1966), 341-54.

This essay reviews most of Swift's attacks on Dryden, then goes on
to argue that the naval battle and firefighting in Gulliver's
Travels, Book I, chapter v, are partly references to Dryden's
"forced and askew conjunction" of the Dutch Wars and the London fire
in Annus Mirabilis.

1054. Ogawa, Yasuhiro. "Curse of Never Dying: Swift's Struldbrugg
      Episode." Essays in Foreign Language and Literature, 24 (1978),
      85-117.

1055. Orwell, George. "Politics vs. Literature: An Examination of
       Gulliver's Travels." Pp. 166-85 of Fair Liberty Was All His Cry: A
       Tercentenary Tribute to Jonathan Swift 1667-1745. Edited by A.
       Norman Jeffares. London: Macmillan; New York: St. Martin's Press,
       1967.

       Orig. pub. in Shooting an Elephant and Other Essays (1950); rept.
       as pp. 192-209 of Item 332; in The Collected Essays, Journalism
       and Letters of George Orwell, 4 vols., eds. Sonia Orwell and Ian
       Angus (London: Secker and Warburg; New York: Harcourt, 1968), IV,
       223; as pp. 342-61 of Item 285.

       Recoiling from Swift's "perverse" conservativism, his "totalitarian"
       Houyhnhnms, and his "anti-human" sentiments, Orwell nevertheless
       claims the highest admiration for Gulliver's Travels and for
       Swift--a "diseased writer," who nevertheless appeals to the "inner
       self" in all of us, "which at least intermittently stands aghast at
       the horror of existence."

1056. Osella, Giacomo. "Gli 'Immortali' di Gionata Swift e la loro
       origine." Lares, 166, pp. 27-31.

1057. Otten, Robert M. "Lemuel Gulliver, Projector." Notre Dame English
       Journal, 5, no. 1 (Winter, 1969-70), 5-15.

       Gulliver's plan to eradicate Yahooism in England is seen as his
       motivation throughout the four books. How this might affect
       interpretation of Gulliver's Travels is ignored.

1058. Pagetti, Carlo. "Gulliver da Uomo a Cavallo." Il Gazzettino, Aug.
       14, 1967.

1059. Palomo, Delores J. "The Dutch Connection: The University of Leiden
       and Swift's Academy of Lagado." HLQ, 41 (1977), 27-35.

       Also pub. in Transactions of the Samuel Johnson Society of the
       Northwest, 7 (1974), 119-34.

       The case for the University of Leiden as a specific target of satire
       in Book III is based on its pre-eminence as an exponent of the new
       learning, the abbreviation of its Latin name ("Acad. Lugd."), and
       similarities between the work of some Leiden scientists and that of
       Swift's projectors.

1060. Passon, Richard H. "Gay to Swift on Political Satire." American
       Notes and Queries, 3 (1965), 87.

       The idea for satirizing political pedantry in Book II, chapter 7,
       may have come from Gay's letter of 16 August 1714, facetiously
       discussing the reduction of politics to a science.

1061. Passon, Richard H. "Legal Satire in <u>Gulliver</u> from <u>John Bull</u>."
      <u>American Notes</u> <u>and</u> <u>Queries</u>, 5 (1967), 99-100.

      See the reply by P. Köster (Item 342).

      Book IV, chapter v, is said to echo passages of legal satire from
      <u>John Bull</u>.

1062. Patterson, Anne. "Swift's Irony and Cartesian Man." <u>Midwest</u>
      <u>Quarterly</u>, 15 (1974), 338-50.

      Argues a case for the continuing relevance of Swift's satire on
      science and materialism in Book III and in <u>The Mechanical Operation</u>
      <u>of the Spirit</u>.

1063. Peake, Charles. "The Coherence of <u>Gulliver's Travels</u>." Pp. 171-196
      of <u>Focus</u>: <u>Swift</u>. Edited by C.J. <u>Rawson</u>. London: Sphere Books,
      1971.

      Rejecting the imposition of modern ideas of consistency on
      Gulliver's character, Peake argues for a "progressive change in the
      formal characteristics of the Voyages, and some kind of consecutive
      argument underlying the diversity." Thus, Book I's higher proportion
      of narrative to satire and its rise and falling action is succeeded
      by Book II's comparative devotion to incident but without a process
      of rising and falling; in Book III Gulliver operates more as an
      observer than a participant, satire predominating over narrative;
      while in Book IV, the essence of Gulliver's life is the enjoyment of
      peace and quiet, without involvement in personal or public strife.
      The essay contains additional pages of less original discussion of
      Swift's attitudes towards and attack on pride.

1064. Phillipson, John S. "Sir Samuel Morland; 'Gulliver's Travels'." <u>N&Q</u>,
      216 (1971), 227-28.

      Swift's book-writing machine in Book III, chapter 2, may be
      ridiculing the computing machine that Leibnitz demonstrated before
      the Royal Society on 22 January 1672/3.

1065. Phillipson, John S. "Swift's Half-way House." <u>Medical History</u>, 13
      (1969), 297-98.

      Swift has "anticipated a development of modern psychiatry" by giving
      Gulliver, in the personality and dwelling of Pedro de Mendez, a
      "half-way house" on his return from confinement to the world
      outside.

1066. Philmus, Robert M. "The Language of Utopia." <u>Studies in the Literary</u>
      <u>Imagination</u>, 6, no. 2 (Fall 1973), 61-78.

      To assume that the Houyhnhnm utopia is simply an "ultimate" order is to overlook its "dialectical" relations to the preceding three books of the Travels. (The terms are adopted from Kenneth Burke.) In its "dialectical" context, the Houyhnhnmland is itself "the thing which is not," disclosing the ironic equivocality of the expression. Saying "the thing which is not" can be a synonym for lying; but in an open, mortal universe, it also expresses the possibility of conveying transcendent truths. Ultimately, in Swift as in Orwell, "the limits of a closed social order, utopian or anti-utopian, coincide with the limits where language becomes intractable as a means of expressing 'the Thing which is not'."

1067. Philmus, Robert M. "Swift, Gulliver, and 'The Thing Which Was Not'." ELH, 38 (1971), 62-79.

Gulliver's repudiation of saying "the thing which was not" displays his ignorance of the value of indirection in language—of fiction itself, therefore, and of irony in all its forms—to bring truth home to an audience. Swift, on the other hand, warns the reader against abuse of interpretation precisely because interpretation is always necessary. Illustrations include the quotation from the Aeneid in which Gulliver is identified with Sinon, Gulliver's expulsion from Houyhnhnmland (at least partly for disconcerting use of language), and the Tribnia episode, which exposes the consequences of assigning arbitrary meaning to an author's words.

1068. Pierre, Gerald J. "Gulliver's Voyage to China and Moor Park: The Influence of Sir William Temple upon Gulliver's Travels." TSLL, 17 (1975), 427-37.

Temple's Of Heroic Virtue is apparently echoed in chapter vi of Book I and in places throughout Book IV. Unless Swift is satirizing Temple's values, which seems unlikely, Gulliver's misanthropy is not the product of an absurd delusion about false ideals, but rather is an expression of Swift's admiration for a civilization as superior in its way as Temple's China.

1069. Pinkus, Philip. "Sin and Satire in Swift." Bucknell Review, 13, no. 2 (1965), 11-25.

Rept. as pp. 186-201 of Swift: Gulliver's Travels: A Casebook. Edited by Richard Gravil. London: Macmillan, 1974.

The purpose of Gulliver's Travels is to make us aware of evil, not to "conquer" or "diminish" it, hence Swift's concentration on pretensions ("sartorism") in language and reason. Swift's satire is no mere affirmation of faith, but rather it "protests the ways of God to man with all the passion of [Swift's] faith."

1070. Pinkus, Philip. Swift's Vision of Evil: A Comparative Study of A Tale of a Tub and Gulliver's Travels. Vol. 2: Gulliver's Travels. (English Literary Studies Monograph Series, 4.) Victoria, British Columbia: U. of Victoria, 1975. Pp. 138.

Rev. (severely) by C.J. Rawson in MLR, 73 (1978), 884-85; by
Patricia Köster in Scriblerian, 8 (1976), 79-80.

As distinguished from A Tale of a Tub, Gulliver's Travels is what
Pinkus calls a "satire of fear." Its images of destruction document
the leakage of humanity from acts of reason. In the Travels, "man is
lost in an indifferent universe, a cosmic nihilism created by
mathematics"--the book is "an act of desperation." An Appendix on
"Battle of the Books" and "Mechanical Operation of the Spirit" is
included.

1071. Piper, William Bowman. "The Sense of Gulliver's Travels." Rice
      University Studies, 61, no. 1 (Winter 1975), 75-106.

Piper admonishes that "Critics have not, at least not in a formal
and persistent and self-conscious way, bent themselves to the
painstaking task of narrow and intense scrutiny" of Gulliver's
Travels. Then he goes on to analyze a number of passages in which
the reader is irked or surprised through Gulliver's unreliableness,
before concluding that "the force of this inexhaustible vexation,
this inescapable instruction, which Swift has provided the world, is
this: that the reader is himself animal rationis capax ... who at
any moment and in confronting even the most obvious challenge to his
understanding can fail, can fall into absurdity."

1072. Pollin, Burton R. "Dean Swift in the Works of Poe." N&Q, 218 (1973),
      244-46.

Surveys a dozen references to Swift by Poe.

1073. Pons, Jacques, and Maurice Pons. "Les clés du langage imaginaire
      dans l'oeuvre de Swift." Europe, 463 (1967), 98-108.

Carrying on Emile Pons's work, Jacques and Maurice Pons decide that
much of Swift's secret language in Gulliver's Travels derives from a
code used by both Stella and Vanessa. The different peoples in the
four books all speak roughly alike.

1074. Probyn, Clive T. "Gulliver and the Relativity of Things: A
      Commentary on Method and Mode, with a Note on Smollett."
      Renaissance and Modern Studies, 18 (1974), 63-76.

Argues for Boyle's "Upon the Eating of Oysters," from Occasional
Reflections upon Several Subjects (1664), as the most likely source
of Swift's use of the travel book genre as a vehicle for satire by
moral relativity.

1075. Probyn, Clive T. "Man, Horse and Drill: Temple's Essay on Popular
      Discontents and Gulliver's Fourth Voyage." English Studies, 55
      (1974), 358-60.

In his essay (1697), Temple dismisses apparent similarities between men and beasts, probably an allusion to the Locke-Stillingfleet controversy, and probably influential on Swift's thought in Gulliver's Travels.

1076. Probyn, Clive T. "Swift and Linguistics: The Context Behind Lagado and Around the Fourth Voyage." Neophilologus, 58 (1974), 425-39.

The first part of this essay explains that the ostensibly disjunct linguistic satires in the Lagadan academy "imitate a mode and parody a group of schemes," common in seventeenth-century linguistics (the work of John Wilkins is typical). Then Probyn attempts "to chart the terminological continuity of the noun series Man, Horse and Monkey," finding that Gulliver fails to make Aristotelian distinctions concerning this grammatical and logical triad.

1077. Probyn, Clive T. "Swift and the Physicians: Aspects of Satire and Status." Medical History, 18 (1974), 249-61.

Swift goes beyond merely satirizing incompetent physicians, linking medicine with modern madness, literally as well as metaphorically, because the surgeon works at the surface level, unconcerned with moral anatomy. Modish and without humanist inhibitions, medicine is, ironically, appropriate only for moral incurables.

1078. Pullen, Charles H. "Gulliver: Student of Nature." Dalhousie Review, 51 (1971), 77-89.

Whatever Gulliver stands for as a symbol, by the end of Book IV he is a character of some substance, enabling Swift to stack the deck against himself in exploring Gulliver's experience. Swift "is quite prepared to take on the task of watching not only a good man, but an intelligent and scientifically-trained man under the pressure of increasingly bewildering shifts of perception."

1079. Pyle, Fitzroy. "Yahoo: Swift and the Asses." Ariel, 3, no. 2 (April, 1972), 64-69.

"Yahoo" represents the sound of an ass braying, balancing "Houyhnhnm," the sound of a horse.

1080. Quinlan, Maurice J. "Lemuel Gulliver's Ships." PQ, 46 (1967), 412-17.

Adventure, the name of two different ships in which Gulliver sails, was also the name of the ship of Captain Kidd, whose piratical exploits were well known to Swift.

1081. Quinlan, Maurice J. "Treason in Lilliput and in England." TSLL, 11 (1970), 1317-32.

The impeachment of Gulliver is a very specific satire on the Whigs' recrimination against Swift's Tory friends. This essay focuses on Swift's attacks on the needlessly cruel penalties for treason, on the customary jargon of the laws, and on specific enemies. Whenever the parallels between England and Lilliput break down, Quinlan has an explanation.

1082. Quintana, Ricardo. "Gulliver's Travels: The Satiric Intent and Execution." Pp. 78-93 of Jonathan Swift 1667-1967: A Dublin Tercentenary Tribute. Edited by Roger McHugh and Philip Edwards. Dublin: Dolmen Press; London: Oxford U. Press, 1967.

A case, contra soft school, is made for the "range of mood and voice" of Gulliver's Travels, including discussion of Swift's "rhetoric of realism," his utopias, his "comedy of exclusion" and absurdity through entrapment.

1083. Quiròs, Jorge Molina. "La novela utópica inglesa (Tomás More, Swift, Huxley, Orwell). Madrid: Prensa Espanola, 1967.

1084. Quiròs, Jorge Molina. "Misantopia y Utopia en 'Gulliver's Travels'." Filologia Moderna, 7 (1967), 179-84.

"Soft school" commentary.

1085. Rader, Ralph W. "Fact, Theory, and Literary Explanation." Critical Inquiry, 1 (1974), 245-72.

See the exchange among Stanley E. Fish, Jay Schleusener, and Rader in Critical Inquiry, 1 (1975), 883-911.

In the course of a theoretical discussion of literary hypotheses, Rader points out that the distinctive quality of Book IV is a function of merging the second and third persons of the usual satiric triangle (Rader does not mention the work of Henry W. Sams or Claude Rawson). He argues against "revisionist" ("soft-school") readings of the Houyhnhnms' imperfections. Having the horses do human-like things in a distinctively equine way runs the risk of making the horses seem clumsy, even ludicrous; but "this was an entirely minor risk compared with the need to maintain the imaginative probability of the fictional premise essential to the special satiric attack."

1086. Radner, John B. "The Struldbruggs, the Houyhnhnms, and the Good Life." SEL, 17 (1977), 419-33.

Gulliver's initial infatuation with the "ideal" Struldbruggs reveals his nominal Christianity and shallow conception of virtue; he is attracted to the security, superiority and emotional detachment he imagines the Struldbruggs to possess. This episode, rather than

underscoring a true enlightenment for Gulliver in Houyhnhnmland,
foreshadows the inadequate values and understanding that underlie
his obsession in Book IV.

1087. Rawson, C.J. "Diagonal Handwriting: An Allusion to Swift by Lord
      Chesterfield." N&Q, 212 (1967), 189.

      A letter by Chesterfield to his godson alludes to the Lilliputians'
      slanted handwriting in Book I, chapter vi.

1088. Rawson, C.J. "Gulliver and the Gentle Reader." Pp. 51-90 of Imagined
      Worlds: Essays on Some English Novels and Novelists in Honour of
      John Butt. Edited by Maynard Mack and Ian Gregor. London: Methuen,
      1968.

          Rept. as pp. 1-32 of Item 391; (in part) as pp. 688-93 of Item
          125; (in part) in Gulliver's Travels: An Authoritative Text.
          Edited by Robert A. Greenberg. New York: Norton, 1961, 1970.

      Rawson's analysis of a reader's response leads to hard school
      conclusions. Rather than springing a trap on them, Swift disconcerts
      his readers, denying them distance from his satiric targets and from
      his satiric values. Therefore Gulliver's Travels lacks coherent
      organization, except insofar as it works to make its readers
      vulnerable and thereby more receptive.

1089. Reed, Gail Simon. "Dr. Greenacre and Captain Gulliver: Notes on
      Conventions of Interpretation and Reading." Literature and
      Psychology, 26 (1976), 185-90.

          Rev. (favorably) in review art. ("Augustan Studies in 1976") by
          William Kupersmith in PQ, 56 (1977), 470-97.

      Criticizes Greenacre (Swift and Carroll, 1955) for equating Swift's
      fictional creations with a patient's dreams and free associations,
      therefore confusing Swift and Gulliver. Salutary advice to
      psychoanalyst-critics.

1090. Reichard, Hugo M. "Gulliver the Pretender." Papers on English
      Language and Literature, 1 (1965), 316-26.

      A well-documented case for Gulliver's fraudulence, discernible only
      in Book IV, with the usual soft school conclusion that to "see at
      last through Gulliver's game is to laugh away the oppressiveness and
      to find Swift's achievement all the more extraordinary."

1091. Reichard, Hugo M. "Satiric Snobbery: The Houyhnhnms' Man." Satire
      Newsletter, 4 (1967), 51-57.

      Because Gulliver is "a very monster of a snob," he drastically over-values those perfect objects of snobbery, the Houyhnhnms. As a result, the satire of Book IV achieves only a "delimited indictment" of humankind.

1092. Reichert, John F. "Plato, Swift, and the Houyhnhnms." PQ, 47 (1968), 179-92.

Though Houyhnhnmland does not stand for Plato's Republic, the "markedly Platonic cast" of the Houyhnhnms' lives suggests that Swift is not satirizing deism or Cartesianism or neo-stoicism. Moreover, Swift's own satiric technique is reminiscent of Socratic irony. "Just as Socrates, by feigning ignorance, leads his friends to articulate knowledge they did not know they possess, so the Houyhnhnm, by his very real ignorance of human ways, forces Gulliver to abandon circumlocution." The upshot is a hard-school reading of Book IV: virtue is not an imaginary ideal; rather, it is vice that is incomprehensible.

1093. Reiju, Tokiwai. "The Unity of Gulliver's Travels: A Reconsideration of Book III." Pp. 125-39 of Studies in Eighteenth-Century English Literature. Kyoto: Apollon Press, 1968.

Noted in Scriblerian, 1, no. 1 (Autumn 1968), 7.

Had the Struldbruggs episode been somehow assimilated to the stories of Laputa and Balnibarbi, Gulliver's Travels would have been a unified work! The essay is in Japanese.

1094. Reinhold, Heinz. Der englische Roman im 18. Jahrhundert: soziologische, geistes- und gattungsgeschichtliche Aspekte. Stuttgart: Verlag W. Kohlhammer, 1978. Pp. 206.

Noted by Heinz J. Vienken in Scriblerian, 13 (1981), 82.

"In his ill-organized and undocumented article on Gulliver's Travels, Mr. Reinhold touches on genesis, anonymous publication, genre, sources, obscenity, realism and Swift's misanthropy—hardly more than a paraphrase of the views of Case, Ehrenpreis and others." (Vienken)

1095. Reisner, Thomas A. "Swift's Gulliver's Travels." Explicator, 26, no. 5 (January 1968), Item #38.

Several coinages in Book II may be traced to Erse and Gaelic originals. Glumdalclitch may be related to the substantive glum or glumadh ("a large mouthful of liquids"); Grildrig may derive from grileag ("a grain of salt, any small matter, a small potato") and from driog ("a drop"). Grultrud (Brobdingnagian for "towncrier") may be the fusion of grullagan ("a ring of people") and trudaire ("one who speaks haltingly, a stammerer").

1096. Renaker, David. "Swift's Laputians as a Caricature of the
      Cartesians." PMLA, 94 (1979), 936-44.

      The Laputians' haunting fear of the sun's extinction may derive from
      Descartes's cosmology of vortices in Principes de la philosophe.
      This detail and others suggest that the Laputians represent
      Cartesians and Laputa, France, while the Balnibarbians represent
      England and the Royal Society. If so, Swift is implying that the
      Royal Society was significantly influenced by Descartes, contrary to
      Thomas Sprat's influential account in History of the Royal Society.

1097. Rexroth, Kenneth. "Gulliver's Travels." Saturday Review, 52 (March
      22, 1969), 12; 16.

      Contains the remarkable assertions that Swift's "'savage
      indignation' is just outraged innocence" and that children are
      usually charmed by Book IV.

1098. Riely, John. "Scribleriana at the Yale Center for British Art."
      Scriblerian, 10 (1977), 47-50.

      Notes three Gilpin illustrations of Gulliver's Travels.

1099. Rogers, J.P.W. "Swift, Walpole, and the Rope-Dancers." PLL, 8
      (1972), 159-71.

      The picture of the Lilliputian games (Book I, chapter 3) conjures up
      several species of theatrical entertainment, all dominated by
      senseless or balletic spectacle. High-wire agility connoted
      elasticity of conscience to an eighteenth-century audience: the word
      "dexterity" was packed with associations of fraud and chicanery.
      Rogers concludes that unless a modern reader is "alive to the
      suggestions of both folly and turpitude which are evoked by the
      rope-dancing episode, he will miss much of the satiric impact that
      the passage carrried with it."

1100. Rogers, Pat. The Augustan Vision. London: Weidenfeld and Nicolson,
      1974. Pp. 318.

      This general introduction stresses the particularity of "social
      forms," "physical environment," "literary situation," and
      "psychological states" of the period and pursues the implications of
      the eighteenth-century mind's habit of stratifying experience. A
      Tale of a Tub and Gulliver's Travels are seen as "dense
      agglomerative" works constructed of segments.

1101. Rogers, Pat. "Gulliver and the Engineers." MLR, 70 (1975), 260-70.

      All four of Gulliver's adventures are "Southern Journeys," raising
      memories of the South-Sea Bubble and the contemporary world of

entrepreneurs and inventors. The buildings of the Academy of Lagado, for example are a sustained allusion to engineering innovations; Gulliver's fire-fighting in Lilliput plays off a controversy over new equipment in the years 1723-25. From these allusions, Rogers concludes that <u>Gulliver's Travels</u> "<u>derives</u> not just from a course of philosophic reading, but from a lively engagement in contemporary life, and a ready exposure to the popular news-stories of the day."

1102. Rogers, Pat. "Gulliver's Glasses." Pp. 179-88 of <u>The Art of Jonathan Swift</u>. Edited by Clive T. Probyn. New York: Barnes & Noble; London: Vision Press, 1978.

Also pub. as pp. 179-88 of <u>A Centenary Symposium,</u> ed. Alice Shalvi (Jerusalem: Jerusalem Academic, 1976).

A brief survey of eighteenth-century attitudes towards spectacles and of what they seem to symbolize leads to a discussion of the faculty of sight in <u>Gulliver's Travels</u>. Gulliver's glasses represent the intrusive modern intelligence, peering into what is better left unexamined. At the same time, they are, literally and symbolically, aids to Gulliver's survival, means to disguise physical infirmities and to repress the body's urges.

1103. Ross, Angus. <u>Swift: Gulliver's Travels</u>. (Studies in English Literature, 38.) London: Edward Arnold, 1968. Pp. 62.

Rev. (favorably) by J.T. Boulton in <u>Scriblerian</u>, 1, no. 2 (Spring, 1969), 6-7.

A pluralist reading for an undergraduate audience.

1104. Rudat, Wolfgang E.H. "Pope's Clarissa, the Trojan Horse, and Swift's Houyhnhnms." <u>Forum for Modern Language Studies</u>, 13 (1977), 6-11.

The Houyhnhnms' rationality constitutes a sort of Trojan horse (as does Clarissa's moralizing). Readers too well-pleased with this ambiguous gift, presented by Sinon-like Gulliver, may find themselves tricked.

1105. Ryley, Robert M. "Gulliver, Flimnap's Wife, and the Critics." <u>Studies in the Literary Imagination</u>, 5, no. 2 (October 1972), 53-63.

This attack on critics who treat the <u>Travels</u> as a novel focuses on the anatomical incongruities of Gulliver's defense of Flimnap's wife. Swift's motive in creating Gulliver is not novelistic consistency so much as "comic opportunism."

1106. Sackett, S.J. "Gulliver Four: Here We Go Again." <u>Bulletin of the Rocky Mountain Modern Language Association</u>, 27 (1973), 212-18.

This Freudian soft-school analysis identifies the Houyhnhnms with
reason, innocence, and the super-ego, the Yahoos with sin,
self-love, and the id. Searching for a third, mediating term, Swift
nevertheless failed to discover the concept of the ego; Gulliver, in
this view, is merely ridiculous at the end.

1107. Saito, Keiko. "Revaluation of Soseki's Essay on Swift." Etudes de
      Littératures Comparées, 5 (1969), 55-92.

      Noted by Zenzo Suzuki in Scriblerian, 3 (1970), 10.

      "Miss Saito argues that Soseki's [Soseki Natsume (1867-1916)]
      explanation of the Travels as an expression of a misanthropic
      satirist who despaired of mankind is essentially correct." (Suzuki)

1108. Schachterle, Lance. "The First Key to Gulliver's Travels." Revue des
      Langues Vivantes, 38 (1972), 37-45.

      "Signor Corolini's" key of 1726 demonstrates that at least some of
      Swift's contemporaries were aware of the specific political satire
      in Book I.

1109. Schlösser, Anselm. "Gulliver in Houyhnhnmland." Zeitschrift für
      Anglistik und Amerikanistik, 15 (1967), 375-82.

      Rept. (in an English translation prepared by the author) in Dublin
      Magazine, 6, nos. 3-4 (Autumn/Winter 1967), 27-36.

      Part of an introduction to a German edition of Swift's prose works,
      this essay works hard to establish a well known point: Gulliver is
      no simple equivalent of Swift himself.

1110. Scholes, Robert, and Robert Kellogg. The Nature of Narrative. New
      York: Oxford U. Press, 1966. Pp. 326.

      Pp. 113-16 discuss the affinities of Gulliver's Travels with
      allegorical romances and with realistic narratives.

1111. Schwandt, J.A. "The Love of Learning and the Lust for the
      Marketplace: Reflections on Swift and the Grand Academy of
      Lagado." Discourse, 10 (1967), 405-13.

      Lessons for undergraduates from Book III: the life of learning is
      always in conflict with the customary life of societies; the life of
      learning strictly requires organization to survive; there is a vast
      difference between the life of learning and its end product,
      critical awareness, and the organizational use of intelligence and
      its end product, social utility.

1112. Scobie, Steven. "Concerning Horses; Concerning Apes." Riverside
      Quarterly, 4 (1971), 258-62.

      This comparison between Gulliver's Travels and two films in the
      "Planet of the Apes" series surprisingly emphasizes the positiveness
      of Swift's vision compared to the "nihilism" of the films.

1113. Sena, John F. "Another Source for the Yahoos." Research Studies, 41
      (1973), 278-79.

      In Genesis, ch. 25, Esau is described as a (rash and angry) hunter
      who is covered with red hair. This may remind us of the Yahoos.

1114. Sena, John F. "Gulliver-Suite." Scriblerian, 3 (1971), 77.

      Describes Telemann's 1729 musical adaptation.

1115. Sena, John F. "Illustrations of Gulliver's Travels: An Addition and
      Correction." PBSA, 74 (1980), 258-79.

1116. Sena, John F. "Swift, the Yahoos and 'The English Malady'." PLL, 7
      (1971), 300-03.

      The Yahoos' susceptibility to spleen identifies them with
      eighteenth-century Englishmen (the disorder was so common that it
      came to be called the "English Malady").

1117. Shamsuddoha, M. "Swift's Moral Satire in the Fourth Book of
      Gulliver's Travels." Dacca University Studies, 23 (1975), (Part
      A), 83-94.

      Hard-school survey of critical opinions up to 1968, relying mostly
      on Twentieth-Century Views and Twentieth-Century Interpretations.
      Shamsuddoha's main point is that Gulliver is Swift's weapon, not his
      target.

1118. Shaw, Patrick W. "The Excrement Festival: Vonnegut's
      Slaughterhouse-Five." Scholia Satyrica, 2 (1976), 3-11.

      Briefly compares the similarly hopeless situations of Gulliver and
      Billy Pilgrim and distinguishes Vonnegut's "excremental vision"
      ("all the waste matter discharged from the body including semen")
      from Swift's.

1119. Shaw, Sheila. "The Rape of Gulliver: Case Study of a Source." PMLA,
      90 (1975), 62-68.

      Rev. in review art. ("Studies in Augustan Literature") by William
      Kupersmith in PQ, 55 (1976), 533-52.

An episode in <u>Hassan-al-Bassri</u>, supposed to have been a source for Gulliver and the Brobdingnagian Maids of Honor, was in fact not available to Swift. Moreover, not until the Frenchman J.C. Mardrus published his translation in 1900–1904 did giants appear in the text of <u>Hassan</u>.

1120. Sherbo, Arthur. "Swift and Travel Literature." <u>Modern Language Studies</u>, 9, no. 3 (Fall, 1979), 114–27.

A careful study of sources ("<u>in travel literature known to have been in Swift's possession</u>") of Lilliput and Brobdingnag, of Gulliver's ships, of Gulliver himself, of the prefatory matter.

1121. Shugg, Wallace. "The Beast Machine in English Literature (1663–1750)." <u>JHI</u>, 29 (1968), 279–92.

Mentions Book II of <u>Gulliver's Travels</u> and "The Beasts Confession to the Priest" as instances of widespread criticism of Descartes's theories about animals.

1122. Simons, Mary L. "Daniel's <u>Voyage to the World of Cartesius</u> and Swift's <u>Gulliver's Travels</u>." Pp. 24–28 of <u>1967 Proceedings of the Conference of College Teachers of English of Texas</u>. Vol. 32. Edited by Martin Shockley. Lubbock: Texas Tech College, 1967.

1123. Skau, Michael W. "Flimnap, Lilliput's Acrobatic Treasurer." <u>American Notes and Queries</u>, 8 (1970), 134–35.

Notes that Flimnap is an anagram for "flipman" and sounds like "flipflap."

1124. Skau, Michael W. "Glumdalclitch, Gulliver's 'Little Nurse'." <u>American Notes and Queries</u>, 8 (1970), 116.

Glumdalclitch is an anagram of the Anglo-Saxon phrase "mucg tall child".

1125. Smith, Raymond. "Swift's Utopias." <u>Discourse</u>, 9 (1966), 389–98.

Smith's method, comparing Swift's "obvious" ideals with what happens in the four voyages, leads to the conclusion that Swift treats even his sincerest values with exaggeration and comedy, requiring flexibility on the part of his readers.

1126. Smith, Raymond J., Jr. "The 'Character' of Lemuel Gulliver." <u>Tennessee Studies in Literature</u>, 10 (1965), 133–39.

Although it is barely possible to study Gulliver as a novelistic

character, Swift's main intent is to manipulate him as an instrument
of satire--thus Gulliver's naiveté, his "hyperbolic subservience,"
his pedanticism, his bravado, and his naive pride.

1127. Söderlind, Johannes. "The Word Lilliput." Studia Neophilologica
      (Uppsala), 40 (1968), 75-79.

      Rev. by Adina Forsgren in Scriblerian, 1, no. 2 (Spring 1969),
      8-9.

      The Swedish words "lille Putte" mean "little boy."

1128. Soriano, Marc. "Comment et pourquoi les deux premières parties des
      Voyages de Gulliver sont devenues un livre pour la jeunesse."
      Europe, 463 (1967), 131-52.

      The success of Gulliver's voyages among children is due to the
      wonderlands they present, analogues for which Soriano discovers in
      both early folklore and eighteenth-century texts. Children perceive
      their own process of growth in the dialectics of big and little,
      strong and weak, and in the reversals of these relationships: a
      process that ultimately comforts by assuring the benignity of the
      movement towards adulthood.

1129. Steele, Peter. "Terminal Days Among the Houyhnhnms." Southern Review
      (Australia), 4 (1971), 227-36.

      Reading the Travels as a novel, Steele focuses on how Gulliver's
      "ambiguous consciousness" develops by its experience of the Yahoos
      and Houyhnhnms. The final irony of Book IV is that Gulliver comes to
      exemplify the very human pride he despises, capping a series of
      unresolvable contradictions that nevertheless illuminate the human
      condition.

1130. Steensma, Robert C. "Swift's Model for Lord Munodi." N&Q, 210
      (1965), 216-17.

      Steensma notes similarities between Munodi and Sir William Temple in
      (1) political career; (2) attitudes towards the origin, growth, and
      characteristics of earlier civilizations; (3) estate; (4) views on
      science and progress.

1131. Steeves, Harrison R. Before Jane Austen. New York: Holt, Rinehart &
      Winston, 1965.

      Rev. by E.M. Jennings in South Atlantic Quarterly, 65 (1966),
      300-01.

      Pp. 43-52 ("Saeva Indignatio") are a conventional discussion of
      Gulliver's Travels as pre-Austenian fiction.

1132. Stéphane, Nelly. "Nous ne sommes pas Gulliver." Europe, 463 (1967), 16-26.

Arguing that the world Swift (and Gulliver) inhabited was radically different from our own, Stéphane supplies background on eighteenth-century English letters for modern French readers.

1133. Sturm, Norbert A. "Gulliver: The Benevolent Linguist." University of Dayton Review, 4, no. 3 (Autumn 1967), 43-54.

This labored and unoriginal plea for Swift's positive intentions is based on the extraordinarily naive charge that "the critics have forgotten Swift's characteristic method of writing behind a mask ... most, if not all, have read the book as though Swift were the narrator.... They have overlooked the possibility that Gulliver, and not Swift, may have created Houyhnhnmland." This, in 1967!

1134. Suits, Conrad. "The Role of the Horses in 'A Voyage to the Houyhnhnms'." University of Toronto Quarterly, 34 (1965), 118-32.

A witty and forceful argument (à la hard school) that, far from displaying his lunacy, Gulliver rather makes valid inferences about human nature from the evidence before him. Suits also undertakes to show that the Houyhnhnms represent an unattainable ideal, and that the virtues of Pedro de Mendez merely reveal the "hopeless distance between even the best human beings and rational creatures." Concludes Suits: if the "conclusion is in any sense a retraction on Swift's part or anything but one lash the more, then I am a sorrel nag."

1135. Sutherland, W.O.S., Jr. The Art of the Satirist: Essays on the Satire of Augustan England. Austin: U. of Texas, 1965. Pp. 134.

Pp. 107-25 are "Satire and the Use of History: Gulliver's Third Voyage." More inclusive than is generally credited, Book IV expresses "a world view based upon the assumptions of the modern philosopher." The third voyage "fails," because "although we think Swift 'right' in his moral platitudes, we consider his concept of the scientific world view to be 'wrong'." Of Book IV, Sutherland remarks that "the Houyhnhnms are symbols of hope, not despair," since they represent what has been, not what is.

1136. Svintila, Vladimir. "Gospodin Swift i Kapitan Galivar." ["Mr. Swift and Captain Gulliver: Between Imaginary and Real Worlds."] Septemvii, 12 (1967), 229-37.

1137. Swaim, Kathleen M. A Reading of Gulliver's Travels. (De Proprietatibus Litterarum, Series Didactica, 1.) The Hague: Mouton, 1972. Pp. 219.

Rev. by Frank Brady in Scriblerian, 7 (1975), 107-08; (with another work) by Colin J. Horne in Yearbook of English Studies, 6 (1976), 275-78.

A very detailed and rather schematic reading, which sees Books I-IV as centering on the physical, the emotional, the intellectual, and the moral aspects of human nature, respectively. Swaim herself focuses on three principle areas: food and eating; physicality, especially defecation and urination; and language.

1138. Takase, Fumiko. "The Houyhnhnms and the Eighteenth-Century Goût Chinois." English Studies, 61 (1980), 408-17.

Book IV in particular may have been influenced by the contemporary enthusiasm for Chinese history and culture. Perhaps Houyhnhnmland is modeled after China governed by a philosopher king under the dictates of Confucianism.

1139. Taylor, Sheila. "The 'Secret Pocket': Private Vision and Communal Identity in Gulliver's Travels." Studies in the Humanities, 6 (1978), 5-11.

If the eighteenth-century novel is defined as "fictions about individuals placed in situations where they must discover or re-define their relationship to society," then Gulliver's Travels is both a novel and a criticism of novels, according to Taylor. "Whereas Gulliver moved from the proposition that identity is private and absolute to a belief that identity is social and relative, the reader infers an enlarged view which harmonizes these two extremes."

1140. Tchekalov, I.I. "Gulliver's Travels and the Fantastico-Satiric Genres in Eighteenth-Century English Literature." Vestnik Liningradskogo Universiteta (Leningrad U. Review), 20 (1968), 104-15.

Noted in Scriblerian, 1, no. 2 (1969), 2-3.

Fantastic, fabulous, utopian, and burlesque features are well represented in Gulliver's Travels. Not merely different from his contemporaries, Swift used these elements of familiar stories, but also further developed the "fantastico-satiric" genre, influencing Fielding and Smollett.

1141. Thomas, W.K. "Brave New World and the Houyhnhnms." Revue de l'université d'Ottawa, 37 (1966), 688-96.

1142. Thomas, W.K. "Satiric Catharsis." University of Windsor Review, 3, no. 2 (Spring 1968), 33-44.

Satiric catharsis, rather than opening our eyes, anesthetizes pain and makes us more tolerant. The Struldbruggs episode, for example, by ridiculing the desire to live forever, eases the pain of our awareness of death. In Book IV, "by directing our ribald and derisive laughter at the Yahoos," Swift stimulates that part of us which is superior to the extremes of human depravity. Through the manifestly imperfect Houyhnhnms, Thomas claims, Swift ridicules the doctrine of moral self-sufficiency. "We are left purged of pain and tolerant of man's morality, compounded as it is of the absurdly evil and potentially glorious." Both naïve and tendentious.

1143. Thomsen, Christian W. Das Groteske im englischen Roman des 18. Jahrhunderts: Erscheinungsformen und Funktionen. [The Grotesque in the Eighteenth-Century English Novel: Themes, Forms, and Functions.] (Impulse der Forschung, 17.) Darmstadt: Wissenschaftliche Buchgesellschaft, 1974. Pp. ix + 350.

Rev. by Arthur Clayborough in English Studies, 58 (1977), 166-68; by Walter Kluge in Archiv für das Studium der neueren Sprachen und Literaturen, 215 (1978), 173-75; by Hermann J. Real in Scriblerian, 9 (1976), 88-89.

1144. Thorpe, Peter. "The Economics of Satire: Towards a New Definition." Western Humanities Review, 23 (1969), 187-96.

In Gulliver's Travels, as in most satires, the satirist portrays himself as an economically wise man of humble means; the means of wealth are generally controlled by undesirables. Only occasionally, as in Book IV, does the satirist try to trick the reader into agreeing with poor or false economy. What is poor or false about the Houyhnhnms' economy?

1145. Thorpe, Peter. "Great Satire and the Fragmented Norm." Satire Newsletter, 4 (1967), 89-93.

Swift plants fragments of the "norm" in Gulliver's Travels, which readers can bring together by examining the interplay between Gulliver and his foils and by always keeping the whole of Gulliver's Travels in mind. The norm is "not likely to be found in any one character but among characters."

1146. Tintner, Adeline R. "Lady into Horse: James's 'Lady Barberina' and Gulliver's Travels, Part IV." Journal of Narrative Technique, 8 (1978), 79-96.

In addition to the basic premise of pitting horses against mankind, specific details of James's "Lady Barberina" suggest that he was using Gulliver's fourth voyage as a model or parallel, which Tintner thinks may explain the unusual bitterness of James's story.

1147. Todd, Dennis. "Laputa, the Whore of Babylon, and the Idols of Science." SP, 75 (1978), 93-120.

The real brilliance of Book III is that Swift found in contemporary science the "damning evidence to link it to Babylon and Jerusalem." "Laputa is the eighteenth-century wasteland, and its features are drawn from the desolate Jerusalem." Thus Book III is more coherent than has often been thought: it is framed by denials of religion; the organization of its episodes parodies the course of divine history. The theme of the book is hopelessness, and Swift attacks the mentality which rejects the spirit, leaving man "confined to the dead-ends of his own limitations and mortality."

1148. Torchiana, Donald T. "Jonathan Swift, the Irish, and the Yahoos: The Case Reconsidered." PQ, 54 (1975), 195-212.

English accounts of Irish peasants read "pretty much like Swift's depictions of the Yahoos"; in some reports, the Irish character seems to resemble pure evil; these images had persisted long before as well as after Gulliver's Travels. Moreover, Swift's hatred of Ireland scarcely needs to be documented. Finally, in A Modest Proposal Swift "is forced to admit his folly in countering a general Irish folly, a fact of life like the evil of the Yahoos who are also bent upon pitiless self-destruction."

1149. Traldi, Ila Dawson. "Gulliver the 'Educated Fool': Unity in the Voyage to Laputa." PLL, 4 (1968), 35-50.

A "double theme" unites the episodes of Book III as well as connecting them to the other voyages. Human pride futilely defies the limits of nature, especially human nature; but at the same time, man ignores the possibilities that are inherently and uniquely his own.

1150. Treadwell, J.M. "Jonathan Swift: The Satirist as Projector." TSLL, 17 (1975), 439-60.

In Balnibarbi, and above all in the Grand Academy of Lagado, "we are offered a history and an anatomy of projecting in all its forms from the giant fraud practiced by a Whig government upon a whole nation, right down to that ludicrous and inconsequential 'political' projection which was Swift's own weakness." Some of the identifications are sketchy.

1151. Trigona, Prospero. "Funzioni e dimensioni nel III viaggio di Gulliver." ["Functions and Dimensions in Gulliver's Third Voyage."] Pp. 93-110 of Studi inglesi: Raccolta di saggi richerche. Edited by Agostino Lombardo. Bari: Adriatica, 1974.

Rept. as pp. 87-110 of Trigona, Prospero. Swift: Le Metamorfosi dell'arcangelo Gionata: II Gulliver. Rome: Bulzoni, 1979.

"Functions" refers primarily to Gulliver's changed role in Book III as comparatively reliable and enterprising observer who can render

Swift's own judgments more directly. "Dimensions" refers to the duality of weight and air in Book III, a less complex and subtle opposition than the large and small dimensions of the first two books.

1152. Trigona, Prospero. Swift: Le Metamorfosi dell'arcangelo Gionata: II Gulliver. Rome: Mario Bulzoni, 1979. Pp. 159.

Contains a chapter on each voyage.

1153. Trimmer, Joseph F. "A Note on Gulliver and the Four Captains." Ball State University Forum, 12, no. 2 (Spring 1971), 39-43.

The thesis here is that Gulliver's interaction with each captain helps the reader to judge his character and his story.

1154. Trousson, Raymond. Voyages aux pays de nulle part: Histoire littéraire de la pensée utopique. Second Revised Edition. Bruxelles: Editions de l'Université de Bruxelles, 1979. Pp. xxvii + 298.

Rev. by Aubrey Rosenberg in University of Toronto Quarterly, 50 (1981), 336-37.

1155. Tsukamoto, Toshiaki. "The Problem of Soseki's Bungaku Hyoron." Journal of Comparative Literature, 12 (1969), 12-47.

Noted by Zenzo Suzuki in Scriblerian, 3 (1970), 10.

"Tsukamoto contends that Soseki's [Soseki Natsume (1867-1916)] view of Swift, despite recent scholarship, remains convincing. Though highly individualistic, Soseki dogmatically interprets A Tale of a Tub with a preconceived prejudice against Christianity. His thesis about Gulliver's Travels is pretty much in line with the Victorians' view; like them he found misanthropic man in it and believed that Swift's satire projected a complete negativism." (Suzuki)

1156. Turner, Paul. "The Meaning of Gulliver's Travels." Bati Dil ve Edebiyatlari Arastirmalari Dergisi [Journal of Modern Languages and Literatures], 2 (1971), 53-66.

Noted by Necla Aytür in Scriblerian, 6 (1973), 5-6.

"... this paper emphasizes Swift's clericalism and makes a good case for reading the Travels as a sermon against pride, each of the four parts showing pride of a different kind." (Aytür)

1157. Uchida, Takeshi. "Swift's 'Voyage to Laputa' and 'Playfulness'." Bulletin of the Department of Literature, Tokai University, 14 (1970), 59-68.

Noted by Zenzo Suzuki in Scriblerian, 3 (1971), 51.

The essay is in Japanese. "Notwithstanding Mr. Uchida's assertion of Swift's playfulness, he fails to consider the overall dark impression of Part III." (Suzuki)

1158. Urnov, D. "Polozhenie Gullivera." ["Gulliver's Condition: To Celebrate the 300th Anniversary of the Birth of Jonathan Swift."] Yunost, 12 (1967), 70-72.

Noted by Leonid Arinshtein in Scriblerian, 2 (1970), 39.

1159. Urnov, D.M. Robizon i Gulliver: Sud'by dvux literaturnyx geroev. Moscow: Mauka, 1973. Pp. 89.

1160. Vance, John A. "'The Odious Vermin': Gulliver's Progression towards Misanthropy." Enlightenment Essays, 10 (1979), 65-73.

This soft school reading traces Gulliver's use of the word "odious" to show him "progressing" towards the perspective represented by the King of Brobdingnag's condemnation of men as "odious little vermin."

1161. Van Tine, James. "The Risks of Swiftian Sanity." University Review (Kansas City, Mo.) 32 (1966), 235-40; 275-81.

Swift's "shaping struggle toward a sane viewpoint" challenged his Christian asceticism, part of the general conflict between artifice and nature in his satire. Gulliver's Travels demonstrates how revulsion to death renders man more vulnerable to its terrors, while the Houyhnhnms' simple integrity enables them to accepte death. Similarly, with regard to the bowels and sexuality, the horses' genuine shamelessness allows them to go beyond Yahoo hatred to acceptance. By contrast, readers are trapped into the same impossible standards that cause Gulliver to reject human reality and isolate him from his family, by their abhorrence of Swift's scatology.

1162. Vickers, Brian. "The Satiric Structure of Gulliver's Travels and More's Utopia." Pp. 233-57 of The World of Jonathan Swift: Essays for the Tercentenary. Edited by Brian Vickers. Cambridge, Ma.: Harvard U. Press; Oxford: Basil Blackwell, 1968.

The closest existing parallel to Gulliver's Travels, More's Utopia shares with it satiric devices, an instinct for comparison, and ethical criticism. On the other hand, Swift does not provide a positive alternative system as does More, and his method of comparison inverts that of More, i.e., a traveller tells other societies about English weaknesses.

1163. Walker, Lewis. "A Possible Source for the Linguistic Projects in the Academy of Lagado." N&Q, 20 (1973), 413-14.

To wit: John Wilkins's An Essay Towards a Real Character and a Philosophical Language (1668), especially Wilkins's idea of basing language on things, and his division of all discourse into 40 "Genus's"--perhaps the original of the 40 handles on Swift's machine.

1164. Walton, J.K. "The Unity of the Travels." Hermathena, 104 (Spring, 1967), 5-50.

Arguing away as if all previous critics had insisted on the total incoherence of Gulliver's Travels, Walton identifies the underlying theme of the whole work as "the nature of power, of those who in different ways wield it, and the discrepancies between power and reason"; he also misses the irony in Swift's comment that the book would "wonderfully mend the world," and he insists continually on the "constructive power" of Swift. An unilluminating survey of familiar ground.

1165. Washington, E. "The Habsburgs and Gulliver's Travels." American Notes and Queries, 16 (1978), 83-85.

The Emperor of Lilliput's protruding lower jaw and drooping lower lip together with his pettiness constitute a satire on the Habsburg emperors.

1166. Weidhorn, Manfred. "Clothes and the Man." Connecticut Review, 3, no. 2 (April 1970), 41-57.

Discusses the moral nature of the sheer act of removing garments in Gulliver's Travels.

1167. Welcher, Jeanne K., and George E. Bush, Jr. (eds.). Gulliveriana: I. Gainesville: Scholars' Facsimiles & Reprints, 1970. Pp. xv + 204.

Includes A Trip to the Moon (1728), by Murtagh McDermot, and A Trip to the Moon (1764-5) by Sir Humphrey Lunatic.

1168. Welcher, Jeanne K., and George E. Bush, Jr. (eds.). Gulliveriana: II. Jr. Gainesville: Scholars' Facsimiles & Reprints, 1971. Pp. xv + 636.

Includes The Travels of Mr. John Gulliver, Son to Capt. Lemuel Gulliver (1731), by Pierre François Guyot Desfontaines; Modern Gulliver's Travels: Lilliput (1796), by Lemuel Gulliver, Jun. (pseud.).

1169. Welcher, Jeanne K., and George E. Bush, Jr. (eds.). Gulliveriana:
      III. Delmar, N.Y.: Scholars' Facsimiles & Reprints, 1972. Pp. xiii
      + 465.

      Includes Travels into Several Remote Nations of the World, vol. III
      (1727) and Memoirs of the Court of Lilliput (1727)--Grub Street
      imitations.

1170. Welcher, Jeanne K., and George E. Bush, Jr. (eds.). Gulliveriana:
      IV. Delmar, N.Y.: Scholars' Facsimiles & Reprints, 1973. Pp. xxx +
      384.

      Includes A Voyage to Cacklogallinia (1727), by Capt. Samuel Brunt; A
      Journey to the World Under-Ground (1742), by Ludwig Holberg; Kanor,
      a Tale Translated from the Savage (1750), by Marie Antoinette
      Fagnan; Gulliver Revived (5th ed., 1787); Mammuth; or, Human Nature
      Displayed on a Grand Scale in a Tour with the Tinkers, into the
      Inland Parts of Africa (1789), by William Thomson.

1171. Welcher, Jeanne K., and George E. Bush, Jr. (eds.). Gulliveriana V:
      Shorter Imitations of Gulliver's Travels. Delmar, N.Y.: Scholars'
      Facsimiles & Reprints, 1974.

1172. Welcher, Jeanne K., and George E. Bush, Jr. (eds.). Gulliveriana VI:
      Critiques of Gulliver's Travels and Allusions Thereto. 3 vols.
      Delmar, N.Y.: Scholars' Facsimiles & Reprints, 1976. Pp. lxxxiv +
      unnumbered pages.

      Includes numerous Critiques, Works Attributed to Lemuel Gulliver and
      Martin Gulliver, Miscellaneous Gulliveriana, Lilliputiana for
      Children, and Other Allusions to Gulliver's Travels.

1173. White, Douglas H. "Swift and the Definition of Man." MP, 73 (1976),
      S48-S55.

      Contemporary attacks on man as animal rationale, the third of three
      stages of attack on natural religion, were more urgent and
      controversial than even R.S. Crane realized (in Item 915). How this
      information ought to affect interpretation of Gulliver's Travels is
      not made entirely clear.

1174. White, John H. "Swift's Trojan Horses: 'Reasoning But to Err'." ELN,
      3 (1966), 185-94.

      A standard soft-school argument that Swift satirizes the Houyhnhnms
      for displaying typically human mental processes, for their snap
      judgments and preoccupation with Gulliver's superficial form. The
      Houyhnhnms "do not balk at concealing the truth"; they are capable
      of logical and semantic confusion.

1175. White, Robert B., Jr. "Gulliver, Sir Hudibras, and the Logicians."
      N&Q, 225 (1980), 33.

      Hudibras, i, 71-72, exemplifies R.S. Crane's famous argument (Item
      915) that Book IV is mocking the logic books' cliché that man is
      distinct from horse.

1176. Wilding, Michael. "The Politics of Gulliver's Travels." Pp. 303-22
      of Studies in the Eighteenth Century. Vol. II. Edited by R.F.
      Brissenden. Canberra: Australian National U. Press; Toronto: U. of
      Toronto Press, 1973.

      Gulliver's Travels progresses in political sophistication, from
      Lilliputian politics in which no idea can be taken seriously, to a
      presentation of mixed monarchy, with innate conflicting interests,
      to a "modern" analysis of the Houyhnhnms' society as one founded on
      economic oppression. Book IV may be read as an attack on British
      colonialism, in which the Yahoos are human beings brutalized and
      debased by a cruel caste system. Because Gulliver's ambiguous status
      challenges the validity of that system he must be expelled.
      Furthermore, once freed, these "slaves" might well be able to
      develop their innate virtues.

1177. Williams, Kathleen M. "Gulliver's Voyage to the Houyhnhnms." Pp.
      247-57 of Swift: Modern Judgements. Edited by A. Norman Jeffares.
      London: Macmillan, 1969; Nashville, Tenn.: Aurora, 1970.

      Orig. pub. in Journal of English Literary History, 18 (1951).

      A classic statement of the soft-school position: "if Swift did
      intend the Houyhnhnms to stand as an ideal contrast, he has badly
      mismanaged the matter"; "Swift makes it plain that the Portuguese
      sailors are admirable human beings, and emphasizes in them the very
      qualities which the Houyhnhnms neither possess nor would
      understand"; "In Gulliver's Travels there is not only a traditional
      Christian pessimism; there may well be a positive Christian ideal
      suggested in the conduct of the good humans, though it is presented
      with Swift's habitual obliquity and restraint."

1178. Winter, Michael. Compendium Utopiarum: Typologie und Bibliographie
      literarischer Utopien. Vol. 1: Von der Antike bis zur deutschen
      Frühaufklärung. (Repertorien zur deutschen Literaturgeschichte,
      8.) Stuttgart: J.B. Metzler, 1978. Pp. lx + 287; 9 illustrations.

      Rev. by J.L. Hibberd in MLR, 75 (1980), 694-96.

      Intended primarily for German readers interested in social thought,
      this reference work combines a chronological bibliography of
      literary utopias with extended commentaries. Gulliver's Travels
      receives about ten thousand words.

1179. Wood, James O. "Gulliver and the Monkey of Tralee." SEL, 9 (1969), 415-26.

Gulliver's kidnapping by a Brobdingnagian monkey plays off a family myth of the Fitzgeralds, Earls of Kildare, perhaps to irk the contemporary Earl with whom Swift's relations were strained. A similar story from 1660 allegorizes the kidnapping ape as the enemies of the Church of England, though what this implies about Gulliver's Travels is not made clear.

1180. Wray, William R. "Swift's Gulliver's Travels, Book I, Chapter 1." Explicator, 26, no. 1 (September 1967), Item #7.

The sexual pun "Master Bates" is Swift's way of undercutting Gulliver's dullness without becoming dull himself.

1181. Yeomans, W.E. "The Houyhnhnm as Menippean Horse." College English, 27 (1966), 449-54.

Rept. as pp. 258-66 of Item 332; as pp. 202-11 of Item 956.

A clear summary of the case against reading Gulliver's Travels as a novel. Swift combines burlesque and solemn elements in the Houyhnhnms, allowing them to be "altogether subservient to his intellectual purposes," with much Menippean precedent behind him.

1182. Zall, Paul M. "Lolita and Gulliver." Satire Newsletter, 3 (1965), 33-37.

Perceptive remarks on Nabokov's "neo-Swiftian way of engaging the reader himself as a satiric hero." Both writers "lead us up to a point of expectation and then stop dead in their tracks," leaving readers to go "barreling along solo." The strategy satirizes human minds running in grooves of their own devising.

1183. Zimansky, Curt A. "Gulliver, Yahoos, and Critics." College English, 27 (1965), 45-49.

The "dominating satiric formula" of Gulliver's Travels is: "Swift's readers believed that man is distinguished from animals by his gift of reason, and is no better than a beast unless he uses that reason." Zimansky praises a rigorous use of historical method for allowing us to understand this "formula."

1184. Zimmerman, Everett. "Gulliver the Preacher." PMLA, 89 (1974), 1024-32.

In Swift's view, the preacher's main duty is "to suppress, rather than to express, himself." Because it makes clear what position the satire comes from, Gulliver's Travels becomes, as well as a satire,

a psychological study of Gulliver, as we compare his "often
unexceptionable statements to his devious ends." Soft-school
opinions.

1185. Zimmerman, Lester F. "Lemuel Gulliver." Pp. 61–73 of <u>Jonathan Swift:</u>
   <u>Tercentenary Essays</u>. (U. of Tulsa Department of English Monograph
   Series, 3.) Tulsa: U. of Tulsa, 1967.

   Argues for the unity of the voyages based on Gulliver's changing
   character, projected against the motif of "man is the measure."

1186. Zirker, Herbert. "Lemuel Gullivers <u>Yahoos</u> und Swifts Satire."
   <u>Anglia</u>, 87 (1969), 39–63.

   Explores the "whole disposition of the word" <u>Yahoo</u> from a compound
   of common expressions of disgust—"yah," "ugh"—to the Hebrew
   tetramorph for Jahweh. Gulliver's revulsion from the Yahoos may thus
   be a parody of those Christians who divorce themselves utterly from
   the Hebrew Jehovah. Thus Gulliver's idealizing of the Houyhnhnms
   renders them suspect as genuine ideals.

   See also Items 34, 36, 37, 40, 57, 58, 82, 95, 102, 206, 218, 246,
   249, 253, 265, 267, 268, 269, 271, 286, 294, 304, 311, 313, 314,
   316, 341, 354, 357, 361, 364, 376, 379, 380, 381, 385, 391, 396,
   398, 402, 406, 410, 414, 417, 422, 430, 431, 441, 442, 444, 453,
   456, 460, 463, 607, 652, 687, 706, 716, 856.

INDEX